XXI

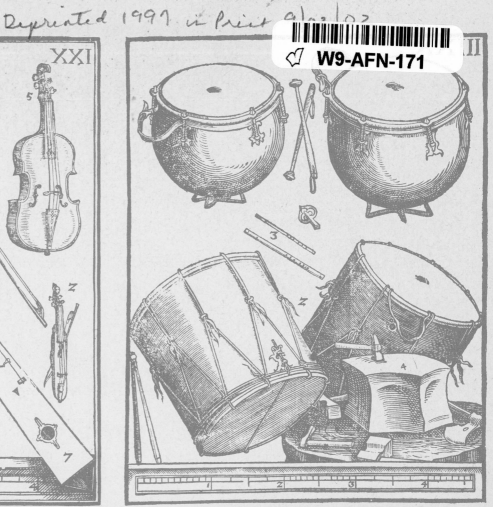

II

XXIX

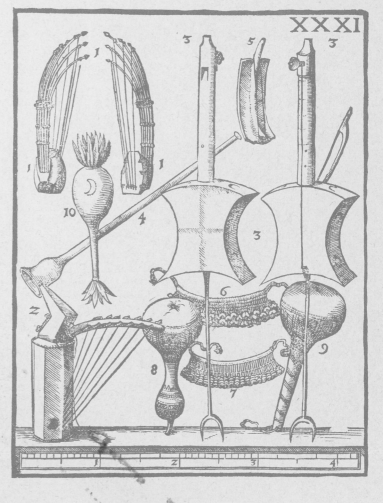

XXXI

MUSICAL INSTRUMENTS
OF THE WORLD

MUSICAL INSTRUMENTS
OF THE WORLD

An Illustrated Encyclopedia
by the Diagram Group

**PADDINGTON
PRESS LTD**

**THE TWO CONTINENTS
PUBLISHING GROUP**

Library of Congress Cataloging in Publication Data

Diagram Group
  Musical instruments of the world

  Includes index
  1.Musical instruments — Dictionaries. I. Title
ML102.15D5   781.9'1'03   76-21722
ISBN 0--8467—0134—0

Printed and bound in Holland by Smeets Offset, B.V., Weert

In the United States
Paddington Press Ltd
Two Continents Publishing Group

In the United Kingdom
Paddington Press Ltd

In Canada
Distributed by
Random House of Canada Ltd

In Australia
Distributed by
Angus & Robertson Pty Ltd

the Diagram Group

Managing editor Ruth Midgley

Research editor Susan Sturrock

Associate editor Linda Proud

Art director Trevor Bounford

Art editor Roger Kohn

Artists Jeff Alger, Peter J. Golding, Richard Hummerstone, Susan Kinsey, Pavel Kostal, Kathleen McDougall, Graham Rosewarne

Art assistants Eileen Batterberry, Jonathan Beck, Robert Galvin, Jim Kane, Jill Moore, Annabel Praeger, Diana Taylor, Margaret Wells

Editorial contributors Joyce Becker, Gaik See Chew, Jean Cooke, Joan Faller, David Heidenstam, David Lambert

Contributing artists Olivia Beasley, Thea Nockels, Martin Swaine, Michael Turner

Picture researcher Enid Moore

The authors and publishers wish to extend their warmest thanks to the many institutions, manufacturers, retailers and individuals without whose kind and generous assistance this encyclopedia could not have been compiled. A fuller list of museums and collections is included on page 314, but special thanks are due to:

Acknowledgments Musikinstrumentensammlung des Staatlichen Instituts für Musikforschung, Berlin
Musée Instrumental, Brussels
Göteborgs Museum, Gothenburg
Gemeentemuseum, The Hague
Vystavkya Musikalnych Instrumentov, Leningrad
British Museum, London
British Piano Museum, Brentford (London)
Finnish Embassy, London
Grey Coat Hospital, London
Horniman Museum, London
Japan Information Centre, London
London Library, London
Nigeria High Commission, London
Royal College of Music, London
Royal Military School of Music, Kneller Hall, Twickenham (London)
Royal Netherlands Embassy, London
Westminster Central Music Library, London
Civiche Raccolte d'Arte Applicata Ed Incisione, Castello Sforzesco, Milan
Glinka Museum, Moscow
Metropolitan Museum of Art, New York City
Museum of the American Indian, New York City
Pitt Rivers Museum, Oxford
Conservatoire de Musique, Paris
Národní Museum, Prague
Smithsonian Institution, Washington DC
Kunsthistorisches Museum, Vienna

Boosey & Hawkes
John Broadwood & Sons
Crabb Concertinas
Arnold Dolmetsch
Ian Harwood & John Isaacs
Robert Morley & Co
Henri Selmer & Co
Steinway & Sons

E. N. Alexeiev
Wendy Bird
James Cummings
Helen Rice Hollis
Val Podlasinski
Semon Levin
Nina A. Lissova
Raymond Man
Alfred Mirek
Julia Moore

Habit de Musicien

o. Valck. Excudit

Foreword

Throughout history only a very few books have attempted to depict the vast range of man's inventiveness in his search for music-making objects. Michael Praetorius' "Syntagma Musicum" of 1618 stands as the first major attempt to illustrate and document a large number of instruments. His knowledge, however, was almost entirely restricted to Europe: today, of course, it is possible to include numerous examples from all corners of the world.

In the late 18th and 19th centuries independent collectors began amassing collections of musical instruments. Although their origins and characteristics were often inadequately documented, these instruments became the nucleus of many splendid collections housed in major museums throughout the world.

The 20th century brought attempts to develop a comprehensive system of classification for this store of material, and the system of Erich von Hornbostel and Curt Sachs — which groups instruments according to how the sound is produced — has provided the basis on which our encyclopedia is organized. The variety of instruments is truly staggering even within one group — for example, the simple tin whistle is shown to be related to the vast church organ.

It is perhaps strange that in the midst of 20th century technology the traditional skill of drawing has proved the clearest method of depiction. Working from actual instruments or from numerous picture references the artists have been able to convey precise details of form, decoration, and methods of sounding. In many cases small figure drawings have been included to show playing positions and relative sizes.

Complementing the illustrations are short paragraphs of clearly written text, providing the reader with a wealth of information. Individual panels of additional reference material are included for the instruments of the symphony orchestra. Wherever possible, instruments displayed in museums or other collections have been identified to encourage the reader to examine them for himself.

A different perspective is provided by the encyclopedia's later chapters. Here, instruments are presented according to geographical distribution, historical period, and use in groups. Finally included are brief biographies of personalities important in the development of musical instruments.

The study of musical instruments is a relatively new science and the editors hope that this new encyclopedia will help stimulate general interest in this fascinating field.

Left Instruments of the 16th century in a French popular illustration.

Classification

The basic classification of instruments within this encyclopedia is derived from the system published in 1914 by Erich von Hornbostel and Curt Sachs. Under this system — now accepted by musicologists all over the world — instruments are categorized according to the way in which sound is produced. Each of the encyclopedia's first five chapters is devoted to instruments of a particular category.

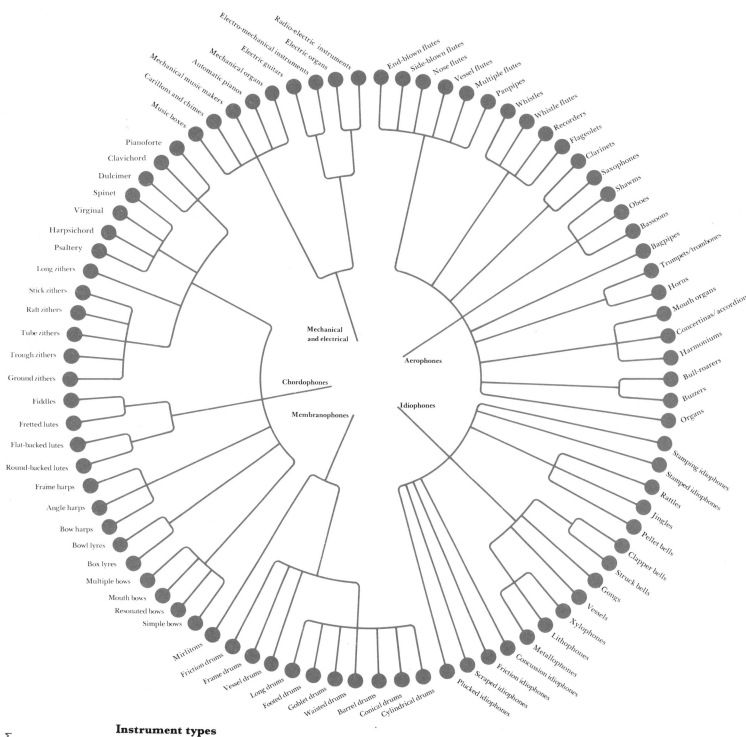

Instrument types
Subdivisions are shown radiating from the five major categories at the center of the diagram.

Contents

Aerophones

Idiophones

Membranophones

Chordophones

Mechanical and electrical instruments

Instruments around the world

Instruments through the ages

Musical ensembles

Makers, virtuosi, writers

Aerophones: introduction

Aerophones are instruments in which the sound is produced by the vibration of air. They are classified according to how the vibration is generated, and include flutes, reeds, cup mouthpiece instruments, and free aerophones. Since the Stone Age, flutes have been endowed with magical significance, and some peoples still use them in ritual associated with storms, crops, and death. Reed instruments originated in the East. More complex than flutes, they are less widely distributed, appearing today in Europe, Africa, and the East. Cup mouthpiece instruments have a very ancient history. Found in varying degrees of sophistication throughout the world, they are today most commonly used for ritual, military, and signaling purposes. Free aerophones, typified by the bull-roarer, are still used by some tribes as magical instruments.

Aerophones family tree
The aerophone family includes blow hole and whistle mouthpiece flutes, single reeds, double reeds, instruments with cup mouthpieces, free reeds, and free aerophones. Bagpipes and organs are hybrid instruments with pipes of different kinds.

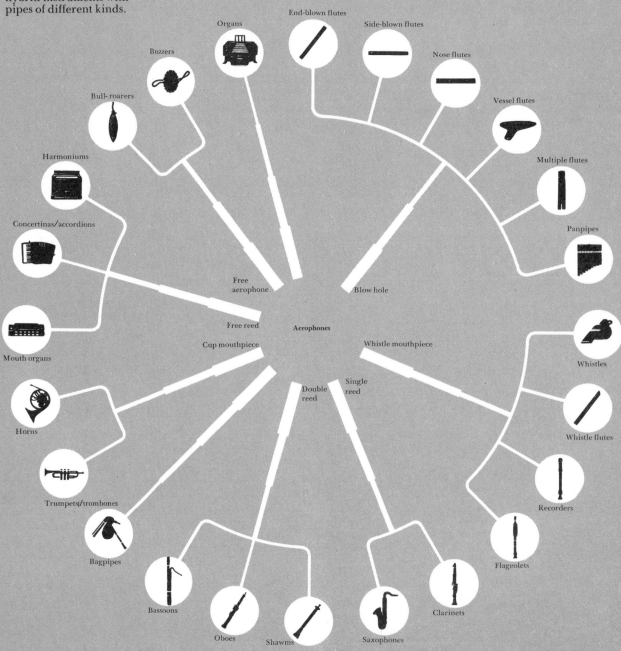

Organs

Buzzers

Bull-roarers

Harmoniums

Concertinas/accordions

Mouth organs

Horns

Trumpets/trombones

Bagpipes

Bassoons

Oboes

Shawms

Saxophones

Clarinets

Flageolets

Recorders

Whistle flutes

Whistles

Panpipes

Multiple flutes

Vessel flutes

Nose flutes

Side-blown flutes

End-blown flutes

Free aerophone

Free reed

Cup mouthpiece

Aerophones

Blow hole

Whistle mouthpiece

Single reed

Double reed

Making the air vibrate In all types of aerophone sound is made by vibrating air, and instruments are classified according to how the air is set into vibration. In instruments with a blow hole (a) or whistle mouthpiece (b) the air vibrates after being directed against a sharp edge. Vibrations in a tube may also be produced by reeds — single (c), double (d), or free (e). In cup mouthpiece instruments (f) air is made to vibrate by the action of the player's lips. In a free aerophone (g) there is no enclosed air column — the air vibrates around the instrument as it travels through the air.

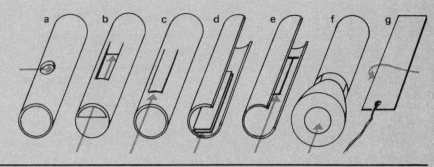

Body shapes Most aerophones have a tubular or vessel-shaped body in which vibrating air is enclosed during play. The shape of the body affects the character of the sound produced. The most common body type is the hollow tube, which may be cylindrical (a) as in the clarinet, tapering (b) as in the recorder, or flared (c) as in the oboe. Less common are aerophones with a vessel body (d) like that of the ocarina.

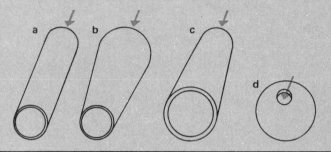

Pitch The pitch produced depends on the length of the tube containing the vibrating air column. The tube's length determines the length of the sound waves and consequently the number of waves (frequencies) produced in a second. Any tube is theoretically capable of producing a pitch appropriate to its length. This pitch is called the fundamental. A 2ft tube will sound middle C (1), while a tube twice as long will sound one octave lower (2). A stopped (closed) pipe will sound one octave lower than an unstopped pipe of the same length.

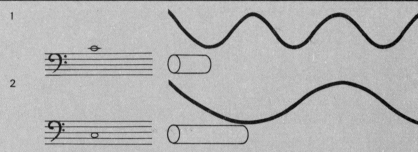

Harmonic series When a column of air is activated it vibrates not only as a whole but also in sections. These secondary vibrations produce pitches other than the fundamental. Known as harmonics, these additional pitches are produced by increasing the intensity of the airstream so that the air vibrates more quickly in the tube. Harmonics occur in a sequence called the harmonic series. Although the distance between one harmonic and the next is fixed, the actual pitches vary with the size and shape of the tube. The example given here is for a hypothetical 8ft tube.

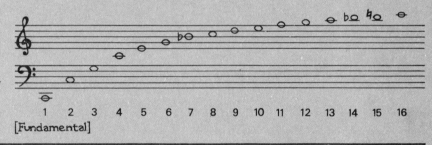

1　2　3　4　5　6　7　8　9　10　11　12　13　14　15　16
[Fundamental]

Altering the pitch Only by shortening or lengthening the tube can an aerophone be made to produce pitches other than its fundamental and associated harmonics. A tube is "shortened" by the use of finger holes: opening holes at the lower end of the tube has the effect of reducing the total length of tube to the point at which the air can first escape (a). A longer tube may be obtained by means of a simple slide mechanism (b), or by the use of crooks or valves to divert the air through an extra length of tubing (c).

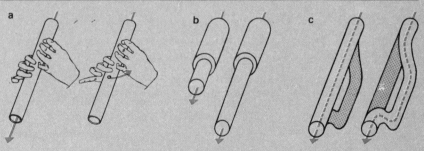

Tone color Every aerophone has its own distinctive sound quality or "tone color." When any pitch is played the actual sound produced is colored by the presence of harmonics associated with this pitch. The presence of different harmonics is determined by the shape of the tube. For example, the conical tube of the oboe emphasizes the lower harmonics (a) while the stopped cylindrical tube of the clarinet emphasizes the odd-numbered harmonics (b). (In each case the harmonic composition of the instrument's lowest pitch has been illustrated.)

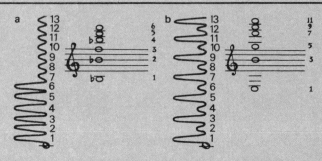

End-blown flutes

An end-blown flute is a variety of flute in which the airstream is directed against the sharp rim of the open upper end of a pipe by the player's lips. Despite its unsophisticated appearance it is very difficult to play. The pipe is often fairly long and the number of finger holes is frequently only two or three. The main materials are bone, horn, wood, bamboo, or occasionally metal, and the bore is usually cylindrical. The angle at which the instrument is held varies according to the style of the upper rim. End-blown flutes are found in every continent but especially in South America and Asia, and examples exist dating from the Stone Age.

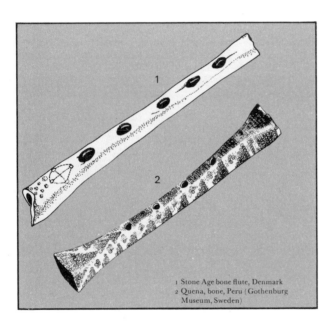

1 Stone Age bone flute, Denmark
2 Quena, bone, Peru (Gothenburg Museum, Sweden)

Above Examples of bone flutes. Flutes made from bone are among the oldest surviving instruments. They were used by primitive peoples as decoy instruments, and for making music. They were often played in pairs—a practice that continues today.

Below End-blown flutes are usually rested against the chin (a) or lower lip (b). With his lips pursed or drawn tightly over his teeth, the player directs a concentrated stream of air against the sharp edge of the blow hole. This can be demonstrated by blowing across the top of a bottle.

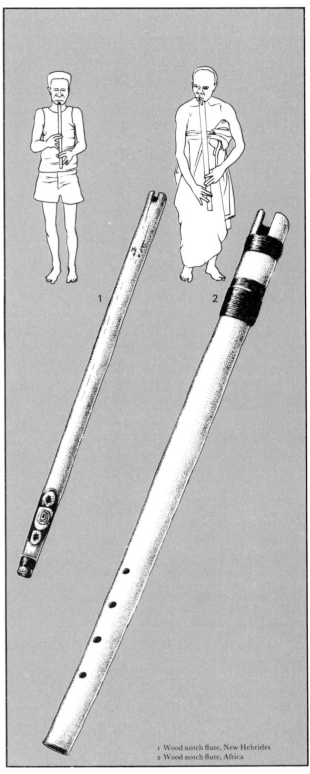

1 Wood notch flute, New Hebrides
2 Wood notch flute, Africa

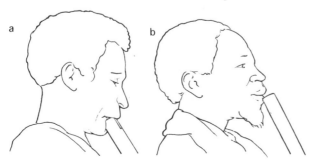

Above and above right Examples of modern folk instruments. Wood or bamboo are the most usual materials, though in some countries a length of metal tubing is used. Made of bamboo, the Japanese **shakuhachi** (6) has an uncharacteristic wide bore that is internally lacquered.

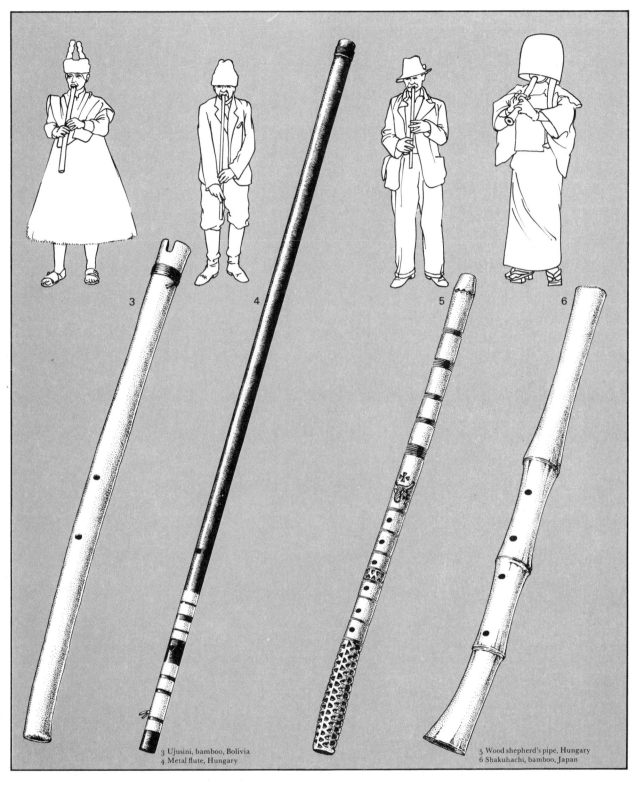

3 Ujusini, bamboo, Bolivia
4 Metal flute, Hungary
5 Wood shepherd's pipe, Hungary
6 Shakuhachi, bamboo, Japan

© DIAGRAM

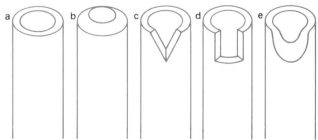

Right Types of blow hole. The simple blow hole (a) is often modified to create a sharper edge against which to direct the airstream. Common types are the beveled blow hole (b) or blow holes with notches that are V-shaped (c), square-shaped (d), or rounded (e).

Whistle flutes

A whistle flute, sometimes called a fipple flute, is an end-blown flute in which the air is directed through a simple mouthpiece against the sharp edge of a hole cut in the pipe just below the mouthpiece. It can be made of clay, wood, cane, or metal, and the most familiar European version is the recorder. Finger holes or some other means of sounding more than one pitch distinguish the whistle flute from the simple whistle.

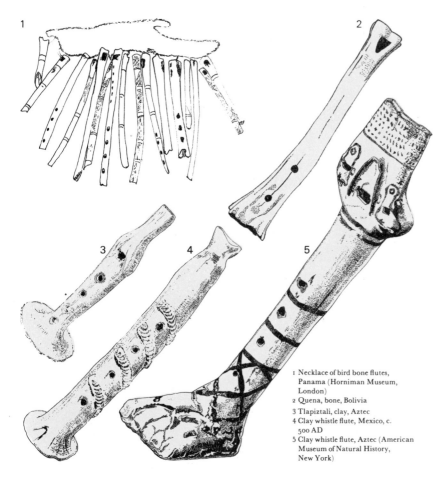

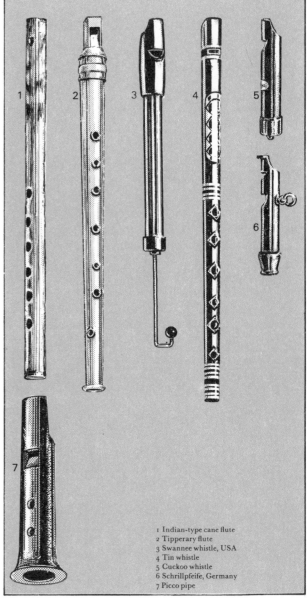

1 Necklace of bird bone flutes, Panama (Horniman Museum, London)
2 Quena, bone, Bolivia
3 Tlapiztali, clay, Aztec
4 Clay whistle flute, Mexico, c. 500 AD
5 Clay whistle flute, Aztec (American Museum of Natural History, New York)

1 Indian-type cane flute
2 Tipperary flute
3 Swannee whistle, USA
4 Tin whistle
5 Cuckoo whistle
6 Schrillpfeife, Germany
7 Picco pipe

Above Whistle flutes from Central and South America. The necklace (1) is made up of tiny flutes made from bird bones. The quena (2) is a bone whistle flute from Bolivia. The clay whistle flutes (3, 4, and 5) are typical of numerous Mexican examples dating from 300–1500AD.

Below Bosun's whistle used for piping senior naval officers aboard ship. Slung on a cord around the bosun's neck, it is grasped in one hand when played. The opening and closing of the hand causes the pitch to rise and fall.

Below Wood pitch pipe used to give starting pitches to singers. This pipe has a calibrated plunger pushed in or pulled out to give the pitch required. Pipes without plungers give only a single pitch.

Above Examples of commercial whistle flutes from the USA and Europe. The whistle flute's mouthpiece makes it easier to play than most other types of flute and cheap toy versions can be bought in many countries. The cuckoo whistle (5) can be used for orchestral effects.

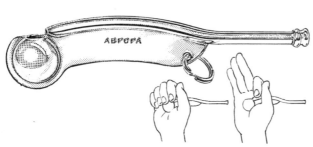

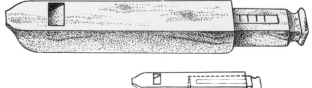

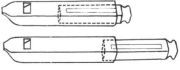

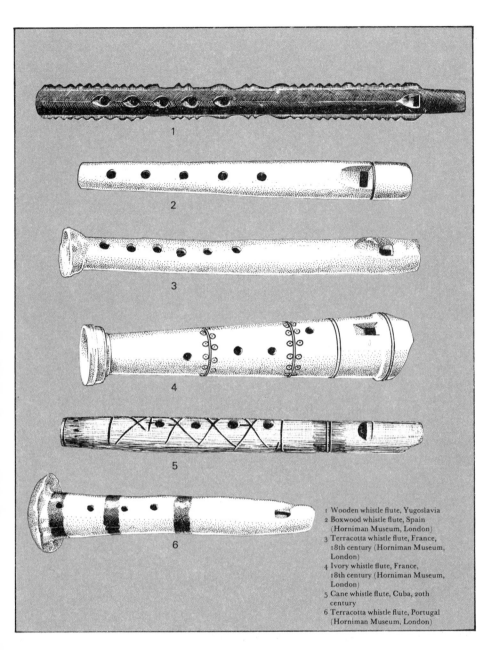

Above Fujara player.

Right Slovakian fujara. Made from wood, the fujara is exceptionally large for a whistle flute. The projecting mouthpiece, at some distance from the upper end of the pipe, enables the player to reach all the finger holes.

1 Wooden whistle flute, Yugoslavia
2 Boxwood whistle flute, Spain (Horniman Museum, London)
3 Terracotta whistle flute, France, 18th century (Horniman Museum, London)
4 Ivory whistle flute, France, 18th century (Horniman Museum, London)
5 Cane whistle flute, Cuba, 20th century
6 Terracotta whistle flute, Portugal (Horniman Museum, London)

Above Examples of folk whistle flutes from Europe and Cuba (5). Most common in Europe, this type of instrument is known in all continents. Many whistle flutes are straight-sided but others are markedly tapered, like the ivory flute (4), or flared, like the terracotta flute (6).

Below One-handed pipes used with a drum—a modern replica of a tabor (drum) pipe (1) and a Basque folk instrument, the txistu (2). One-man pipe and tabor ensembles became popular in parts of Europe in the 12th century but were later superseded by fifes and drums.

Right An 18th century pipe and tabor player.

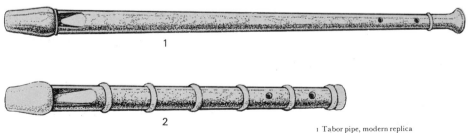

1 Tabor pipe, modern replica
2 Txistu, Basque

Vessel flutes and whistles

A vessel flute is characterized by its body shape, which is globular instead of tubular. The sound is produced by directing the airstream either across the sharp edge of a blow hole as in the end-blown flute, or into a whistle mouthpiece as in the whistle flute. Some vessel flutes, for instance the ocarina, have finger holes and sound different pitches. Others are simple whistles and produce only a single note.

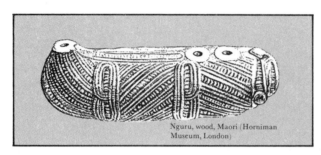

Nguru, wood, Maori (Horniman Museum, London)

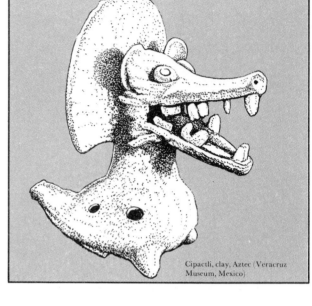

Cipactli, clay, Aztec (Veracruz Museum, Mexico)

Above Maori nguru from New Zealand—an intricately carved wood vessel flute with two finger holes.

Below Examples of primitive whistles. All are simply constructed, and bone, horn, cane, and wood are the most usual materials. Single-note whistles have a history dating back as far as the Stone Age, when they were commonly used as signal and decoy instruments.

Below Examples of the great variety of practical and novelty whistles. The referee's whistle (2) contains a captive pellet and the "surprise" whistle (3) has a bulb for regulating the sound. The bird whistle (7) is a tiny vessel flute that is filled with water for playing.

Above Aztec cipactli in the form of a lizard. Animal and human shapes were particularly popular with Aztec and Inca instrument makers.

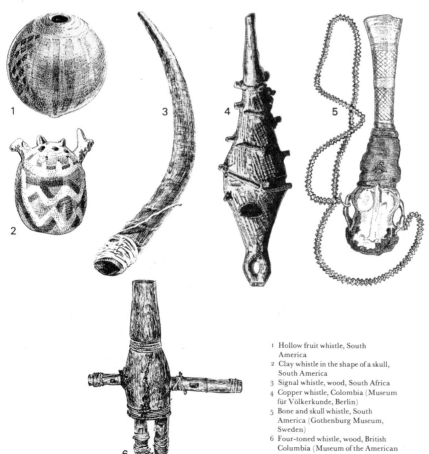

1 Hollow fruit whistle, South America
2 Clay whistle in the shape of a skull, South America
3 Signal whistle, wood, South Africa
4 Copper whistle, Colombia (Museum für Völkerkunde, Berlin)
5 Bone and skull whistle, South America (Gothenburg Museum, Sweden)
6 Four-toned whistle, wood, British Columbia (Museum of the American Indian, New York)

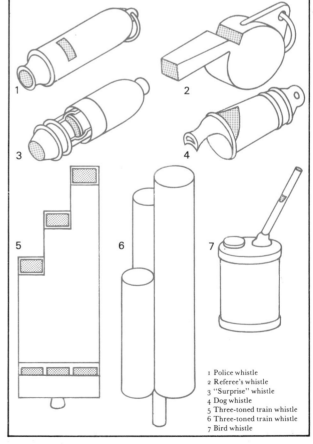

1 Police whistle
2 Referee's whistle
3 "Surprise" whistle
4 Dog whistle
5 Three-toned train whistle
6 Three-toned train whistle
7 Bird whistle

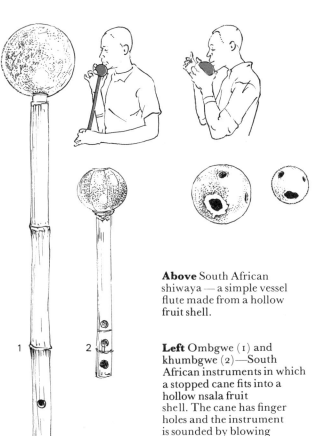

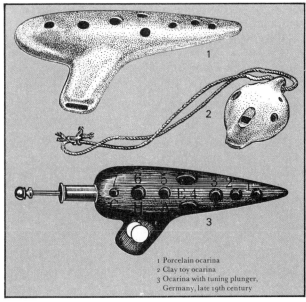

Above South African shiwaya — a simple vessel flute made from a hollow fruit shell.

Left Ombgwe (1) and khumbgwe (2)—South African instruments in which a stopped cane fits into a hollow nsala fruit shell. The cane has finger holes and the instrument is sounded by blowing across a hole in the shell.

1 Porcelain ocarina
2 Clay toy ocarina
3 Ocarina with tuning plunger, Germany, late 19th century

Above Ocarinas—vessel flutes with a whistle head and up to eight finger holes. The name ocarina was first used by Giuseppe Donati, who invented such an instrument in the late 1800s. Ocarinas of different sizes were used in ensembles in the early 1900s.

Below Peruvian clay jug in the form of a seated figure playing a notched flute. The shape of the hollow handle suggests that it was used as a whistling pot.

Whistling pot, clay, Peru
(Metropolitan Museum of Art, New York)

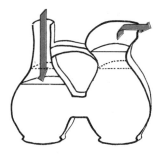

Above Double-vesseled whistling pot from Peru.
Left The connecting chambers are half-filled with water and air blown through the narrow neck into the first chamber. This forces water into the second chamber, which in turn forces air through the whistling head.

Whistling pot, clay, Peru
(Metropolitan Museum of Art, New York)

© DIAGRAM

Side-blown flutes

A side-blown flute is a pipe with the blow hole pierced in its side. The pipe is usually stopped at the end nearest the blow hole. It is usually held to the right of the player though occasionally this position is reversed. Such flutes are often made from wood or bamboo and the bore is roughly cylindrical. Side-blown flutes originated in Asia, where they were depicted as early as the 9th century BC. The side-blown flute is difficult both to make and to play, but is pleasant to listen to and can perform highly intricate melodies.

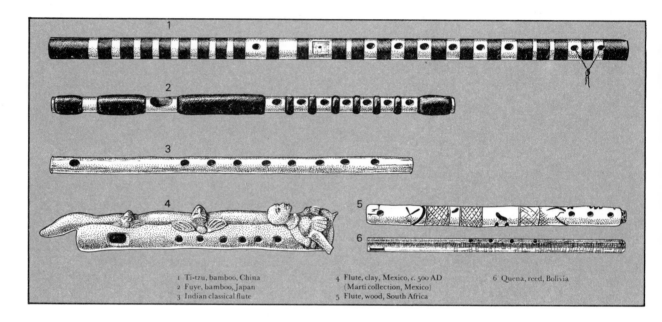

1 Ti-tzu, bamboo, China
2 Fuye, bamboo, Japan
3 Indian classical flute
4 Flute, clay, Mexico, c. 500 AD (Marti collection, Mexico)
5 Flute, wood, South Africa
6 Quena, reed, Bolivia

Above Sophisticated and simple side-blown flutes. The Chinese ti-tzu (1) and Japanese fuye (2) are equivalents of the Western orchestral flute. The ti-tzu has a vibrating membrane near the blow hole and this gives a characteristic reedy quality to the sound.

Left Statue of the Indian god Krishna playing a side-blown flute.

Right The South African naka ya lethlake (a) and the Panamanian flute (b) are typical primitive side-blown flutes. The Slovakian flute (c) is attractively finished with a carved ram's head.

Right Examples of hole arrangements. The number and position of finger holes varies in relation to the position of the blow hole and the length of the tube. The bottom example is stopped with a blow hole slightly off center to provide in effect two flutes of different lengths.

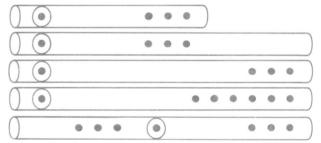

a

b

c

Fifes

A fife is a type of small side-blown flute. It has a cylindrical bore and is made in one piece. From the 16th century it has been associated with military and processional music. From about 1850 a small B♭ flute generally replaced the fife as a processional instrument, but a one-keyed instrument is still in use in some countries.

Right Military boy fifer.
Below Development of the fife. In the 19th century an E♭ key was added and experiments made regarding the shape of the bore (2), but the marching flute (3) soon became a serious rival. Recently, school instrument manufacturers have begun making plastic fifes (5).

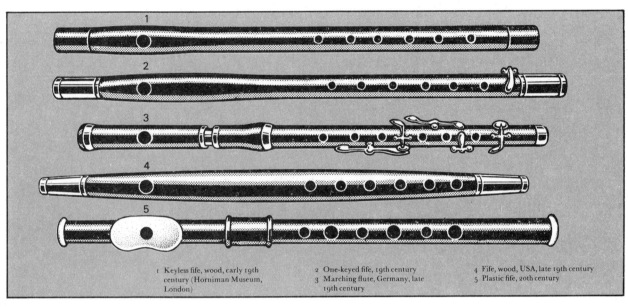

1 Keyless fife, wood, early 19th century (Horniman Museum, London)
2 One-keyed fife, 19th century
3 Marching flute, Germany, late 19th century
4 Fife, wood, USA, late 19th century
5 Plastic fife, 20th century

Nose flutes

A nose flute is an instrument sounded by breath from the nostril instead of from the mouth. The nose is obviously a less efficient projector of breath than the mouth, but among some primitive peoples of the Pacific nose breath is thought to have special powers. These flutes are found in other regions but particularly in Polynesia where the nose flute is the "national" instrument. The player generally plugs one nostril with tobacco or rag, or presses it closed with a finger. The most common version is side-blown, but end-blown nose flutes are played by the aboriginals of Borneo.

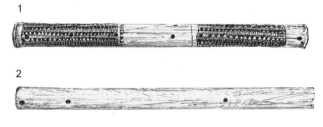

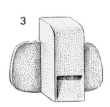

1 Nose flute, bamboo, Polynesia
2 Nose flute, bamboo, Tahiti
3 Novelty nose flute, plastic, 20th century

Above Nose flutes from Polynesia (1) and Tahiti (2). The Tahitian flute was brought home by the explorer Captain Cook. The novelty flute (3) works by the same principle.
Left Different playing techniques for the Malaysian nose flute (a), party novelty (b), and Polynesian nose flute (c).

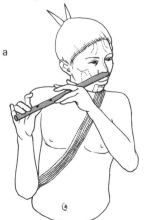

a

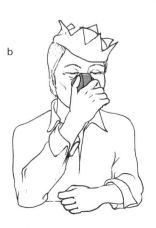

b

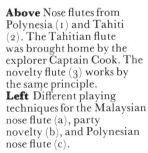

c

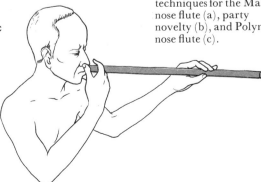

Multiple flutes

Pairs of flute players have been common since earliest times, and sometimes a single player would perform on two flutes at the same time. Later this gave rise in some areas to the development of multiple flutes, though with the exception of South American examples from antiquity the multiple flute has a much shorter history than the multiple reed pipe.

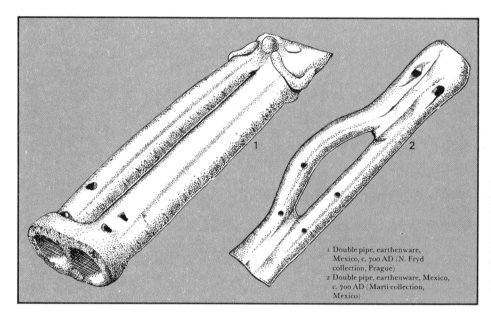

1 Double pipe, earthenware, Mexico, c. 700 AD (N. Fryd collection, Prague)
2 Double pipe, earthenware, Mexico, c. 700 AD (Marti collection, Mexico)

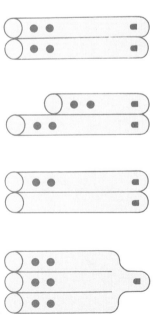

Above Slovakian peasant playing a double flute.
Below Some of the many forms of multiple pipe. Simple identical pipes produce the same pitch or set of pitches: different pitches are produced when the pipes vary in length or have differently placed finger holes.

Above Mexican double flutes made of clay. Such instruments in a great variety of shapes were common from the 4th–9th centuries AD. The use of a curved pipe in conjunction with a straight one is a neat way of "disguising" the different lengths of the two pipes.

Below Triple flutes. The Mexican triple flute (1) has one longer pipe that was probably unfingered and used as a drone. The South American triple whistle (2) has sound holes near the center of the pipes. The Tibetan gling-bu (3) has identically placed finger holes on each pipe.

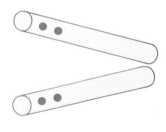

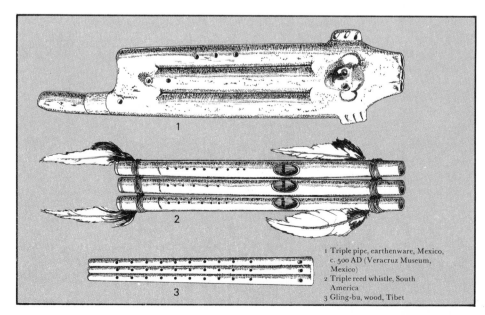

1 Triple pipe, earthenware, Mexico, c. 500 AD (Veracruz Museum, Mexico)
2 Triple reed whistle, South America
3 Gling-bu, wood, Tibet

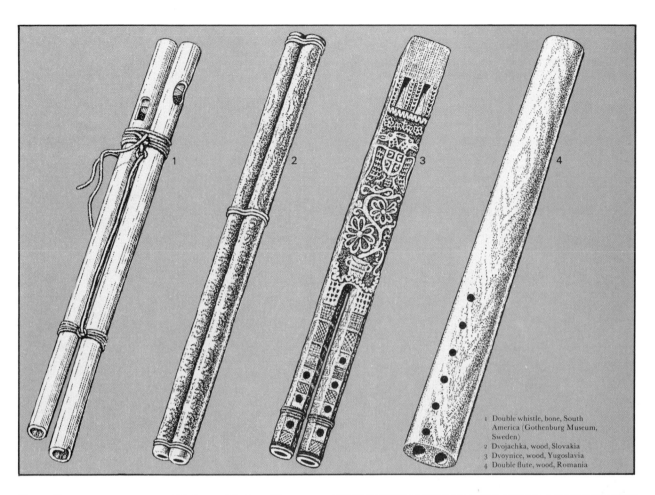

1 Double whistle, bone, South
   America (Gothenburg Museum,
   Sweden)
2 Dvojachka, wood, Slovakia
3 Dvoynice, wood, Yugoslavia
4 Double flute, wood, Romania

Above Contemporary
double flutes. The South
American whistle (1) and
the Slovakian dvojachka (2)
consists of two separate pipes
lashed together. The
intricately carved dvoynice
from Yugoslavia (3) and the
Romanian double flute (4)
are both fashioned from solid
blocks of wood.

Right and below Clay
quadruple pipes from
ancient Mexico. Because of
their width these instruments
have a narrow windway to
direct the air into all four
pipes simultaneously. This
principle is also fairly
common in triple pipes.

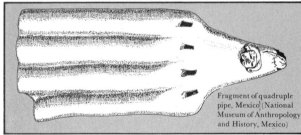

Fragment of quadruple
pipe, Mexico (National
Museum of Anthropology
and History, Mexico)

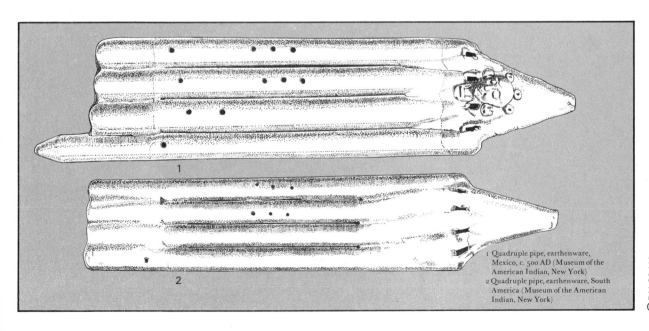

1 Quadruple pipe, earthenware,
   Mexico, c. 500 AD (Museum of the
   American Indian, New York)
2 Quadruple pipe, earthenware, South
   America (Museum of the American
   Indian, New York)

©DIAGRAM

Panpipes

Panpipes are sets of graduated flutes that are joined together in a raft or bunch shape. The sound is produced by blowing across the top of the holes. The tubes have no finger holes and the lower end is usually stopped. Panpipes have been known for over 2000 years and specimens have been found in most parts of the world. Materials include clay, stone, cane, wood, and, more recently, metal and plastic.

Left Pan, god of the ancient Greeks, playing the syrinx or "panpipe." According to legend, Pan was in love with a nymph who, fleeing from him, was turned into a reed by a protecting deity. Pan used this reed to make the first syrinx and played upon it for consolation.

1 Pottery panpipe, Peru, 200 BC–400 AD (Horniman Museum, London)
2 Stone panpipe, Peru (Merseyside County Museums)

Above Ancient Peruvian panpipes of clay (1) and stone (2). Both belong to the basic raft type but the clay example has a very simple external appearance compared with the decorative geometric design typical of stone panpipes.

Below Panpipers from Bolivia (left) and Northern Italy (right). Groups of folk musicians playing instruments of different sizes—with correspondingly different pitch capabilities—are found in many parts of the world.

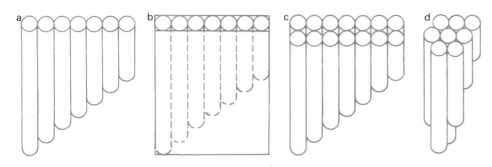

Left The four basic forms of panpipe. Simple raft panpipes include those made from separate pipes bound together (a) and those carved from a single block (b). The double panpipe (c) and the bundle panpipe (d) are more difficult to play and are less commonly found.

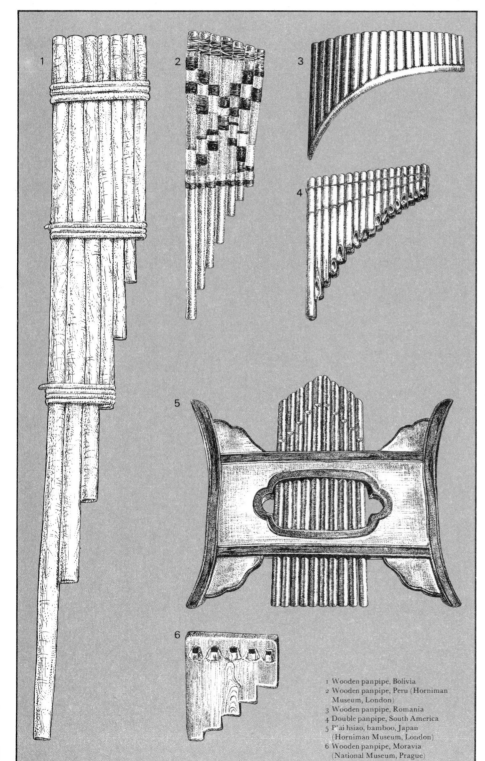

Left Wood and bamboo panpipes illustrating this instrument's wide distribution and diversity of shape.

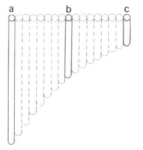

Above The relationship between the lengths of individual pipes and the notes sounded. Pipe (b) is half as long as pipe (a) and sounds a note one octave higher than pipe (a). Pipe (c) is half as long as pipe (b) and sounds one octave above pipe (b) and two octaves above pipe (a).

1 Wooden panpipe, Bolivia
2 Wooden panpipe, Peru (Horniman Museum, London)
3 Wooden panpipe, Romania
4 Double panpipe, South America
5 P'ai hsiao, bamboo, Japan (Horniman Museum, London)
6 Wooden panpipe, Moravia (National Museum, Prague)

Above Toy panpipe. Made of metal or plastic, these instruments are usually tuned to produce notes of the major scale. It is difficult to sound the pipes separately so it is usual to blow into them in quick succession in the style of a flourish. This effect can be heard in Mozart's "The Magic Flute."

©DIAGRAM

Recorders

The recorder is a type of whistle flute that was very important in renaissance and baroque music. It is usually made from wood and has a wide tapering bore. Despite the increasing complexity of other woodwind instruments, the recorder remained comparatively simple. Having been generally discarded from around 1750 in favor of the transverse flute, interest in the recorder was revived by the instrument maker Arnold Dolmetsch in 1919.

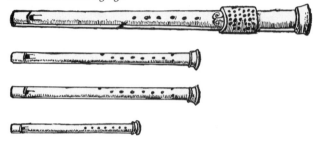

Above Woodcut showing four recorders, taken from Sebastian Virdung's book "Musica getutscht und Ausgezogen" published in 1511. The recorders illustrated are a bass (top), two means, and a treble (bottom).

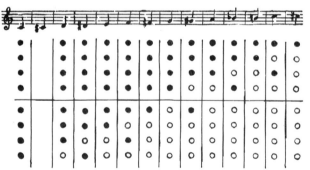

Above Fingering chart, after Virdung.

Left Illustrations of fingering from Virdung (top) and Hotteterre. In his book Virdung included illustrations showing each hand uppermost. By the time of Hotteterre's book, in 1707, playing right hand uppermost had almost died out.

Right A consort (set) of renaissance recorders. These instruments were characterized by their simple profile and by the absence of a pronounced bell. They produced a sweet and quiet tone, but the narrow windway and wide bore meant that the player had to blow quite strongly.

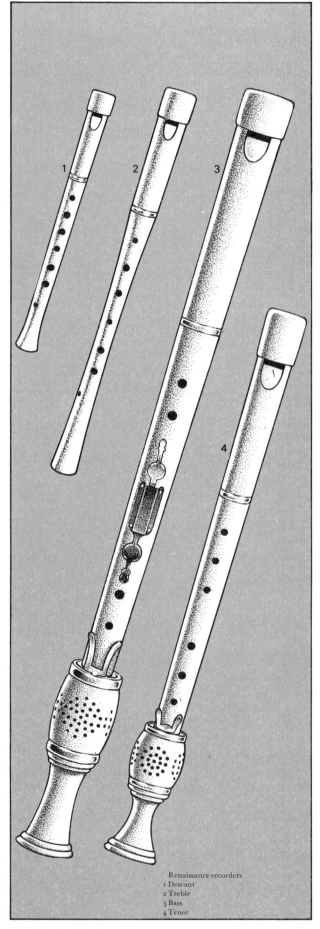

Renaissance recorders
1 Descant
2 Treble
3 Bass
4 Tenor

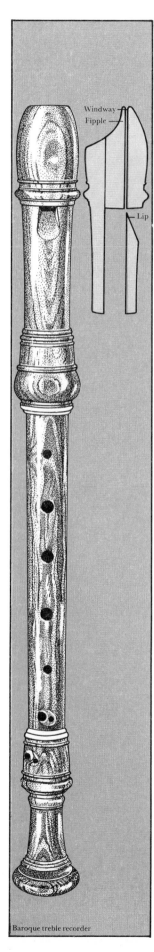

Baroque treble recorder

Left Baroque recorder and diagram of the mouthpiece. In this type of recorder, still used today, the upper end of the tube is plugged with a wood block called a fipple and the slit between this plug and the mouthpiece forms the windway. The air is thus directed against the sharp edge of the lip.

Right Consort of baroque recorders with their pitch ranges. The two new instruments—the great bass and the sopranino—were not usually used with the regular members of the consort. The sopranino was usually a solo instrument and the great bass was used to add richness to the bass line.

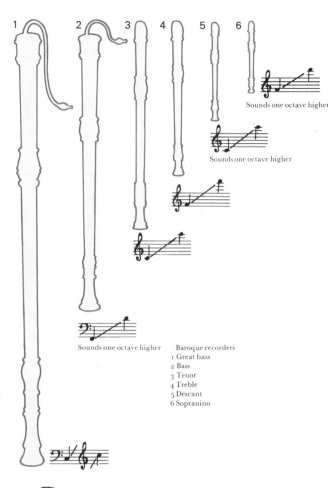

Sounds one octave higher

Sounds one octave higher

Sounds one octave higher

Baroque recorders
1 Great bass
2 Bass
3 Tenor
4 Treble
5 Descant
6 Sopranino

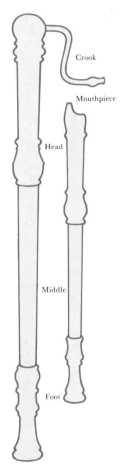

Crook

Mouthpiece

Head

Middle

Foot

Left Identification of recorder parts. The crook on bass instruments enables the player to reach all the finger holes.

Above Groups of recorder players. In the 16th and 17th centuries recorders were widely played by groups of amateurs. The 20th century revival of interest in the recorder has led to the development of cheap plastic recorders that are particularly useful in schools.

©DIAGRAM

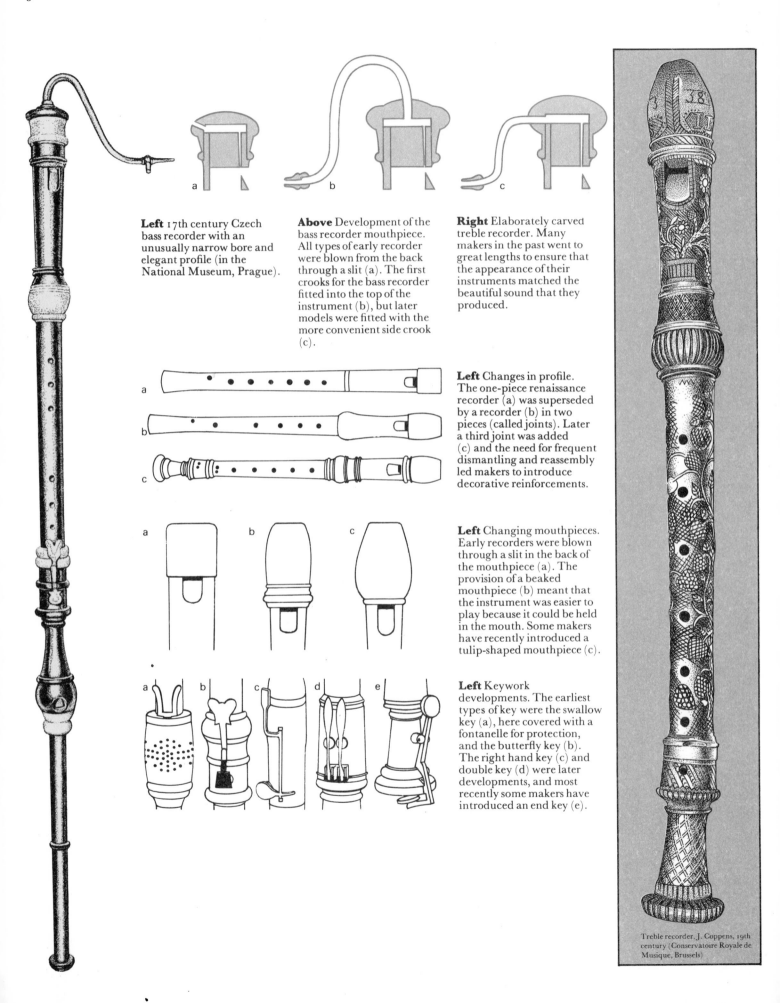

Left 17th century Czech bass recorder with an unusually narrow bore and elegant profile (in the National Museum, Prague).

Above Development of the bass recorder mouthpiece. All types of early recorder were blown from the back through a slit (a). The first crooks for the bass recorder fitted into the top of the instrument (b), but later models were fitted with the more convenient side crook (c).

Right Elaborately carved treble recorder. Many makers in the past went to great lengths to ensure that the appearance of their instruments matched the beautiful sound that they produced.

Left Changes in profile. The one-piece renaissance recorder (a) was superseded by a recorder (b) in two pieces (called joints). Later a third joint was added (c) and the need for frequent dismantling and reassembly led makers to introduce decorative reinforcements.

Left Changing mouthpieces. Early recorders were blown through a slit in the back of the mouthpiece (a). The provision of a beaked mouthpiece (b) meant that the instrument was easier to play because it could be held in the mouth. Some makers have recently introduced a tulip-shaped mouthpiece (c).

Left Keywork developments. The earliest types of key were the swallow key (a), here covered with a fontanelle for protection, and the butterfly key (b). The right hand key (c) and double key (d) were later developments, and most recently some makers have introduced an end key (e).

Treble recorder, J. Coppens, 19th century (Conservatoire Royale de Musique, Brussels)

Flageolets

The flageolet is a whistle flute with a narrow tapering bore, and was popular in England and France from the 17th to 19th centuries. It is similar both in use and appearance to the recorder, but in the 18th century the flageolet's beaked mouthpiece was replaced by a slim nozzle of bone or ivory. Though primarily an unsophisticated solo instrument it was often used in bands or orchestras to play the highest part.

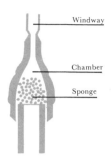

Windway
Chamber
Sponge

Left Section through the head of a flageolet with a nozzle mouthpiece. The tiny sponge absorbed the player's saliva.
Below right Modern toy flageolet made from metal with a plastic mouthpiece. These instruments are available in a variety of sizes and are very similar to the tin whistle.

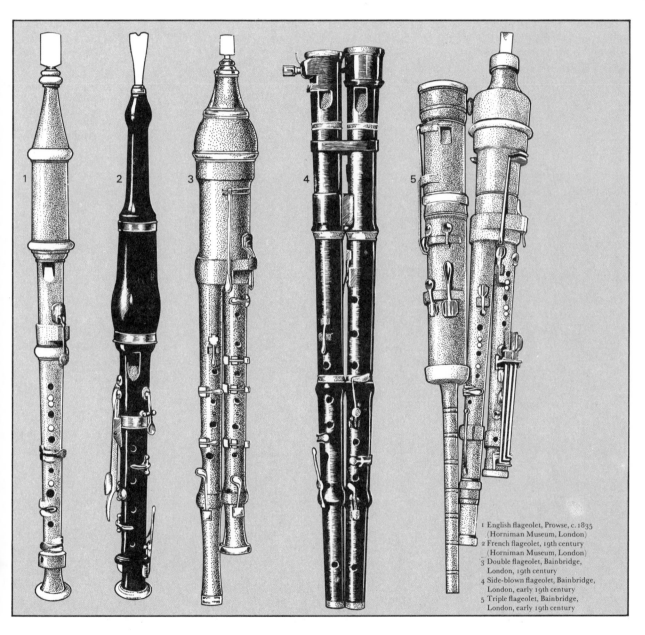

1 English flageolet, Prowse, c. 1835 (Horniman Museum, London)
2 French flageolet, 19th century (Horniman Museum, London)
3 Double flageolet, Bainbridge, London, 19th century
4 Side-blown flageolet, Bainbridge, London, early 19th century
5 Triple flageolet, Bainbridge, London, early 19th century

Above Different types of flageolet. The two basic types were the English flageolet (1) with six finger holes, and the French flageolet (2) with four finger holes and two thumb holes. The double flageolet (3) enjoyed some popularity in England in the early 1800s.

It had one mouthpiece leading to two pipes and was therefore capable of playing chords. The side-blown flageolet (4) was a rarity, and Bainbridge's triple flageolet (5) was too complex ever to become popular.

Orchestral flutes

The Western classical flute is a side-blown, or transverse, flute that first reached Europe from the East in the 12th century. During the Middle Ages it was chiefly associated with military music, but by the middle of the 17th century had become more important as an instrument of the opera and court orchestra. The first major changes in Western flute design were made in the late 17th century by the French Hotteterre family. Even more important were the radical developments introduced by Theobald Boehm of Munich in the early 1830s. His design has remained largely unaltered until the present day, and "Boehm flutes," made of wood or metal, are today played in symphony orchestras all over the world.

Left Flute player from a medieval military band.

Below The development of keywork on the orchestral flute. The earliest flutes had no keys and some notes were poor in quality and inaccurate in pitch. The addition of keys to correct these defects was a gradual process over 150 years—the earliest keys being added at the instrument's lower end.

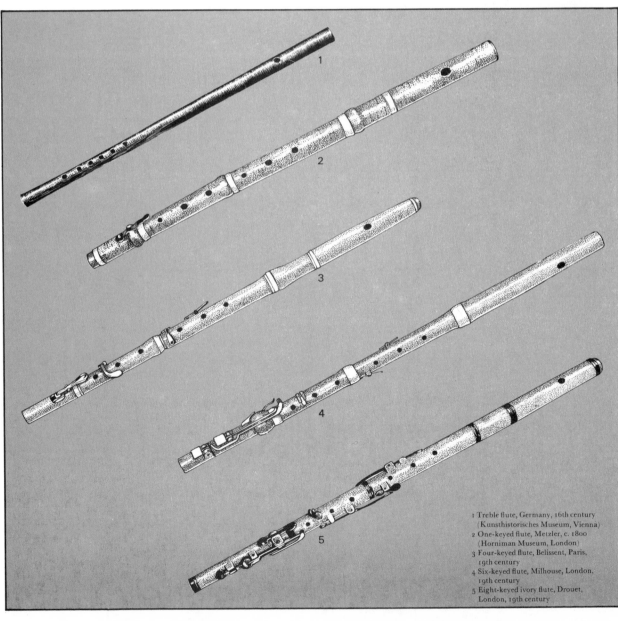

1 Treble flute, Germany, 16th century (Kunsthistorisches Museum, Vienna)
2 One-keyed flute, Metzler, c. 1800 (Horniman Museum, London)
3 Four-keyed flute, Belissent, Paris, 19th century
4 Six-keyed flute, Milhouse, London, 19th century
5 Eight-keyed ivory flute, Drouet, London, 19th century

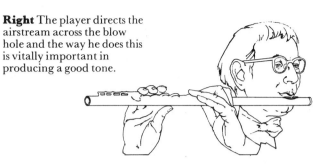

Right The player directs the airstream across the blow hole and the way he does this is vitally important in producing a good tone.

Above Illustration based on Agricola's "Musica Instrumentalis deudsch" of 1528. These cylindrical flutes are, from top to bottom, the descant, alto, tenor, and bass.

Below Illustration of a Hotteterre flute dating from the early 1700s. This instrument is in three sections, has one key, and was the type used for most of the 18th century.

Below The development of flutes of different sizes. The piccolo (1) and flute in F (5) extended the range up, and the alto (2) and bass flutes (3 and 4) extended it down. Of these instruments the most useful has been the piccolo, which sounds one octave higher than the standard orchestral flute.

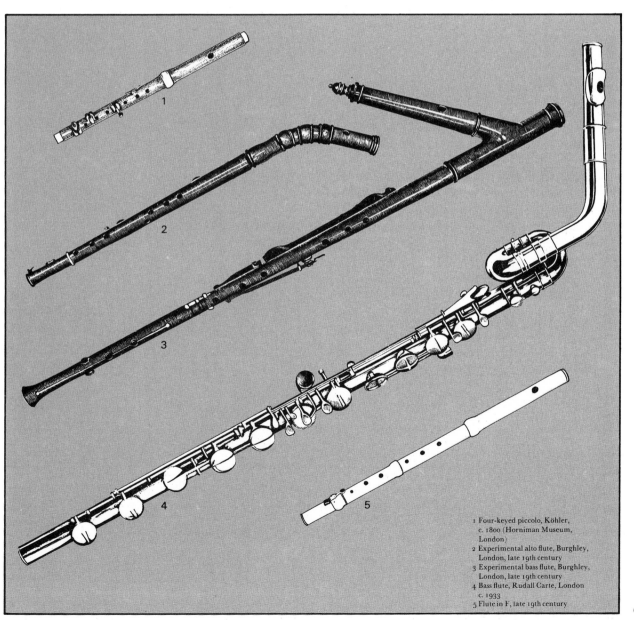

1 Four-keyed piccolo, Köhler, c. 1800 (Horniman Museum, London)
2 Experimental alto flute, Burghley, London, late 19th century
3 Experimental bass flute, Burghley, London, late 19th century
4 Bass flute, Rudall Carte, London c. 1933
5 Flute in F, late 19th century

Above Blow hole changes. The earliest flutes had a simple, circular blow hole (a). Later, an oval hole (b) was found to produce a more vibrant tone. The modern flute has a lip plate (c) to help direct the airstream.

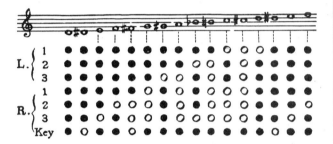

Above Flute fingering chart drawn from that by Jean Hotteterre, and an illustration of this famous French instrument maker playing the flute.

Blow hole

Head joint

Middle joint

Foot joint

Left Naming of parts of the flute. (The word joint is used for each section.)
Right Members of the orchestral flute family. The standard flute (1) is prominent in the instrumental texture of chamber and orchestral music, and is also a favorite solo instrument. The piccolo (2) is occasionally used for orchestral solos and for doubling a flute or violin melody an octave higher. As the lower notes of the bass flute (3) and alto flute (4) do not carry well through the orchestral texture, these instruments are usually used in quieter passages where their mellow sound can best be heard.

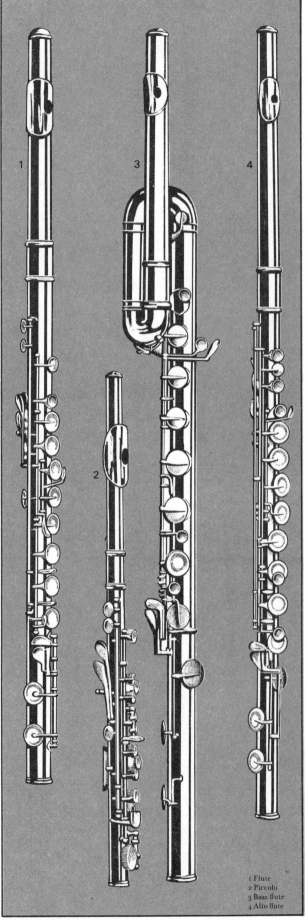

1 Flute
2 Piccolo
3 Bass flute
4 Alto flute

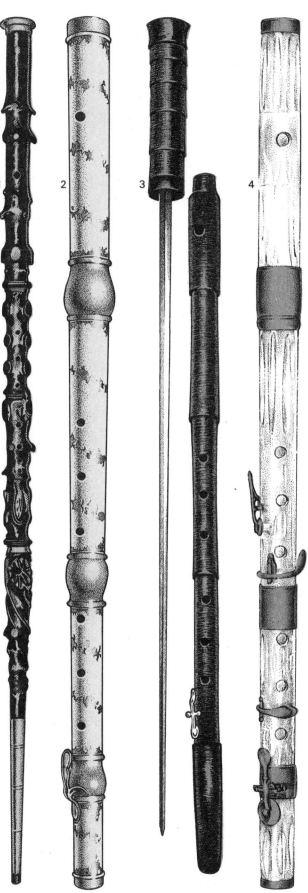

Left Unusual flutes from the late 18th and early 19th centuries. Of these, only the **glass flute (4)** represented a serious attempt to produce an instrument to rival the standard contemporary flute. (Not drawn to scale.)

1 Walking stick flute, late 19th century (Castello Sforzesca, Milan)
2 Porcelain flute, Germany, 18th century (Prague State Academy of Music)
3 Flute and dagger, late 18th century (Horniman Museum, London)
4 Four-keyed glass flute, Laurent, 1826 (Horniman Museum, London)

Right Two Giorgi flutes dating from around 1900. Giorgi was an imaginative Italian instrument maker who sought to develop an alternative to the Boehm flute. These flutes were made of ebonite and were end-blown. Some of his models were without keys whereas others had an unusually large number.

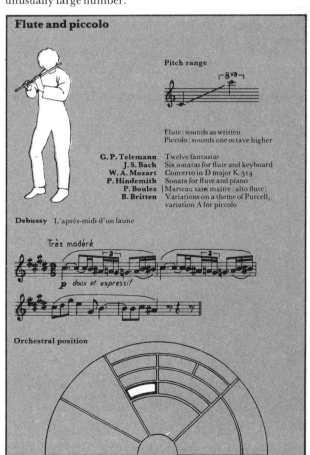

Flute and piccolo

Pitch range

Flute: sounds as written
Piccolo: sounds one octave higher

G. P. Telemann   Twelve fantasias
J. S. Bach   Six sonatas for flute and keyboard
W. A. Mozart   Concerto in D major K.314
P. Hindemith   Sonata for flute and piano
P. Boulez   Marteau sans maître (alto flute)
B. Britten   Variations on a theme of Purcell, variation A for piccolo

Debussy   L'après-midi d'un faune

Très modéré

p doux et expressif

Orchestral position

Folk clarinets

Instruments in the clarinet family are characterized by a single beating reed, or tongue, which is cut out of, or attached to, a cylindrical tube. This type of instrument probably originated in ancient Egypt and from there spread through North Africa and Europe. Clarinets are less common elsewhere in Africa, in Asia, and in North America, but appear in a great variety of forms in South America.

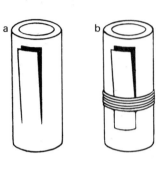

Left Diagrams showing the two basic types of clarinet. In an idioglottal instrument the reed is cut from the tube (a). The heteroglottal type has an attached reed (b).

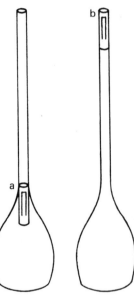

Left Different reed positions. Sometimes the reed is in the lower part of the tube (a). More usually it is at the top of the tube (b) and is held in the player's mouth.

Right Heteroglottal clarinets from the Indians of North and South America. The North American Haida clarinet (1) has a reed between two hollowed out lengths of cedar wood. The South American clarinets are gourd and cane (2 and 3), and gourd and bone (4).

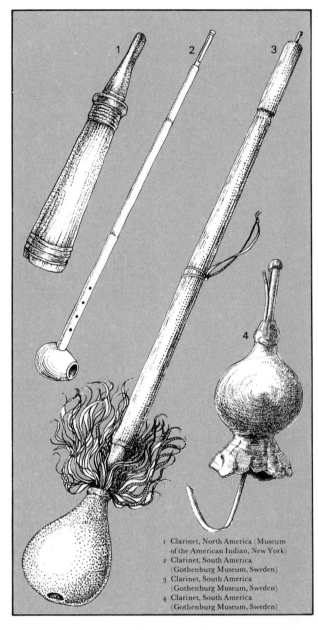

1 Clarinet, North America (Museum of the American Indian, New York)
2 Clarinet, South America (Gothenburg Museum, Sweden)
3 Clarinet, South America (Gothenburg Museum, Sweden)
4 Clarinet, South America (Gothenburg Museum, Sweden)

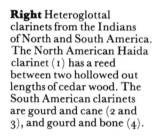

Left Simple idioglottal clarinets from the Goajiro Indians of South America (1) and from Cyprus (2). The Goajiro cane clarinet has a down-cut reed and four finger holes. The Cypriot reed clarinet has an up-cut reed and two finger holes.

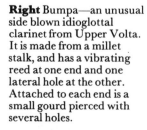

Right Bumpa—an unusual side blown idioglottal clarinet from Upper Volta. It is made from a millet stalk, and has a vibrating reed at one end and one lateral hole at the other. Attached to each end is a small gourd pierced with several holes.

Right Single-reed horn-pipes. Found in many parts of the world, hornpipes may be simple or very elaborate. The simplest type has a beating reed cut from a single length of cane fitted into a cow horn (1). More elaborate examples have finger holes, protective mouth horns, and, sometimes, more than one pipe. The Welsh pibcorn (2) fell into disuse in the 18th century.

Below Diagram showing a hornpipe reed protected by a mouth horn.

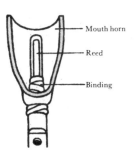

— Mouth horn

— Reed

— Binding

Below Hornpipes and players. The Basque alboka (1) has two cane pipes, a wood handle, and a horn at each end. The Moroccan double hornpipe (2) has two cane pipes, each fitted with a cow horn. The obsolete Scottish stock-and-horn (3) had a wood or bone pipe and a horn at the end.

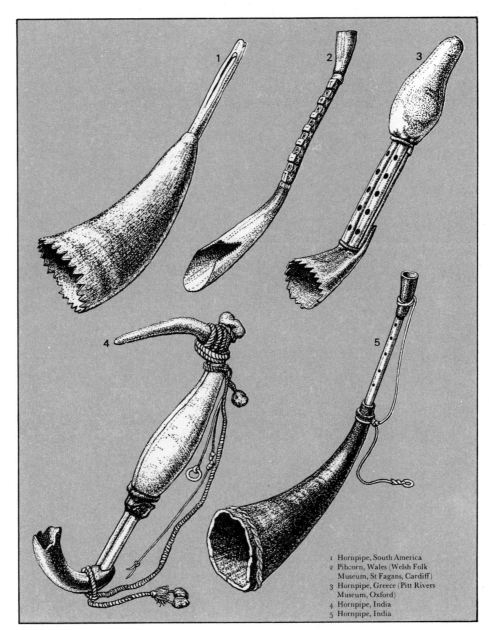

1 Hornpipe, South America
2 Pibcorn, Wales (Welsh Folk Museum, St Fagans, Cardiff)
3 Hornpipe, Greece (Pitt Rivers Museum, Oxford)
4 Hornpipe, India
5 Hornpipe, India

© DIAGRAM

Multiple clarinets

The widespread practice of playing wind instruments in pairs led in some parts of the world to the development of double, and even triple or quadruple, clarinets. Instruments of this kind are particularly important in Arab countries, but examples are also found elsewhere —notably in the Balkans, India, Sardinia, and South America. The combination of melody and drone pipes is often found in these instruments.

Right Tiktiri—a double clarinet of a kind found throughout the Indian sub-continent. It has two cane pipes fitted into a gourd that acts as both blowpipe and wind chamber. This instrument's strange melodic sound is popularly associated with the art of the snake charmer.

Right Double clarinets from the Balkans. The diple šurle (1) has two divergent wood pipes fitted into a wood mouth horn. The diplice (2) has a traditionally decorated mouth horn, and two pipes carved from one piece of wood. The leather-bound clarinet (3) has two pipes of different lengths.

Below Yugoslavian musician playing a double clarinet.

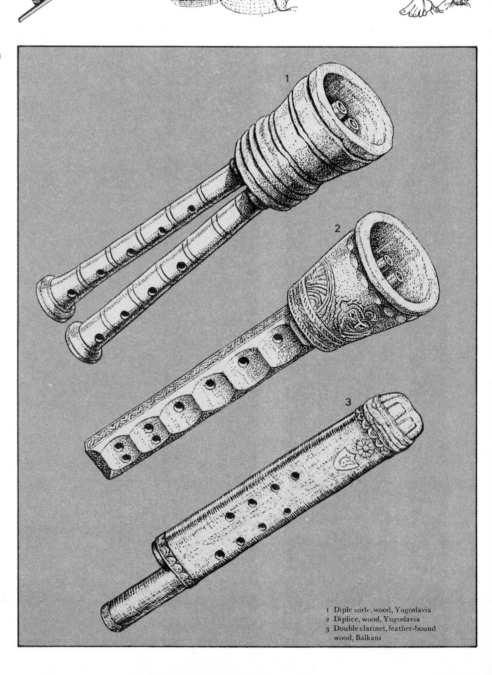

1 Diple šurle, wood, Yugoslavia
2 Diplice, wood, Yugoslavia
3 Double clarinet, leather-bound wood, Balkans

Right Brazilian Camayura
Indians playing the urua—
an enormous double clarinet.
The urua (illustrated far
right) is made of two unequal
lengths of cane, with inset
idioglottal reeds (shown in
the diagram). In rituals the
longer pipe is considered
male and the shorter pipe
female.

Below Multiple clarinets.
The Sardinian launeddas (1)
has two melody pipes and
one longer drone pipe. The
Egyptian double clarinet (2)
and arghul (3) also have
drones. The ancient
Egyptian example (4),
Tunisian zummara (5), and
Palestinian clarinet (6) all
have two similar pipes.

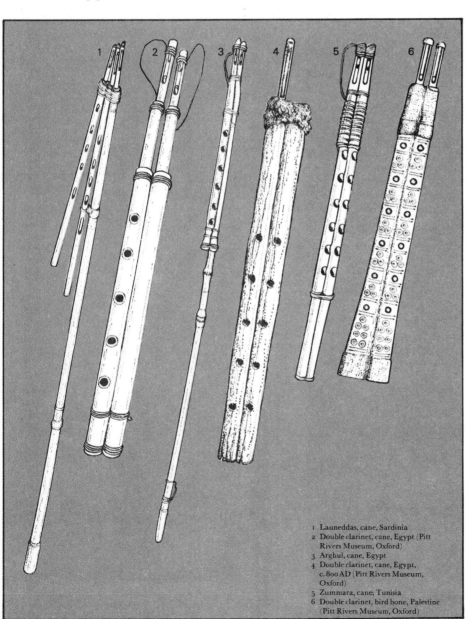

1 Launeddas, cane, Sardinia
2 Double clarinet, cane, Egypt (Pitt
  Rivers Museum, Oxford)
3 Arghul, cane, Egypt
4 Double clarinet, cane, Egypt,
  c. 800 AD (Pitt Rivers Museum,
  Oxford)
5 Zummara, cane, Tunisia
6 Double clarinet, bird bone, Palestine
  (Pitt Rivers Museum, Oxford)

© DIAGRAM

Orchestral clarinets

The orchestral clarinet is one of the most versatile of all orchestral instruments. It was first developed from the chalumeau around 1700 by the German instrument-maker J. C. Denner. Over a period of about 20 years the clarinet became distinguishable from the chalumeau by its separate mouthpiece, its bell, and the addition of extra keys which enabled it to play higher notes. In the 1840s the Boehm system of keys, already successfully applied to the orchestral flute, was added to the clarinet. It brought a new facility to clarinet playing and remains the favored system for modern instruments. Throughout its history the clarinet has been made in different sizes. There are also a number of related single-reed instruments, of which the basset horn is the most important.

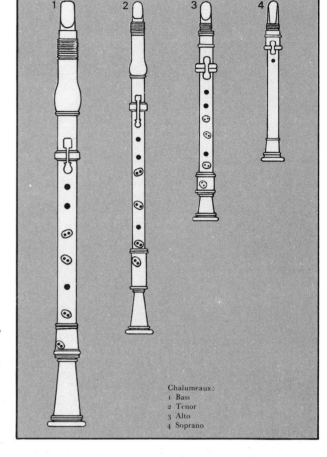

Chalumeaux:
1 Bass
2 Tenor
3 Alto
4 Soprano

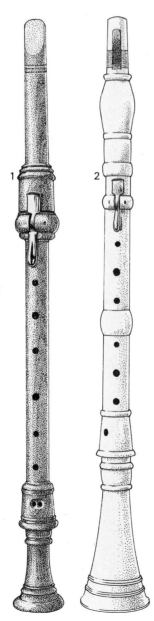

Right Modern replicas of a family of chalumeaux—bass, tenor, alto, and soprano. The chalumeau, a simple single-reed instrument made of wood, was the direct ancestor of the orchestral clarinet. Even after the development of the clarinet, chalumeaux were used in opera orchestras.

Left Early clarinets with two keys—the other key is on the back, opposite the front key. The clarinet by J. C. Denner (1) is one of his earliest models and is not very different from a chalumeau. Scherer's ivory clarinet of about 1725 (2) shows the shape more typical of later clarinets.

Right Modern clarinet family, comprising E♭, B♭, A, alto, bass, and contrabass instruments. The B♭ (2) and A (3) are the most often used, and professional players have matched pairs. The E♭ (1) clarinet is less common and is used for special effects. It appears in Berlioz's Fantastic Symphony.

1 Two-keyed clarinet, J. C. Denner, early 18th century (Bavarian National Museum, Munich)
2 Two-keyed clarinet, ivory, Scherer, c.1725

Modern clarinets:
1 E♭
2 B♭
3 A
4 Alto
5 Bass
6 Contrabass

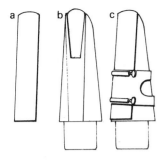

a b c

Above Diagrams of the clarinet reed (a), separate mouthpiece (b), and the reed fixed to the mouthpiece by the metal ligature (c). Mouthpieces are usually made of wood or ebonite. Reeds are usually natural cane, but plastic or fiberglass are sometimes used.

Right The B♭ (1) and alto (2) clarinets show the two basic shapes of modern clarinets. The B♭ clarinet is the most commonly used of all clarinets and is a versatile instrument well suited to the expression of different moods. The alto clarinet appears only rarely in orchestral scores.

Left Contrabass player. The contrabass clarinet is made in a variety of styles but is seen only very occasionally. It plays extremely low notes and has an easily distinguishable soft, round tone. It is sometimes used in Tchaikovsky's 6th symphony.

Clarinet

Written pitch range
(Clarinet in B♭ sounds one tone lower; clarinet in A sounds a minor third lower)

W. A. Mozart	Concerto in A major, K.622
W. A. Mozart	Adagio for clarinets and basset horns, K.411
F. Schmitt	Sextet for clarinets (E♭, two B♭, E♭ alto, bass, and contrabass)
J. Brahms	Quintet for clarinet and strings, op. 115
C. Debussy	Rhapsody for clarinet and piano
A. Copland	Concerto for clarinet, harp, and strings

Mozart Symphony no. 39, 3rd movement

Allegretto

Clarinet 1

Clarinet 2

Orchestral position

1

2

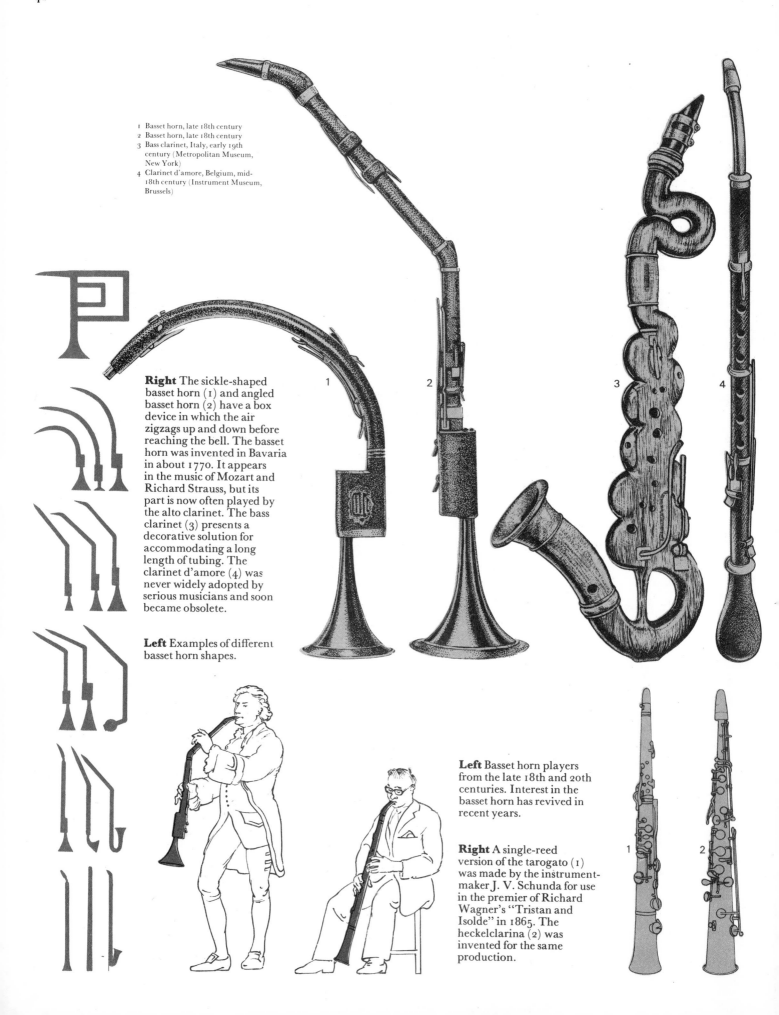

42

1 Basset horn, late 18th century
2 Basset horn, late 18th century
3 Bass clarinet, Italy, early 19th
   century (Metropolitan Museum,
   New York)
4 Clarinet d'amore, Belgium, mid-
   18th century (Instrument Museum,
   Brussels)

Right The sickle-shaped
basset horn (1) and angled
basset horn (2) have a box
device in which the air
zigzags up and down before
reaching the bell. The basset
horn was invented in Bavaria
in about 1770. It appears
in the music of Mozart and
Richard Strauss, but its
part is now often played by
the alto clarinet. The bass
clarinet (3) presents a
decorative solution for
accommodating a long
length of tubing. The
clarinet d'amore (4) was
never widely adopted by
serious musicians and soon
became obsolete.

Left Examples of different
basset horn shapes.

Left Basset horn players
from the late 18th and 20th
centuries. Interest in the
basset horn has revived in
recent years.

Right A single-reed
version of the tarogato (1)
was made by the instrument-
maker J. V. Schunda for use
in the premier of Richard
Wagner's "Tristan and
Isolde" in 1865. The
heckelclarina (2) was
invented for the same
production.

Saxophones

Saxophones are classified with clarinets as members of the single-reed family, but they are actually a hybrid of the clarinet and the oboe. Like the clarinet the saxophone has a single reed attached to a beaked mouthpiece, but its conical tube and flared bell are more typical of the oboe family. The saxophone was invented about 1840 by Adolphe Sax, a Belgian instrument-maker working in Paris. Sax's original family of saxophones comprised 14 members, but only eight of these are normally made today. These eight are, starting with the smallest, the sopranino, soprano, alto, tenor, baritone, bass, contrabass, and subcontrabass. Only the soprano, alto, tenor, and baritone are widely used. Saxophones are regular members of dance bands and military bands, and occasionally they are used to play distinctive solos in orchestral works.

Below Tenor, or melody, saxophone (1)—with the bent tube and upturned bell characteristic of all but the smallest two members of the saxophone family. Along with the alto and baritone, the tenor saxophone features prominently in the full-bodied sound of the big band.

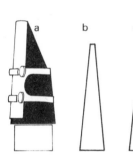

Left Diagram emphasizing the hybrid nature of the saxophone. A single-reed clarinet-type mouthpiece (a) and an instrument with the conical bore typical of the oboe family (b) were brought together (c) to produce an instrument of great versatility.

Right Soprano saxophone (2). Like the smaller sopranino, the soprano saxophone has a straight conical tube. The soprano saxophone is used particularly in jazz bands as a melody instrument along with the clarinet and trumpet. The sopranino is used in military bands.

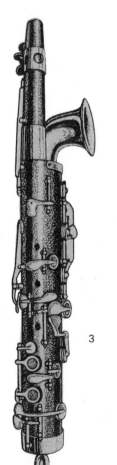

1 Tenor saxophone
2 Soprano saxophone
3 Octavin, late 19th century
  (Horniman Museum, London)

Left Octavin (3)—an unusual wood instrument that in various parts resembles the saxophone, clarinet, and bassoon. First made in Germany in 1894, this complicated instrument had little popular appeal. It has a reedy tone similar to the soprano saxophone.

Folk shawms

Instruments of the shawm family date back to the ancient civilizations of the Middle East and Europe. These instruments were usually played in pairs. Today, folk shawms made of wood or metal are common in Europe, Asia, and parts of Africa. All these instruments, like the modern oboe, have double reeds made from dried cane. Shawms produce a strident buzzing tone and are usually played outdoors.

Left A simple double reed. The two blades of dried cane are bound together and fitted into the top of the instrument. The reeds vibrate when the player blows through the aperture between them.

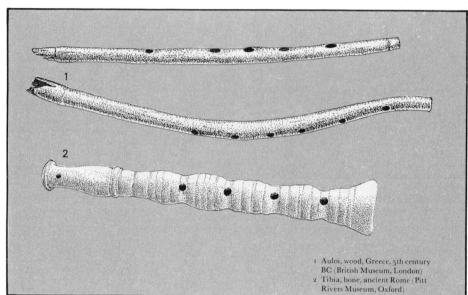

Left Ancient double-reed instruments. The auloi (1) are a pair of double-reed pipes from ancient Greece. Few examples survive, and these are shrunk and warped with age. Auloi players wore a characteristic chin strap (far left). The tibia (2) is one of a pair of Roman double-reed pipes.

1 Auloi, wood, Greece, 5th century BC (British Museum, London)
2 Tibia, bone, ancient Rome (Pitt Rivers Museum, Oxford)

Below Examples of folk shawms from Europe and the USSR. Their variety is emphasized by the two shawms from Yugoslavia (1 and 2). The Catalan tiple (4) is a more sophisticated keyed instrument. The Breton bombarde (5) and Italian piffaro (6) are used to accompany bagpipes.

1 Zurla, Yugoslavia
2 Sopile, Yugoslavia
3 Surnaj, USSR (Museum of Folk Art, Tashkent)
4 Tiple, Spain (Conservatorio Municipal, Barcelona)
5 Bombarde, France
6 Piffaro, Italy
7 Tarogato, Hungary

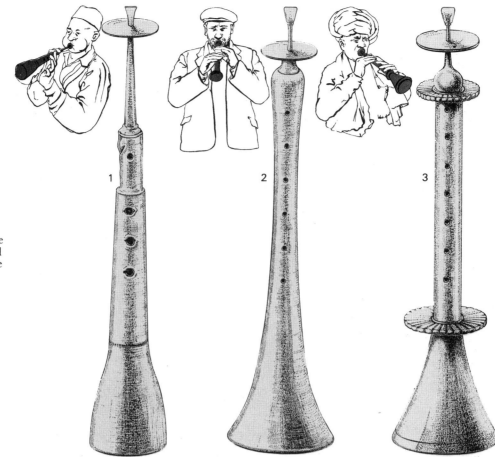

Right The Nigerian alghaita (1) has a metal mouthpiece and leather-covered wood body. Its player puffs out his cheeks to form a wind chamber. The Turkish zurna (2) is a typical Middle Eastern shawm. The Indian shanai (3) has decorative rings where its sections are fitted together.

Below Examples of folk shawms from the Far East. These instruments show an even greater variety of shape than Western examples. The Indian shawm (4) is a double version of the shanai. The pi nai (6) has an unusual quadruple reed made from dried palm leaf.

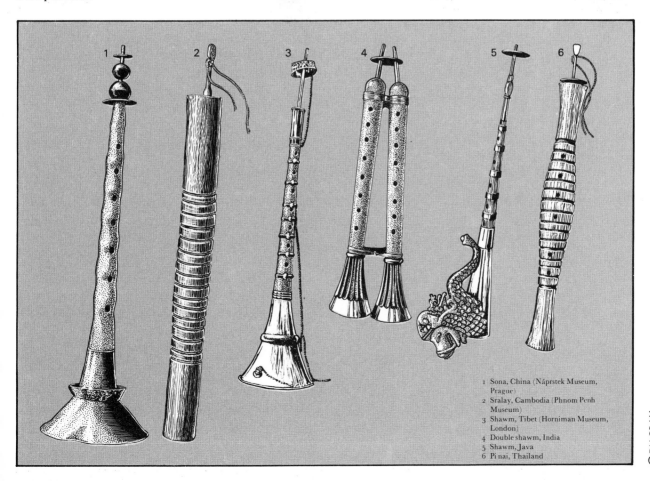

1 Sona, China (Náprstek Museum, Prague)
2 Sralay, Cambodia (Phnom Penh Museum)
3 Shawm, Tibet (Horniman Museum, London)
4 Double shawm, India
5 Shawm, Java
6 Pi nai, Thailand

©DIAGRAM

Renaissance double reeds

The shawm, the most important early double-reed instrument, was played in Europe as early as the 13th century. This instrument was made in different sizes and produced a loud sound that was best suited to outdoor music. In the 16th century there developed a wide and unusual range of different double-reed instruments more suited to indoor playing. A characteristic feature of some of these instruments was a reed-cap, which protected the reed and acted as a wind chamber. This made them easy to blow and a favorite instrument for consort playing. Limited tone quality and range, however, later led them to be replaced by the more responsive instruments of the baroque period. Also developed in the 16th century were deeper double-reed instruments characterized by the doubled-back bore now seen in the modern bassoon.

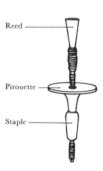

Left Double reed mounted on a conical metal staple and fitted with a wood pirouette. The player takes the reed into his mouth and rests his lips against the pirouette.

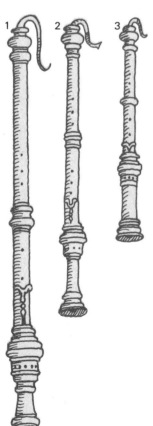

Left Family of basanelli, taken from Praetorius's book "Syntagma Musicum" (1618–20). Basanelli were a type of shawm and were made in three sizes—bass (1), alto tenor (2), and treble (3). They had a slightly conical bore ending in a false bell. All sizes were blown through a crook.

Right The three commonest sizes of renaissance shawm —treble (1), alto (2), and tenor (3). The tenor, with the less common bass and great bass, is sometimes called a pommer—the German name for larger types of shawm.
Below Musician playing the unwieldy great bass shawm.

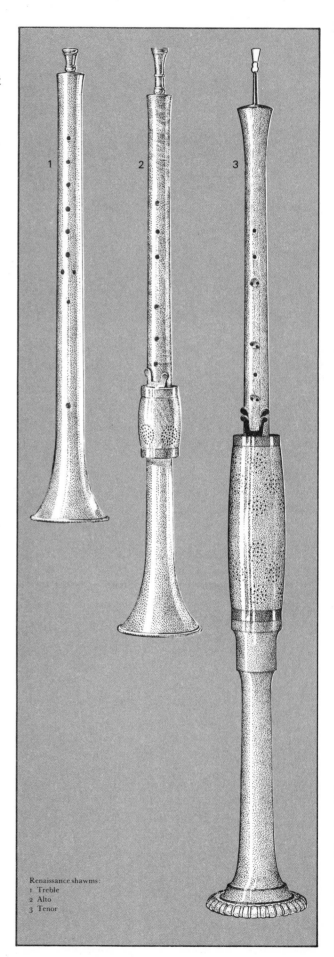

Renaissance shawms:
1 Treble
2 Alto
3 Tenor

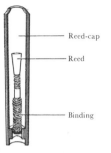

Above Diagram of the top of a reed-cap instrument. The cap acts as a wind chamber, in which the reed vibrates when the player blows through a small opening. Instruments with reed-caps produce notes that are always of uniform strength and quality.

Left Common renaissance double-reed instruments. The courtaut (1) has two channels in a single piece of wood. The cornemuse (2) is a modern reproduction of an instrument described by Praetorius. The crumhorn (3) has a slender, hooked tube, and was the most popular of the reed-cap instruments. The rauschpfeife (4) was a German reed-cap instrument with a small bell. The deutsche schalmei (5) had a narrow bore, long flaring bell, and a single key covered by a fontanelle. The curtal (6) and the sordone (7) had double-backed tubes and were blown through a crook.

Below A racket, with a diagram showing the long air channel that produced its very deep sound.

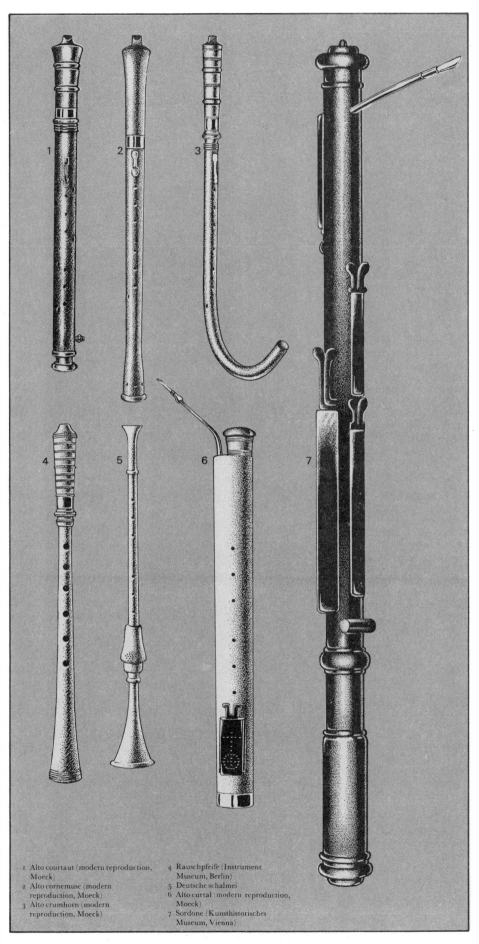

1 Alto courtaut (modern reproduction, Moeck)
2 Alto cornemuse (modern reproduction, Moeck)
3 Alto crumhorn (modern reproduction, Moeck)
4 Rauschpfeife (Instrument Museum, Berlin)
5 Deutsche schalmei
6 Alto curtal (modern reproduction, Moeck)
7 Sordone (Kunsthistorisches Museum, Vienna)

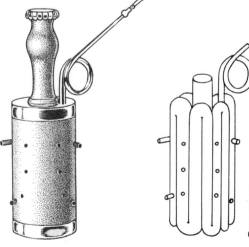

© DIAGRAM

Orchestral oboes

The oboe was developed from the treble shawm in the 17th century to meet the demand for a shawm-like instrument suitable for indoor use. The first oboes are thought to have been made by the Hotteterre family and were used by musicians at the court of Louis XIV. They were made in three sections, and had accurately calculated bore dimensions and finger hole positions. During the 18th century several different sizes of oboe were introduced into the orchestra. Among them was an alto version—the cor anglais—which remains in regular use today. The main development in the 19th century was the application of key mechanisms to the oboe. German makers generally preferred a fairly simple mechanism, whereas French makers produced a variety of more complicated systems. Even today, key systems for the oboe vary considerably from maker to maker.

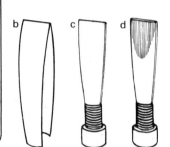

Left Making an oboe reed. A short length of dried-out cane is split into three (a). One piece is gouged and shaped to exact measurements, bent over (b), and then bound tightly to a metal staple (c). The tip is cut off and the separate blades scraped very thin (d) so that they will vibrate.

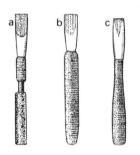

Left The modern reed (a) and the 18th century reed (b) both have a U-shaped scrape and are mounted on a metal staple. The modern staple is covered in cork for a firmer fit in the top of the oboe. The 19th century French reed (c) illustrates a less usual V-shaped scrape.

Above The oboist draws his lips between the teeth into the mouth, and then forces air through the reed at high pressure. Only a little air can be exhaled through such a small opening, and before inhaling again the player must take care to expel unused air from the lungs.

Right Early oboes. The two-keyed oboe (1) dates from the 17th century and closely resembles the Hotteterre model used in the operas of Lully. The six-keyed oboe of about 1820 (2) has the bulging upper end characteristic of earlier oboes. Its bulbous bell is more typical of larger oboes. The Triébert-system oboe of about 1850 (3), named after its designer, has the smooth elegant profile of the modern instrument.

1 Two-keyed oboe, c. 1680
2 Six-keyed oboe, J. Power, c. 1820 (Horniman Museum, London)
3 Oboe, Triébert, Paris, c. 1850

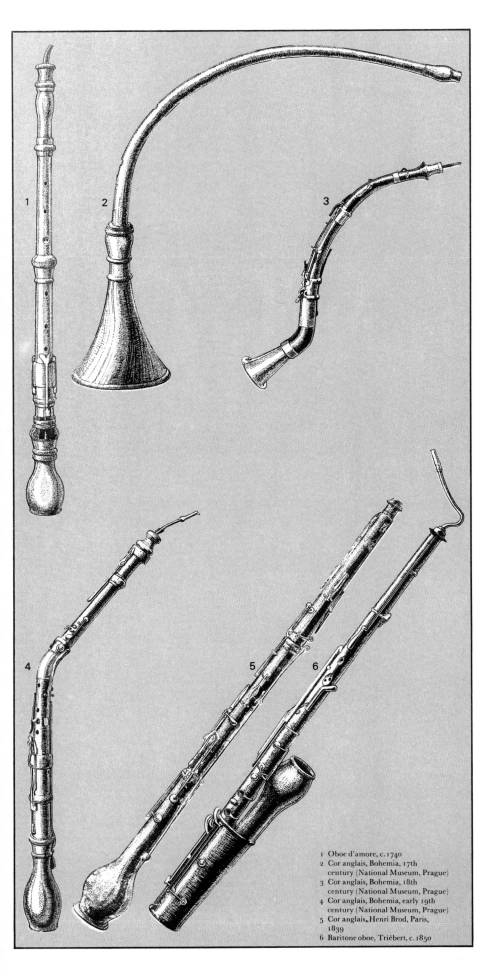

Left Early larger oboes. The oboe d'amore (1) was first developed in Germany around 1720 and has a bulbous bell and short brass crook. It often appears in the music of J. S. Bach. The cor anglais of the 17th and 18th centuries was curved (2 and 3), whereas the 19th century instrument was angled (4) and later straight (5). The baritone oboe (6) has an obscure history. Early versions had an upturned bell but later examples were straight.

1 Oboe d'amore, c.1740
2 Cor anglais, Bohemia, 17th century (National Museum, Prague)
3 Cor anglais, Bohemia, 18th century (National Museum, Prague)
4 Cor anglais, Bohemia, early 19th century (National Museum, Prague)
5 Cor anglais, Henri Brod, Paris, 1839
6 Baritone oboe, Triébert, c.1850

Right Modern reproduction (by Moeck) of an early 18th century oboe da caccia. The oboe da caccia is probably the ancestor of the cor anglais, and is thought originally to have been used in pairs for hunting purposes. It was occasionally used by J. S. Bach in his religious music.

© DIAGRAM

1

2

3

Left Illustrations of modern orchestral oboes and a diagram showing their relative sizes and pitch ranges. The cor anglais (1) is particularly effective when playing melancholy solos. The oboe d'amore (2) was revived in the 19th century for performances of music by J. S. Bach. It has also been used occasionally by 20th century composers. The regular orchestral oboe (3) has been a favorite instrument with composers for almost 300 years. Its reedy sound is heard best either in plaintive melodies or in quick staccato passages.

Right An oboe of the type favored until recently by members of the Vienna Philharmonic Orchestra. This 15-keyed instrument is little different from the model made by Sellner around 1850. It has tuning holes in the bell and extra thickness at each end.

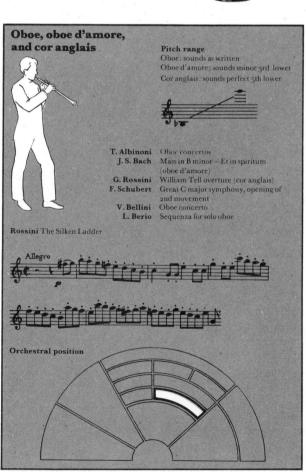

Oboe, oboe d'amore, and cor anglais

Pitch range
Oboe: sounds as written
Oboe d'amore: sounds minor 3rd lower
Cor anglais: sounds perfect 5th lower

T. Albinoni	Oboe concertos
J. S. Bach	Mass in B minor—Et in spiritum (oboe d'amore)
G. Rossini	William Tell overture (cor anglais)
F. Schubert	Great C major symphony, opening of 2nd movement
V. Bellini	Oboe concerto
L. Berio	Sequenza for solo oboe

Rossini The Silken Ladder

Allegro

Orchestral position

Left Modern baritone oboe (1) and heckelphone (2). The baritone oboe is pitched one octave below the regular orchestral oboe. It is only rarely used. The heckelphone was invented by Heckel in 1904 and has a wide conical bore and bulbous bell. It is usually pitched at baritone range.

Right Soprano sarrusophone (3) and contrabass sarrusophone (4). These brass instruments are members of a group of eight double reeds designed by Sarrus in 1856 for use in military bands.
Their ranges correspond approximately to those of the oboe and contrabassoon.

Below The musette (5) is a simple oboe-like instrument developed from the chanter (melody pipe) of the bagpipe. It is not usually associated with art music and is more commonly found as a toy.

©DIAGRAM

Bassoons

The bassoon is a bass wind instrument developed during the 17th century from the curtal. It is characterized by two separate parallel tubes joined at one end by a U-tube. Early bassoons had only two keys but in the 19th century German makers experimented with a variety of key mechanisms. Most successful was the system perfected by Heckel and this still remains popular with players all over the world.

1 Three-keyed bassoon, 17th century
2 Four-keyed bassoon, Milhouse, Newark, c. 1780
3 Bassoon, Switzerland, 18th century
4 Bassonore, Winnen, Paris, 1844
5 Contrabassoon, Stanesby Jr, London, 1739

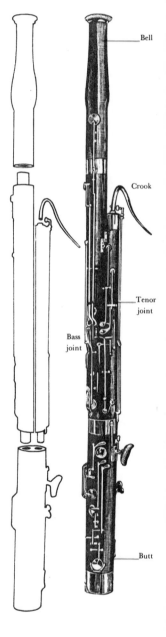

Bell

Crook

Tenor joint

Bass joint

Butt

Above Three-keyed bassoon (1) and four-keyed bassoon (2). Made in four sections, these 17th and 18th century instruments had a narrow bore and were played with a large reed. Four-keyed bassoons were used in the orchestra for most of the 18th century, appearing in works by J. S. Bach and Mozart.

Above Bassoons with unusual bells. The 18th century Swiss bassoon (3) was used in church. The powerful-toned bassonore (4), invented by Winnen of Paris in the 1830s for military band use, has a wide bore and large bell.
Right English contrabassoon of 1739 (5).

Above Identification of the parts of a bassoon and a diagram showing how the bassoon is dismantled.

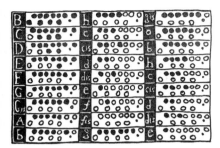

Above An 18th century fingering chart for a four-keyed bassoon. Bassoons with only a few keys were fingered in many different ways to correct inaccurate tuning. The sophisticated keywork of modern bassoons reduces the need for such alternative fingering.

Below Examples of bassoon and contrabassoon reeds. The early 19th century bassoon reed (a) is longer and slimmer than the late 19th century reed (b). The modern bassoon and contrabassoon reeds (c and d) have a shorter staple and squatter profile.

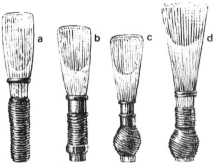

a b c d

Bassoon and contrabassoon

Pitch range
Bassoon: sounds as written
Contrabassoon: sounds one octave lower

J. B. Boismortier	Duos for bassoons
A. Vivaldi	Bassoon concertos
W. A. Mozart	Concerto in B♭ major, K.191
C. M. von Weber	Concerto in F major, op. 75
P. Dukas	The Sorcerer's Apprentice—main theme
I. Stravinsky	Rite of Spring (opening)
G. Vinter	The Playful Pachyderm

Haydn Symphony no. 98, 3rd movement

Menuetto

Orchestral position

Above Modern bassoon—the lowest sounding regular member of the orchestral wind group. The mellow notes of the bassoon's lower register provide a firm bass for orchestral harmony. Its higher notes, corresponding to the range of the tenor voice, are well suited for solos.

Above Modern contrabassoon or double bassoon. This instrument can play notes one octave lower than the standard bassoon, and extensions are available to extend the range even farther down. Despite its very low pitch, the tone of the contrabassoon is rich and gentle.

©DIAGRAM

Bagpipes

Bagpipes are reed instruments characterized by an air reservoir in the form of a bag. The bag is inflated by air from the mouth or by bellows operated by the player's arm. Because the reeds are sounded by air from the bag, and not directly from the mouth, the player can breathe while playing and so produce an uninterrupted sound. The bag is usually made of animal skin into which the chanter, or fingered melody pipe, and the unfingered drone pipes are inserted. The chanter and drones may be either cylindrical or conical, and have a single or double reed at their upper ends where they fit into the bag. The history of the bagpipe is obscure but it is related to instruments in which the whole reed is taken into the mouth. Known as early as Roman times, bagpipes are now found in Asia, North Africa, and Europe.

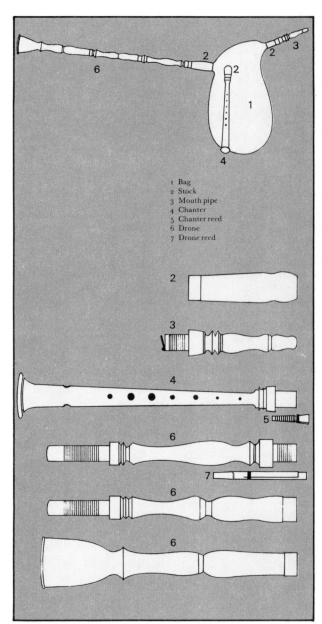

1 Bag
2 Stock
3 Mouth pipe
4 Chanter
5 Chanter reed
6 Drone
7 Drone reed

Left A medieval bladder pipe player. This instrument, a simple type of bagpipe used in the Middle Ages, is now played only as a toy. Air is blown through the short mouth pipe into the bladder which acts as a reservoir. The airstream sounds the reed enclosed in the chanter pipe.

Left A medieval bagpipe player. The air reservoir of this instrument is made from the whole skin of a pig. The mouth pipe is stuck into the back and the chanter protrudes from the animal's mouth. The chanter terminates in a decorative animal's head carved out of wood.

Left Bellows-blown and mouth-blown bagpipes. The bellows-blown bagpipe (a) has a small skin bag inflated by bellows strapped to the right arm. The large bag of the mouth-blown bagpipes (b) is inflated through a short mouth pipe fixed in one of the skin's forelegs.

Above A diagram showing the construction of a simple bagpipe. Into holes in the bag (1) are inserted the stocks (2). These hold in place the mouth pipe (3), the chanter (4) and its reed (5), and the sectioned drone (6) and its reed (7).

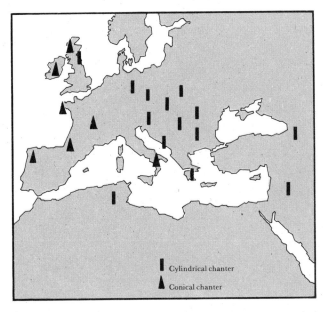

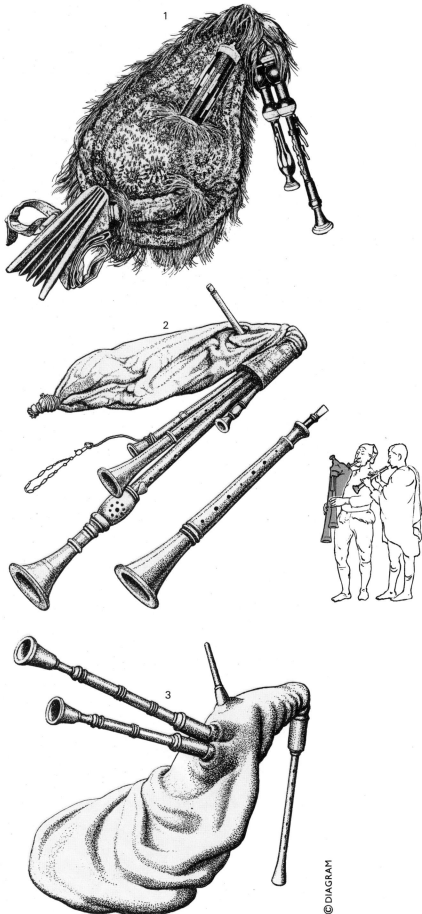

Below Diagrams showing the two types of chanter. The chanter is the melody pipe of the bagpipe and may be cylindrical (a) or conical (b). Cylindrical chanters are usually fitted with a single reed and conical chanters with a double reed. Chanters are made of cane, wood, bone, or metal.

Above Map showing the distribution of bagpipes with different types of chanter. The bagpipes of Eastern Europe usually have a cylindrical chanter fitted with a single reed, whereas the bagpipes of Western Europe usually have a conical chanter fitted with a double reed.

Right Historical bagpipes. The French musette (1) has a velvet-covered bag and was popular at the court of Louis XIV. The Italian zampogna (2) has two drones and two chanters, each fitted with double reeds. It is often played with a piffaro (far right). The German dudelsack (3) has a goatskin bag, a chanter, and two drone pipes.

Below Dudelsack player, after an engraving by Dürer.

© DIAGRAM

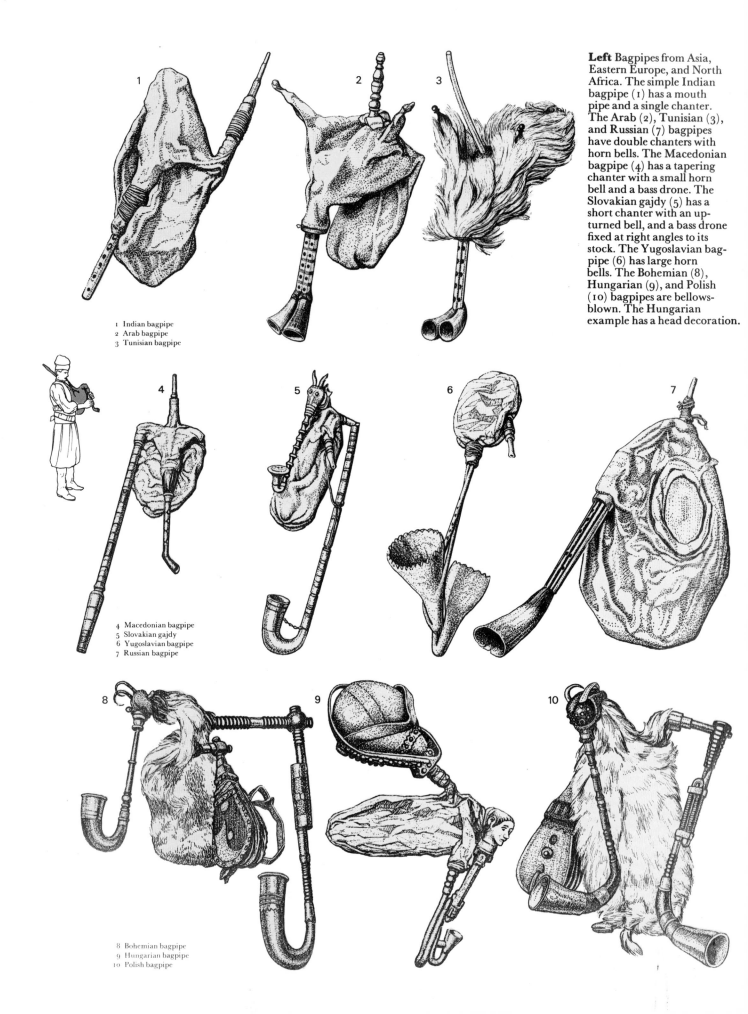

Left Bagpipes from Asia, Eastern Europe, and North Africa. The simple Indian bagpipe (1) has a mouth pipe and a single chanter. The Arab (2), Tunisian (3), and Russian (7) bagpipes have double chanters with horn bells. The Macedonian bagpipe (4) has a tapering chanter with a small horn bell and a bass drone. The Slovakian gajdy (5) has a short chanter with an up-turned bell, and a bass drone fixed at right angles to its stock. The Yugoslavian bag-pipe (6) has large horn bells. The Bohemian (8), Hungarian (9), and Polish (10) bagpipes are bellows-blown. The Hungarian example has a head decoration.

1 Indian bagpipe
2 Arab bagpipe
3 Tunisian bagpipe

4 Macedonian bagpipe
5 Slovakian gajdy
6 Yugoslavian bagpipe
7 Russian bagpipe

8 Bohemian bagpipe
9 Hungarian bagpipe
10 Polish bagpipe

Right British and Irish bagpipes. The Scottish Highland pipes (1) are mouth-blown and have a conical chanter and three drones fitted into a tartan-covered bag. They are a feature of Scottish regimental bands. The bellows-blown Irish Union pipe (2) is played in a sitting position. It has a four-keyed chanter and three drones inserted into a common stock. Regulators in the stock allow a chordal accompaniment. The Northumbrian small pipe (3) is bellows-blown. The chanter has nine keys, and in a common stock are four drones of which only three are played at one time.

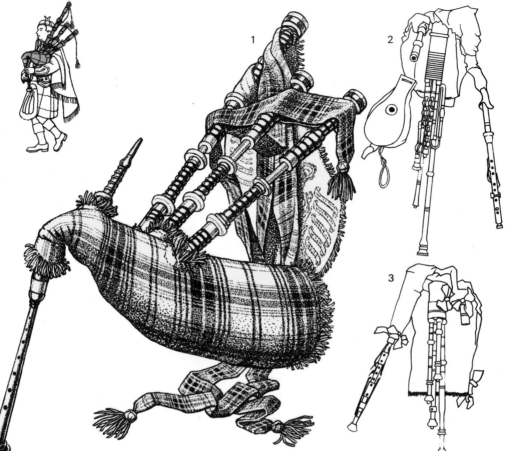

1 Scottish Highland pipes
2 Irish Union pipe
3 Northumbrian small pipe

Right Bagpipes from France and Spain. The French cornemuse (4) has a stock carrying the chanter and a small drone. The Breton biniou (5) is usually played with the bombarde, a Breton shawm. The Spanish gaita (6) is traditionally played at feasts and weddings.

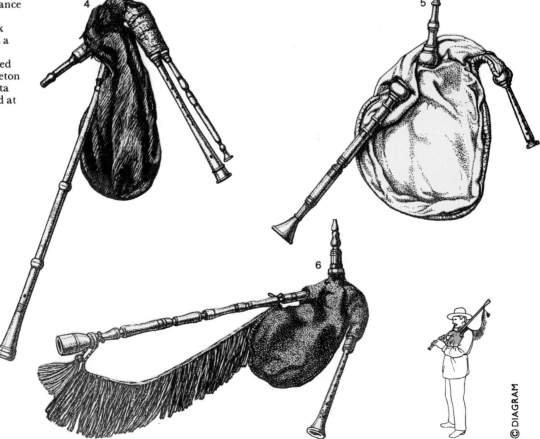

4 French cornemuse
5 Breton biniou
6 Spanish gaita

© DIAGRAM

Simple trumpets

It is often difficult to make a distinction between primitive trumpets and horns, for in each case the sound is produced by the vibration of the player's lips. In general, however, a trumpet is predominantly straight and cylindrical whereas a horn tends to be curved and conical. Primitive trumpets are found in every continent and are usually associated with ritual and magic.

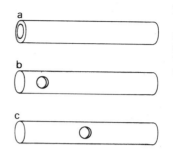

Left Blow hole positions. Most primitive trumpets are end-blown (a). Rarer side-blown examples have the blow hole near one end (b) or at the center (c).

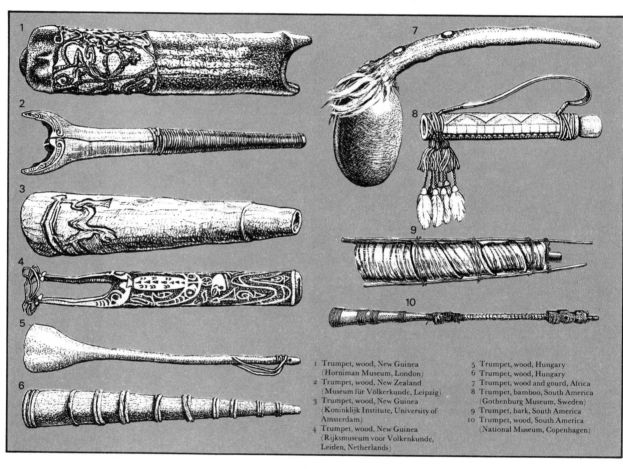

1 Trumpet, wood, New Guinea (Horniman Museum, London)
2 Trumpet, wood, New Zealand (Museum für Völkerkunde, Leipzig)
3 Trumpet, wood, New Guinea (Koninklijk Institute, University of Amsterdam)
4 Trumpet, wood, New Guinea (Rijksmuseum voor Volkenkunde, Leiden, Netherlands)
5 Trumpet, wood, Hungary
6 Trumpet, wood, Hungary
7 Trumpet, wood and gourd, Africa
8 Trumpet, bamboo, South America (Gothenburg Museum, Sweden)
9 Trumpet, bark, South America
10 Trumpet, wood, South America (National Museum, Copenhagen)

Above Primitive trumpets made from natural materials. Wood trumpets are found in many parts of the world, and are usually made from a single piece of wood. More unusual are the wood and gourd trumpet (7), bamboo trumpet (8), and the trumpet made from spiral-wound bark (9).

Right Players of large trumpets. The South American trumpets (a, f) are made of bark. The Burmese trumpet (b) is metal, and the Bolivian trumpet (c) and South African trumpet (e) are wood with horn bells. The Australian didgeridoo (d) and Swiss alphorn (g) are wood.

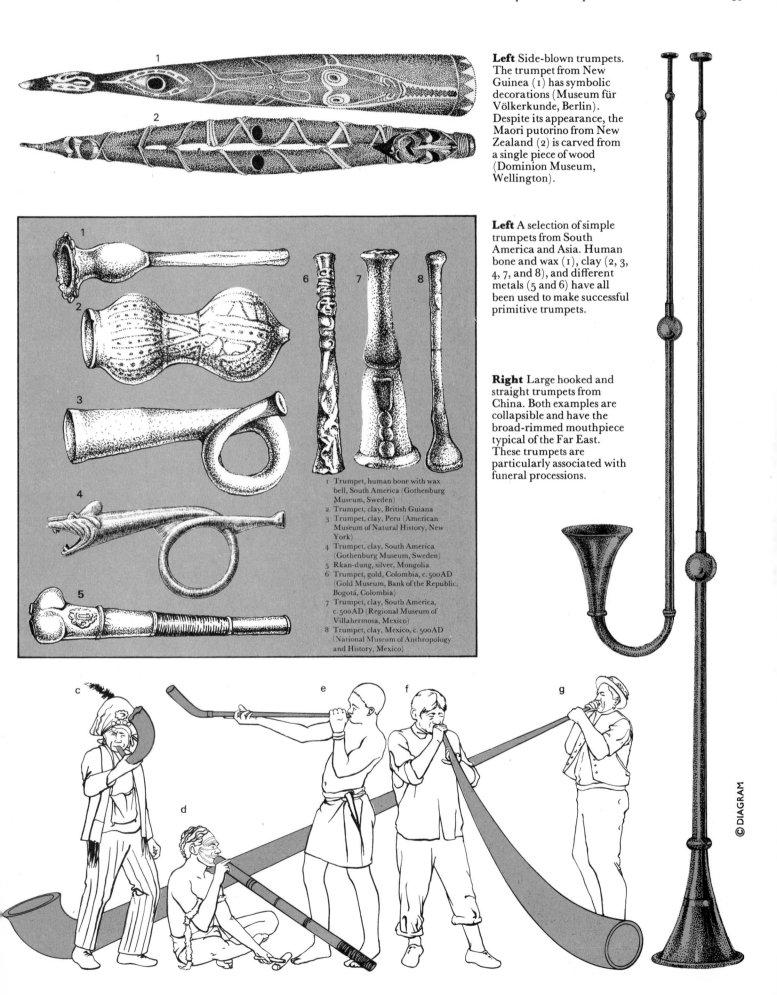

Left Side-blown trumpets. The trumpet from New Guinea (1) has symbolic decorations (Museum für Völkerkunde, Berlin). Despite its appearance, the Maori putorino from New Zealand (2) is carved from a single piece of wood (Dominion Museum, Wellington).

Left A selection of simple trumpets from South America and Asia. Human bone and wax (1), clay (2, 3, 4, 7, and 8), and different metals (5 and 6) have all been used to make successful primitive trumpets.

Right Large hooked and straight trumpets from China. Both examples are collapsible and have the broad-rimmed mouthpiece typical of the Far East. These trumpets are particularly associated with funeral processions.

1 Trumpet, human bone with wax bell, South America (Gothenburg Museum, Sweden)
2 Trumpet, clay, British Guiana
3 Trumpet, clay, Peru (American Museum of Natural History, New York)
4 Trumpet, clay, South America (Gothenburg Museum, Sweden)
5 Rkan-dung, silver, Mongolia
6 Trumpet, gold, Colombia, c. 500AD (Gold Museum, Bank of the Republic, Bogotá, Colombia)
7 Trumpet, clay, South America, c. 500AD (Regional Museum of Villahermosa, Mexico)
8 Trumpet, clay, Mexico, c. 500AD (National Museum of Anthropology and History, Mexico)

© DIAGRAM

Historical trumpets

The development of the modern trumpet can be traced back over thousands of years. All the major civilizations of the past produced trumpets, although our knowledge of these instruments relies more on contemporary illustrations and sculptures than on surviving instruments. Most ancient trumpets were straight or hooked and had a long, almost cylindrical tube and a slightly flaring bell.

Right Ancient and medieval trumpets. The Greek salpinx (1) is ivory with bronze strengthening rings. The metal lituus (2) was a Roman military trumpet. The Egyptian trumpet (3) came from the tomb of Tutankhamun. The buisine (4) is a fanfare trumpet from medieval Europe.

Left Celtic carnyx from 1st century Britain. Made of bronze, these trumpets had a characteristic bent-back bell in the form of an open-mouthed animal.

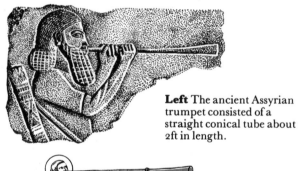

Left The ancient Assyrian trumpet consisted of a straight conical tube about 2ft in length.

Left Angels are traditionally depicted with musical instruments—among them the medieval buisine.

Left Fanfare trumpet of the kind still used on ceremonial occasions.

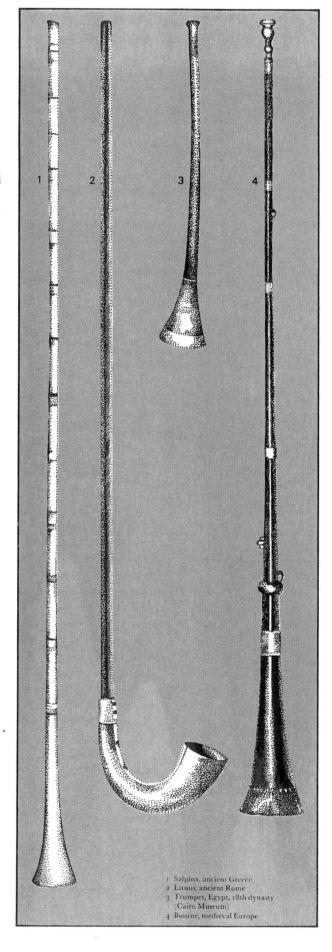

1 Salpinx, ancient Greece
2 Lituus, ancient Rome
3 Trumpet, Egypt, 18th dynasty (Cairo Museum)
4 Buisine, medieval Europe

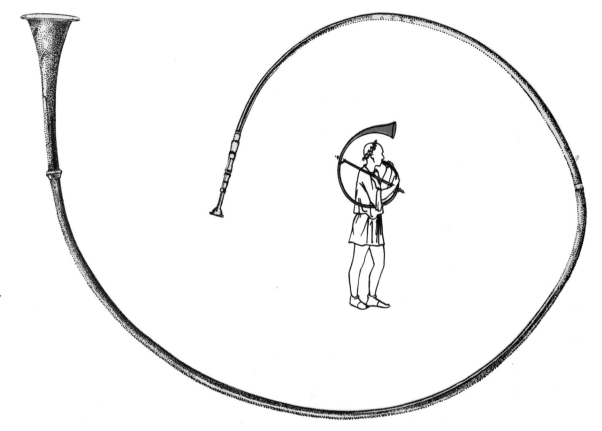

Right Roman cornu (or buccina). Associated with high-ranking military personnel, it was up to 11ft long and had a gently flaring bore. A wood rod was sometimes attached diagonally across the coil so that the instrument could rest on the player's shoulder.

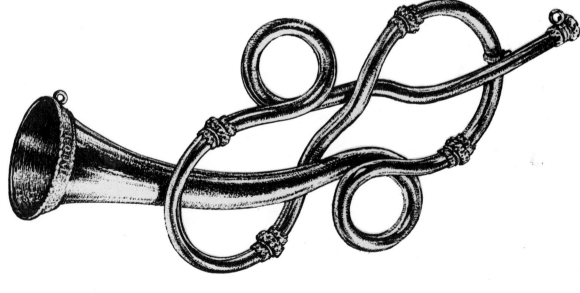

Right An elaborately looped trumpet made by Antonius Schnitzer of Nuremberg in 1598 (Museum of Art, Vienna). Looped trumpets were less cumbersome than straight trumpets and were often designed as decorative objects.

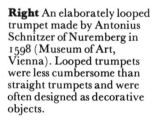

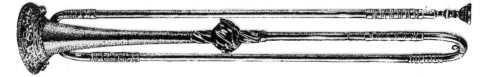

Right An 18th century "natural" trumpet. These trumpets, with no valves, could only play tunes comprised of high notes. The high breath pressure required and the strain on the player's lips combined to make this instrument very difficult to play.

©DIAGRAM

Orchestral trumpets

In the late 18th century makers of brass instruments became particularly interested in the problems of producing a trumpet without the limitations of the "natural" trumpet. A satisfactory solution was found early in the 19th century, when Stölzel and Blühmel produced the first valved trumpets. These trumpets were more versatile and enabled players to play tunes including a far greater range of notes.

1 Hand trumpet, Sautermeister et Müller, Lyon, c.1820
2 Slide trumpet, Köhler, London, c.1865 (Horniman Museum, London)
3 Keyed trumpet, Sandbach, London, 1812 (Royal Military School of Music, London)

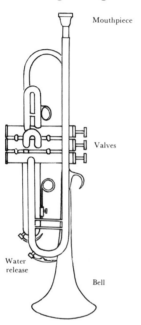

Mouthpiece

Valves

Water release

Bell

Right The curved trumpet (1) allowed the hand to be placed in the bell to lower the pitch. Slide trumpets (2) used the lengthening-tube principle of the trombone, and keyed trumpets (3) the shortening-tube principle of the flute. All were superseded by valved instruments.

Left Identification of parts of a valved orchestral trumpet.

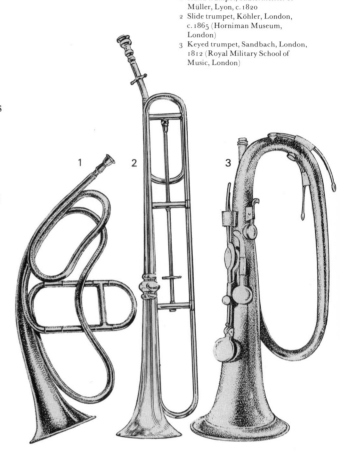

Below Diagrams demonstrating the valve mechanism of a trumpet. When the valve is at rest (a) air passes directly through the main tube. When the valve is depressed (b) the air column is lengthened because air is now diverted through the extra length of tubing.

Right An early valved trumpet—with Stölzel piston valves. Most valved trumpets have three valves, which may be depressed singly or in any combination. The operation of these valves allows the player to produce all the notes of the scale.

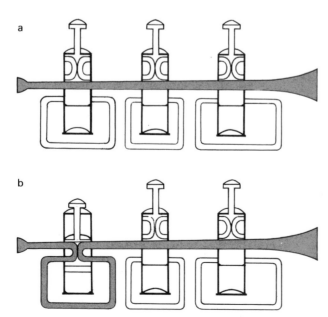

a

b

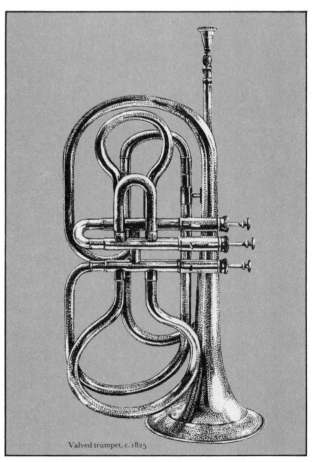

Valved trumpet, c.1825

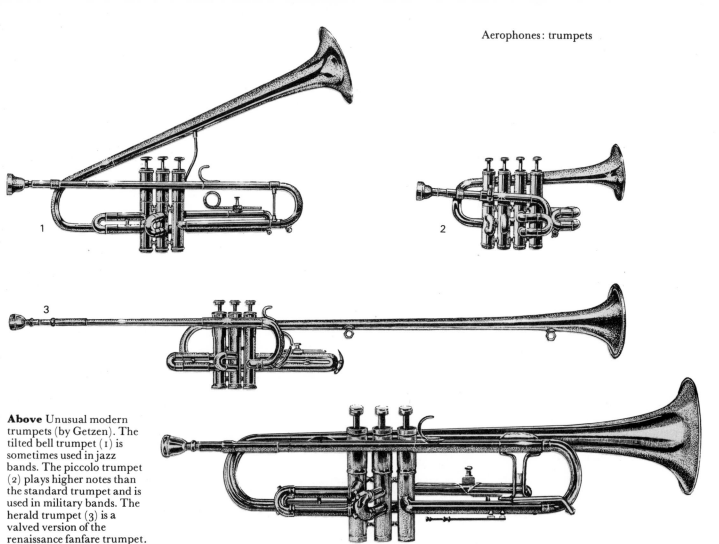

Above Unusual modern trumpets (by Getzen). The tilted bell trumpet (1) is sometimes used in jazz bands. The piccolo trumpet (2) plays higher notes than the standard trumpet and is used in military bands. The herald trumpet (3) is a valved version of the renaissance fanfare trumpet.

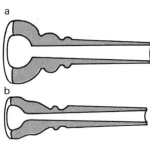

Above The modern B♭ trumpet used in orchestras and in jazz, dance, and military bands. Mainly associated with stirring solos, it is also used in the orchestral background texture.
Left The shallow-cup mouthpiece (a) has been replaced by the smaller, deeper mouthpiece (b).

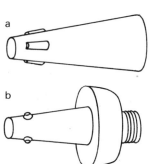

Left Straight (a), cup (b), and wow-wow (c) mutes. Made from wood, metal, rubber, or polystyrene, mutes of many different styles can be fitted into the trumpet's bell to diminish the volume or produce unusual sounds. They are particularly popular with jazz musicians.

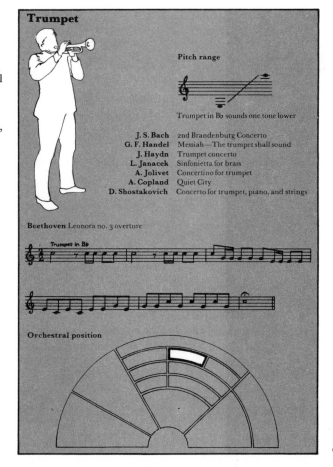

Trumpet

Pitch range

Trumpet in B♭ sounds one tone lower

J. S. Bach   2nd Brandenburg Concerto
G. F. Handel   Messiah—The trumpet shall sound
J. Haydn   Trumpet concerto
L. Janacek   Sinfonietta for brass
A. Jolivet   Concertino for trumpet
A. Copland   Quiet City
D. Shostakovich   Concerto for trumpet, piano, and strings

Beethoven Leonora no. 3 overture

Orchestral position

© DIAGRAM

Trombones

A trombone is a brass instrument in which the sound is produced by the vibrations of the player's lips. In this respect it is similar to the trumpet, but the trombone is characterized by its telescopic slide used for lengthening the tube. The trombone—then called the sackbut—first appeared in Europe in the 1400s, and still retains its simple basic design. It is popular in orchestras and different types of bands.

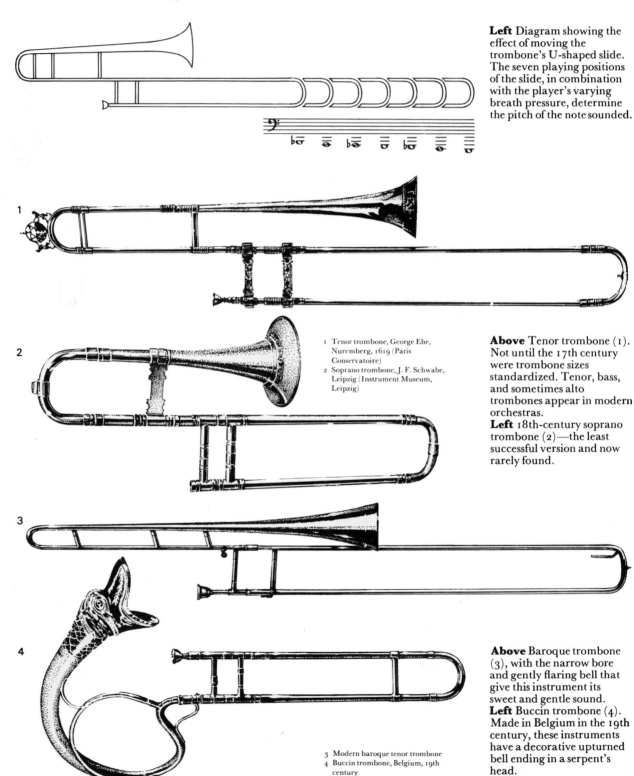

Left Diagram showing the effect of moving the trombone's U-shaped slide. The seven playing positions of the slide, in combination with the player's varying breath pressure, determine the pitch of the note sounded.

1 Tenor trombone, George Ehe, Nuremberg, 1619 (Paris Conservatoire)
2 Soprano trombone, J. F. Schwabe, Leipzig (Instrument Museum, Leipzig)

Above Tenor trombone (1). Not until the 17th century were trombone sizes standardized. Tenor, bass, and sometimes alto trombones appear in modern orchestras.
Left 18th-century soprano trombone (2)—the least successful version and now rarely found.

3 Modern baroque tenor trombone
4 Buccin trombone, Belgium, 19th century

Above Baroque trombone (3), with the narrow bore and gently flaring bell that give this instrument its sweet and gentle sound.
Left Buccin trombone (4). Made in Belgium in the 19th century, these instruments have a decorative upturned bell ending in a serpent's head.

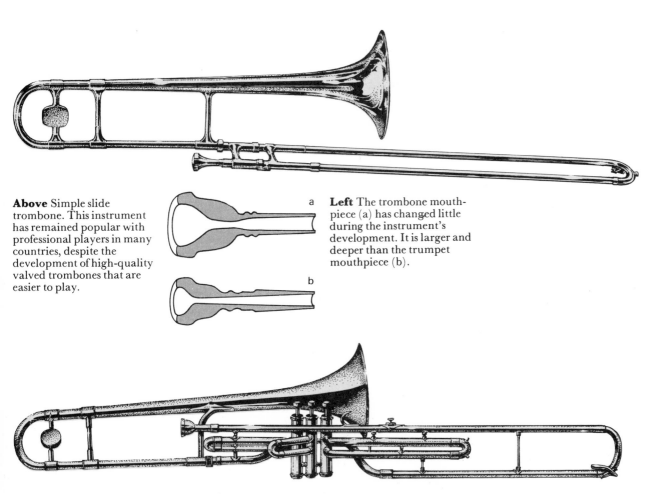

Above Simple slide trombone. This instrument has remained popular with professional players in many countries, despite the development of high-quality valved trombones that are easier to play.

a
b

Left The trombone mouthpiece (a) has changed little during the instrument's development. It is larger and deeper than the trumpet mouthpiece (b).

Above Modern three-valved trombone. The addition of valves to the trombone was made difficult by the fact that any inaccuracy in intonation is exaggerated by the instrument's length. Only with 20th century correcting mechanisms were satisfactory valved trombones produced.

Below The simple trombone (a) has only its slide for changing the pitch of notes. Trombones with one or two valves (b) give the player the choice of different lengths of tubing and retain the slide. The three-valved trombone (c) produces more notes without use of the slide.

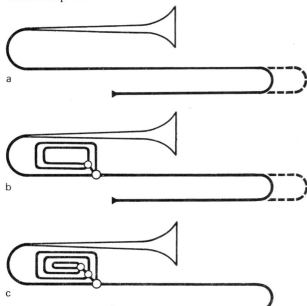

a
b
c

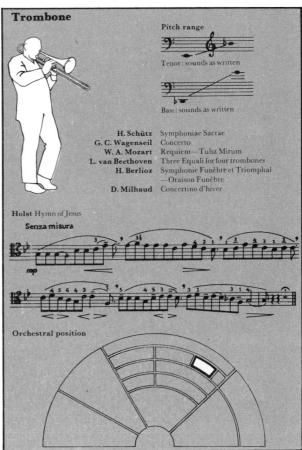

Trombone

Pitch range

Tenor: sounds as written

Bass: sounds as written

H. Schütz	Symphoniae Sacrae
G. C. Wagenseil	Concerto
W. A. Mozart	Requiem—Tuba Mirum
L. van Beethoven	Three Equali for four trombones
H. Berlioz	Symphonie Funèbre et Triomphal —Oraison Funèbre
D. Milhaud	Concertino d'hiver

Holst Hymn of Jesus

Senza misura

Orchestral position

Simple horns

A horn is a curved and conical instrument in which the sound is produced by vibrations of the player's lips. The simplest type is made from an animal horn and animal horns serve as a model for other primitive horns. Examples may be end-blown or side-blown, and unless provided with finger holes have a limited melodic range. They are widely used for signaling and ritual.

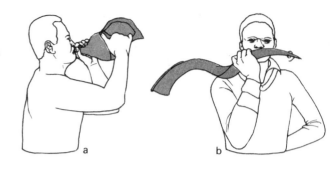

Above Primitive horns are most commonly end-blown, like the shell horn from Hawaii (a). The side-blown horn from South Africa (b) represents a less common type.

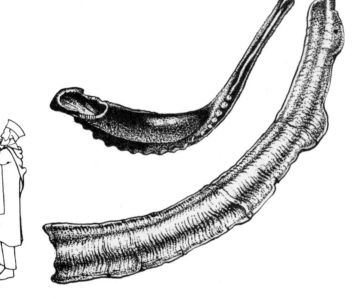

Left Hebrew shofarim, an ancient type of horn still used in Jewish ritual. Made of animal horn, it is usually played with a separate mouthpiece and produces two different notes.

Below Animal horn instruments from different parts of the world. Among the simplest of all folk instruments, examples are found in every continent. The Finnish paimensarvi (8) has finger holes and so plays notes of a wider melodic range than most primitive horns.

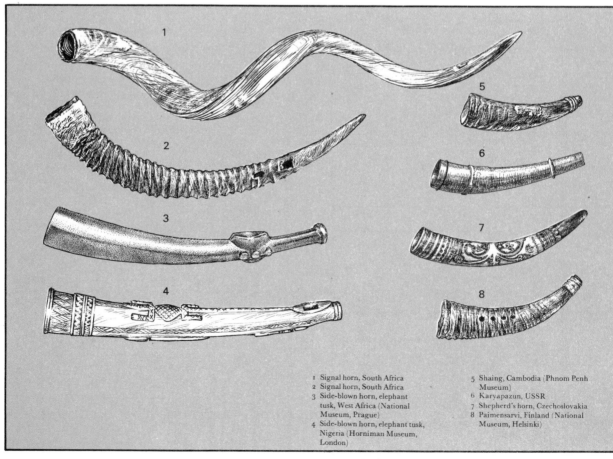

1 Signal horn, South Africa
2 Signal horn, South Africa
3 Side-blown horn, elephant tusk, West Africa (National Museum, Prague)
4 Side-blown horn, elephant tusk, Nigeria (Horniman Museum, London)
5 Shaing, Cambodia (Phnom Penh Museum)
6 Karyapazun, USSR
7 Shepherd's horn, Czechoslovakia
8 Paimensarvi, Finland (National Museum, Helsinki)

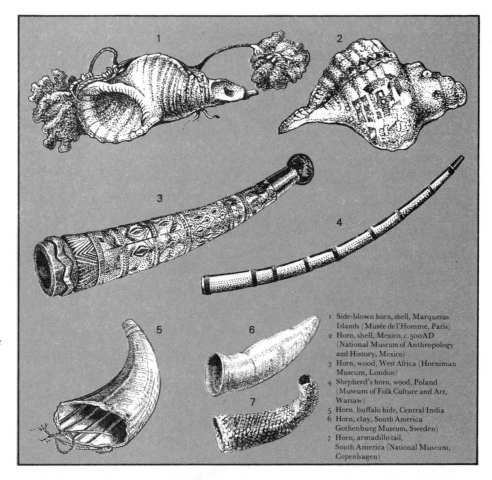

Right Primitive horns made of shells (1 and 2), wood (3 and 4), buffalo hide (5), clay (6), and the tail of an armadillo (7). The clay and armadillo horns are calling tubes rather than true horns—the player calls into the instrument rather than attempting to sound different notes.

1 Side-blown horn, shell, Marquesas Islands (Musée de l'Homme, Paris)
2 Horn, shell, Mexico, c. 500 AD (National Museum of Anthropology and History, Mexico)
3 Horn, wood, West Africa (Horniman Museum, London)
4 Shepherd's horn, wood, Poland (Museum of Folk Culture and Art, Warsaw)
5 Horn, buffalo hide, Central India
6 Horn, clay, South America Gothenburg Museum, Sweden)
7 Horn, armadillo tail, South America (National Museum, Copenhagen)

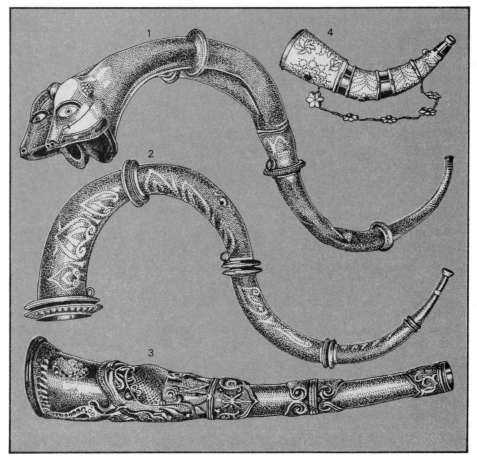

Right Metal horns. These represent the most sophisticated form of folk horn. They are commonest in Asia but are also found elsewhere. The double-belled copper ranasringa (1) is from Nepal (Horniman Museum, London). The single-belled ranasringa (2) is from India (Náprstek Museum, Prague). Another copper horn is the rkan-ling (3) from Tibet (Horniman Museum, London). The Bolivian example (4) is animal horn covered with metal (Náprstek Museum, Prague).

Historical horns

Horns have been known in Europe since very early times. In the Middle Ages they were associated almost exclusively with hunting and military activities. From about the 14th century the development of metal horns with special mouthpieces increased the versatility of the instrument, and led in the 18th century to the horn's acceptance as a regular member of the orchestra.

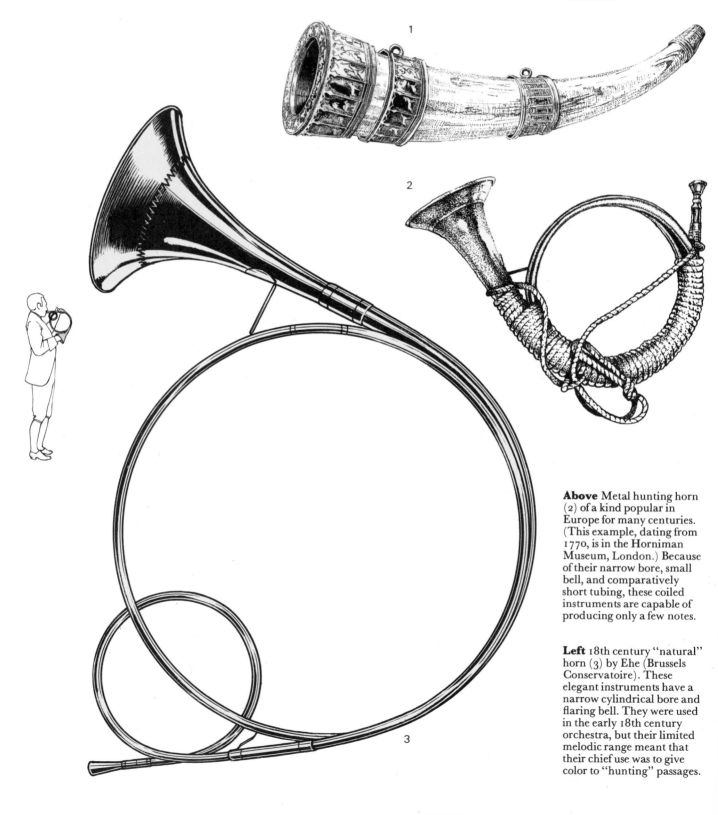

Below The Savernake horn (1). This ivory horn (in the British Museum) is decorated with 14th century English silverwork but is thought to be of 11th century Italian origin. Decorated horns—among them the carved ivory horns known as oliphants—were much sought after by European noblemen.

Above Metal hunting horn (2) of a kind popular in Europe for many centuries. (This example, dating from 1770, is in the Horniman Museum, London.) Because of their narrow bore, small bell, and comparatively short tubing, these coiled instruments are capable of producing only a few notes.

Left 18th century "natural" horn (3) by Ehe (Brussels Conservatoire). These elegant instruments have a narrow cylindrical bore and flaring bell. They were used in the early 18th century orchestra, but their limited melodic range meant that their chief use was to give color to "hunting" passages.

Below Bronze Age lur (1) from Scandinavia (National Museum, Copenhagen). These curious instruments have a conical bore terminating in a flat disk, and a mouthpiece similar to that of the modern trombone. They have usually been found in pairs, with both instruments sounding the same pitch.

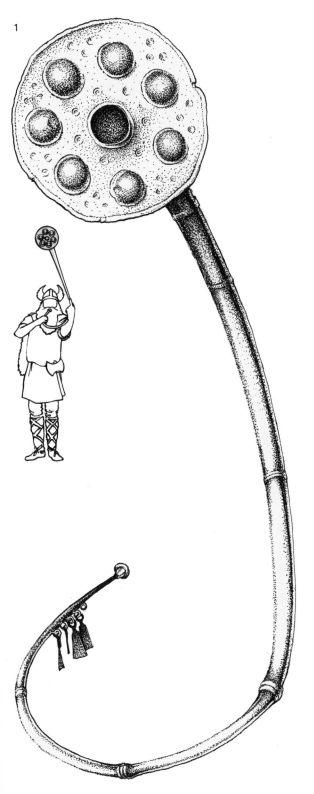

1

Left An early 19th century Belgian hand horn (2) in the Metropolitan Museum, New York. It has a compact shape and large bell. By placing his hand in the bell the player lowered the pitch of the note played by a semitone, and so increased the total number of available pitches.

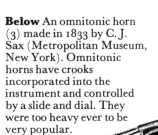

2

Right An 18th century crook horn with a selection of detachable crooks. Different crooks varied the length of tubing and so increased the horn's melodic possibilities. Players became very skilled at rapidly changing crooks.

Below An omnitonic horn (3) made in 1833 by C. J. Sax (Metropolitan Museum, New York). Omnitonic horns have crooks incorporated into the instrument and controlled by a slide and dial. They were too heavy ever to be very popular.

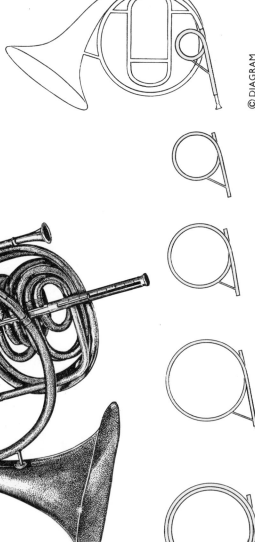

3

© DIAGRAM

Orchestral horns

In the 19th century the application of valves to the horn freed players from the inconvenience of using a wide variety of crooks. The horn in F proved the most useful, and by the late 19th century was the standard instrument for orchestral use. Around the turn of the century the double horn was devised and this meant that at last the horn could take its place as one of the truly melodic instruments of the orchestra.

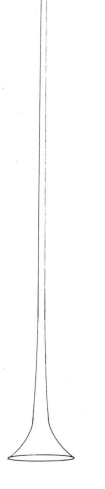

Left Diagrammatic representation of the length of tubing of a horn in F compared with this instrument's overall dimensions.

Right The single horn in F (1) is favored by some players for its simplicity. The Wagner tuba (2) was devised by the composer Richard Wagner for use in "The Ring." Closely related to the horn, Wagner tubas appear in tenor and bass sizes and are played with a horn-like mouthpiece.

Below Double horn in F and B♭—the most usual orchestral horn. The wide bore of the single horn in F makes high notes difficult to play. This led to the incorporation into the F instrument of a horn in B♭ brought into operation by the depression of a thumb valve.

Right The player supports the horn by placing his right hand in the bell (a). Changing his hand position (b) helps to refine the sound and check imperfections of intonation. The hand can also be used as a mute, to alter a note's pitch, or to achieve different tone color effects.

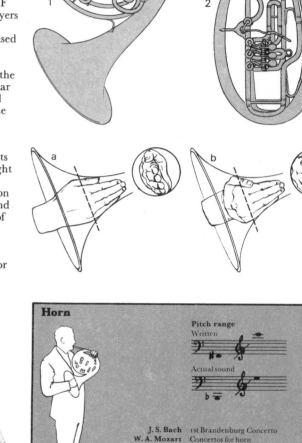

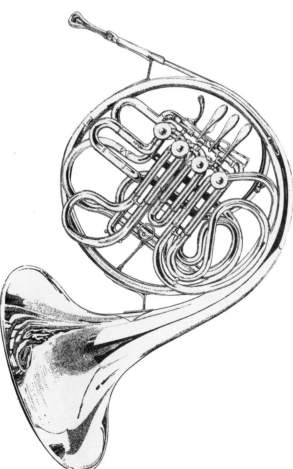

Horn

Pitch range
Written

Actual sound

J. S. Bach	1st Brandenburg Concerto
W. A. Mozart	Concertos for horn
J. Haydn	Concerto in D major
R. Strauss	Concerto no. 1, op. 11
M. Ravel	Pavane for a dead Infanta—main theme
S. Prokofiev	Peter and the Wolf (wolf: three horns)
C. Debussy	La Mer—De l'aube à midi sur la mer

Brahms Symphony no. 3, 3rd movement

Poco allegretto

p espr.

Orchestral position

Tubas

The tuba is a valved brass instrument with a wide conical bore, flared bell, and cup-shaped mouthpiece. It is characterized by its large size and deep sound. The first tubas were made in the 1830s in Berlin, and the instrument has since appeared in various shapes and sizes. One of these—the E♭ bass tuba—is sometimes called the bombardon. Tubas are used in both the orchestra and the military band.

Left The "recording" tuba —an instrument designed for orchestral recordings. Its forward-pointing bell projects the sound more effectively than the standard upright version.
Below The relative sizes of three modern orchestral tubas —contrabass (a), E♭ bass (b), and F bass (c).

Below The orchestral tuba. The bass member of the brass section of the orchestra, this large instrument is surprisingly agile for its size. Invented in the 1820s, it was uncommon before the 1850s. It is at its most effective when playing quick staccato solos, but is equally capable of playing sustained melodies.

Above A "marching" tuba. Designed for military bands, this instrument has a light-weight fiberglass bell. For marching the tuba is rested on the player's shoulder with its bell pointing forward.

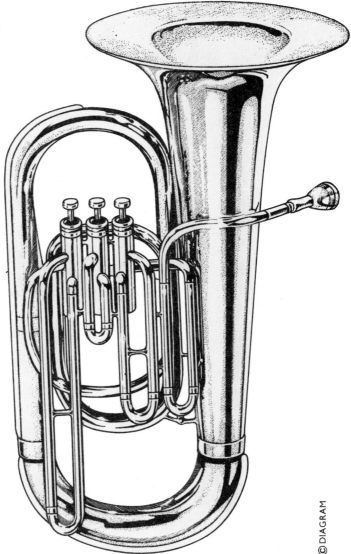

Tuba

Pitch range

Sounds as written

H. Berlioz   Symphonie Fantastique— Dies Irae
              (main theme)
R. Wagner   Götterdämmerung—Funeral March
J. Brahms   Tragic Overture

Mussorgsky-Ravel Pictures from an Exhibition

Sempre moderato pesante

pp   *poco a poco cresc.*

Orchestral position

© DIAGRAM

Cornetts and serpents

The cornett and serpent are wood finger hole horns with cup-shaped mouthpieces similar to those of the trumpet and trombone. The cornett enjoyed considerable popularity in the 16th and 17th century orchestra, while the serpent was still played in churches and military bands in the 19th century. Though not strictly related, the serpent was often used as the bass member of the cornett family.

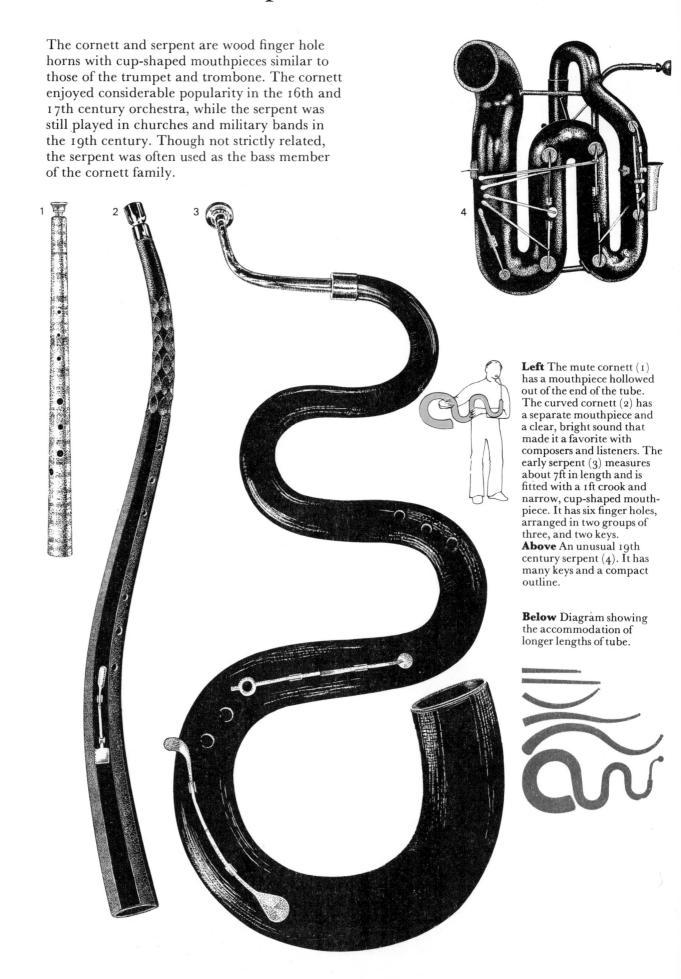

Left The mute cornett (1) has a mouthpiece hollowed out of the end of the tube. The curved cornett (2) has a separate mouthpiece and a clear, bright sound that made it a favorite with composers and listeners. The early serpent (3) measures about 7ft in length and is fitted with a 1ft crook and narrow, cup-shaped mouthpiece. It has six finger holes, arranged in two groups of three, and two keys.
Above An unusual 19th century serpent (4). It has many keys and a compact outline.

Below Diagram showing the accommodation of longer lengths of tube.

Bugles and cornets

The bugle, a simple horn used in medieval times as a hunting and signal instrument, was first used in the military band in the late 18th century. Since then the standard bugle has scarcely changed. Both the cornet, descended from the post horn, and the mellophone, descended from the orchestral horn, entered the military band in the 19th century. The cornet is also occasionally used in the orchestra.

Right 19th century bugles and a US cavalry bugler. The simple bugle (1) is sometimes decorated for special occasions (2). Its limited number of notes makes the bugle call easy to recognize. The keyed bugle (3) never became popular and was ousted by the flugelhorn.

Right Small instruments of the military band. The flugelhorn (4), first made in Vienna in the 1820s is a direct descendant of the keyed bugle. The mellophone (5) is a marching instrument derived from the orchestral horn. The cornet (6), introduced to the military band in the 1820s, still retains its popularity today. In the mid-19th century it was used in orchestral music by Rossini and Berlioz. Usually shaped like a trumpet, the cornet has also been made in a variety of other shapes.

Below A circular cornet—one of the unusual shapes used for this instrument.

© DIAGRAM

Later brass instruments

After the successful application of the valve principle to trumpets and horns in the early 19th century, makers in Europe and the USA began to experiment with brass instruments of different shapes and sizes. Many of the resulting instruments were derived from the orchestral horn and most were designed for marching bands. The more eccentric examples proved shortlived, but others are still commonly played today.

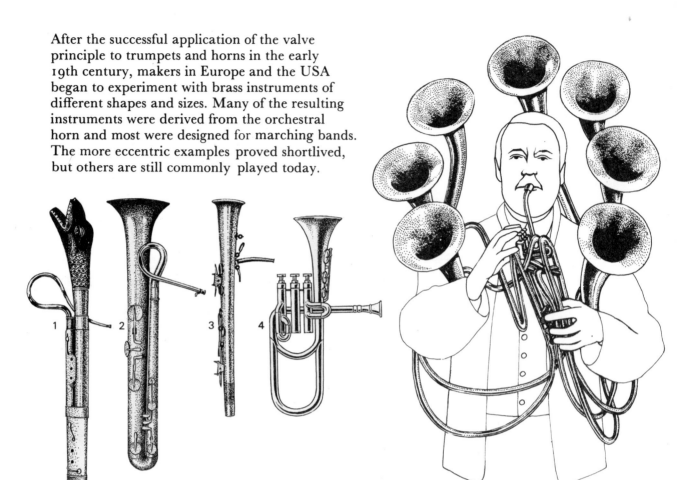

Above Band instruments played in the upright position. The basshorn (1) is a variety of metal serpent shaped like a bassoon. The ophicleide (2) is a large keyed bugle, and the Tuba-Dupré (3) is a treble version. The saxhorn (4) is a type of valved bugle developed by Adolphe Sax.

Above Alto horn. Made about 1880 by Distin, this cumbersome instrument had seven separate horns of different lengths joined by a single cup mouthpiece. Six valves directed the air into the chosen horn. This principle had earlier been applied by Sax to trumpet and trombone variants.

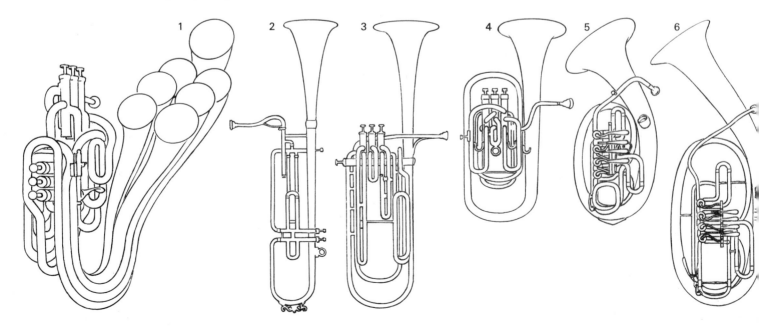

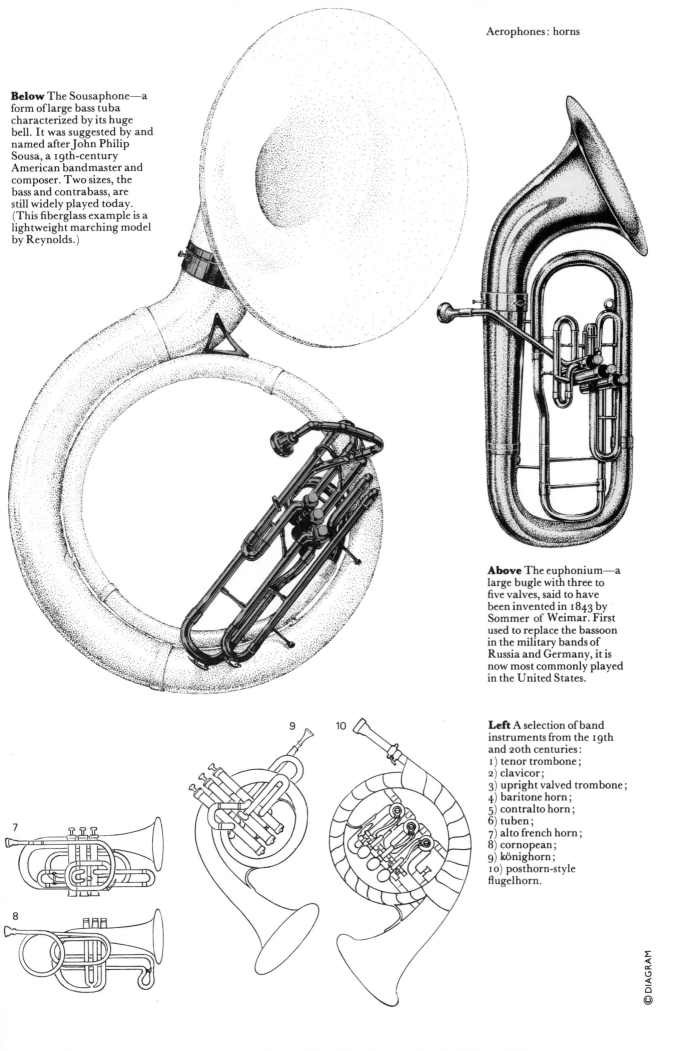

Below The Sousaphone—a form of large bass tuba characterized by its huge bell. It was suggested by and named after John Philip Sousa, a 19th-century American bandmaster and composer. Two sizes, the bass and contrabass, are still widely played today. (This fiberglass example is a lightweight marching model by Reynolds.)

Above The euphonium—a large bugle with three to five valves, said to have been invented in 1843 by Sommer of Weimar. First used to replace the bassoon in the military bands of Russia and Germany, it is now most commonly played in the United States.

Left A selection of band instruments from the 19th and 20th centuries:
1) tenor trombone;
2) clavicor;
3) upright valved trombone;
4) baritone horn;
5) contralto horn;
6) tuben;
7) alto french horn;
8) cornopean;
9) könighorn;
10) posthorn-style flugelhorn.

© DIAGRAM

Bull-roarers

Bull-roarers are one of the world's most ancient instruments, dating back more than 25,000 years. When Stone Age man fastened a thin piece of bone to a cord and whirled it around over his head he created an instrument that has been found among primitive peoples throughout the world. Bull-roarers are made in many different shapes and sizes, but most are now made of wood and conform to the basic elongated disk pattern. Although they do not produce a truly musical or rhythmic sound, it is possible to change the pitch by changing the speed at which the bull-roarer is drawn through the air. The instrument's chief function is as a ritual object, and its roaring sound has been likened to the voice of the wind or thunder, or the cries of gods, spirits, or ancestors. The bull-roarer survives in more sophisticated cultures as a simple children's toy.

Left A native of New Guinea spinning his bull-roarer through the air.

Below Bull-roarers from different continents. Instruments of this type often appear in fertility rites, and many of the symbols used in their decoration are believed to have magical significance. The toy bird whistle (8) works in a similar way to the bull-roarer. It is made of metal.

Right Diagram showing how a bull-roarer works. The bull-roarer disk spins on its axis as it circles around the player. This action causes the air around the bull-roarer to vibrate, and produces a sound which varies with the instrument's size, speed, and angle to the ground.

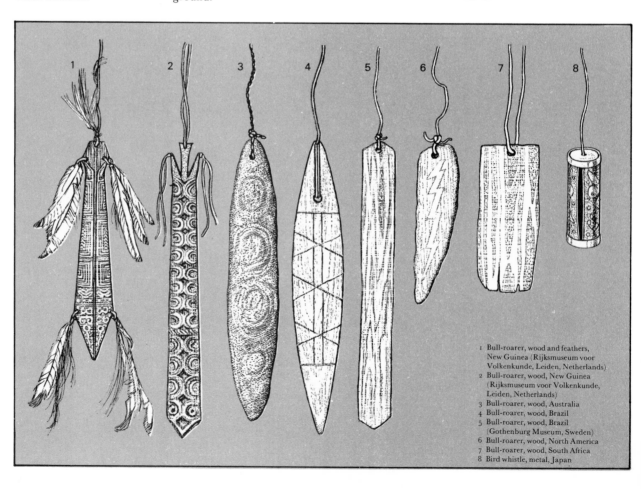

1 Bull-roarer, wood and feathers, New Guinea (Rijksmuseum voor Volkenkunde, Leiden, Netherlands)
2 Bull-roarer, wood, New Guinea (Rijksmuseum voor Volkenkunde, Leiden, Netherlands)
3 Bull-roarer, wood, Australia
4 Bull-roarer, wood, Brazil
5 Bull-roarer, wood, Brazil (Gothenburg Museum, Sweden)
6 Bull-roarer, wood, North America
7 Bull-roarer, wood, South Africa
8 Bird whistle, metal, Japan

Buzzing and humming instruments

Buzzing and humming instruments resemble the bull-roarer in producing a sound as the instrument travels through the air. They have been common since early times and are found in many parts of the world. Buzz-disks are occasionally used as ritual objects, notably in the fertility rites of some South American Indians, but buzzing and humming instruments are now generally more common as toys.

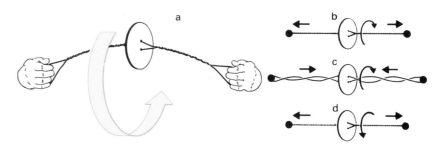

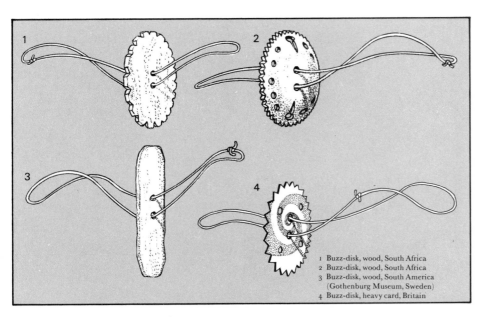

1 Buzz-disk, wood, South Africa
2 Buzz-disk, wood, South Africa
3 Buzz-disk, wood, South America (Gothenburg Museum, Sweden)
4 Buzz-disk, heavy card, Britain

Above Buzz-disk action. The player spins the disk away from himself until the whole length of string is twisted (a). He then pulls his hands farther apart, and the disk spins toward him as the string untwists (b). When the string is completely untwisted the disk continues to spin in the same direction and causes the string to retwist (c). If the player pulls his hands apart when the string is fully twisted, the disk starts to spin in the opposite direction (d)—so allowing the action to be repeated.

Left Buzz-disks from South Africa (1 and 2), South America (3) and Britain (4).

Left Humming tops from different cultures. The South American humming tops (1 and 2) are made from gourd shells. As with the yo-yo (3) and mechanical humming top (4), the sound is produced by air whistling through holes.
Below Child playing with a humming top.

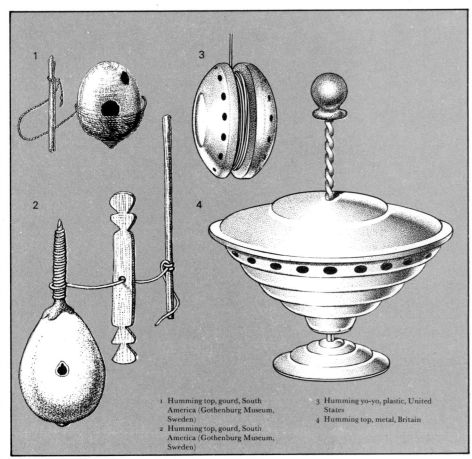

1 Humming top, gourd, South America (Gothenburg Museum, Sweden)
2 Humming top, gourd, South America (Gothenburg Museum, Sweden)
3 Humming yo-yo, plastic, United States
4 Humming top, metal, Britain

©DIAGRAM

Eastern mouth organs

The mouth organ has a very long history in the Far East, having first been described in China about 3000 years ago. Instruments of this kind, of varying degrees of sophistication, are played today in many oriental countries. They are free-reed instruments with a vibrating reed fitted in each playing pipe. The player blows into the wind chamber and sounds individual pipes by covering the finger holes.

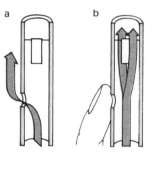

Above Diagram showing how an oriental mouth organ works. If the finger hole is left uncovered (a), air escapes through it so that the air continuing up the pipe is insufficient to make the reed vibrate. When the finger hole is covered (b), sufficient air reaches the reed to make it vibrate.

Left Oriental mouth organ players from Borneo (a), China (b), and Laos (c). The Laotian mouth organ, the khen, has six, 14, or 16 bamboo pipes in a wood or ivory wind chamber. It is made in three sizes, of which the largest has pipes that are 10ft long.

Left Mouth organs from Borneo and China. The Bornean mouth organ with the gourd wind chamber (1) and the Chingmiau mouth organ (2) are more primitive types. The sheng (3) from China and the shô (4) from Japan are more sophisticated classical instruments.

Far left Sheng players.

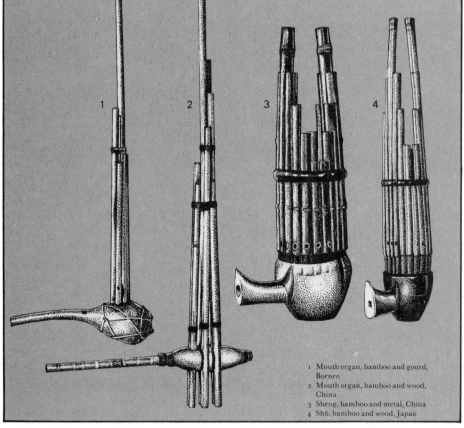

1 Mouth organ, bamboo and gourd, Borneo
2 Mouth organ, bamboo and wood, China
3 Sheng, bamboo and metal, China
4 Shô, bamboo and wood, Japan

Western mouth organs

Western mouth organs date only from the first quarter of the 19th century, and belong to a family that developed as a result of interest in the free-reed instruments of the Far East. The Western mouth organ, or harmonica, is a versatile instrument produced in great numbers for family and professional entertainment. The melodica is an easily played related instrument popular with children.

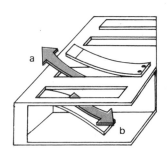

Left Western mouth organ mechanism. When the player blows he activates reeds fixed at the near side of the instrument (a). When he sucks he activates reeds fixed at the far side (b). The pitch of a reed is determined by its length, and the player's tongue covers chambers with reeds he does not wish to sound.

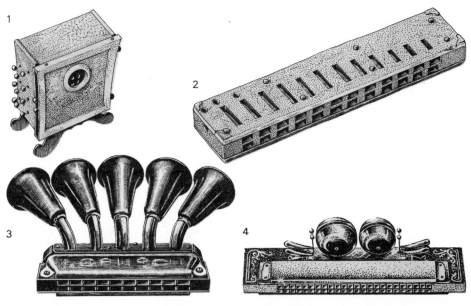

Left Early Western mouth organs. Wheatstone's symphonium (1) of 1829 was blown through the hole at the front. Notes were selected with finger buttons. The German harmonica by Trossinger (2) dates from about 1830 and is an early instrument of more conventional design. The trumpet harmonica (3) and bell harmonica (4) are special effects instruments from the early 20th century.

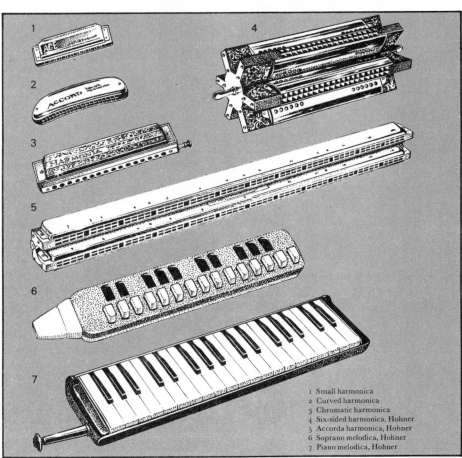

1 Small harmonica
2 Curved harmonica
3 Chromatic harmonica
4 Six-sided harmonica, Hohner
5 Accorda harmonica, Hohner
6 Soprano melodica, Hohner
7 Piano melodica, Hohner

Left Modern harmonicas and melodicas. The small harmonica (1) and curved harmonica (2) are of simple design. Each hole of the chromatic harmonica (3) has four reeds, two for natural and two for chromatic notes. The side button is pushed in to sound chromatic notes. The six-sided harmonica (4) comprises six individual harmonicas each in a different key. The chord harmonica (5) comprises two large harmonicas played together. The soprano button melodica (6) and piano melodica (7) are recent developments of the mouth organ principle.
Right Harmonica player.

Above Free-reed pitch pipes for guitar tuning.

© DIAGRAM

Concertinas and accordions

Concertinas, accordions, and melodeons are free-reed instruments invented in the first decades of the 19th century. All have end keyboards joined by expandable bellows to drive air over the reeds. Simple models have only a few button or piano keys, whereas concertinas and accordions used by professional entertainers are complex instruments capable of playing music in a variety of styles.

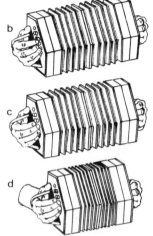

Right Concertina from a German mail order catalog of 1912. Each of the traditionally shaped hexagonal ends has a handle and button keys.

Left Diagrams showing the operation of an English or double-action concertina. The player starts with the instrument in a closed position (a). He depresses the button keys for the notes he wishes to play. This allows him to move his hands apart (b), and so sound the chosen reeds as air is drawn over them into the bellows. The player continues by depressing the keys for the next notes he requires (c). He then moves his hands back together (d), and so forces air out of the bellows over the selected reeds.

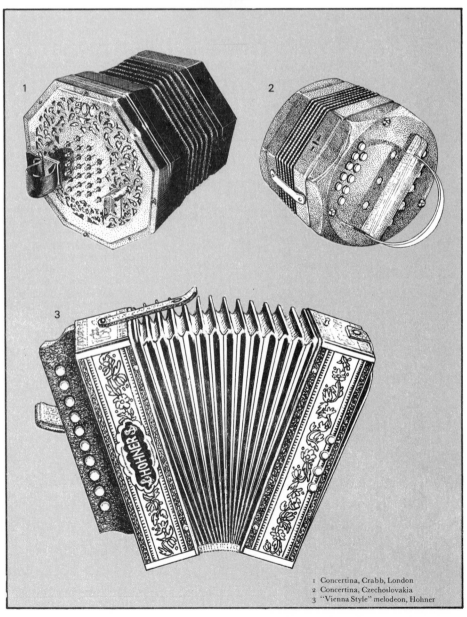

Left Concertinas and a melodeon. The hand-built concertina (1) is a fine example of a craftsman's art. An instrument of this kind takes at least 200 hours to make. The mass-produced concertina (2) is a cheaper but less attractive alternative. The melodeon (3) was originally called a lap organ in the USA. This example has 10 treble keys operated by the right hand, and bellows and four bass keys operated by the left hand. Each key produces a different note on the press and the draw.
Below Concertina player, and an inexpensive novelty concertina.

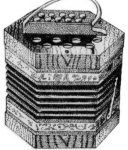

1 Concertina, Crabb, London
2 Concertina, Czechoslovakia
3 "Vienna Style" melodeon, Hohner

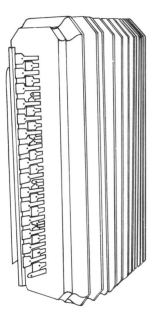

Left A very early accordion (Horniman Museum, London). Made in France about 1820, it has unusual lever-like keys.

1

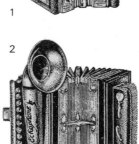

2

Right Two accordions from the early 20th century. The Empress accordion (1) appears in an American store catalog of 1902. It measured only 8in by 6½in. The Echophone accordion (2), with its trumpet amplifier, appears in a German catalog of 1912.

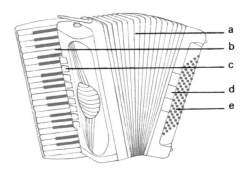

a
b
c
d
e

Above Diagram identifying parts of a modern piano accordion.

a) Bellows
b) Keyboard
c) Treble registers
d) Bass registers
e) Basses

1

2

3

1 Shand Morino accordion, Hohner
2 Galotta 12 accordion, Hohner
3 "Gola" accordion, Hohner

Left Modern accordions. The accordion with button keys (1) is a sophisticated professional model. The small piano accordion (2) is a beginner's model with 25 piano keys and 12 basses. The piano accordion (3), a professional model, has 41 piano keys, 11 treble registers and a master coupler, 120 basses, and seven bass registers. Registers change the tonal quality of the notes played. Basses sound either a single note, or chords built on a particular note.

Below Accordion player.

Organs

The organ is one of the oldest instruments still played today. In all its forms it consists of pipes, levers or keys, and a wind supply. Its origin can be traced back to the simple panpipe, though details of the transition from panpipes blown by man to pipes blown by mechanical means are lost in antiquity. The earliest true organ was the 3rd century BC hydraulis. The craft of organ building, developed by the ancient Greeks and Romans, passed to the peoples of the Middle East. From medieval times it was confined almost exclusively to Europe, extending later to the USA. The most important stages in the development of the modern organ span 2000 years and include the introduction of keys, the addition of stops, and the mechanization of the action. The most recent development is the use of electricity to power the mechanism.

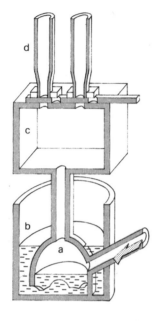

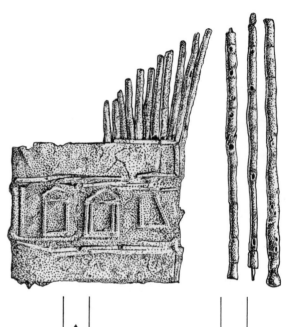

Right Part of the Pompeii hydraulis—a type of water organ invented by Ctesibios of Alexandria about 250 BC.

Left Hydraulis mechanism. The pnigeus (a) was an upturned funnel standing on feet in a container half full of water (b). Its upper end led to the arcula, or wind chest (c). Air from hand pumps entered the pnigeus, filled the arcula, and then forced water in the pnigeus back into the container. If pumping was halted, the air pressure in the pnigeus fell and water entered it from the container. This restored the air pressure in the arcula and ensured a steady supply of air to the pipes (d).

Left Illustration of a Byzantine organ, taken from that on the 4th century AD obelisk of Theodosius. After the Roman Empire organ-making survived as a Byzantine art. This organ has eight pipes of different lengths. Two men are shown operating the pipes and two the bellows.

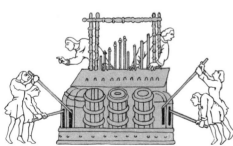

Left Illustration of a 6th century hydraulic organ, based on that in the Utrecht Psalter. This organ worked on a similar principle to Ctesibios's hydraulis of 800 years earlier. Four men pumped air into receivers, where it was trapped under water pressure.

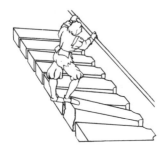

Left Foot-operated bellows, after an illustration by Pretorius (1618–20). As early as the 15th century some organs were fitted with 16ft and even 32ft pipes. This led to the abandoning of hand-operated bellows in favor of more powerful foot bellows. The bar helped the operator to balance.

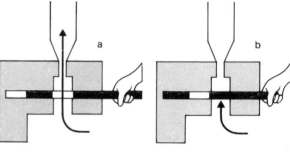

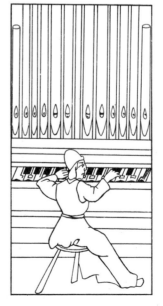

Above Early slider action. When the wood slider was pulled out so that a hole bored in it lined up with the bottom of a pipe, air entered the pipe from the windchest and produced a note (a). To stop the sound the slider was pushed back in to cut off the wind supply (b).

Left Broad-keyed organ, from an illustration in "Theorica Musica" by Gaffurius (1492). Keys on organs developed from the huge levers introduced in the 11th century to replace the cumbersome hand-operated sliders. By the late 1500s broad keys were replaced by narrow ones.

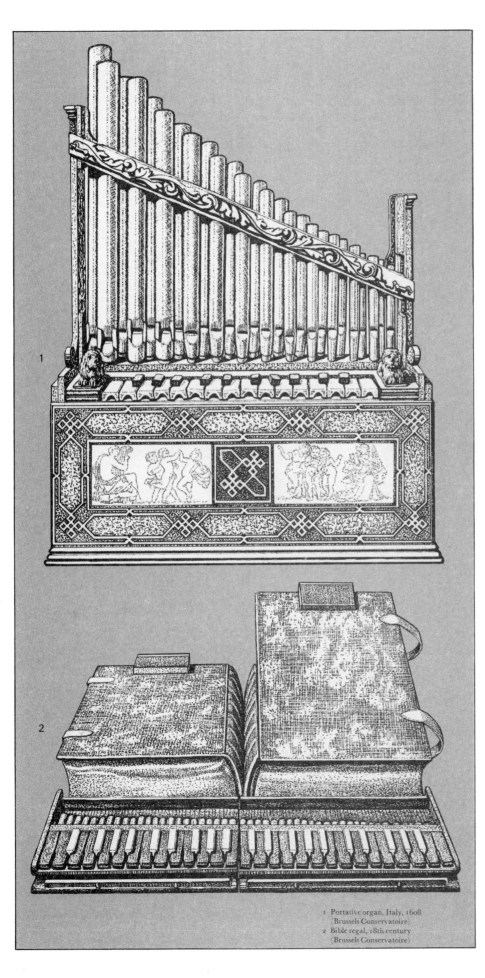

Above Portative organ and player taken from a 14th century manuscript.
Left Portative organ (1) and bible regal (2). Portatives were small portable organs made from the 12th to mid-17th centuries. They were played by one person, who operated the bellows with the left hand and the keys with the right hand. All its pipes were flue pipes. The bible regal was book-shaped and could be folded away after use. Every type of regal had all reed pipes.

Below Pumping the bellows of a bible regal.

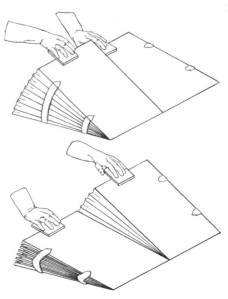

1 Portative organ, Italy, 1608
(Brussels Conservatoire)
2 Bible regal, 18th century
(Brussels Conservatoire)

©DIAGRAM

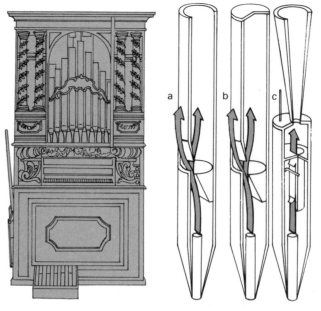

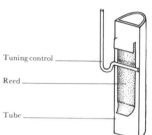

Above Positive organ, from a 15th century manuscript. Positive organs were non-portable flue-pipe organs designed for church or home use. A second person operated the bellows.

Right An 18th century chamber organ, a later form of positive organ (Castello Sforzesco, Milan).

Left Types of pipe. Flue pipes are open (a) or stopped (b), and work like whistle flutes. A stopped pipe sounds an octave below an open pipe of the same length. A reed pipe (c) has a beating reed in a frame.

Below An organ reed—a curved tongue over an opening in the brass tube.

Tuning control

Reed

Tube

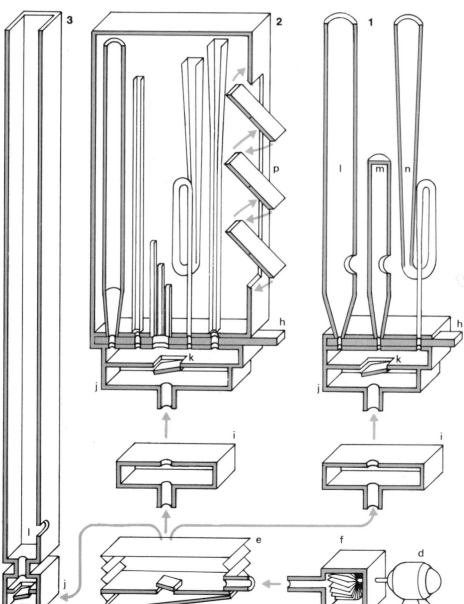

Left How an organ works. The three sections of the organ, the great organ (1), the swell organ (2), and the pedal organ (3), are controlled by a player at the console (4). Each section has its own keyboard or manual. The great manual (a) operates the great organ, and the swell manual (b) the swell organ. The pedal board (c) operates the pedal organ. An electric generator (d) feeds air to the bellows (e) by means of a fan (f). By means of stops (g) which control sliders (h) in the great and swell organs, the player selects a rank of pipes. When a key or pedal is pressed, air passes from the reservoir (i) into the wind chest (j), through open pallet holes (k), and then into the selected pipes— open (l), stopped (m), or reed (n). The swell pedal (o) opens and closes shutters (p) in the swell box, allowing gradual changes of volume. By means of a complex coupling mechanism, all sections of the organ can be sounded simultaneously.

Right An organ console—the instrument's control panel. Often the console is at some distance from the organ pipes, but its manuals (keyboards), stops, and pedalboard all control the sounds produced. Some organs have as many as five manuals, each operating a different set of pipes.

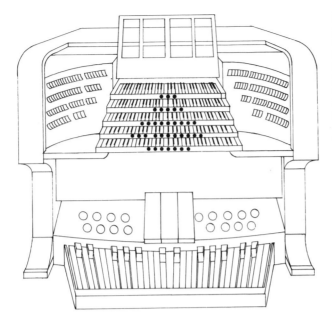

Right Diagram showing the principle behind the use of organ stops. Each stop, when extended, brings into action one or more sets, or ranks, of pipes. The choice of stops determines the tonal quality of any note played on the manual or pedalboard. In the diagrams, stop (a) operates the front rank of pipes, and stop (b) the rear rank. If both stops are out, both ranks of pipes sound. Thus three different tonal qualities can be obtained from two stops. The number of possibilities increases cumulatively with the number of stops. Some organs have as many as 2000 stops.

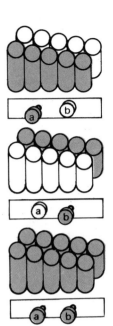

Below Swallow's nest organ built for Abondance Abbey, Savoy and now in the church of St Valère, Sion, Switzerland. Organs of this type were built in several European countries during the Renaissance. They are fixed high on the wall, and the organist climbs a ladder to reach the console.

Below Organ of the chapel of the Massachusetts Institute of Technology, USA. This modern organ reflects current interest in reviving the tonal qualities of baroque organs and the trend toward simplicity in case design. It is a good example of the modern organ-builder's work.

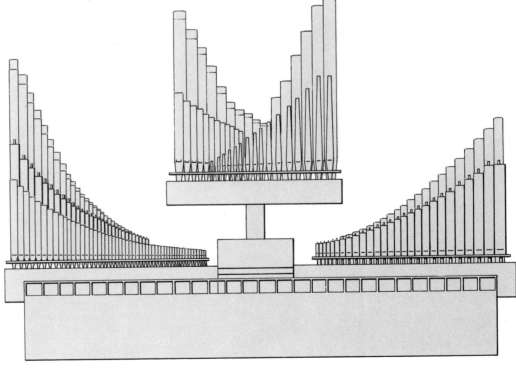

©DIAGRAM

Organ

G. Frescobaldi	Ricercari e canzoni francesi
J. S. Bach	Preludes, toccatas, fugues, chorale preludes
G. F. Handel	Organ concertos
F. Mendelssohn	Six organ sonatas
F. Liszt	Prelude and Fugue on the name Bach
C. Franck	Six pièces pour grand orgue
C. M. Widor	Organ Symphonies
O. Messiaen	Les Corps glorieux

J. S. Bach   Canonic Variation on "Von Himmel hoch da komm'ich her"

Left The elaborately decorated 17th century organ of the New Cathedral, Salamanca, Spain. Many of the front pipes are for decoration only. Very distinctive are the rows of trumpet-stop pipes projecting horizontally forward outside the case.

Harmoniums

The harmonium is a free-reed instrument patented by Debain of Paris in 1848. Though resembling a small organ, and frequently used as a substitute for one, the harmonium is directly related to the free-reed mouth organ and concertina. It consists of a set of free reeds, whose length determines their pitch, activated by a wind supply from foot-operated compression bellows, and controlled by a keyboard.

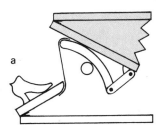
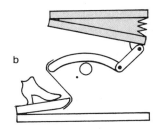

Above Diagrams showing the bellows action of a harmonium. With the pedal in the "up" position the bellows are open (a). Depressing the pedal operates the lever that closes the bellows (b). Each pedal operates a different bellows. The player uses a "heel and toe" action.

Right Identification of parts of a harmonium, and arrows showing the passage of air through the instrument.

a) Pedal
b) Bellows
c) Wind trunk
d) Reservoir
e) Wind chest
f) Bellows board
g) Reed
h) Pallet hole
i) Key
j) Stop

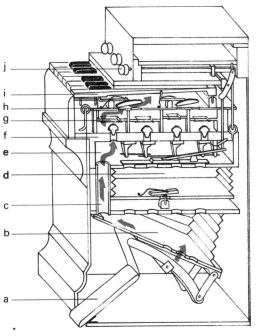

Below French harmonium by Debain (Instrument Museum, Brussels). Made about 1870, it has a simple compact case and very large pedals. Its range is five octaves and there is a single "expressive" stop. The free reeds are fitted with a special mechanism to help them vibrate more easily.

Right "Acme Queen Parlor Organ"—a large American home organ dating from the early 20th century. It has a range of five octaves and eleven stops. Its grandiose carved case was designed to complement the furniture of the period.

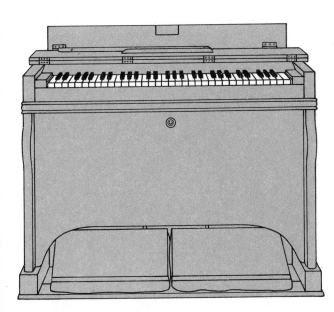

Idiophones: introduction

Idiophones are instruments made of naturally sonorous material, sounded in a variety of different ways. Their development began many thousands of years ago when early man first clashed together sticks, stones, and bones to emphasize the rhythms of his clapping hands and stamping feet. Similar primitive idiophones made of natural materials are today used by many peoples to accompany singing and dancing and to act as signaling instruments. Interest in the different sounds and pitches produced by objects of varying sizes and materials led to the development of such instruments as the xylophone and gong chime. The Western symphony orchestra includes a wide variety of "percussion" instruments, ranging from the simple wood block to tuned instruments like the tubular bells and glockenspiel.

Idiophones family tree
There are eight basic types of idiophone: stamping, stamped, shaken, percussion, concussion, friction, scraped, and plucked. The largest group — percussion idiophones — has a major subdivision according to shape.

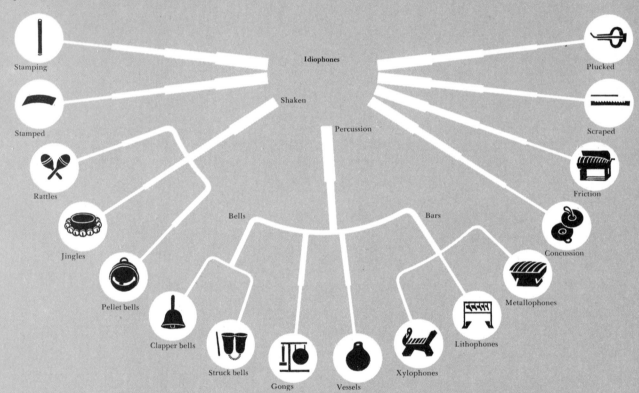

Shapes Idiophones are made in numerous shapes. Common examples include the tubular stamping stick (a), bells (b), gongs (c), vessels (d), and bar idiophones like the xylophone (e). Along with material and sounding method, shape affects the type of sound produced.

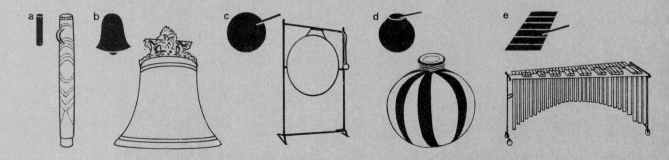

Sounding Idiophones are classified according to the ways in which they are made to produce sound. The eight sounding methods used for this classification are illustrated below: stamping (a), stamped (b), shaken (c), percussion (d), concussion (e), friction (f), scraped (g), and plucked (h).

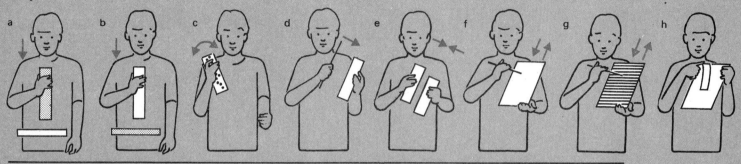

Stamping idiophones are instruments sounded by banging them on the ground or another hard surface. They include sticks, tubes, and tap shoes.

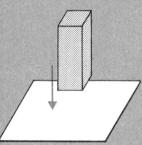

Stamped idiophones In this case the sound comes from the surface on which the stamping takes place. Stamped pits and boards are good examples.

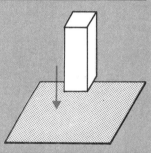

Shaken idiophones Of the instruments sounded by shaking, rattles and jingles are two common types. They are made from many different materials in a great variety of styles.

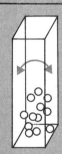

Percussion idiophones Also called struck idiophones, these instruments are made to sound by striking them with a stick or beater. Gongs and xylophones are characteristic examples.

Concussion idiophones An idiophone that produces sound when two or more similar parts hit together is called a concussion idiophone. Examples are cymbals and clappers.

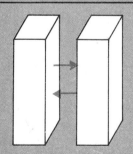

Friction idiophones are instruments sounded by rubbing. Sometimes, as with the musical saw, two objects are rubbed together. Other instruments, such as musical glasses, are rubbed with a moistened finger.

Scraped idiophones These instruments have a notched or ridged surface, and produce a series of short taps when a stick is drawn over them. Examples include bone scrapers and the washboard.

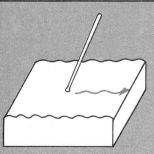

Plucked idiophones Also called linguaphones, these instruments have one or more flexible tongues attached to a frame. They are sounded by plucking the tongues. Jew's harps and sansas are examples.

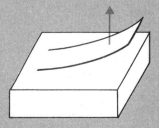

©DIAGRAM

Stamping sticks

Stamping sticks are among the simplest and oldest of all rhythm instruments. Usually beaten on the ground they may be sticks chosen at random or be specially fashioned lengths of hollow wood or bamboo. Sometimes they are used specifically to produce a rhythm for dancing, but often, as when used for grinding corn, the rhythm both arises from and helps along a job of work.

Left Conductor of a 17th century French court orchestra marking time by tapping a stick on the floor. The composer Lully died after injuring his foot with his baton.

Above Stamping sticks in play. Australian aborigines (a) beat on the ground with sticks picked up at random. New Britain islanders (b) beat time with their spears. In Fiji two hollow tubes are stamped on the ground (c). In Bali rhythm is produced while grinding corn in a trough (d).

Right Examples of different types of stamping instrument. Some peoples, like the Australian aborigines, use an ordinary stick (1). Common in Oceania and South America is the more resonant hollow tube, made of cane (2) or wood (3, 4, and 5). A gourd (6) is a good alternative.

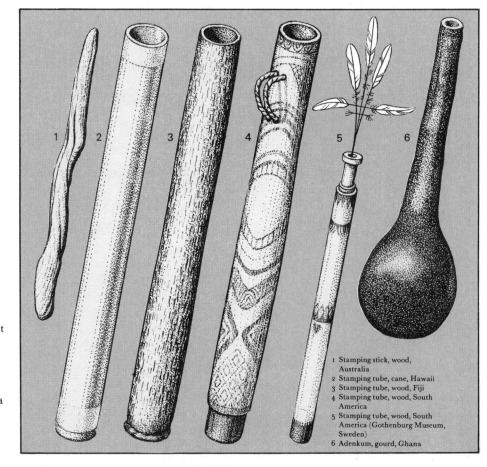

1 Stamping stick, wood, Australia
2 Stamping tube, cane, Hawaii
3 Stamping tube, wood, Fiji
4 Stamping tube, wood, South America
5 Stamping tube, wood, South America (Gothenburg Museum, Sweden)
6 Adenkum, gourd, Ghana

Tapping feet

The stamping or tapping of the feet, even the sound of people walking or marching, has its own rhythmic quality. Peoples from many different cultures have throughout history sought to emphasize the natural rhythmic patterns produced by such simple activities. Specially designed footwear is sometimes worn to increase the volume and give a more definite quality to the sounds thus produced.

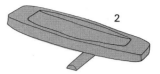

Above Two examples of special footwear used to emphasize the rhythmic tapping of the feet. The tap shoe (1) is fitted with metal plates at the toe and heel. The Hawaiian "shoe" (2) is made of wood and produces a clicking sound when the foot is rocked back and forward (right).

Left Clog dancing (a) is a traditional folk art still occasionally found in the North of England. Tap dancing (b) acquired an enthusiastic following after the great Hollywood musicals of the 1930s and 1940s. (Fred Astaire is drawn here from a still out of the film "Top Hat.")

Pits and boards

In the ceremonies and festivities of many different peoples a rhythmic accompaniment is set up by the stamping feet of the participants. The sound of their stamping is greatly amplified when the dancers stamp over a board or a covered pit.

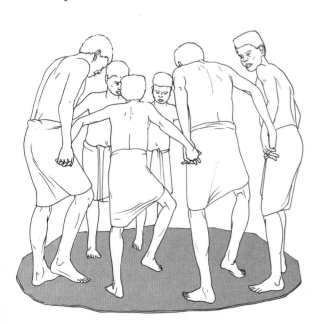

Left Solomon Islanders dancing over a bark-covered pit. Stamped pits are common in Oceania and are also found elsewhere. They produce a deep thudding accompaniment during ceremonial dancing.

Right Dancer from the New Hebrides using an inverted curved board to emphasize the rhythm of his steps. The hollow cavity under the board acts as a resonator and amplifies the sound.

©DIAGRAM

Rattles

Rattles are shaken idiophones which for many thousands of years have played an important role in the music and magical rites of primitive peoples all over the world. The simplest rattles are no more than dried gourds or pods containing rattling seeds. Other materials used for rattles include animal hide, wood, basketwork, clay, and metal, and the shape of these rattles often echoes that of a gourd.

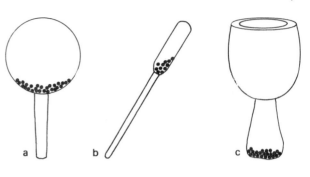

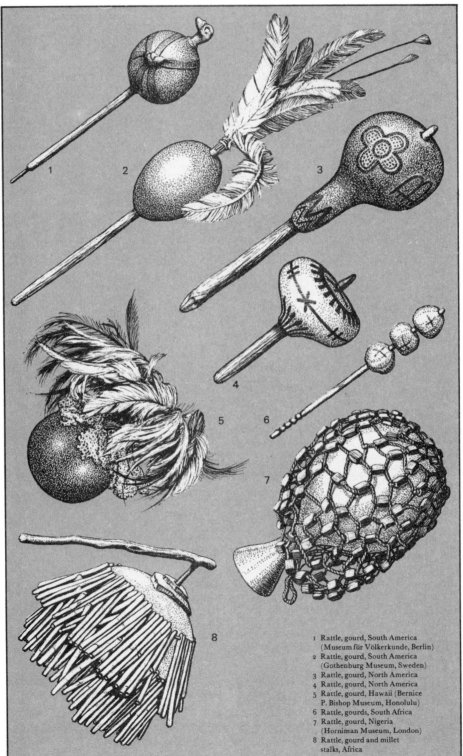

Above Diagrams showing three basic types of rattle—simple (a), stick (b), and cup (c). The simple rattle is spherical, often a gourd, with a wood handle. The stick rattle may be partially or completely hollowed out. The cup rattle, or rattling cup, has a hollow base filled with rattling substances.

Left Gourd rattles from America and Africa. Many of these simple rattles are decorated with carvings (1 and 6), the addition of feathers (2 and 5), or by painting (3 and 4). More unusual are rattles with external rattling devices, like the net rattle (7) and millet stalk rattle (8).

Below A very simple rattle—a large dried seed pod from Queensland, Australia (Horniman Museum, London).

1 Rattle, gourd, South America (Museum für Völkerkunde, Berlin)
2 Rattle, gourd, South America (Gothenburg Museum, Sweden)
3 Rattle, gourd, North America
4 Rattle, gourd, North America
5 Rattle, gourd, Hawaii (Bernice P. Bishop Museum, Honolulu)
6 Rattle, gourds, South Africa
7 Rattle, gourd, Nigeria (Horniman Museum, London)
8 Rattle, gourd and millet stalks, Africa

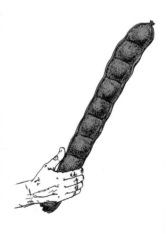

Left Rattles made from animal materials. The turtle shell rattle (1) and the carved horn rattle decorated with cords (2) are ceremonial instruments from North America (Museum of the American Indian, New York). The carved ivory rattle (3) is from Nigeria (Horniman Museum, London).

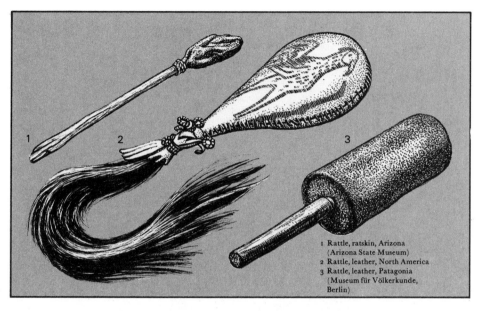

Left Rattles made from animal hide. The rattle from Arizona (1) has a small ratskin pouch tied to a stick. Also from North America is the stitched rattle with a horse's tail handle (2). The Indians of Patagonia make cylindrical rattles (3) by stretching wet leather over a frame.

1 Rattle, ratskin, Arizona (Arizona State Museum)
2 Rattle, leather, North America
3 Rattle, leather, Patagonia (Museum für Völkerkunde, Berlin)

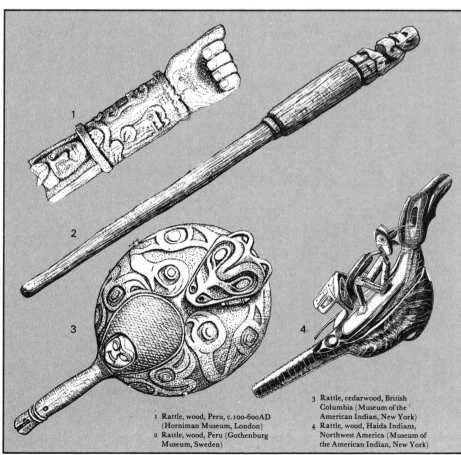

Left Wood rattles from Peru (1 and 2) and Northwest America (3 and 4). Many rattles in this material are beautifully carved with images of magical significance. For example, the rattle from British Columbia (3) symbolizes the human metamorphosis of a beaver.

Below North American Indian with a carved wood rattle.

1 Rattle, wood, Peru, c.100-600AD (Horniman Museum, London)
2 Rattle, wood, Peru (Gothenburg Museum, Sweden)
3 Rattle, cedarwood, British Columbia (Museum of the American Indian, New York)
4 Rattle, wood, Haida Indians, Northwest America (Museum of the American Indian, New York)

© DIAGRAM

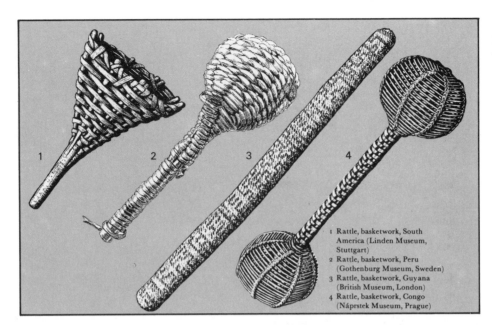

Left Basketwork rattles from America and Africa. Many basketwork rattles imitate the shape of a gourd—like the Peruvian single-ended rattle (2) and the African double-ended rattle (4). The stick rattle from Guyana (3) is intricately woven to give a two-color geometric pattern.

1 Rattle, basketwork, South America (Linden Museum, Stuttgart)
2 Rattle, basketwork, Peru (Gothenburg Museum, Sweden)
3 Rattle, basketwork, Guyana (British Museum, London)
4 Rattle, basketwork, Congo (Náprstek Museum, Prague)

Left Clay rattles. The mushroom-shaped rattle (1) was found in Northern Europe and dates from the 8th century BC. Rattles made of clay are, however, more particularly associated with the ancient Indian civilizations of South and Central America. Among the many unusual forms taken by American examples are rattling cups (4 and 6) and rattling vessels (5), each containing clay pellets in its base.

1 Rattle, clay, Silesia, 8th century BC (Moravian Museum, Brno, Czechoslovakia)
2 Rattle, clay, Mexico, c.500AD
3 Rattle, clay, Mexico, c.500AD (National Museum of Anthropology and History, Mexico)
4 Rattling cup, clay, Peru (Museum für Völkerkunde, Berlin)
5 Rattling vessel, clay, Peru (Gothenburg Museum, Sweden)
6 Rattling cup, clay, Peru

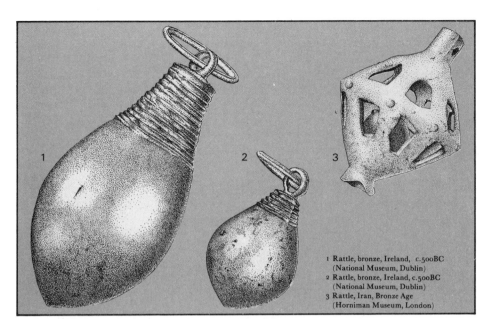

Left Ancient rattles made of bronze. The pear-shaped rattles (1 and 2) were part of an archaeological find in County Offaly, Ireland. Each contains a number of bronze pellets. The lantern-shaped Persian bell rattle (3) was found in Luristan and contains a single bronze pellet.

1 Rattle, bronze, Ireland, c.500BC
  (National Museum, Dublin)
2 Rattle, bronze, Ireland, c.500BC
  (National Museum, Dublin)
3 Rattle, Iran, Bronze Age
  (Horniman Museum, London)

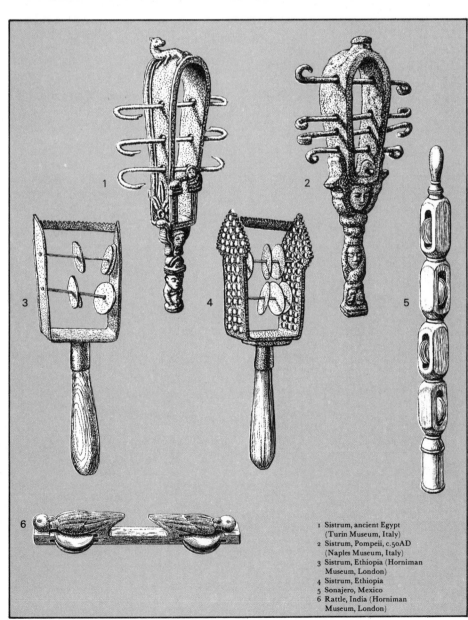

1 Sistrum, ancient Egypt
  (Turin Museum, Italy)
2 Sistrum, Pompeii, c.50AD
  (Naples Museum, Italy)
3 Sistrum, Ethiopia (Horniman
  Museum, London)
4 Sistrum, Ethiopia
5 Sonajero, Mexico
6 Rattle, India (Horniman
  Museum, London)

Left Sistra—rattles with jingling metal disks threaded on rods. Examples survive from ancient Egypt (1) and Pompeii (2), and similar instruments (3 and 4) are still used today in Ethiopian churches. The Mexican sonajero (5) and Indian bird rattle (6) have similar jingling disks.

Below Javanese anklung—a highly refined bamboo rattle. Carefully tuned vertical bamboo tubes slide in a groove in a horizontal bamboo and produce a pleasant sound on striking its rim. Instruments are made in different sizes and are often played in groups.

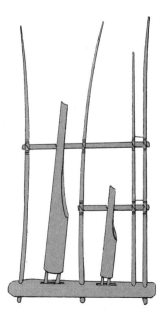

© DIAGRAM

Jingles

Jingles comprise a number of small rattling
objects or bells which on their own would
produce very little sound but which together
make a significant contribution to music making.
Usually worn about the body or attached to
clothing, jingles often provide a dancer's
own accompaniment. Less common are stick
or frame jingles, including the spectacular
Turkish crescent or jingling johnny.

Right Dancers with three
types of jingle. Ankle
jingles (a) are worn in many
parts of the world. The
dancer's jingling apron (b)
is more unusual, but jingles
on clothing are very
common. The stick jingle
(c) is shaken during dancing.

Below Jingles made from
plant and animal materials.
Very common among the
many types of jingle made
from nuts are necklaces (1),
belts (3), and anklets (5).
More unusual are jingles
made from animal materials,
like the jingles made from
springbok ears (6) and
from hooves (7).

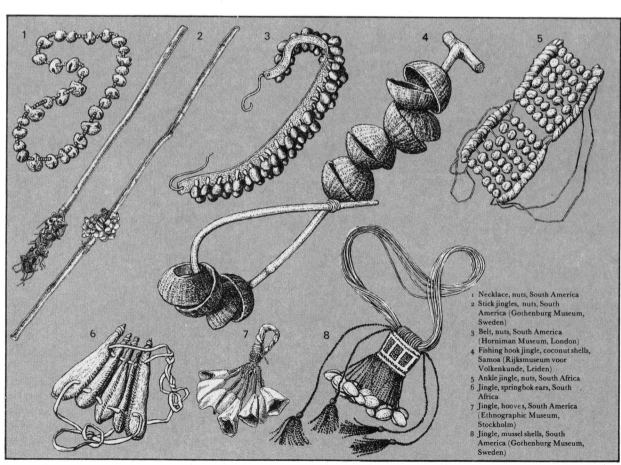

1 Necklace, nuts, South America
2 Stick jingles, nuts, South
America (Gothenburg Museum,
Sweden)
3 Belt, nuts, South America
(Horniman Museum, London)
4 Fishing hook jingle, coconut shells,
Samoa (Rijksmuseum voor
Volkenkunde, Leiden)
5 Ankle jingle, nuts, South Africa
6 Jingle, springbok ears, South
Africa
7 Jingle, hooves, South America
(Ethnographic Museum,
Stockholm)
8 Jingle, mussel shells, South
America (Gothenburg Museum,
Sweden)

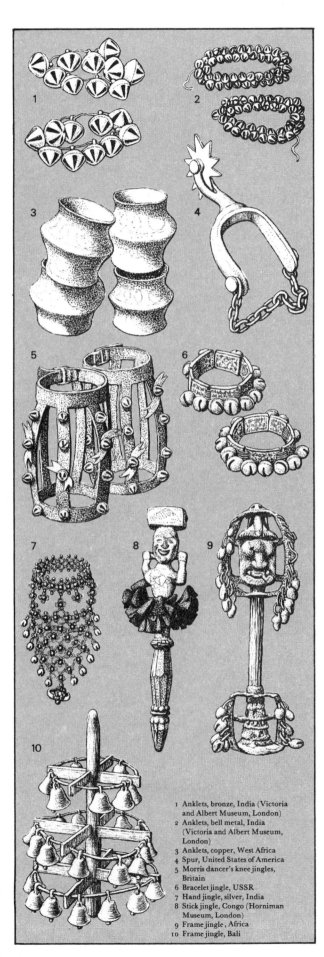

Left Jingles made from metal. Jingles comprised of small metal bells are found in many countries. Included here are examples from India (1, 2, and 7), Britain (5), the USSR (6), and Bali (10). Another interesting form of jingle is the metal spur (4) worn for horse riding.

Right Turkish crescent or jingling johnny—an impressive stick jingle adopted as a military band instrument by British and German armies in the 18th and 19th centuries.

Below Jingles used by orchestras, bands, and by school groups. Illustrated here are a tambourine jingle (1) and different styles of "sleigh bells" (2, 3, and 4). Sleigh bells were occasionally used by Mozart and appear in the scores of a number of 20th century composers.

1 Anklets, bronze, India (Victoria and Albert Museum, London)
2 Anklets, bell metal, India (Victoria and Albert Museum, London)
3 Anklets, copper, West Africa
4 Spur, United States of America
5 Morris dancer's knee jingles, Britain
6 Bracelet jingle, USSR
7 Hand jingle, silver, India
8 Stick jingle, Congo (Horniman Museum, London)
9 Frame jingle, Africa
10 Frame jingle, Bali

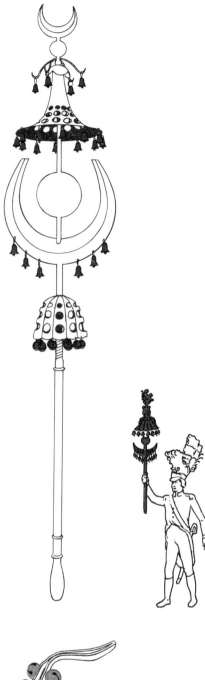

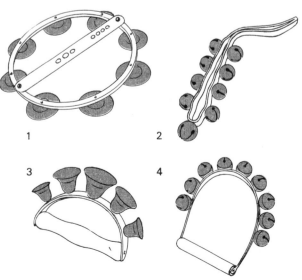

© DIAGRAM

Pellet and clapper bells

Individual bells with an integral sounding device were known as early as the 9th century BC. There are two basic forms—pellet bells and clapper bells—which are found today in a great variety of shapes and sizes. Wood or metal bells are most common but more unusual materials are also found. Most bells are untuned, but sets of tuned handbells provide popular entertainment in some countries.

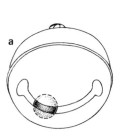

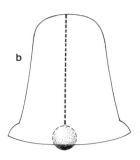

Left Diagrams showing the basic characteristics of pellet and clapper bells. The pellet bell (a) is sounded by an unattached pellet inside the bell cavity. Clapper bells are sounded by a swinging clapper which may be attached either internally (b) or externally (c).

Above Diagram showing the area of greatest vibration when a clapper bell is struck. The bell vibrates most around the rim, or sound bow, and is dead at the center, or vertex. This pattern distinguishes a bell from a hollow gong, in which the vibrations are greatest at the center.

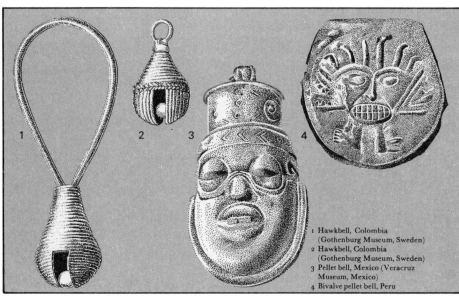

1 Hawkbell, Colombia (Gothenburg Museum, Sweden)
2 Hawkbell, Colombia (Gothenburg Museum, Sweden)
3 Pellet bell, Mexico (Veracruz Museum, Mexico)
4 Bivalve pellet bell, Peru

Left Pellet bells from pre-Columbian America. The simple hawkbells (1 and 2) are from Colombia. The Mexican god's head bell (3) is made of copper. The Peruvian bivalve bell (4) is made from two connected pieces of hammered metal.
Below European claw bell, popular early this century.

Left Animal bells. Pellet bells are used for some small animals, as on the dog collar (1), but animal bells are more usually of the clapper type. The Thai bullock bell (4) is about 18in high. The attractive Russian saddle chimes (7) have four external clappers to each bell.

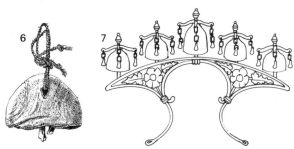

1 Dog collar bell, USA
2 Horse harness bell, England
3 Cowbell, Switzerland
4 Bullock bell, Thailand
5 Camel bell, Somalia
6 Camel bell, Africa
7 Saddle chimes, USSR

Right Ancient clapper bells. The Assyrian bells (1 and 2) date from c.800BC and were found at Nimrud (British Museum, London). The Egyptian bells (3 and 4) date from about 200BC. The Greek bell (5) is in the museum on the holy island of Delos. The Roman bell (6) is a handbell of more modern appearance.

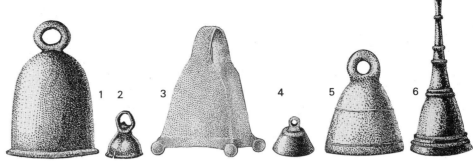

Right Examples of clapper bells from different countries. Simple clapper bells with a single clapper (1,2, and 3) are commonest, but multiple clapper bells are also found in many parts of the world. The Congolese bell (5) has three chambers each with its own clappers. Usually bell and clapper are made of similar material but sometimes quite different materials are used. The nut bell from New Britain (1) has a clapper made from a boar's tooth, while the South American wood bell (6) has bone clappers. The delicate Burmese bell chime (8) and Korean bell (9) are sounded by the action of the wind.

Above Ethiopian temple bell with subsidiary bells acting as clappers.

1 Bell, nut, New Britain (Museum für Völkerkunde, Leipzig)
2 Bell, bronze, India (Victoria and Albert Museum, London)
3 Bell, wood, Nigeria (Horniman Museum, London)
4 Bell, wood, Liberia (Metropolitan Museum, New York)
5 Bell, wood, Congo (Horniman Museum, London)
6 Bell, wood, South America (Gothenburg Museum, Sweden)
7 Bell, wood, Bali (Tropen Institute, Amsterdam)
8 Wind bells, metal, Burma
9 Wind bell, metal, Korea (Horniman Museum, London)

© DIAGRAM

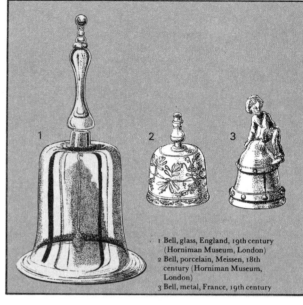

Above Bellringers through the ages—a medieval musician, a 16th century beggar, a town crier, and a 20th century schoolboy. The use of bells for signaling purposes has been common since the earliest times.

Right Decorative bells. The 19th century English glass bell (1) and the 18th century Meissen porcelain bell (2) are fine examples of bells made as collector's pieces. The bell with the handle shaped like a climbing boy (3) is a 19th century French table bell originally used for summoning servants.

1 Bell, glass, England, 19th century (Horniman Museum, London)
2 Bell, porcelain, Meissen, 18th century (Horniman Museum, London)
3 Bell, metal, France, 19th century

Right Identification of parts of a bell of the type used by groups of handbell ringers. This activity has been practiced by enthusiasts for at least 800 years.

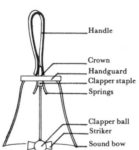

Handle
Crown
Handguard
Clapper staple
Springs
Clapper ball
Striker
Sound bow

Right Two styles of handbell handle—the older solid wood handle (a), and the now more popular leather strap attached to a wood crown (b). The strap is gripped firmly by the hand and the thumb placed against the crown to help support the bell and give greater control.

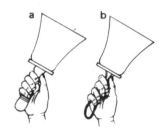

a   b

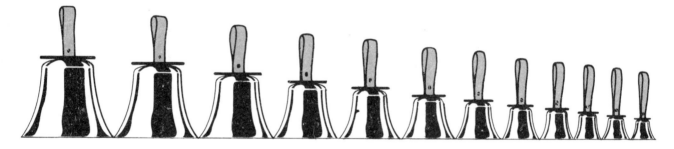

Above Set of handbells showing typical gradations in size. The bells are usually tuned to the notes of a major scale. Simple harmonic accompaniments can be provided by the larger deeper bells while the melody is usually divided among the smaller higher pitched bells.

Left Group of handbell players. Each player rings two or four bells, which may be sounded individually or together. Usually the sound of each bell is allowed to die away naturally but bells may be damped against the chest. Surprising volume control is achieved by good players.

Church bells

From about the 8th century large tower bells have been a feature of Christian churches. Simple ringing techniques include swinging a clapper or hammer against an almost stationary bell by means of a rope, or gently swinging the bell to hit a clapper. Sophisticated change ringing was developed in England in the 17th century and remains popular there. Elsewhere mechanical bell ringing has been preferred.

Left Wheel of "sacring" bells. A feature of Spanish churches, these small bells are sounded during the Mass.
Right The bell from Caversfield, Oxfordshire (1) dates from around 1200 and is one of England's oldest church bells. More elaborate is the cathedral bell from Meissen, East Germany (2).

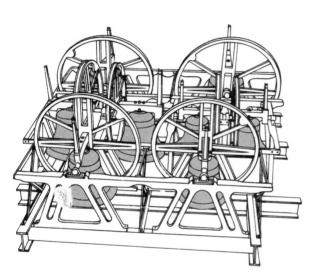

Right Identification of parts of an English bell-ringing mechanism. The English method of hanging bells is distinguished by the full-circle wheel and the stay—both essential if the bells are to be used for "change ringing."
Left Bells in an English iron and steel frame.

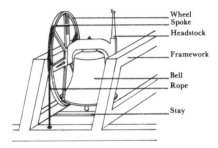

Wheel
Spoke
Headstock
Framework
Bell
Rope
Stay

Right Diagram showing the variations in thickness of a well shaped bell. The bell is thickest at the sound bow, where it is struck, and tapers to one-third of that thickness toward the top. The overall dimensions are also scientifically calculated in relation to the bell's weight.

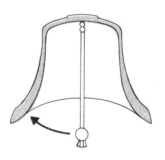

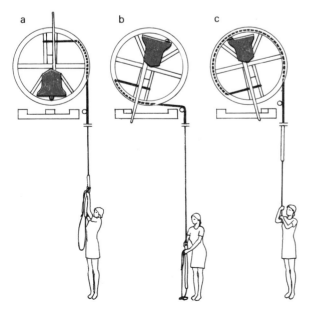

Left Ringing action. The rope, attached to the bell wheel, reaches into the ringing chamber below the belfry. Before ringing can begin, the bellringer must move his bell from its down position (a) to the set position—upside down, resting slightly off balance. A gentle pull on the rope—hand stroke (b)—causes the bell to swing down, strike, and continue up in the same direction. A stay on each bell wheel, catching in a slider, stops the bell from swinging over the top. A further pull—back stroke (c)—causes the bell to return to its first position, ringing as it travels.

Right Example of a change for five bells. Without interrupting the rhythm two bells will sound in a different order if one ringer slows his back stroke while his neighbor pulls harder at his hand stroke.
Below Operating a carillon —a mechanical means of sounding bells (see p. 246).

```
12345
21435
24153
42513
45231
54321
53412
35142
31524
13254
12345
```

©DIAGRAM

Struck bells

Struck bells sounded by a separate striker have been known in China for some 4000 years, and today bells of this type remain very popular in Far Eastern countries. Elsewhere struck bells are less common, although interesting hand-held examples are found in parts of Africa. Most Far Eastern struck bells are suspended in a frame, either singly or grouped together to produce a tuned bell chime.

Below Asian struck bells. The Chinese bell with the decorative stand (1) has a distinctive crescent-shaped mouth. The Chinese bell (2) is over 2000 years years old. The Korean bell (3) was taken to Japan by pirates. The Japanese resting bell (4) sits rim up on a pillow on a lacquered stand.

Right Striking mechanism for a very large Japanese temple bell. The monk pulls on the rope and so causes the horizontally suspended wood beam to swing and strike the bell. Large bells of this kind are typically housed in a separate building in the grounds of the temple.

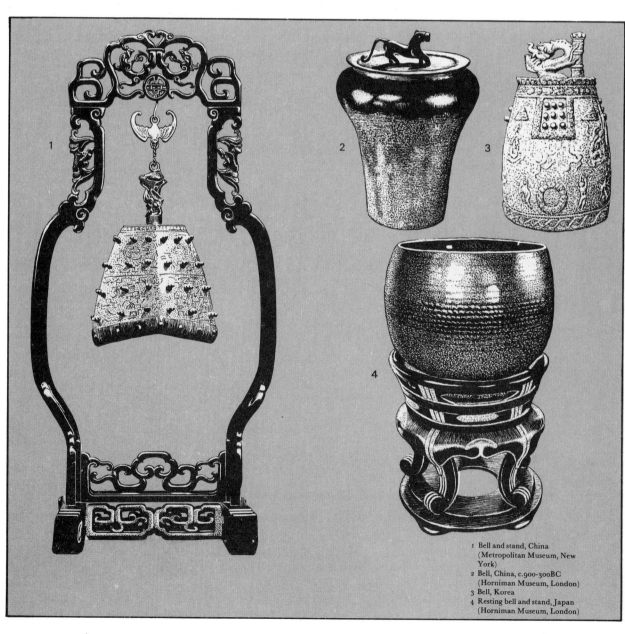

1 Bell and stand, China (Metropolitan Museum, New York)
2 Bell, China, c.900-300BC (Horniman Museum, London)
3 Bell, Korea
4 Resting bell and stand, Japan (Horniman Museum, London)

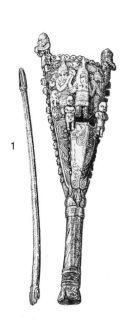
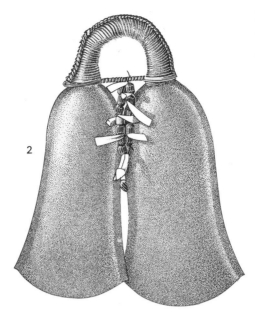

1

2

Left Struck bells from Africa. The carved ivory bell (1) is from the Benin culture of Nigeria and probably dates from the 16th century (British Museum, London). It has two internal chambers producing different pitches. The large metal double bell (2) is a type commonly played today.
Below Double bell player.

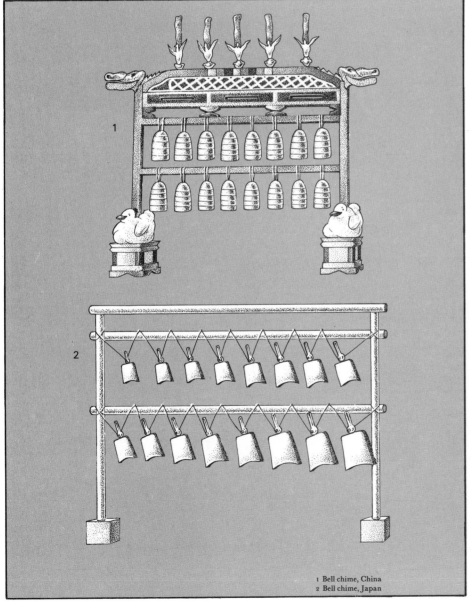

Left Bell chimes from the Far East. Sometimes the bells are the same size but of differing thickness (1). Other chimes have bells hung in order of size (2). Bell chimes are sometimes played in conjunction with hanging stone chimes.
Below Part of a vertically hung Japanese bell chime.

Below Medieval manuscript illustration showing a European struck bell chime. In Europe the struck bell has never been as popular as the clapper type.

1 Bell chime, China
2 Bell chime, Japan

© DIAGRAM

Gongs

A gong is a metal percussion disk struck by a beater. Found most commonly in Southeast Asia, the gong was known in China in the 6th century AD. The earliest examples were flat bronze plates although many later gongs have a bulging surface or a raised central boss. Single suspended gongs are now found in many parts of the world. Horizontal gongs and sets of gong chimes are largely confined to Asia.

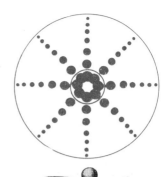

Left Diagram showing the vibration pattern of a gong. The gong is struck at the center to give maximum sound and its vibrations diminish toward the rim. This pattern distinguishes a hollow gong from a bell—which is dead at the center and vibrates most around the rim.

Right A selection of novelty gongs from Europe and the United States. Brought to Europe from Asia the gong became a member of the Western orchestra and has also enjoyed widespread popularity as a domestic novelty and signal instrument.

Left Ethiopian gong made of iron. Large suspended gongs of this kind are used in the Ethiopian Coptic church, but elsewhere in Africa gongs are of only minor significance.

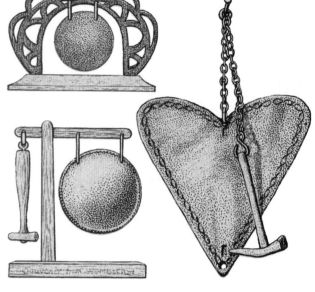

Left Gongs from India (Victoria and Albert Museum, London). Indian gongs are made in a variety of shapes but most examples are small with a flat surface. They give a high pitch and are used for signaling the time and during Hindu ritual.

Left An unusual cast bronze gong from China. This solid gong is similar in outline to a common form of Chinese bell. It dates from the Han dynasty (200BC–224AD).

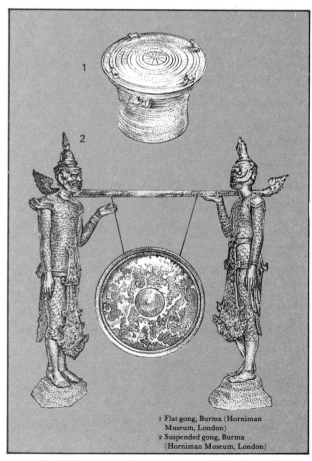

Right Two styles of gong from Burma. The "Shan drum" (1) is a flat bronze gong set on a drumlike base with concave sides. The striking surface is decorated with tiny frogs. The carved and gilded figures carrying the suspended gong (2) are approximately 4ft high.

1 Flat gong, Burma (Horniman Museum, London)
2 Suspended gong, Burma (Horniman Museum, London)

Below Gongs used in the Japanese gagaku ensemble. These bronze gongs, made in different sizes, are suspended in decorative frames and hit with hard beaters. They are used to give emphasis to important beats in each phrase.
Right The seated player hits the gong from behind.

Below Typical gong of the Dayak peoples of Borneo. This comparatively small, double-bossed gong is suspended from a simple frame and struck with a padded beater. Gongs are believed by some Borneans to be effective in warding off storms.
Right Dayak gong player.

Right Javanese kenong. This deep-rimmed gong with a central boss rests on crossed cords over a decorated hollow box frame. It produces a clear, high-pitched note. The very fine example illustrated here is from the Raffles gamelan in the British Museum, London.

Kenong, Java (British Museum, London)

©DIAGRAM

Left Javanese gong ageng (Raffles gamelan, British Museum, London). The gong ageng consists of two suspended bossed gongs of slightly different sizes, usually between 2ft and 3ft in diameter. Struck on the boss with a padded beater each gong produces a slightly different pitch.

Left Javanese bonnang (Raffles gamelan, British Museum, London). The bonnang is a gong chime made up of two rows of wide-rimmed bossed gongs resting on cords in a wood frame. They are tuned to the notes of a diatonic scale, and are used to accompany the melody.

Left Gong chime from Borneo. The gongs are wide-rimmed and bossed like those of the Javanese bonnang. Their pitch may be raised by shaving the boss or lowered by shaving the edge of the rim.

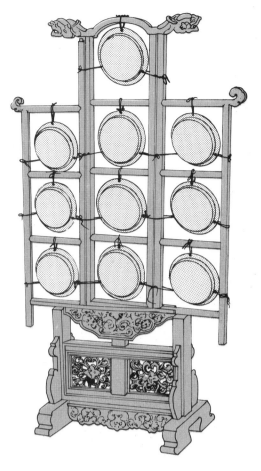

Above Set of Javanese gongs suspended in random order from a wood frame. Although not deliberately tuned, each gong produces a different tone of distinct pitch.

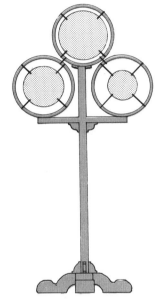

Right Tam âm la—a Vietnamese gong chime with three small gongs suspended in metal circles on a wood frame. The gongs are of slightly different diameters, with the largest gong at the top. The tam âm la became a member of the Vietnamese court orchestra in the late 18th century.

Right Yun lo, or yun ngao. This Chinese gong chime consists of nine or ten small gongs suspended in rows in a wood frame. The gongs have the same diameter, about 4in, but are of different thicknesses to produce different tones. They are played with a felt-covered beater.

Below Gong chimes from Thailand (1) and Burma (2) consisting of tuned gongs resting on cords in a low circular wood frame. The player sits inside the frame (right) and uses beaters with disk ends. The lowest pitched gong is to the player's left and the highest to his right.

©DIAGRAM

1

2

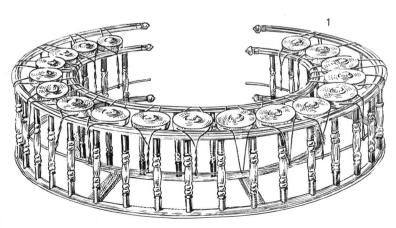

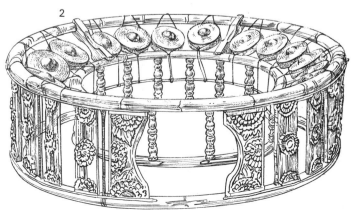

Steel drums

The steel drum is popularly considered the national instrument of Trinidad. The development of the steel drum in the 1940s soon led to the replacement of the traditional carnival bamboo stick bands by groups of steel drum players. Within a few years steel bands were established throughout the Caribbean and elsewhere, giving a distinctive new sound to music in a variety of different styles.

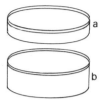

Left Steel drum beaters—fitted with a small hard sponge-rubber ball (a), or wrapped with rubber bands (b).

Right An oil drum—predecessor of the West Indian steel drum.

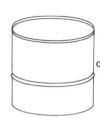

Right Steel drum depths. The "ping pong" (a) is cut off about 5in below the rim of the barrel, and the "guitar" (b) about 9in below the rim. The "cello" (c) is two-thirds to three-fourths of the total barrel depth. A bass drum is made from the full depth of the barrel without its bottom.

Right Making a steel drum. The end of the barrel is sunk by means of a sledge hammer to form a basin (a). The tuning pattern is then traced on (b) and with a nail punch thousands of tiny impressions are hammered over the tracing (c). These hammered grooves "insulate" the tone of each section. When the barrel has been cut to the correct depth (d) each section is hammered up from below (e). The pan is heated over a fire (f) and plunged into cold water (g) to temper the steel. The maker then tunes the drum by tapping each section, so producing the finished product (h).

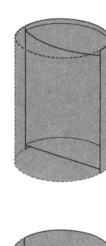
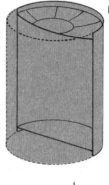
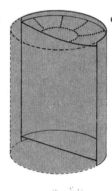
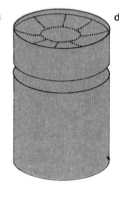
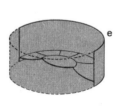
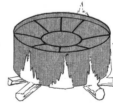
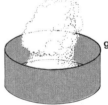

Right Diagrams showing common tuning patterns for steel drums—rhythm (a), ping pong (b), second pan (c), cello (d), guitar (e), and bass (f). The ping pong usually gives 25 different pitches: the bass pan only five.
Below Musician playing a marching bass steel drum.

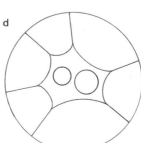
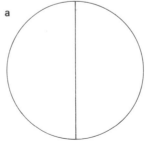
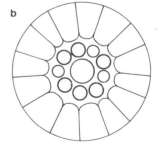
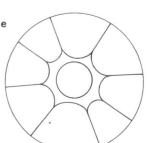
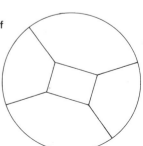
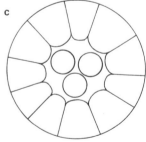

Right Steel drummers with ping pong (a), second pan (b), and bass (c). For marching, smaller drums are supported on straps around the neck. For stationary performances, they are fitted on stands. The bass, rarely used in processions, usually rests on sponge-rubber feet.

Right Ping pong (a), guitar pan (b), bass pan (c), and rhythm pan (d). The ping pong plays the melody while the guitar pan usually provides the background accompaniment. Bass pans are often played in groups of four, giving a total of 20 pitches. The rhythm pan is usually left untuned.

Below Musician playing triple cello pans—designed to give a chromatic range of almost two octaves.

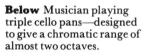

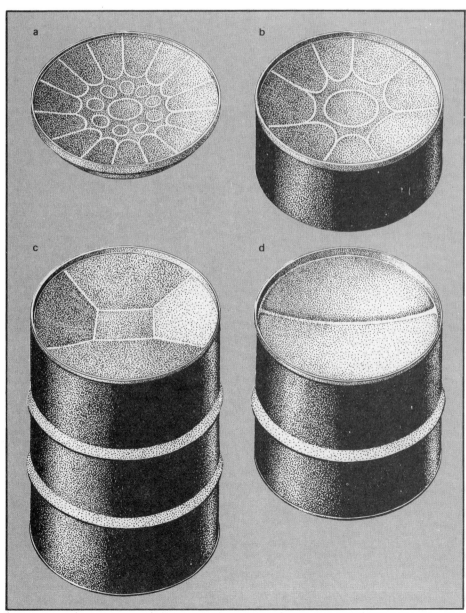

Percussion vessels

Pots, cans, and bottles are just a few of the everyday objects that have been adopted for making music. Sound is produced from these "percussion vessels" by beating or tapping with the hands or with a small stick. By using vessels of different sizes or by filling vessels of the same size with varying amounts of water the player can produce different notes allowing him to play simple tunes.

Right Different playing methods for percussion vessels—sitting with the vessel on the lap (a) or kneeling beside it (b) and beating with the hands, or wearing the vessel around the neck and beating it with sticks (c).

Right Simple percussion vessels. Among the everyday objects commonly used as rhythm instruments are gourds, pots, cans, and mugs. Different notes are produced from objects of different sizes, thicknesses, and materials, and several vessels are often played together.

Below Sand drum. Found in Ethiopia and New Guinea this unusual "drum" is made by tunneling out sand to form a small bridge which is beaten by the hands.

1 Gourds, Africa
2 Percussion pots, Nigeria
3 Hula ipu, Hawaii
4 Suspended cans
5 Suspended mugs

Right Indian jaltarang, porcelain bowls filled with different amounts of water and played by tapping with bamboo sticks tipped with cork or felt. Water in the cups modifies their pitch and helps sustain the tone.

Right Water drums. The example from New Guinea (1) is a lidded, carved wood vessel filled with water. It is beaten on the lid with the hands. The African water drum (2) is made from two half gourds. The smaller gourd, beaten with the hands, floats in water in the larger one.

Right Bottles or glasses can be used for playing simple tunes if each one is filled with water to a different level. Small wood sticks make the best beaters.

© DIAGRAM

Slit drums

Slit drums are made from a length of wood or bamboo hollowed out through a slit along one side. Beaten with sticks or the hands they are generally used for ceremonial or signaling. Sizes range from small instruments that can be carried by one man to the enormous slit drums of Assam each in its own roofed house. Slit drums are largely confined to Southeast Asia, Africa, South America, and Oceania.

Right Playing methods for three types of slit drum—beating on the outside of a small drum placed on the ground (a), scraping the interior of a larger drum resting on supports for greater resonance (b), and beating on a hollowed out tree trunk rooted in the ground (c).

Right Examples of different types of slit. Simple straight slits are most common but many other patterns are also found. Sounds of differing tone quality can be produced by varying the point at which a drum is struck.

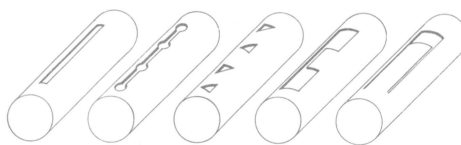

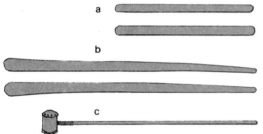

Above Slit drum beaters—small sticks (a), club-shaped beaters (b), and the hammer-headed beater of China and Japan (c).

Right African slit drums. The Congolese drum in the form of a man (1) is played by moving the attached stick up and down in the slit. The double-slitted drum (2) and drum with animal head ends (3) are from Cameroon. Most African slit drums are used as signal instruments.

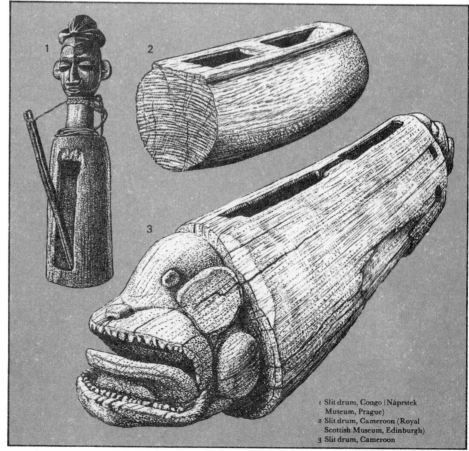
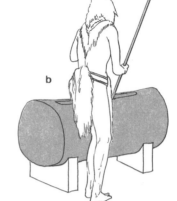

1 Slit drum, Congo (Náprstek Museum, Prague)
2 Slit drum, Cameroon (Royal Scottish Museum, Edinburgh)
3 Slit drum, Cameroon

Right Slit drums from Central America. Mexican examples tend to be small, and modern examples (1 and 2) have similar slit shapes and carvings to pre-Conquest teponaztli (3 and 4). The Costa Rican example (5) was carved from a tree trunk.
Below Mexican playing a small slit drum.

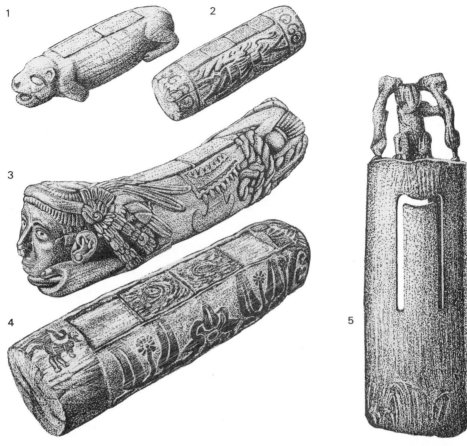

1 Slit drum, Mexico
2 Slit drum, Mexico
3 Teponaztli, Mexico, pre-1520 (National Museum of Anthropology and History, Mexico)
4 Teponaztli, Mexico, pre-1520 (Regional Museum of Toluca, Mexico)
5 Slit drum, Costa Rica (Archaeological Museum, San José, Costa Rica)

Right Japanese slit drums. The fish-shaped mokugyo (1) is struck to mark important points in temple services. The mu yü (2), an abstract fish shape, has a handle formed by the head and tail. Both instruments are carved from camphor wood and lacquered in red and gold.

Above Mu yü player.

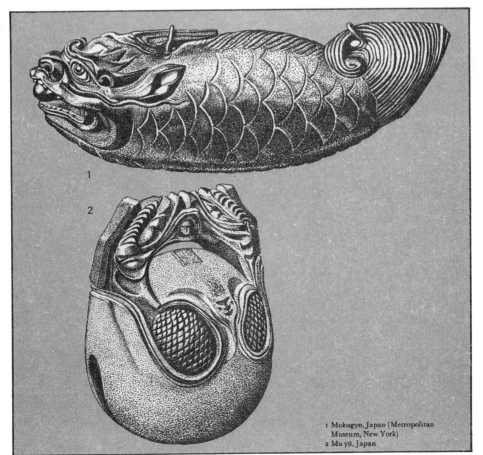

1 Mokugyo, Japan (Metropolitan Museum, New York)
2 Mu yü, Japan

©DIAGRAM

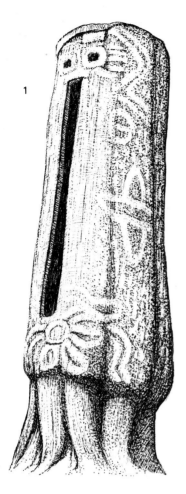

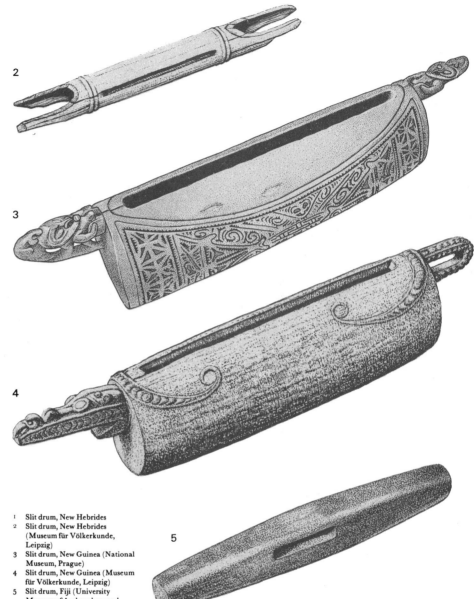

Above and right Slit drums
from Oceania. Drums with
human features are carved
from standing tree trunks
in the New Hebrides (1). A
great variety of more
typical slit drums are also
found in Oceania, like the
examples from New Guinea
(3 and 4) decorated with
symbolic carvings.

1 Slit drum, New Hebrides
2 Slit drum, New Hebrides
   (Museum für Völkerkunde,
   Leipzig)
3 Slit drum, New Guinea (National
   Museum, Prague)
4 Slit drum, New Guinea (Museum
   für Völkerkunde, Leipzig)
5 Slit drum, Fiji (University
   Museum of Archaeology and
   Ethnology, Cambridge, England)

Right A trough drum from
Fiji. Played by beating the
interior with sticks it is
similar in function to a slit
drum. This example has
ends cut from separate
pieces of wood.

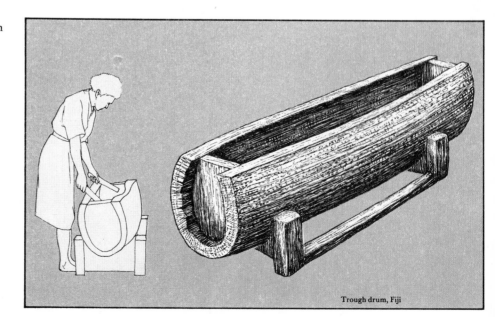

Trough drum, Fiji

Percussion boards

The simple action of beating on a board with a stick is an effective means of producing a strong emphatic rhythm. Found in many parts of the world, percussion boards are commonly used to accompany singing or dancing. The beating of the warrior's shield, known in armies since very early times, is similarly successful as a means of heightening battle fury and instilling fear in the enemy.

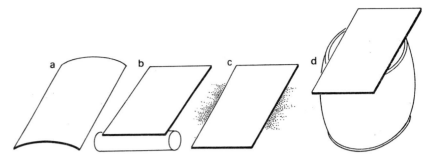

Above Diagrams showing ways of increasing the resonance of a percussion board. A curved board (a) is more resonant than a flat one. The resonance of a board can be increased by raising it from the ground (b), or by placing it over a pit (c) or large vessel (d).

Left Percussion board and shields used for making music. In many parts of Africa and also in Oceania boards and shields are beaten with sticks to produce a strong rhythm for dancing and singing.
Right South Africans making music by beating on their shields.

Below A single bar percussion instrument from Zambia. It consists of a shaped wood bar held between supports over a hollow gourd or pottery resonator. An instrument built on this principle but with several bars producing different notes would be classified as a xylophone.

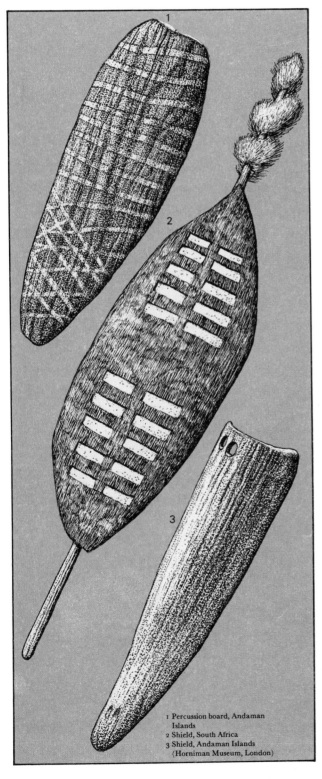

1 Percussion board, Andaman Islands
2 Shield, South Africa
3 Shield, Andaman Islands
(Horniman Museum, London)

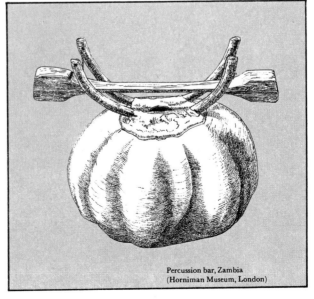

Percussion bar, Zambia
(Horniman Museum, London)

©DIAGRAM

Xylophones

A xylophone is a set of tuned wood bars beaten with sticks. The bars usually rest in a frame and are arranged in order of pitch. Most xylophones are provided with resonators, either in the form of a cradle-shaped box under the bars, or in the form of a separate gourd for each bar. Xylophones are common in Africa, and also in Southeast Asia where they feature in the Indonesian gamelan orchestra.

Right Tuning of xylophone bars. Xylophones produce different pitches by having bars of different lengths (a), thicknesses (b), or densities (c). The longer, thicker, or denser the bar, the lower the pitch it produces. A bar's pitch can be raised by paring wood from under the bar (d).

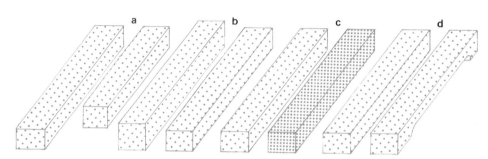

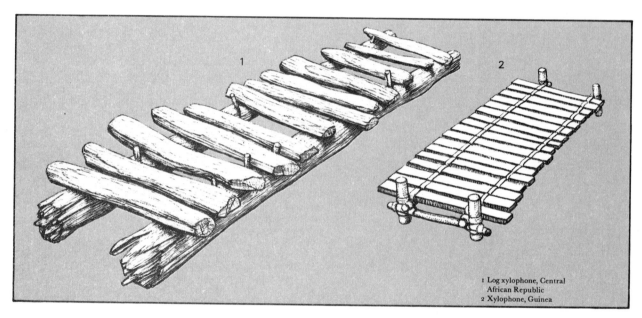

1 Log xylophone, Central African Republic
2 Xylophone, Guinea

Above Primitive African xylophones. The Central African log xylophone (1) is dismantled after each performance. It is a large instrument usually played by two or three musicians. The xylophone from Guinea (2) is a more compact instrument with tied bars of more regular shape.

Right Two less common playing positions. The simple leg xylophone (a) consists of a number of logs rested on the player's outstretched legs. Some xylophones, like the example from the Ivory Coast (b), have neck-straps that allow them to be carried about during play.

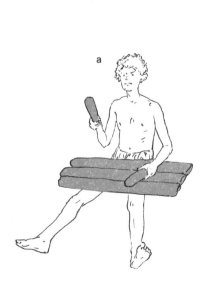

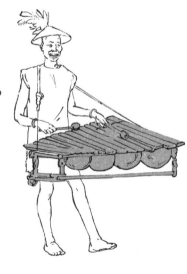

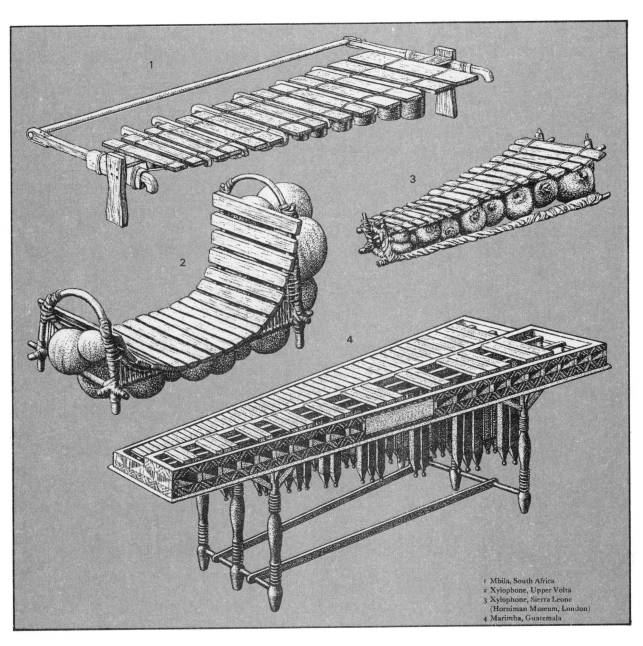

1 Mbila, South Africa
2 Xylophone, Upper Volta
3 Xylophone, Sierra Leone
  (Horniman Museum, London)
4 Marimba, Guatemala

© DIAGRAM

Above Xylophones with
resonators for each bar.
The mbila from South Africa
has tin can resonators (1),
but xylophones with gourd
resonators (2 and 3) are more
usual in Africa. The
marimba from Central
America (4) is characterized
by its carved wood
resonators.

Right Playing positions.
Very commonly the player
sits or kneels on the floor
behind his instrument (a).
Other instruments are
played from a standing
position—like the large
marimba played by several
musicians (b).

Right Xylophones from
Southeast Asia. The
Cambodian ronéat-ek (1)
and Javanese gambang kayu
(2) are typical Asian examples with bars suspended
over a decorative cradle
resonator. More accurately
tuned than most African
xylophones, they are often
played in groups.

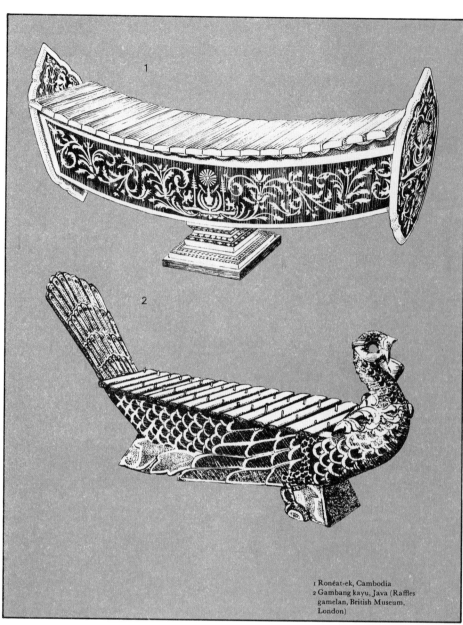

Above Javanese musician
playing a peacock-shaped
gambang kayu.

1 Ronéat-ek, Cambodia
2 Gambang kayu, Java (Raffles
  gamelan, British Museum,
  London)

Right Xylophones of the
kind used in the teaching
system devised by the
composer Carl Orff to
encourage children to
improvise their own music.
Players may use a single
diatonic xylophone (1) or a
a chromatic instrument made
up of two xylophones (2).
Below A young player.

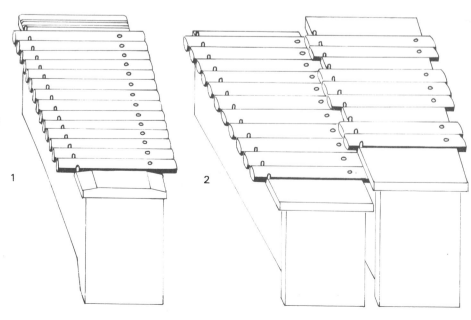

Lithophones

Lithophones are percussion instruments consisting of sets of sonorous stones struck with beaters. The earliest known examples, found in Vietnam, date from Neolithic times. Today lithophones of varying degrees of sophistication are found in the Far East and parts of Africa. Lithophones modeled on a simple xylophone enjoyed a limited popularity in Northern England in the late 19th century.

Above Simple lithophone—percussion stones from Northern Togo. Sonorous stones of different sizes produce different notes when struck with small stones held in the player's hands.

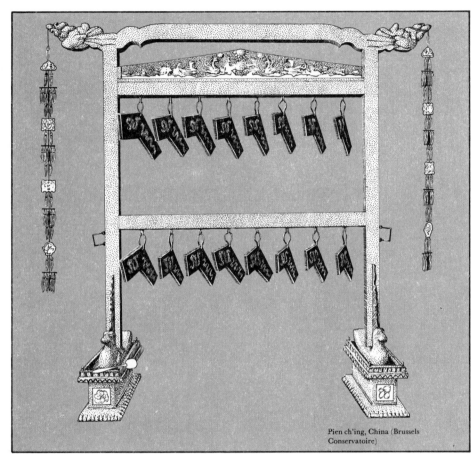

Pien ch'ing, China (Brussels Conservatoire)

Left Pien ch'ing—a Chinese lithophone with two rows of L-shaped stone slabs hung in a frame. The stones are the same size but of different thicknesses to produce different notes. The pien ch'ing is often played with the Chinese bell chime called the pien chung.
Below Pien ch'ing player.

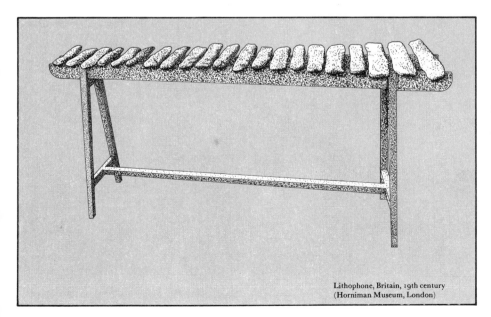

Lithophone, Britain, 19th century (Horniman Museum, London)

Left Lithophone from England's Lake District. A number of these unusual instruments, modeled on the xylophone, were made in the 19th century from locally found rocks. It was played in concert tours of Britain and Europe and in two command performances before Queen Victoria.

© DIAGRAM

Metallophones

Although similar in general appearance to the xylophone, the metallophone has bars made of metal instead of wood. Particularly important in the Far East, metallophones of different kinds and sizes form the largest section in the gamelan orchestras of Java and Bali. In America and Europe instruments with metal bars include chime bars, toy "xylophones," and different types of glockenspiel.

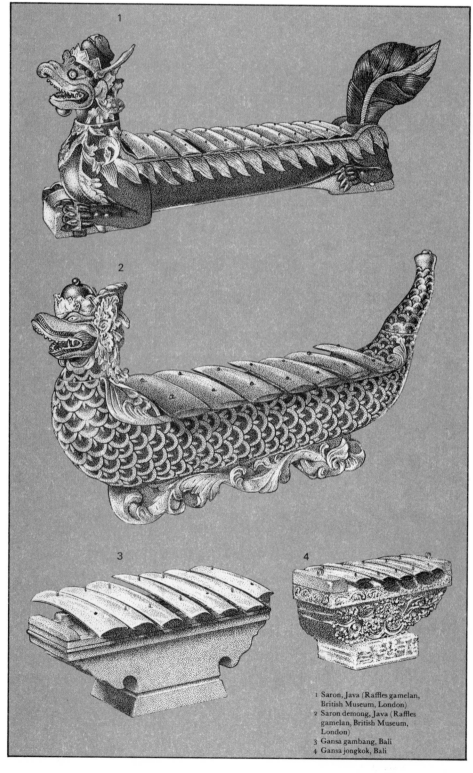

Above Balinese musician playing a gansa gambang. **Left** Javanese sarons (1 and 2) and Balinese gansa gambang (3) and gansa jongkok (4). Distinguished by their cradle-shaped box resonators, these sophisticated metallophones are used to provide the melody in Indonesian gamelan orchestras. Many examples are highly ornamental, like these two dragon-shaped examples from the Raffles gamelan.

Below Types of beater used for playing Indonesian metallophones. Sarons and gansas are played with hammer-shaped beaters made of wood (a). The other important Indonesian metallophone, the gender, is played with beaters with padded disk ends (b).

1 Saron, Java (Raffles gamelan, British Museum, London)
2 Saron demong, Java (Raffles gamelan, British Museum, London)
3 Gansa gambang, Bali
4 Gansa jongkok, Bali

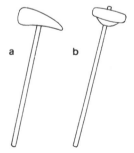

a   b

Above Gender player from the island of Bali.
Left Genders from Bali (1 and 4) and Java (2 and 3). The gender is distinguished from the saron by having individual bamboo resonators for each bar. The gender's rather muted tone is used to elaborate the gamelan melody.

Below Metallophones are found in Western countries in a variety of forms. Chime bars (1) are used in schools and may be played singly or in sets. Many toy "xylophones" (2) are really metallophones. The lyra glockenspiel (3) is a lightweight instrument found in marching bands.

©DIAGRAM

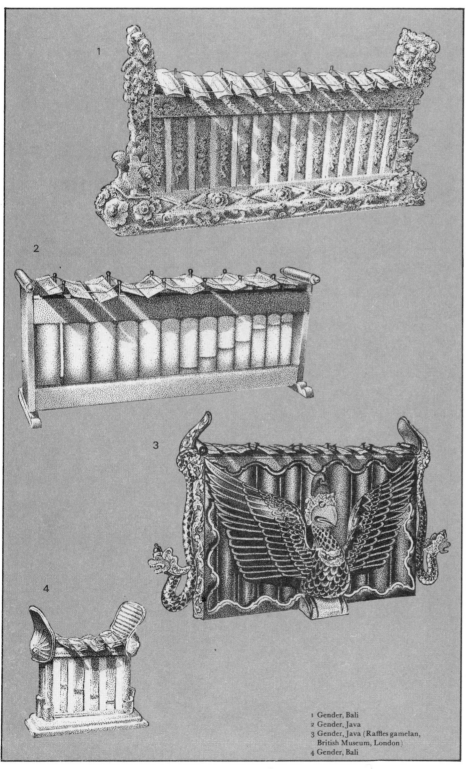

1 Gender, Bali
2 Gender, Java
3 Gender, Java (Raffles gamelan, British Museum, London)
4 Gender, Bali

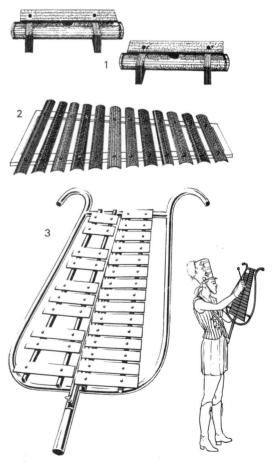

Cymbals and castanets

Cymbals and castanets are common members of the concussion family, in which pairs of similar objects are sounded by clashing together. Cymbals, made of metal, have a long history in Asia, the Middle East, and Europe. Sizes range from large cymbals, held one in each hand, to tiny cymbals worn on the fingers. Castanets, very popular in Spain, are wood shells usually clicked together in the palm of the hand.

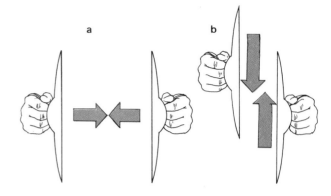

a b

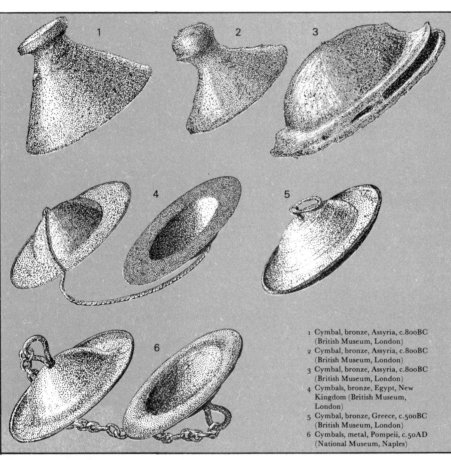

Above Different playing techniques for the cymbals. Sometimes the instruments are clashed together in a horizontal movement (a). Brushing the cymbals together in a vertical movement (b) produces a less strident sound.

Left Ancient cymbals. The Assyrian cymbals (1, 2, and 3) were found at Nimrud. These small cymbals, approximately 2½ in in diameter, were held one in each hand. Small cymbals were also played by the ancient Egyptians (4), Greeks (5), and Romans (6).
Below Roman musician.

1 Cymbal, bronze, Assyria, c.800BC (British Museum, London)
2 Cymbal, bronze, Assyria, c.800BC (British Museum, London)
3 Cymbal, bronze, Assyria, c.800BC (British Museum, London)
4 Cymbals, bronze, Egypt, New Kingdom (British Museum, London)
5 Cymbal, bronze, Greece, c.500BC (British Museum, London)
6 Cymbals, metal, Pompeii, c.50AD (National Museum, Naples)

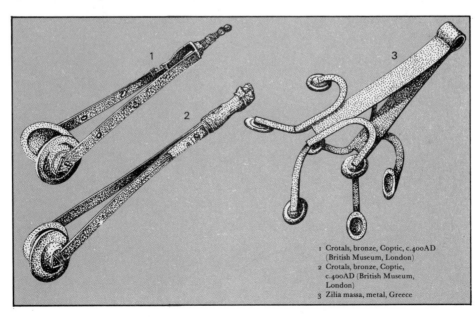

Left Crotals and zilia massa. Crotals (1 and 2) are ancient metal clappers with cymbal-like ends. Known in ancient Egypt, Greece, and Rome, they are particularly associated with the Copts. A similar instrument, the zilia massa (3), survives in present day Greece and Turkey.

1 Crotals, bronze, Coptic, c.400AD (British Museum, London)
2 Crotals, bronze, Coptic, c.400AD (British Museum, London)
3 Zilia massa, metal, Greece

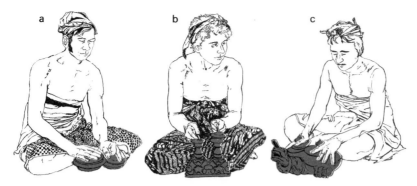

Left Cymbals from Bali—
the chengcheng (a) and
rinchik (b and c). In each
case, cymbals mounted on a
stand are hit from above by
cymbals held in the player's
hands.

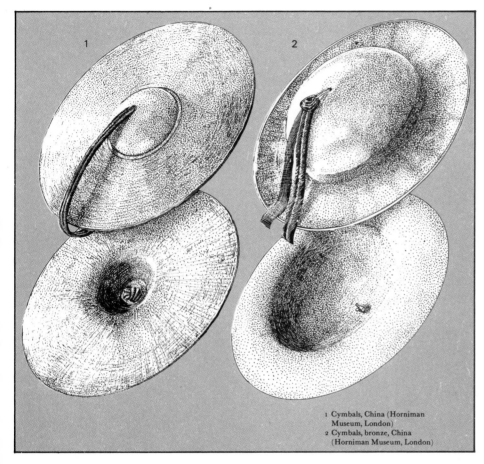

Left Chinese cymbals,
showing the instrument's
two most common forms.
Wide-rimmed cymbals with
a small central boss (1) are
usually held horizontally
and clashed vertically.
Cymbals with a narrow rim
and large central boss (2) are
usually held vertically and
clashed horizontally.

1 Cymbals, China (Horniman
   Museum, London)
2 Cymbals, bronze, China
   (Horniman Museum, London)

Left Castanets—small
shell-shaped clappers made
of wood or ivory. The
traditional form (1, 2, and 3)
are clicked in one hand.
Some modern castanets (4)
are mounted on a handle
and played against the palm
of the other hand.
Right Spanish flamenco
dancer with castanets.

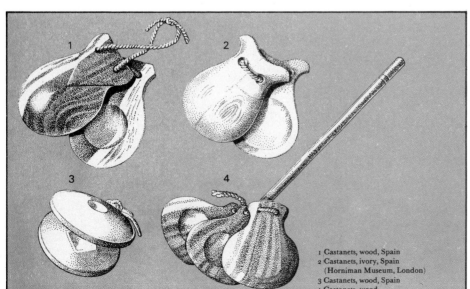

1 Castanets, wood, Spain
2 Castanets, ivory, Spain
   (Horniman Museum, London)
3 Castanets, wood, Spain
4 Castanets, wood

© DIAGRAM

Clappers

The striking together of similar objects is one of the most basic ways of producing a rhythmic accompaniment. Clappers were well known in the ancient world, and Egyptian hand-shaped examples suggest that these instruments were devised as an alternative to clapping the hands. Today, clappers of different materials and varying degrees of sophistication are found in many parts of the world.

Left Wind chime. This instrument of Asian origin has become known in the West as a domestic novelty. Small lengths of wood or ivory, hung from a frame, strike together when blown by the wind.

Right Ancient Egyptian clappers. Made in wood or ivory, many extant examples are carved in the form of human hands or decorated with human or animal heads. The single hand (3) was originally one of a pair.
Below Egyptian with a pair of curved clappers, drawn from a wall frieze.

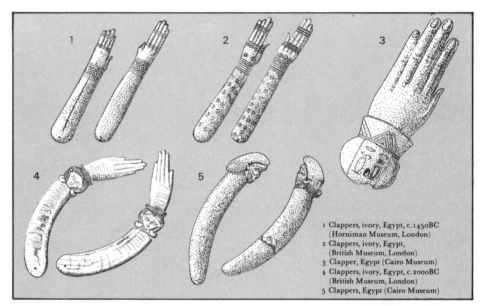

1 Clappers, ivory, Egypt, c.1450BC (Horniman Museum, London)
2 Clappers, ivory, Egypt, (British Museum, London)
3 Clapper, Egypt (Cairo Museum)
4 Clappers, ivory, Egypt, c.2000BC (British Museum, London)
5 Clappers, Egypt (Cairo Museum)

Right Large clappers held one to each hand. The clappers from Australia (1) and Hawaii (2) are simple wood sticks. The Balinese kemanak (3) and the Nigerian castanet-like clappers (4) are worked in metal. The spagane (5) have hide hand-straps.
Below Aboriginal clappers.

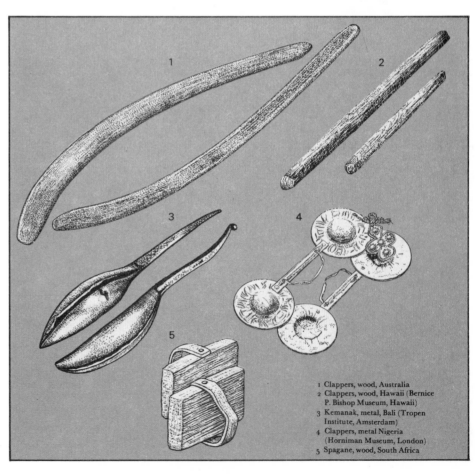

1 Clappers, wood, Australia
2 Clappers, wood, Hawaii (Bernice P. Bishop Museum, Hawaii)
3 Kemanak, metal, Bali (Tropen Institute, Amsterdam)
4 Clappers, metal Nigeria (Horniman Museum, London)
5 Spagane, wood, South Africa

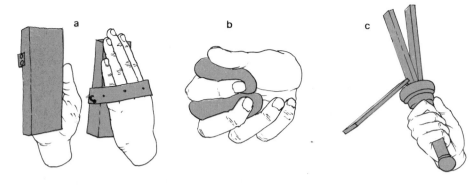

Left Different playing methods for clappers. Some clappers are held one to each hand (a). Other smaller clappers are held between the fingers of one hand and struck together (b). A third type, with a number of clappers attached to a handle, is sounded by shaking (c).

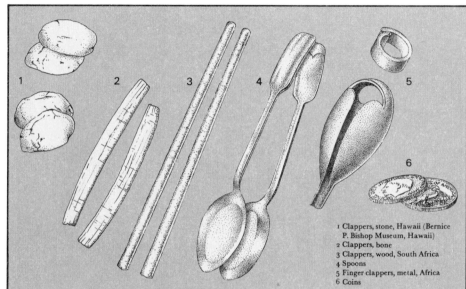

1 Clappers, stone, Hawaii (Bernice P. Bishop Museum, Hawaii)
2 Clappers, bone
3 Clappers, wood, South Africa
4 Spoons
5 Finger clappers, metal, Africa
6 Coins

Left Small clappers held in one hand. Stones (1), bones (2), and sticks (3) are among the simplest one-handed clappers. Spoons (4) and coins (6) also make effective clappers. The African ring clappers (5) are worn on a finger and thumb.
Below Clapper player from a medieval manuscript.

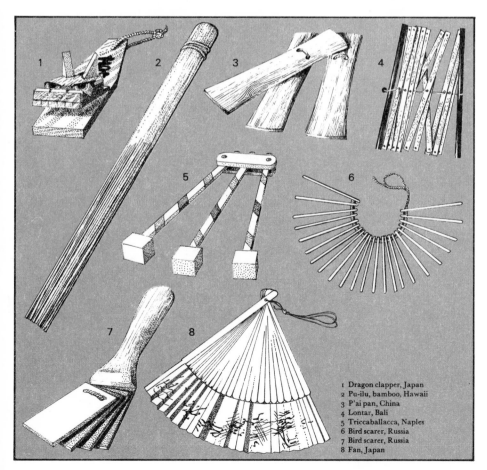

1 Dragon clapper, Japan
2 Pu-ilu, bamboo, Hawaii
3 P'ai pan, China
4 Lontar, Bali
5 Triccaballacca, Naples
6 Bird scarer, Russia
7 Bird scarer, Russia
8 Fan, Japan

Left Clappers with two or more sounding parts that hit together when the instrument is shaken or flicked. The Hawaiian pu-ilu (2) is a bamboo switch sounded by striking against the other hand.
Below A Japanese priest uses a similar sounding technique with his fan.

Friction instruments

A diverse group of instruments, including simple shells and fir cones as well as the musical saw and table-sized glass harmonica, is unified by being sounded by friction. A moistened finger, a piece of cloth or rope, a stick or a bow may be used to play these instruments, but the most primitive examples consist of two like objects rubbed together. The sound produced varies according to the instrument's composition.

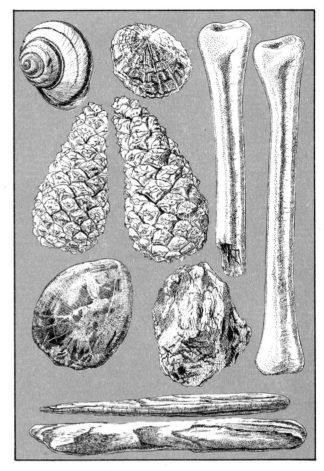

Right Natural objects used as friction instruments. Shells, bones, fir cones, stones, and sticks are among the objects rubbed together for making music.
Left Shells being used as a friction instrument.

Left and below Friction instruments with different sounding devices. The African hollow log (1) is rubbed inside with a bundle of twigs. The waxed tortoise shell (2) is from South America. The carved wood instrument from New Britain (3) is rubbed with moistened hands.

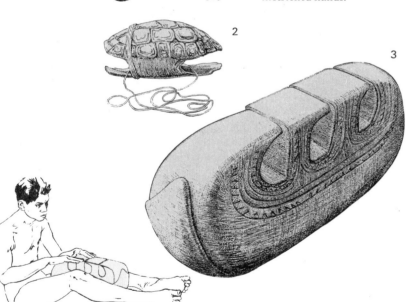

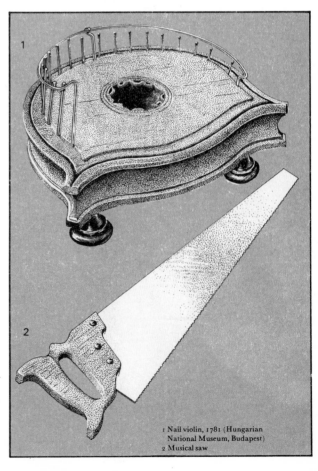

Right Bowed friction instruments. Nail violins (1) were made in 18th and 19th century Europe. Nails of different lengths, giving different pitches, were arranged around a resonator. Notes from a musical saw (2) depend on how much the instrument is bent.
Left Musical saw player.

1 Nail violin, 1781 (Hungarian National Museum, Budapest)
2 Musical saw

Right Making music with a wine glass. Rubbing a moistened finger around the glass's rim causes vibrations in the bowl to produce a high-pitched eerie sound. The thinner the glass the more easily can a sound be produced.

Right Gluck, the 18th century opera composer, who in 1746 attained fame as a performer on the musical glasses. An advertisement in the London press promised that Gluck "performs whatever may be done on a Violin or Harpsichord and thereby hopes to satisfy the Curious as well as the Lovers of Musick."

Right Boxed set of musical glasses from the 19th century. Notes of different pitches are obtained from glasses of different sizes and thicknesses, so enabling the playing of tunes. Although known earlier, musical glasses enjoyed their greatest popularity in the 18th and 19th centuries.

Right Benjamin Franklin, among whose many inventions was an ingenious mechanized version of the musical glasses. Franklin's glass harmonica—or "armonica" as he called it—was invented in the 1760s and sounded by holding the fingers against mechanically rotated glass bowls.

Right Franklin's "armonica," based on a drawing by the inventor. Glass bowls of different sizes fitted on a rod over a trough of water, so that the rims of the bowls just touched the water. A treadle turned the bowls and kept their rims moist for playing.
Below A glass harmonica.

Below Glass trombone by Baschet, Paris (Instrument Museum, Brussels). Its 12 glass rods of different lengths are sounded by rubbing with moistened fingers. Metal rods at right angles to the glass rods modify the sound, and the instrument has a curved sheet metal amplifier.

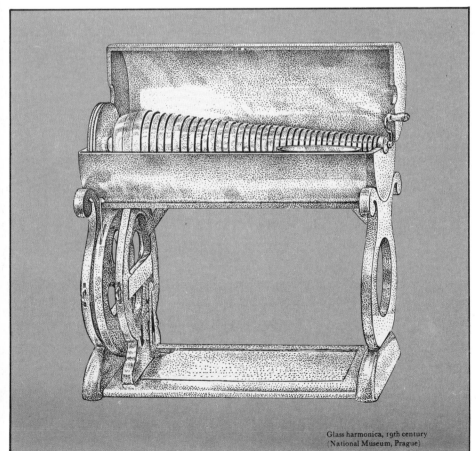

Glass harmonica, 19th century
(National Museum, Prague)

© DIAGRAM

Scraped instruments

When a stick is drawn over a series of notches carved in bone, wood, or some other material, a distinctive rasping sound is produced. Instruments of this kind, known variously as scrapers, stridulators, or rasps, have been found dating back to the Stone Age. Among the scraped instruments commonly found today are simple notched bones and sticks, the washboard, and the cog "rattle."

Right Ancient bone scrapers. These simple notched instruments were sounded by scraping with a stick or another piece of bone. They appear to have been primarily associated with rituals of death and rebirth, being used for example at the funeral ceremonies of Aztec kings.

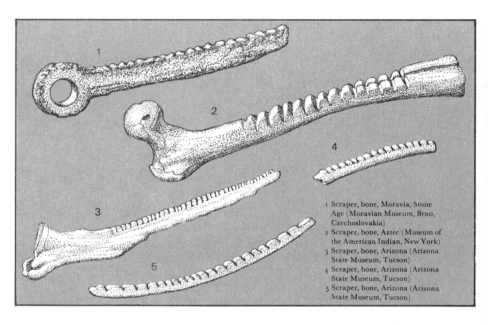

1 Scraper, bone, Moravia, Stone Age (Moravian Museum, Brno, Czechoslovakia)
2 Scraper, bone, Aztec (Museum of the American Indian, New York)
3 Scraper, bone, Arizona (Arizona State Museum, Tucson)
4 Scraper, bone, Arizona (Arizona State Museum, Tucson)
5 Scraper, bone, Arizona (Arizona State Museum, Tucson)

Right Wood scrapers. The scraper from India is sounded with a wood switch (1). The American example (2) is from the Hopi Indians. The East African scraped instrument (3) has a curved notched stick set in a board. The Australian examples (4 and 5) have carved sounding sticks.

Below Hopi Indian making music with a scraper.

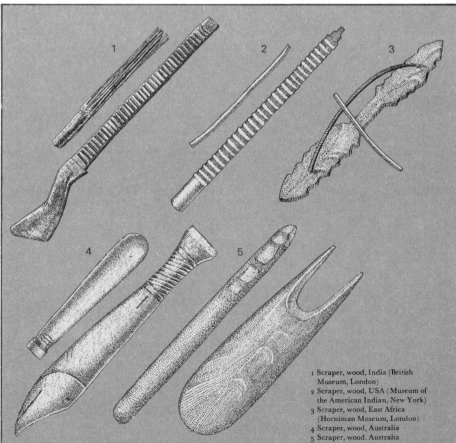

1 Scraper, wood, India (British Museum, London)
2 Scraper, wood, USA (Museum of the American Indian, New York)
3 Scraper, wood, East Africa (Horniman Museum, London)
4 Scraper, wood, Australia
5 Scraper, wood. Australia

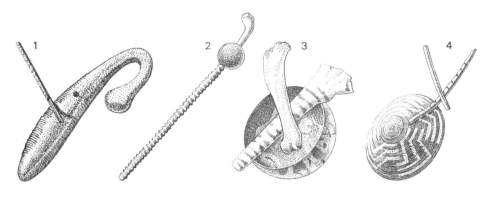

Left Scraped instruments with resonators. The gourd body of the Cuban raspa (1) provides the instrument's own resonator. The African wood scraper (2) is fitted with a fruit shell resonator. The Aztec bone scraper (3) was played over a bowl, and the Papago Indians' wood scraper (4) is played over an upturned basket (right).

Yü, wood, China (Brussels Conservatoire)

Left Yü from China. This scraped wood instrument is carved in the form of a crouching tiger with a series of notches along its backbone. It is sounded by scraping with a bamboo rod split to form a switch. The yü is scraped three times to mark the end of services in Confucian temples.

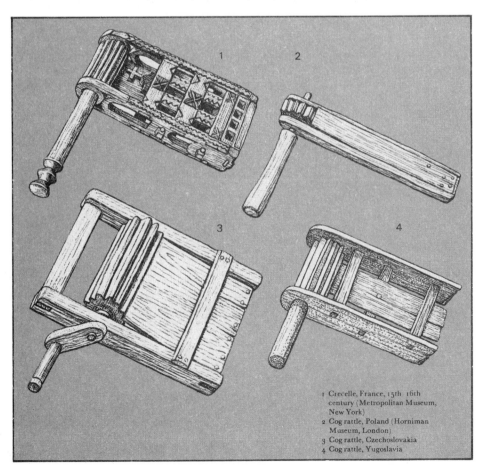

1 Crecelle, France, 15th–16th century (Metropolitan Museum, New York)
2 Cog rattle, Poland (Horniman Museum, London)
3 Cog rattle, Czechoslovakia
4 Cog rattle, Yugoslavia

Left Cog "rattles"— sounded by spinning the rattle around on the handle, so causing a flat piece of wood to flick over a notched cog wheel. The attractive French crecelle (1) dates from the 15th or 16th century. The other examples shown are modern Eastern European folk instruments.

Right Washboard—one of the unconventional instruments employed during the "skiffle" music craze of the 1950s. The notched surface of the washboard was scraped with a metal rod, or more usually with metal thimbles worn on the player's fingers.
Below Washboard player.

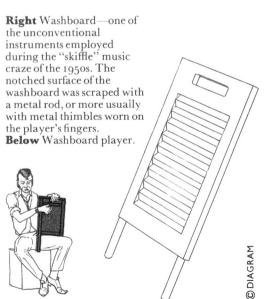

Jew's harps

The jew's harp consists of a flexible tongue cut out of, or attached to, a small frame usually of bamboo or metal. The tongue is free at one end to allow it to be plucked with a finger or cord. The player holds the instrument in his mouth, and the name jew's harp is generally considered to be a corruption of jaw's harp. It produces a quiet but appealing sound, and is commonly used in courtship.

Left Method of playing a jew's harp. The player holds the frame of the instrument between his teeth and plucks its tongue with his finger. The player's mouth acts as a resonator, and the position of his lips, cheeks, and teeth determine the pitch of the note produced.

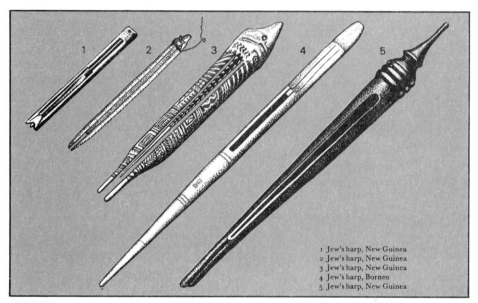

1 Jew's harp, New Guinea
2 Jew's harp, New Guinea
3 Jew's harp, New Guinea
4 Jew's harp, Borneo
5 Jew's harp, New Guinea

Left Jew's harps from New Guinea and Borneo. All these examples are idioglottal—having their tongues cut out of the frame. Jew's harps of this type are particularly common in Oceania, but examples are also found elsewhere. Sizes vary from a couple of inches to over one foot.

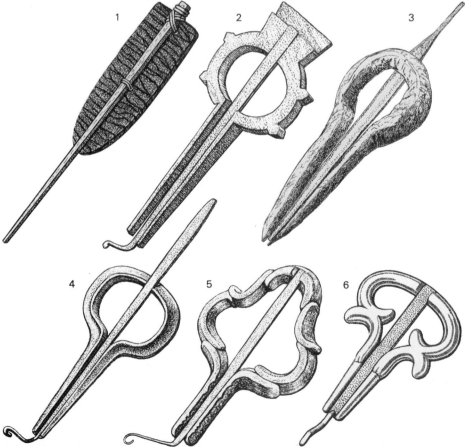

Left Heteroglottal jew's harps—with a separate tongue attached to the frame. Examples of this type are found in many parts of the world. The Hawaiian instrument (1) is made of wood, but most heteroglottal jew's harps are metal. The 19th century German example (5) is made of silver.

1 Jew's harp, Hawaii (Bernice P. Bishop Museum, Hawaii)
2 Jew's harp, USSR
3 Jew's harp, India (Horniman Museum, London)
4 Jew's harp, Italy (Horniman Museum, London)
5 Jew's harp, silver, Germany, 19th century (Pitt Rivers Museum, Oxford, England)
6 Jew's harp, Britain

Sansas

The sansa is a plucked instrument consisting of a number of metal or split cane tongues over a wood board or box resonator. The tongues are held in position by a lateral bar, with one end of each tongue free to be plucked. Plucking is usually with the thumbs, which has led some people to call this instrument a "thumb piano." Although occasionally found elsewhere, the sansa is primarily an African instrument.

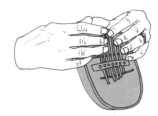

Left Playing method. The sansa is usually held in the hands or rested on the lap, and the player uses his thumbs or forefingers to pluck the tongues. The pitch of a tongue is determined by its length, which can easily be altered by sliding the tongue back and forward under the lateral bar.

Left Examples of sansas from different parts of Africa. Often the board or box is decorated by carving or painting, and sometimes the sound is modified by wrapping wire around each tongue to produce a buzzing effect when plucked.

Below South African sansa in a gourd resonator.

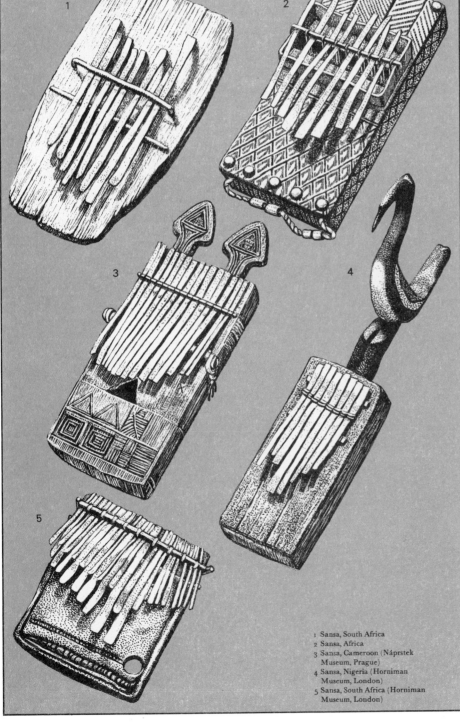

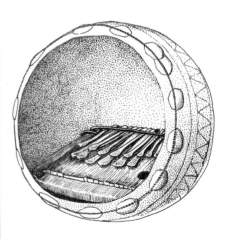

1 Sansa, South Africa
2 Sansa, Africa
3 Sansa, Cameroon (Náprstek Museum, Prague)
4 Sansa, Nigeria (Horniman Museum, London)
5 Sansa, South Africa (Horniman Museum, London)

Orchestral percussion

The percussion section of the modern orchestra includes two basic types of instrument. The simplest type, including the triangle and wood block, are untuned and produce a note of indeterminate pitch. Tuned instruments, including the xylophone and tubular bells, are capable of playing melodies. The history of the orchestral percussion group dates from the mid-18th century when an interest in Turkish—or "Janissary"—music first led to the introduction of such instruments as the cymbals and triangle to supplement the drum section. In the 19th century sophisticated tuned instruments including the xylophone and tubular bells began to appear in the scores of Tchaikovsky and Saint-Saëns. More recently composers like Benjamin Britten have called for a variety of "sound makers" for special effects, including slung mugs struck with wood spoons, cog rattles, and "whips."

Below Tubular bells—a series of brass or steel tubes of varying lengths hanging in a frame. The standard instrument has 18 tubes, giving a range of $1\frac{1}{2}$ octaves. The tubes are struck near the top and a foot-operated damping mechanism can be used to stop the reverberations.

Right Orchestral glockenspiel. The modern instrument, with a range of $2\frac{1}{2}$ octaves, consists of a set of gradated steel bars arranged in two rows like the black and white notes of a piano keyboard. The glockenspiel is played with moderately hard beaters to produce a bell-like tone.

Right Celeste—a keyboard glockenspiel invented by Auguste Mustel in 1886. The metal bars are struck by felt-covered hammers activated by a simplified piano mechanism. Unlike the standard glockenspiel, each bar has its own box resonator which amplifies the tone of the instrument.

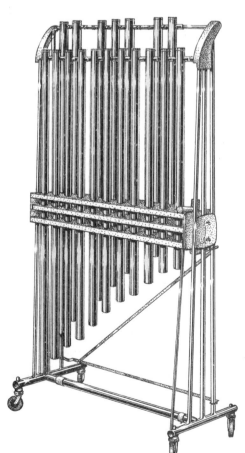

Above Modern orchestral xylophone—the most important tuned percussion instrument, consisting of two rows of wood bars suspended over hollow tube resonators. The commonest orchestral versions have a range of 3½ or 4 octaves, and may be struck with different types of beaters.

Below Modern orchestral marimba. Taking its name from a folk instrument of Africa and Central America, the orchestral marimba is a deep version of the orchestral xylophone. The pitch range of marimbas varies from three to five octaves. Some large models are called xylorimbas.

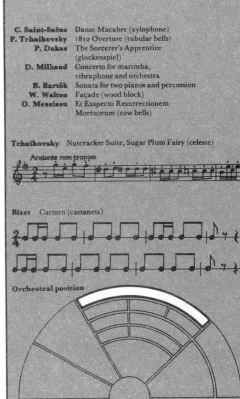

Percussion

C. Saint-Saëns	Danse Macabre (xylophone)
P. Tchaikovsky	1812 Overture (tubular bells)
P. Dukas	The Sorcerer's Apprentice (glockenspiel)
D. Milhaud	Concerto for marimba, vibraphone and orchestra
B. Bartók	Sonata for two pianos and percussion
W. Walton	Façade (wood block)
O. Messiaen	Et Exspecto Resurrectionem Mortuorum (cow bells)

Tchaikovsky Nutcracker Suite, Sugar Plum Fairy (celeste)

Andante non troppo

Bizet Carmen (castanets)

Orchestral position

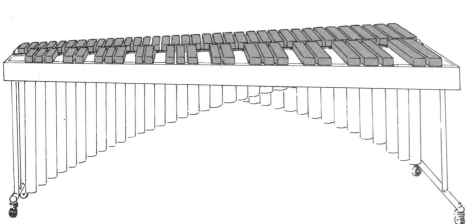

136

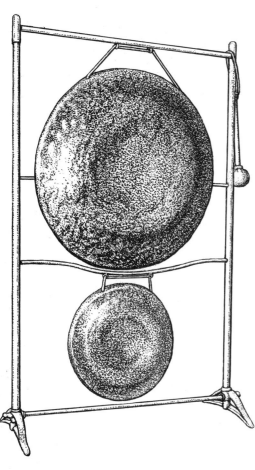

Left Orchestral tam-tams. These bronze gongs, made in a variety of sizes, from 2ft to 5ft in diameter, are suspended in a frame and struck with a soft beater. The sound of the tam-tam, somber and ominous, can be heard to good effect in "Mars" from the suite "The Planets" by Holst.

Right Wood blocks and triangle. The hollow-ended two-tone block (1) and the tulip-shaped block (2) are less common versions of the traditional "Chinese" block (3). All are tapped sharply with a hard beater to give a loud penetrating sound. The metal triangle (4) has been popular for about 200 years.

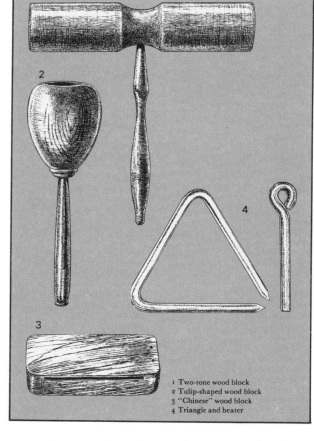

1 Two-tone wood block
2 Tulip-shaped wood block
3 "Chinese" wood block
4 Triangle and beater

Right Cymbals, castanets, and claves. The single cymbal (1) is struck with a stick or wire brush (left). The dance band "hi-hat" (2) is clashed by means of a foot pedal. Castanets (3, 4,5 and 6) are used for a Spanish flavor. Claves (7) are important in Latin American dance music.

Below Cymbal playing methods—clashing two cymbals together (a) and striking a single cymbal with a beater (b).

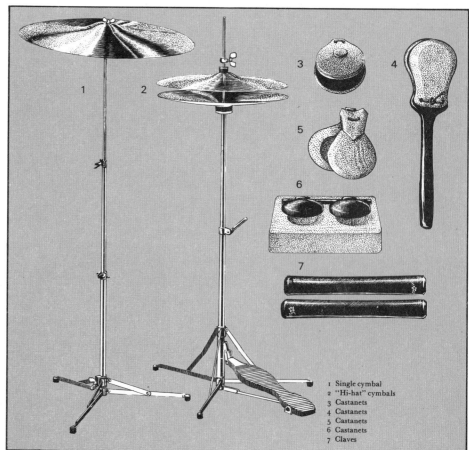

1 Single cymbal
2 "Hi-hat" cymbals
3 Castanets
4 Castanets
5 Castanets
6 Castanets
7 Claves

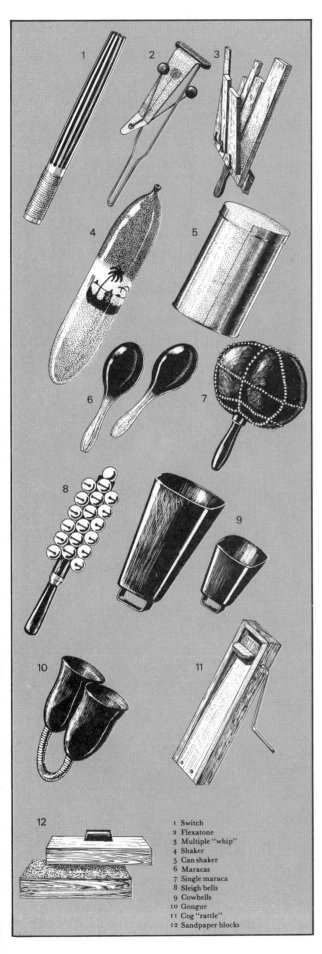

Left Occasional percussion
instruments. The switch (1)
is struck against the hand.
The knobs of the flexatone
(2) strike against the metal
sheet when the instrument is
shaken. The can filled with
dried beans or pebbles (5)
is a simple version of the
dance band shaker (4) and
the Latin American maracas
(6 and 7). The double-belled
gongue (10) produces notes
of two pitches. The
sandpaper blocks (12) are
rubbed together to
imitate the sound of a soft
shoe shuffle.

Right Large thunder sheet
—sounded by shaking or by
beating with a soft drum
stick.

Below Sound makers used
by composers for special
effects. Included here are
coconut shells (1) to
imitate the sound of horses'
hooves, a brake drum (2),
chains rattled against a
metal receptacle (3), an
anvil (4), sand in a tray
(5), a typewriter (6), and
a hammer and plank (7).

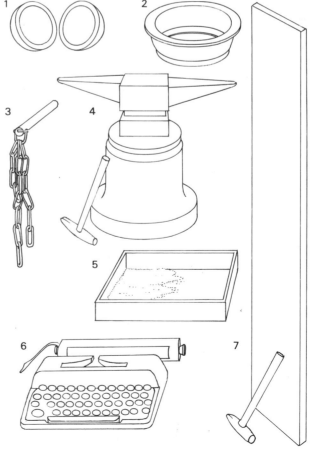

1 Switch
2 Flexatone
3 Multiple "whip"
4 Shaker
5 Can shaker
6 Maracas
7 Single maraca
8 Sleigh bells
9 Cowbells
10 Gongue
11 Cog "rattle"
12 Sandpaper blocks

© DIAGRAM

Membranophones: introduction

Membranophones are instruments in which the sound is made by the vibration of a stretched membrane, or skin. There are two basic types — drums and, much less important, mirlitons. Evidence from art proves the existence of drums at least 4000 years ago in Mesopotamia and Egypt, but the perishable nature of the materials from which drums are made has meant that few ancient examples survive. Today, drums are enormously popular throughout the world, and are made in a great variety of styles. Many peoples consider drums to have magical and ritual significance, using them to ward off evil and to appeal to good spirits. Drums are also important signaling and battle instruments, as well as being popular for accompanying singing and dancing. Since the 1700s drums have been included in the Western orchestra.

Membranophones family tree There are two basic types of membranophone: drums and mirlitons. Drums may be divided according to shape into tubular, vessel, and frame drums, while a separate category is devoted to drums sounded by friction. Tubular drums include cylindrical, conical, barrel, waisted, goblet, footed, and long drums.

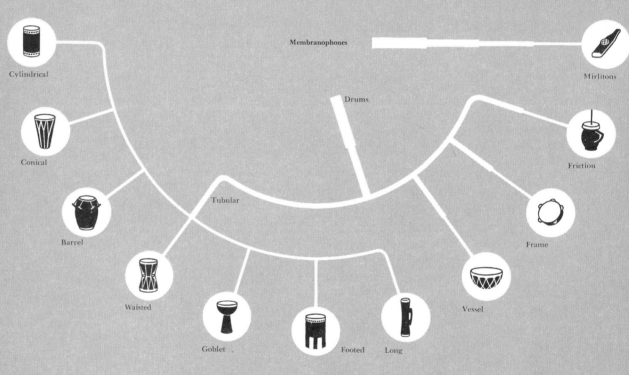

Body shapes
Membranophones are classified by body shape. Cylindrical drums (a) are straight-sided. Conical drums (b) have sloping sides while barrel drums (c) have bulging sides. Waisted or hourglass drums (d) and goblet drums (e) are more elaborate shapes.

Footed drums (f) have legs that are usually cut from the drum body. Long drums (g) are made in a variety of shapes but length is a useful distinguishing feature. In frame drums (h) the skin is stretched over a light frame. Kettledrums (i) have a vessel or pot body and a single playing head.

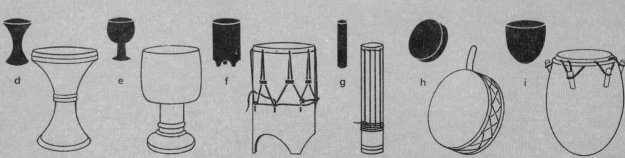

Vibrating membranes In a membranophone sound is produced by the vibration of a stretched membrane. There are two basic types of membranophone: drums (a) and mirlitons (b). A mirliton is sounded by blowing or humming into the instrument.

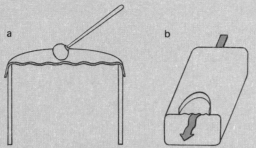

Skin attachment The membrane, or skin, of a drum may be attached in four different ways. It may be glued (a), nailed (b), pegged (c), or laced (d).

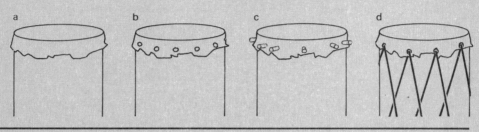

Lacing Different styles of lacing are employed for attaching drum skins. Common patterns are N lacing (1), W lacing (2), X lacing (3), Y lacing (4), or net lacing (5).

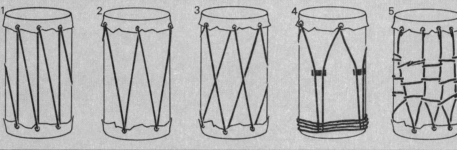

Tuning Drums are tuned by altering the tension of the playing head — by adjusting the lacing (a), moving "chocs" under the lacing (b), or turning keys or taps (c). Tone quality may be changed by applying small sticky balls (1) or paste (2 and 3) to the playing head.

Playing heads Drums may be single-headed with only one skin (a), or double-headed with a skin at each end. Double-headed drums may be played on one head (b) or on both heads (c).

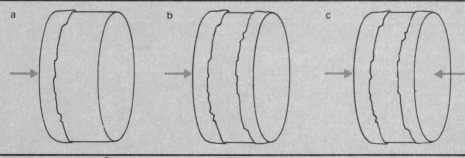

Sounding a drum The skin may be made to vibrate by beating with the hands (a), sticks (b), padded beaters (c), or wire brushes (d). The skins of the clapper drum (e) are struck with small beads as the drum is shaken. Most friction drums are sounded by a stick piercing the skin (f).

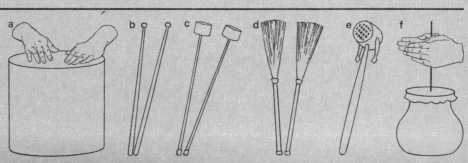

© DIAGRAM

Cylindrical and conical drums

Cylindrical and conical drums are the commonest types of tubular drum. Cylindrical drums vary considerably in size and proportions but have the same diameter throughout. Conical drums also come in a variety of shapes and sizes, ranging from a flattish bowl shape to a long tapering cone. Both types may be single or double headed. They are found throughout the world and date back to prehistoric times.

1 Cylindrical drum, wood, North America (Náprstek Museum, Prague)
2 Cylindrical drum, wood, North America
3 Cylindrical drum, wood, North America
4 Pow-wow drum, wood, North America

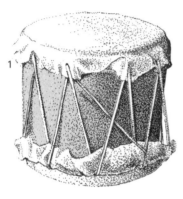

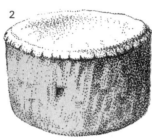

Above Cylindrical drums from Central and South America. The Panamanian drum (1) is a double-headed drum with the two skins laced together. The drum of the Chiriguano Indians (2) has a single membrane stitched to a hoop over a hollow cylinder usually made of palm wood.

Right North American cylindrical drums. The skin of the single-headed drum (1) is glued to the drum's body. Double-headed drums from the Southwest have skins that are stitched together (2) or laced (3). The pow-wow drum of the Chippewa Indians (4) has a decorative cloth skirt.

Left Bolivian musician playing panpipes and a big drum. The drum is double-headed but only one skin is beaten. Short rods, attached to a leather strap across the rear skin, rattle when the instrument is beaten.

Below and right North American Indian drummers. Sometimes the Shawnee big drum (a) is laid on the ground and beaten by several players. The Sioux war drum (b) has two skins laced to a rope around its middle.

a

b

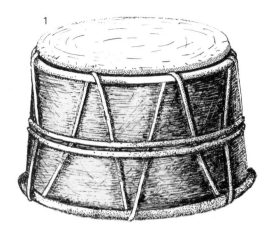

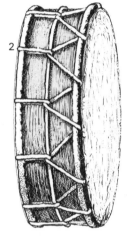

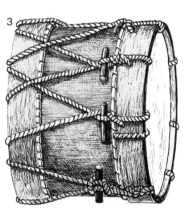

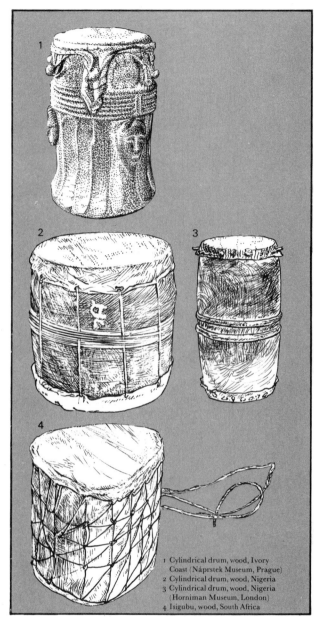

1 Cylindrical drum, wood, Ivory
Coast (Náprstek Museum, Prague)
2 Cylindrical drum, wood, Nigeria
3 Cylindrical drum, wood, Nigeria
(Horniman Museum, London)
4 Isigubu, wood, South Africa

Above Cylindrical folk drums from Europe and the USSR. The Greek dauli (1) and Bulgarian tupan (2) are double-headed drums with laced skins. The Russian tumyr (3) is single-headed.
Below Greek folk musician playing the dauli—the drum is carried on a strap over his left shoulder.

Right Cylindrical drums from Africa. The carved drum from the Ivory Coast (1) is single-headed. The skins of the double-headed drums from Nigeria are laced (2) and pegged (3). The South African isigubu (4) is made from a hollowed out log and has two skins laced together.

Right African musicians with cylindrical drums. The Nigerian drummer (a) carries his instrument by a strap over his left shoulder and strikes one skin with a curved beater. The South African isigubu (b) is carried around the neck and both skins are struck with padded beaters.

a

b

©DIAGRAM

Right Drums from India—
tabla (1 and 2) and a cloth
covered double drum (3).
The tabla consists of one
cylindrical and one conical
drum, each tuned to a
different pitch. Often used
to accompany the sitar, the
tabla is one of India's
most important instruments.

Below Indian tabla player.

1 Tabla, wood, India
2 Tabla, clay, India (Tropen
   Institute, Amsterdam)
3 Double drum, wood, India
   (Victoria and Albert Museum,
   London)

Right Geisha drummer.
Many Japanese drums are
rested on a stand for playing.
Below Japanese cylindrical
drums. The shallow drum
(1) is played in noh drama.
The okedo (2) is a folk
drum used in kabuki theater.
The daibyoshi (3), played
during Shinto worship, is
also used in kabuki.

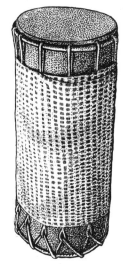

Above Drums from Bali.
Cylindrical drums of
this kind are made in
different sizes and used in
the gamelan orchestras of
Indonesia. They are double
headed with laced skins.
Right Balinese drummer.
The instrument is rested
on the lap and beaten on both
heads with the hands.

Below Single-headed
cylindrical drum from New
Guinea (University of
Amsterdam).

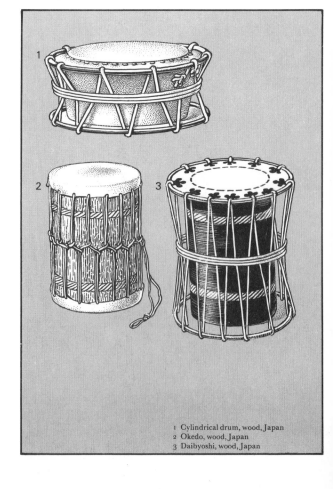

1 Cylindrical drum, wood, Japan
2 Okedo, wood, Japan
3 Daibyoshi, wood, Japan

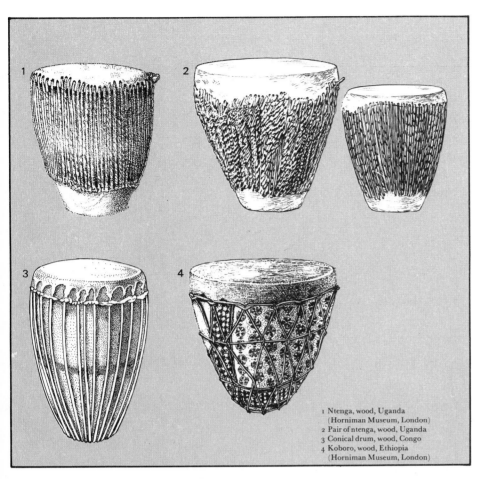

1 Ntenga, wood, Uganda
  (Horniman Museum, London)
2 Pair of ntenga, wood, Uganda
3 Conical drum, wood, Congo
4 Koboro, wood, Ethiopia
  (Horniman Museum, London)

Left Conical drums from
Africa. The ntenga drums
from Uganda (1 and 2) are
double-headed, but only the
larger head is played.
Ntenga are usually found in
pairs of different sizes.
The Congolese drum (3) is
also one of a pair. The
Ethiopian koboro (4) is used
as a church instrument.

Below Congolese drummer
playing a pair of conical
drums fastened to a frame.

Left Conical drums from
Cuba (1) and the Ijca
Indians of South America
(2). Cuban bata drums have
two laced heads. Instruments
of different sizes are often
played together. The conical
drum of the Ijca Indians
is single-headed. It is
held under the arm for
playing.

©DIAGRAM

Below Conical drums from
Indonesia—from Java (1)
and from Nias Island (2,
Horniman Museum, London)

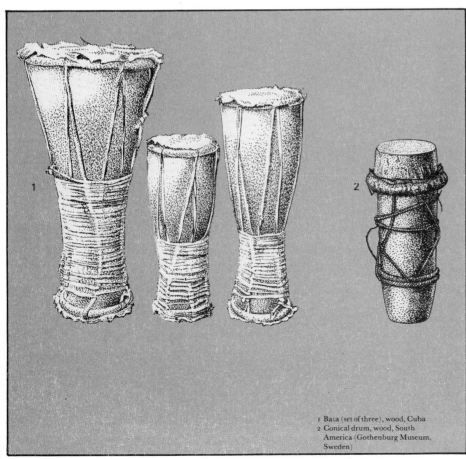

1 Bata (set of three), wood, Cuba
2 Conical drum, wood, South
  America (Gothenburg Museum,
  Sweden)

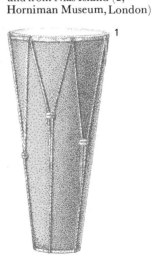

Barrel and waisted drums

Barrel-shaped and waisted drums are important
variations of the simple tubular drum. In each
case the ends are approximately the same size,
and both single and double-headed forms are
found. Though known in Africa barrel drums are
most important in Southeast Asia. Waisted drums
are most common in West Africa and Japan.

Right Barrel drums from
Africa. The double-headed
drum from Nigeria (1) is
set horizontally on the
floor and played with the
hands. The single-headed
drum from Ghana (2) is
played upright. It is tuned
by adjusting the lacing
around the pegs.
Left Nigerian drummer.

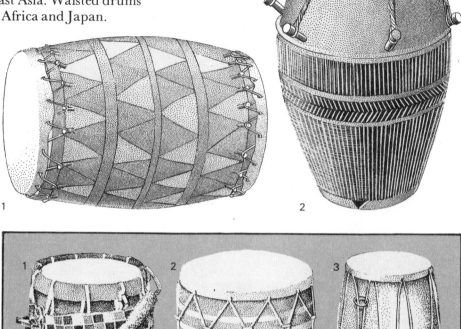

Right Double-headed barrel
drums from India. The
dhola drums (1 and 2) are
played in a horizontal
position. The "tom-tom"
(3) is tuned by rings that
are moved up and down the
lacing to alter the tension on
the drum head. The
mridanga (4), the classical
drum of South India, is used
as a solo and accompanying
instrument. The barrel drum
from Madras (5) is slung
around the neck and played
with the hands.
Left Dhola player using
one hand to beat the drum.

Left Double-headed barrel
drum played by the Chocó
Indians of South America
(Gothenburg Museum,
Sweden).

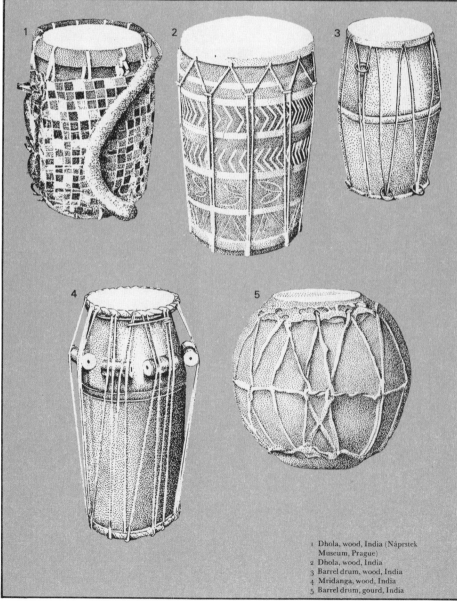

1 Dhola, wood, India (Náprstek
Museum, Prague)
2 Dhola, wood, India
3 Barrel drum, wood, India
4 Mridanga, wood, India
5 Barrel drum, gourd, India

Right and below Drums
from Cambodia (1) and Java
(2 and 3), and a Javanese
drummer. Played with the
bare hands, these double-
headed drums have carrying
handles and are rested on
low wood stands for playing.
Drums of this type are most
commonly found as members
of small instrumental groups.

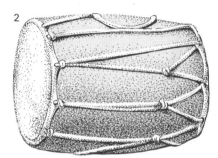

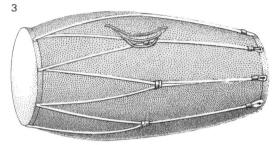

Left Japanese drums. The
tsuri daiko (1 and 2) is a
gagaku drum with a
lacquered body and tacked
heads that are often highly
decorated. Suspended from
a frame (1), or rested on a
wood stand (2), it is beaten
with two sticks on one head
only. The o-daiko (3) is a
Shinto temple drum. Beaten
with sticks, it may be rested
on a stand or carried around
the neck for processional
use. The taiko (4), used for
folk music, has two heads
lashed together with thick
rope. The kakko (5), also a
gagaku instrument, has two
deerskin heads both of
which are beaten.

Right Da-daiko—a huge
gagaku drum. Suspended
in an elaborate frame, it is
struck with heavy lacquered
beaters.

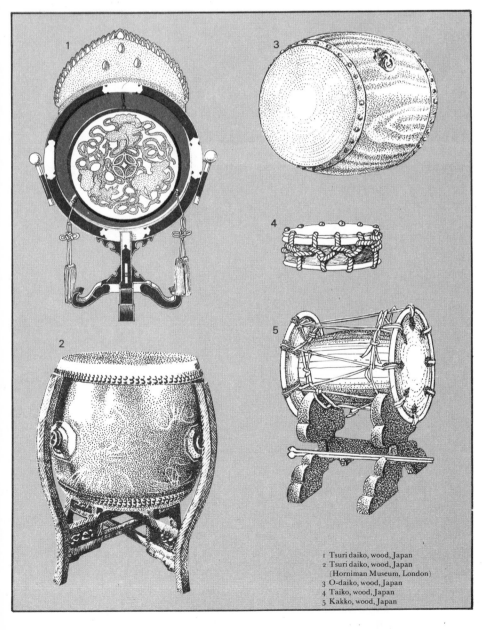

1 Tsuri daiko, wood, Japan
2 Tsuri daiko, wood, Japan
  (Horniman Museum, London)
3 O-daiko, wood, Japan
4 Taiko, wood, Japan
5 Kakko, wood, Japan

©DIAGRAM

Right Waisted drums from Asia and Oceania. The Korean changko (1) has a lacquered wood body and two laced heads. The single-headed drums from New Guinea (2 and 3) have heavy bodies made from one piece of wood. They are played upright. The Tibetan drum (4) is made from two human skulls. Pellets, attached by a cord to its waist, beat against the skulls when the drum is shaken.

Below Musician from New Guinea playing a waisted drum.

1 Changko, wood, Korea
2 Waisted drum, wood, New Guinea (Rijksmuseum voor Volkenkunde, Leiden, Netherlands)
3 Waisted drum, wood, New Guinea (Rijksmuseum voor Volkenkunde, Leiden, Netherlands)
4 Waisted drum, human skulls, Tibet (Horniman Museum, London)

Right Kalungu—African "talking" drums. Beaten with a curved stick, these important drums are used by several West African peoples to imitate the tonal quality of their languages. The pitch of the kalungu can be varied by adjusting the tension of the lacing.
Below Kalungu player.

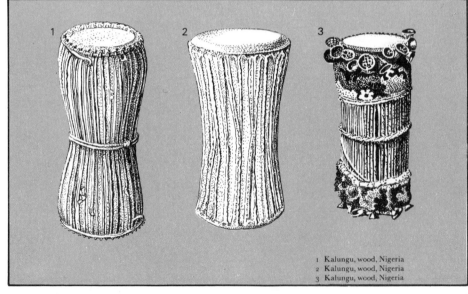

1 Kalungu, wood, Nigeria
2 Kalungu, wood, Nigeria
3 Kalungu, wood, Nigeria

Right Waisted drums from India. The dugdugi of Bengal (1) has a decorated pottery body and two laced heads (Náprstek Museum, Prague). The shallow waisted drum (2) and the huruk (3) have lacquered wood bodies (Victoria and Albert Museum, London).
Left Indian drummer.

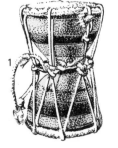

Left Waisted drums from the Middle East. The Iraqi drums (1 and 2) have long wood bodies decorated with metal studs. In each case the playing head is raised above the rim. Drums of this type are usually held under the arm and played with the fingertips. The Turkish drum (3) has a sectioned wood body and a skin over the larger end. Its elegant shape is similar to that of the goblet drum.

Below An Arab drummer.

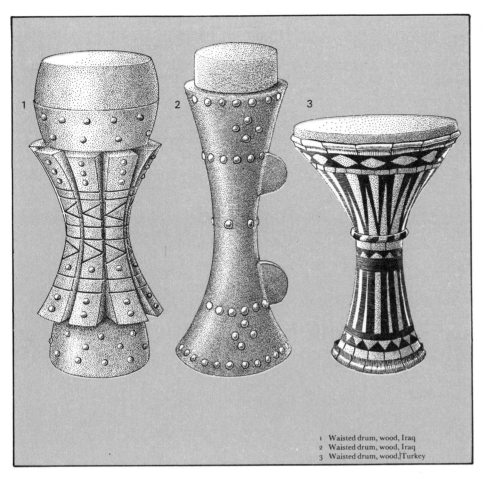

1 Waisted drum, wood, Iraq
2 Waisted drum, wood, Iraq
3 Waisted drum, wood, Turkey

Left Japanese tsuzumis—small waisted drums used in noh drama. Made of cherry or zelkana wood, the hourglass-shaped body is carefully carved on the inside and lacquered on the outside. The two heads, made of hide stretched over iron rings, are held against the body with ropes.

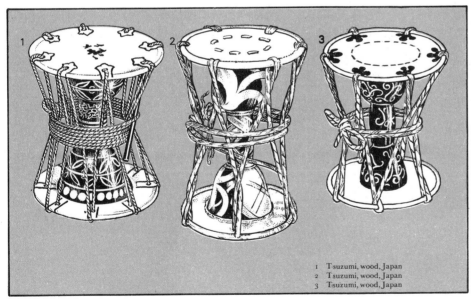

1 Tsuzumi, wood, Japan
2 Tsuzumi, wood, Japan
3 Tsuzumi, wood, Japan

Left Preparations for playing the tsuzumi—a performance begins with a ritual assembling of the instrument.

Above Court musician demonstrating the playing position for the tsuzumi.
Left Playing technique. The drum is gripped by the cords. By relaxing or tightening his grip the player alters the tension on the drum heads and so adjusts the pitch of the instrument during play.

©DIAGRAM

Goblet and footed drums

Goblet drums are a type of single-headed drum particularly important in Arab countries. Made of pottery, wood, or occasionally of metal, they appear in a variety of sizes. Often the skin is glued to the rim of the body—a typical feature of many of these drums. Footed drums, also single-headed, have legs that are usually cut from the wood body of the drum. They are most common in North America, Africa, and Oceania.

Left Clay drum from the Maya culture (Museum of Anthropology and Ethnology, Guatemala City). This drum is shown with a new skin tied on around the rim.

Right European goblet drums. The clay drums from Bohemia (1 and 2) date from about 2000BC. Skins were originally attached to projections molded on the outside of the body. The Greek tarabuka (3) and Yugoslavian darbuk (4) are modern goblet drums beaten with both hands.

Right African goblet drums. The Nigerian example (1) has a wood body decorated with a carved lizard. The Ghanaian drum (2) is a type often played in pairs. The carved drum (3) and the set of small drums (4) are both instruments of the Baule people of the Ivory Coast.
Below Baule drummer.

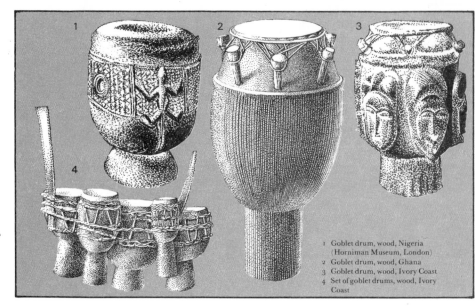

1 Goblet drum, wood, Nigeria (Horniman Museum, London)
2 Goblet drum, wood, Ghana
3 Goblet drum, wood, Ivory Coast
4 Set of goblet drums, wood, Ivory Coast

Above Goblet drums from India (1) and Cambodia (2)
Right Darabukke drums from Islamic countries. The wood or pottery bodies of these goblet-shaped drums are often elaborately decorated with painting or inlaid work. Sizes vary but most are fairly small.
Left Darabukke player.

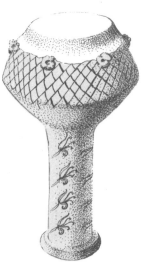

Right Mexican footed
drums and player. The
panhuéhuetl from the
Matlazincan culture (1) has
a carved wood body and a
single membrane of jaguar
skin glued to the upper rim
(Museum of Toluca,
Mexico). The tlalpanhuéhuetl
(2) is a modern Mexican
footed drum.

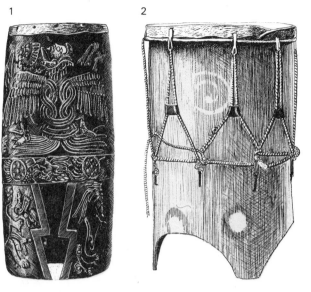

Right Footed drums from
Africa, and a drummer. In
West African examples the
body and "feet" of the drum
are often carved to resemble
the human body (1 and 2).
The examples shown here
from Tanzania (3) and
Central Africa (4) have more
conventionally shaped
bodies and feet.

1 Footed drum, wood, Congo
  (Horniman Museum, London)
2 Footed drum, wood, West Africa
  (Horniman Museum, London)
3 Footed drum, wood, Tanzania
4 Footed drum, wood, Central
  Africa

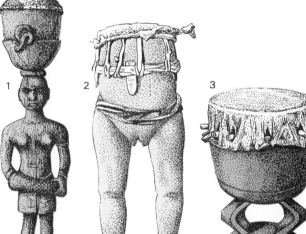

Right Footed drums from
Polynesia (1), the Marquesas
Islands (2), Hawaii (3), and
a Hawaiian drummer. Made
from a single length of
tree trunk, these drums have
carved legs at the base to
give extra resonance when
played. Many examples are
decorated with carving or
tassels.

1 Footed drum, wood, Polynesia
  (British Museum, London)
2 Footed drum, wood, Marquesas
  Islands (Musée de l'Homme, Paris)
3 Footed drum, wood, Hawaii
  (Bernice P. Bishop Museum,
  Honolulu)

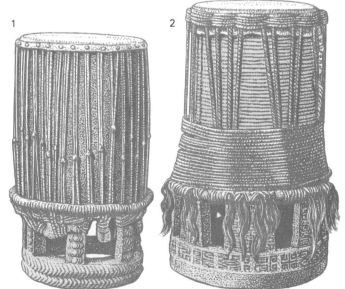

©DIAGRAM

Long drums

Elongated forms of all types of drum may be classified as long drums. In its simplest form, still found today in Africa, the long drum is a length of hollow tree trunk with a single skin head. Other examples are elaborately shaped and decorated. An interesting group of long drums from New Guinea have characteristic handles carved from the side of the wood body.

Left South American long drums, from the Talamanca Indians (1) and Chocó Indians (2, Gothenburg Museum, Sweden). A string threaded with glass beads is stretched across the skin of the Chocó drum.

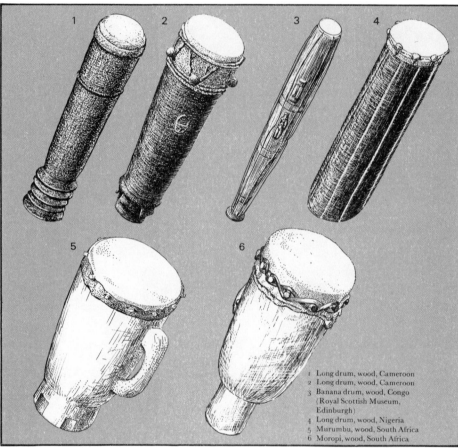

Left African long drums. Examples of this type of drum are sometimes tied to a pole to keep them upright for playing (1 and 2). Others are played in a tilted position (3 and 4). The South African drums (5 and 6) have bodies modeled on the shape of domestic pots. **Below** Nigerian drummer.

1 Long drum, wood, Cameroon
2 Long drum, wood, Cameroon
3 Banana drum, wood, Congo (Royal Scottish Museum, Edinburgh)
4 Long drum, wood, Nigeria
5 Murumbu, wood, South Africa
6 Moropi, wood, South Africa

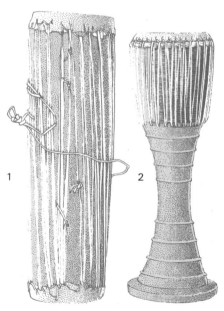

Left Chinese drummer playing a long goblet drum. Instruments of this type are carried horizontally on a strap over the left shoulder and played with the right hand. For celebrations and festivals Chinese drums are often decorated with brightly colored feathers, ribbons, and cords.

Right Long drums from India (Victoria and Albert Museum, London). The two-headed cylindrical drum (1) is carried on a strap over the shoulder. It is beaten with the hands on only one of its heads. The single-headed drum (2) is similar in shape to the Middle Eastern goblet drum.

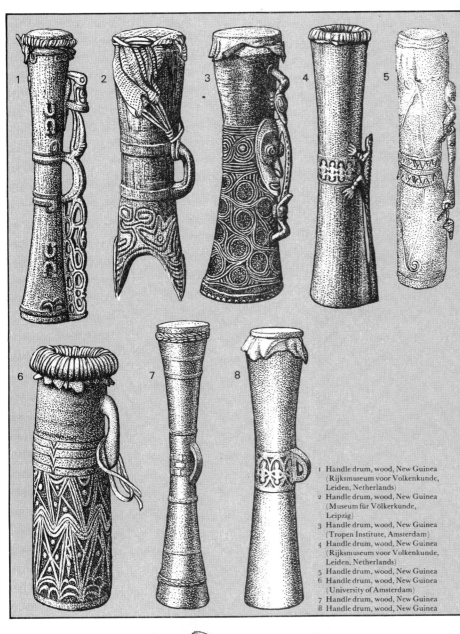

Left Handle drums from New Guinea. Most of the long drums found in New Guinea have a handle for carrying them around. Carved from the same piece of wood as the body of the drum, most handles are near the drum's waist. Many examples are decorated.
Below Long drum player from New Guinea.

Below Tiny balls on the skins of drums from New Guinea. Used to improve a drum's tone, the balls are made of the sticky substance secreted by spiders when making their webs.

1 Handle drum, wood, New Guinea (Rijksmuseum voor Volkenkunde, Leiden, Netherlands)
2 Handle drum, wood, New Guinea (Museum für Völkerkunde, Leipzig)
3 Handle drum, wood, New Guinea (Tropen Institute, Amsterdam)
4 Handle drum, wood, New Guinea (Rijksmuseum voor Volkenkunde, Leiden, Netherlands)
5 Handle drum, wood, New Guinea
6 Handle drum, wood, New Guinea (University of Amsterdam)
7 Handle drum, wood, New Guinea
8 Handle drum, wood, New Guinea

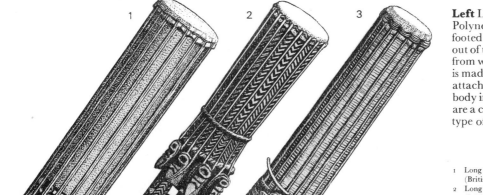

Left Long drums from Polynesia. Each of these footed drums has feet carved out of the block of wood from which the drum body is made. Long cords, attaching the skin to the body in a decorative manner, are a common feature of this type of drum.

1 Long drum, Polynesia (British Museum, London)
2 Long drum, Polynesia (British Museum, London)
3 Long drum, Polynesia (Musée de l'Homme, Paris)

Frame drums

Frame drums consist of one or two membranes stretched over a simple frame. Made of thin wood, the frame is usually shallow and adds little resonance when the skin is beaten. Most frames are circular but other shapes are also found. Drums of this type originated in the Middle East and are still common there. Many frame drums, like the popular tambourine, have metal jingles attached to the rim.

Left Frame drum players from Morocco (a) and South Africa (b). Most frame drums are fairly small and light.

Right Frame drums from the Americas. Drums of this type, often played with the hands, are used in ritual by North American Indians (1 and 2). The Eskimo drum (3) is beaten on the rim with a stick to accompany singing. The deeper drums from Argentina (4) and Panama (5) are played with sticks.

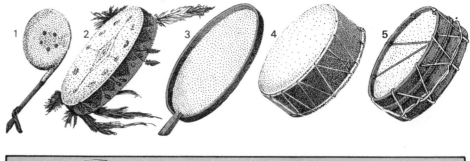

Right European frame drums. The bodhran (1), a popular Irish folk instrument, is played with a double-ended stick. The square frame drum found in Spain (2) and the Middle East, is less familiar than the tambourine (3 and 4). The frame drum with a handle (5) is from Yugoslavia.

Below Frame drums from the USSR and Turkey. The Russian reshoto (1) has a very shallow frame fitted with metal jingle disks. It is held by the handle and played with the fingers or a beater. The Turkish tar (2) has jingle disks in a decorative frame (Horniman Museum, London).

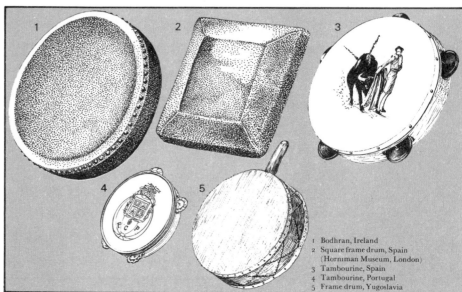

1 Bodhran, Ireland
2 Square frame drum, Spain (Horniman Museum, London)
3 Tambourine, Spain
4 Tambourine, Portugal
5 Frame drum, Yugoslavia

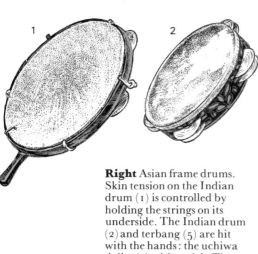

Right Asian frame drums. Skin tension on the Indian drum (1) is controlled by holding the strings on its underside. The Indian drum (2) and terbang (5) are hit with the hands: the uchiwa daiko (3) with a stick. The Javanese kelontong (4) is shaken so that the pellets strike the skins.

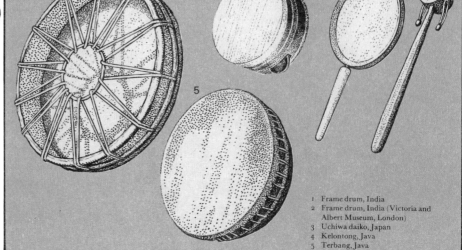

1 Frame drum, India
2 Frame drum, India (Victoria and Albert Museum, London)
3 Uchiwa daiko, Japan
4 Kelontong, Java
5 Terbang, Java

Friction drums

Friction drums include instruments of many shapes and sizes. Some, like those used in African initiation ceremonies, are typically drum-shaped. Others are essentially novelty instruments popular in many parts of the world. All types of friction drum are characterized by a membrane made to vibrate by friction—being rubbed with the fingers or a cloth, or by a cord or stick piercing the membrane.

Left Rommelpot—a simple friction drum formerly popular in many·European countries. Often made by tying an animal bladder over a household pot and then piercing the bladder with a stick, they were commonly played by children at Martinmas and Christmas. **Right** 17th century Flemish rommelpot player.

Right European friction drums. The drums made from clay pots are from Bohemia (1) and Naples (2). The Russian friction drum (3) is sounded with horsehair. The Norwegian thimble drum (4), English mustard **container** drum (5), and French cockerel drum (6) were made as toys.

Below Two ways of sounding a friction drum—pulling the stick up and down (a), and making the stick turn by rubbing it between the hands (b).

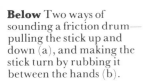

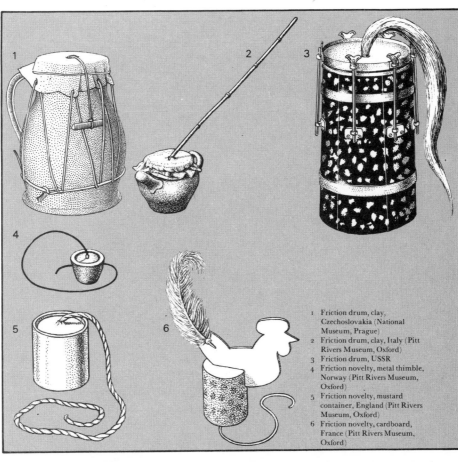

1 Friction drum, clay, Czechoslovakia (National Museum, Prague)
2 Friction drum, clay, Italy (Pitt Rivers Museum, Oxford)
3 Friction drum, USSR
4 Friction novelty, metal thimble, Norway (Pitt Rivers Museum, Oxford)
5 Friction novelty, mustard container, England (Pitt Rivers Museum, Oxford)
6 Friction novelty, cardboard, France (Pitt Rivers Museum, Oxford)

Right African friction drums. The Zambian friction drum (1) and South African ingungu (2) have a sounding stick through a hole in the skin. The South African moshupiane (3) is sounded by rubbing with a bundle of wet corn stalks. **Below** South African ingungu player.

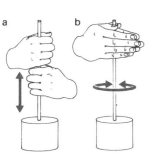

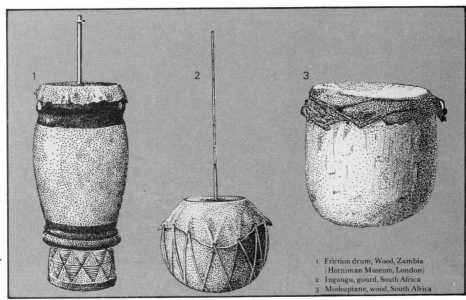

1 Friction drum, Wood, Zambia (Horniman Museum, London)
2 Ingungu, gourd, South Africa
3 Moshupiane, wood, South Africa

© DIAGRAM

Kettledrums

Kettledrums have a single membrane stretched over a pot or vessel body. Known in ancient Egypt, they are commonly found today in Africa, the Americas, Asia, and Europe. Drums of this type are frequently played in pairs. They appear in a variety of sizes, ranging from the very large drums of Africa to the compact and portable Middle Eastern naqara—ancestors of the modern orchestral timpani.

Below African kettledrums. Commonest in Central Africa, kettledrums of many shapes and sizes are found throughout the continent. The shallow drum from the Ivory Coast (1) is carried on a strap around the neck for playing. The other examples shown are played on the lap or on the floor.

Right African drummers playing a gourd drum (a) and a ngoma (b). The simple gourd drum, played in many parts of Africa, consists of a skin stretched over a hole in the top of a gourd. It is usually beaten with the hands. The Venda ngoma, struck with a single beater, is usually played by women.

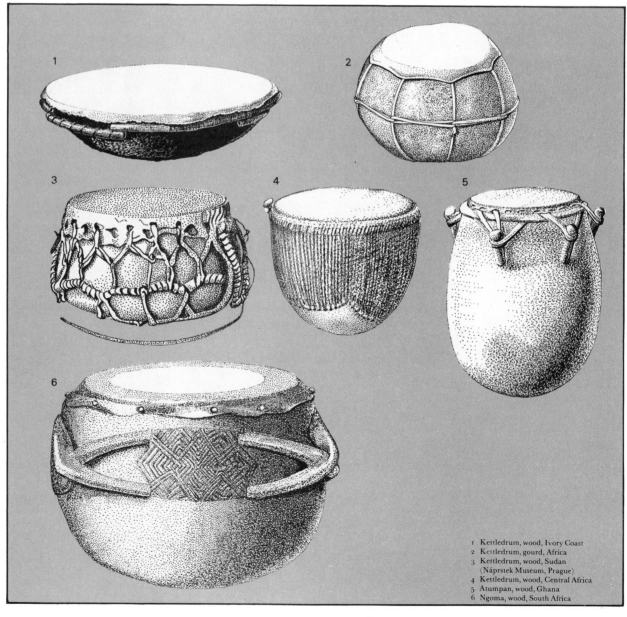

1 Kettledrum, wood, Ivory Coast
2 Kettledrum, gourd, Africa
3 Kettledrum, wood, Sudan
  (Náprstek Museum, Prague)
4 Kettledrum, wood, Central Africa
5 Atumpan, wood, Ghana
6 Ngoma, wood, South Africa

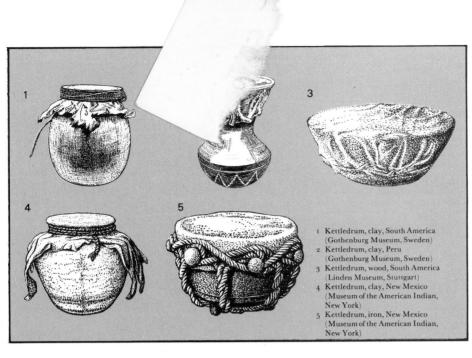

1 Kettledrum, clay, South America
  (Gothenburg Museum, Sweden)
2 Kettledrum, clay, Peru
  (Gothenburg Museum, Sweden)
3 Kettledrum, wood, South America
  (Linden Museum, Stuttgart)
4 Kettledrum, clay, New Mexico
  (Museum of the American Indian,
  New York)
5 Kettledrum, iron, New Mexico
  (Museum of the American Indian,
  New York)

Left American kettledrums.
The South American drums
(1 and 2) and drum from
New Mexico (4) have simple
pot bodies. The shallow
wood drum (3) contains
stones that rattle in play.
The iron-bodied Peyote
drum (5) is filled with water
for playing.
Below Hawaiian kettledrum
(British Museum, London).

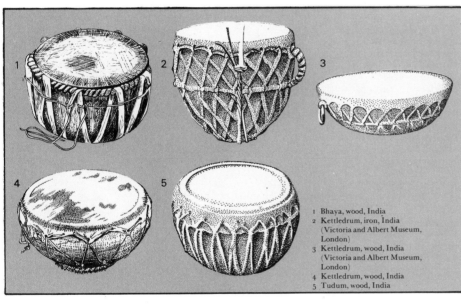

1 Bhaya, wood, India
2 Kettledrum, iron, India
  (Victoria and Albert Museum,
  London)
3 Kettledrum, wood, India
  (Victoria and Albert Museum,
  London)
4 Kettledrum, wood, India
5 Tudum, wood, India

Left Indian kettledrums.
The bhaya (1) is used as the
left hand drum of the famous
Indian tabla. The iron-
bodied drum (2) and shallow
wood drum (3) have rings
through which cords are
threaded for carrying.
Right Indian drummer
striking the tudum with
wedge-shaped beaters.

Left Yugoslavian talambas.
The small kettledrum (1) is
made of metal and played
with two large wood beaters.
The drums (2) are made of
wood covered with leather.

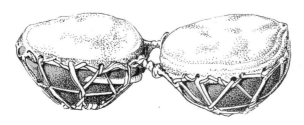

Left Arabic naqara—
predecessors of the modern
Western timpani. Small
pairs of kettledrums with
wood or clay bodies are
found throughout the Arab
world. A stick inserted
through the lacing increases
tension on the head. Naqara
are usually played with small
cloth-covered beaters.

© DIAGRAM

Orchestral and band drums

Drums play an important part in the "percussion" section of Western orchestras and bands. The art and literature of ancient times show that drums were used by all the major civilizations of the past, but the perishable nature of the materials from which most drums are made has meant that few ancient examples survive. Drums had a major role in the music of medieval and renaissance Europe. Especially common were the tabor and side drum, which are still played today. Also common in medieval times were nakers, small kettledrums of Arabic origin that survive as the modern orchestral timpani. In addition to the timpani—most important because they are tuned to specific pitches—the basic orchestral drum group consists of side, tenor, and bass drums. In modern dance bands drums of Latin American origin play an increasingly significant role.

Left Nakers player drawn from a medieval psalter.
Right Kettledrums used in 18th and 19th century orchestras. The 18th century example (1) is tuned by means of a key that fitted over the tuning screws. The 19th century kettledrum (2) has hand-operated tuning screws.

Left 19th century machine timpani. Developed to reduce the amount of time needed for tuning, these instruments were tuned with a single handle. Turning the handle operated a mechanism for turning all the screws at once, so ensuring equal tension at all points on the drum head.

Left Modern hand-screw timpani. Despite the advantages of modern tuning mechanisms these simpler, cheaper drums are still very popular. Although impracticable for most modern music, they are useful for earlier music requiring only three or four different pitches.

1 Drum head
2 Tuning gauge
3 Shell
4 Struts
5 "Crown"
6 Pedal

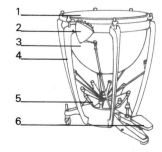

Right Modern orchestral timpanum (Premier).
Left Identification of parts of a modern timpanum. The instrument's tuning is controlled by a foot pedal which alters the tension of the head by means of a "crown" mechanism. A tuning gauge worked by the pedal indicates the pitch.

1 Kettledrum, 18th century
2 Kettledrum, 19th century
(Instrument Museum, Brussels)

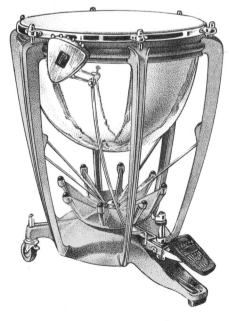

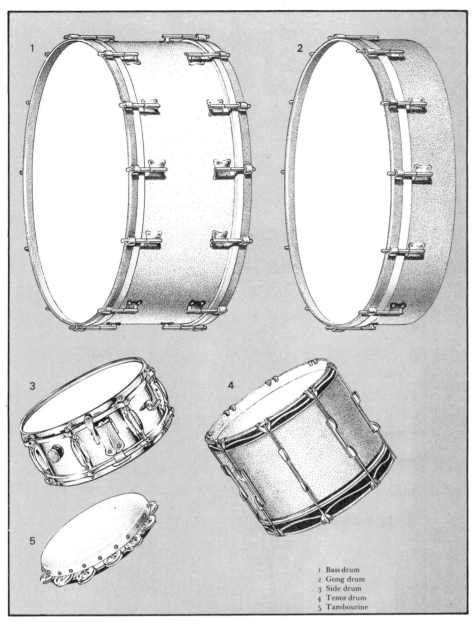

1 Bass drum
2 Gong drum
3 Side drum
4 Tenor drum
5 Tambourine

Drums

J. Haydn	The Creation
G. Verdi	Requiem—Dies Irae (bass drum)
A. Bruckner	Symphony no.9 (timpani)
B. Bartók	Sonata for two pianos and percussion
B. Britten	The Rape of Lucretia—second act (tenor drum)
E. Carter	Six pieces for Kettledrums
Ravel	Bolero (side drum)

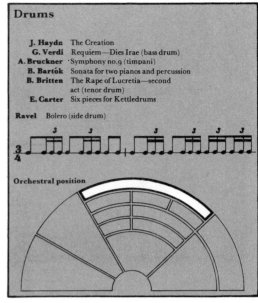

Orchestral position

Left Modern orchestral drums. The double-headed bass drum (1) and single-headed gong drum (2) are played with large padded beaters. The side drum (3) is usually fitted with snares—eight or more lengths of gut, nylon, or wire stretched over the lower head to give extra brilliance to the sound. The side drum and the tenor drum (4) are played with hard wood sticks. The tambourine (5) may be struck, shaken, or less commonly, sounded by friction.

Right Timpani sticks (a), side drum sticks (b), and wire brushes used for special effects (c).

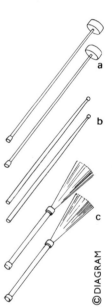

a
b
c

©DIAGRAM

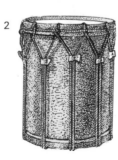

Left Early military drums. The artillery kettledrum (1), dated 1716, has an unusual cylindrical body (Kungl Armémuseum, Stockholm). The long drum (2) is a type of bass drum popular in 18th century England. The side drum (3) has an embroidered cover (Brussels Conservatoire).

Right Set of modern drums of the type used in dance and and jazz bands. This set includes side, tenor, and bass drums, three suspended cymbals, and a pair of hi-hat cymbals. The depression of foot pedals clashes the hi-hats and causes a padded beater to strike the bass drum.

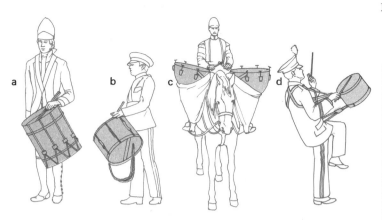

Above Military drummers through the ages. Body-slung drums (a) and (b), and horseback-mounted kettledrums (c) have been important band instruments for several centuries. The hi-stepper attachment (d), used in some marching bands, allows a variety of extreme movements.

Right Three important modern military drums—side (1), tenor (2), and bass (3). These drums are very similar to their orchestral equivalents.

Left Tabor and player. Popular in medieval Europe as a military instrument, and still played in some areas as a folk instrument, the tabor survives in the orchestra as the tambourin de Provence. The upper head is fitted with a snare and the drum is beaten with a single stick.

Left and below Latin American dance band drums. The bongo drums (1) are tuned differently and played with bare hands. The "cocktail" drums (2) are a modern version of the traditional conga drums. The timbales (3), tuned like bongos, are played with thin sticks.

1 Side drum
2 Tenor drum
3 Bass drum

Mirlitons

As well as drums another less familiar group of instruments is characterized by a vibrating membrane. In these "mirliton" instruments, the membrane's function is to modify a sound made in some other way. Usually the membrane is activated by blowing or singing against it, as in the eunuch flute or horn mirliton. Less commonly membranes are used as sound modifiers in instruments such as some African xylophones.

Left Comb and paper—a simple home-made mirliton. The player puts a comb covered with paper in front of his lips and hums or sings against it. This produces a buzzing sound as the paper vibrates.

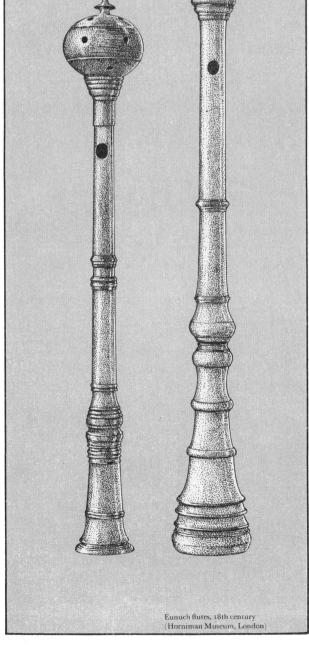

Eunuch flutes, 18th century
(Horniman Museum, London)

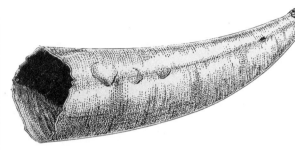

Left Eunuch flutes. Also known as onion flutes, these unusual instruments were made in Europe in the 17th and 18th centuries. A membrane, protected by a removable cap, covers the upper end of the instrument. It is played by speaking or singing into one of the apertures in the cap.

Above Horn mirliton from Nigeria (Horniman Museum, London). Used to modify the sound of the human voice, this instrument consists of a cowhorn tube and a membrane from the substance spun by spiders to protect their eggs.

Above Kazoo and a cross-section showing how it works. This simple toy mirliton is sounded by singing into the blow hole at one end of the tube. The membrane is positioned over a lateral hole halfway down the tube. In the 1930s kazoo bands appeared in some parts of Europe.

Below Zobos and a zobo player. Known as novelties in the USA in the early 20th century, zobos have the external appearance of conventional instruments. Played like a kazoo, their vibrating membranes were intended to give a realistic imitation of the instruments they resembled.

©DIAGRAM

Chordophones: introduction

Chordophones are instruments in which the sound is made by the vibration of strings. There are five basic types: bows, lyres, harps, lutes, and zithers. Of these, the oldest and simplest is the musical bow which is still common in Africa and the Americas. Harps and lyres both appeared about 5000 years ago in ancient Egypt and Sumeria. The harp survives in many parts of the world, although the lyre is now confined almost exclusively to Africa. Plucked lutes also have a long history and are among the most popular of all folk instruments. The bow was first applied to the lute in the 10th century AD, and from these early bowed lutes developed the members of the modern violin family. Zithers appear in a wide variety of styles, ranging from simple tube zithers to the sophisticated keyboard instruments of Western Europe.

Chordophones family tree
The five basic chordophone types are bows, lyres, harps, lutes, and zithers. Lutes have a primary subdivision into plucked and bowed instruments. The large zither family is first divided into simple, long, plucked board, and struck board instruments.

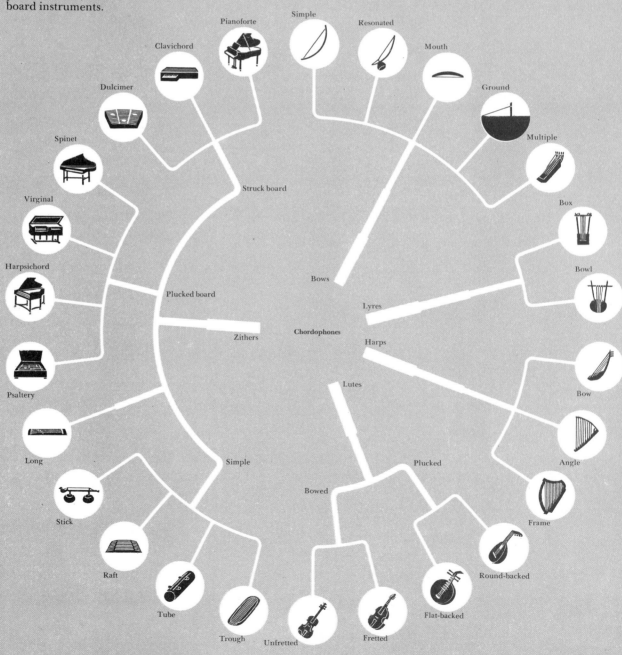

Stringing The relationship of the strings to the body or resonator provides the usual means of classifying chordophones. The musical bow (a) has one or more strings attached to each end of a curved stick. The strings of the lyre (b) run from the resonator to a crossbar supported by two arms. Harp strings run at an oblique angle from the resonator to the neck (c). Instruments of the lute family have strings running from near the base of the body, over a bridge, to the end of the neck (d). Zither strings (e), raised by bridges, run along the instrument's entire length parallel to the body.

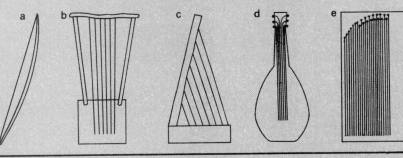

Lifting the strings In order to vibrate freely the strings of lyres, lutes, and zithers must be lifted from the body. On some instruments the strings are attached to the body and then pass over a bridge (a); other examples have a string holder which also acts as a bridge (b).

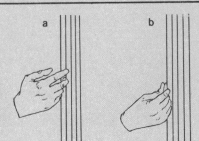

String attachment Several different methods are used for attaching strings to a chordophone's neck. In many primitive examples the string is tied directly to the neck (a). Instruments are easier to tune if the strings are tied to a tuning ring (b) or fastened to a peg (c).

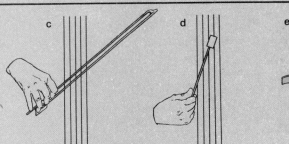

Sounding the strings A variety of playing methods are used for chordophones. Most common are plucking — with the fingers (a) or a plectrum (b) — and bowing (c). Some zithers are played with beaters or hammers (d), while the strings of the aeolian harp (e) are sounded by the wind.

How a string vibrates An activated string vibrates not only as a whole but also in sections — as shown in the diagram (right). The primary, or longest, vibration determines the pitch produced. This pitch is called the fundamental. Secondary vibrations produce harmonics or overtones — pitches which sound in conjunction with the fundamental. The presence of different harmonics gives each instrument its own particular tone color. By touching a string very lightly with his finger while bowing it normally, the player obtains a harmonic in place of the fundamental.

Strings and pitch Pitch is affected by a string's length, tension, and thickness. A short string gives a higher pitch than a long one (a). A string at high tension produces a higher pitch than a less taut string (b). A thin string gives a higher pitch than a thick one (c).

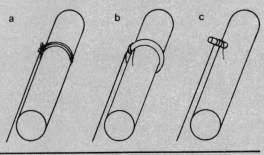

Resonators An activated string gives a better tone if the instrument has a soundbox, or resonator. String vibrations are transferred to the resonator which reinforces and amplifies the tone. Devices like the violin soundpost help spread the vibrations (right).

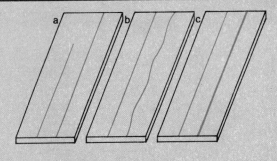

©DIAGRAM

Raising the pitch A higher pitch may be obtained from a string by shortening its vibrating length. In performance this is usually achieved by "stopping" the string — pressing it against the neck or body of the instrument — usually with the finger (a). Some instruments have frets — very low bridges on the neck or body — which show the player where the string should be stopped (b). Many zithers have movable bridges which can be adjusted to give the string a particular vibrating length and thus a particular pitch (c).

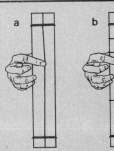

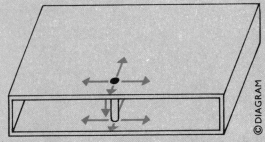

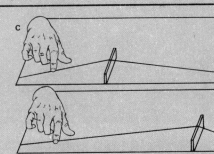

Musical bows

Musical bows are the simplest of all stringed instruments, and are commonly found in Africa, America, and Asia. They are thought to have developed from the hunting bow, and some African peoples use the same bows for shooting and for making music. The simplest bows comprise a single string fastened to each end of a flexible stick. Developments include attached resonators and additional strings.

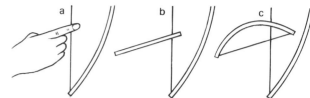

Above Methods of playing the musical bow. The string may be made to vibrate by plucking with the finger (a), tapping or stroking with a stick or plectrum (b), or by playing with a second smaller bow (c).

Right Musical bows without resonators. Simple examples from Africa (1 and 3) and America (4, 5, and 6) lack any musical refinements. More developed are the Southern African bow with the peg string-holder and hollowed out stick (2), and the bridged bow from Alaska (7). The bows from the Solomon Islands (8) and Hawaii (9) are more unusual examples with more than one string.

Below Musical bow players from Africa (a) and Hawaii (b). Holding the bow in the mouth is one of the commonest methods of providing a simple bow with a resonator. The addition of a resonator both amplifies and modifies the sound produced.

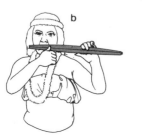

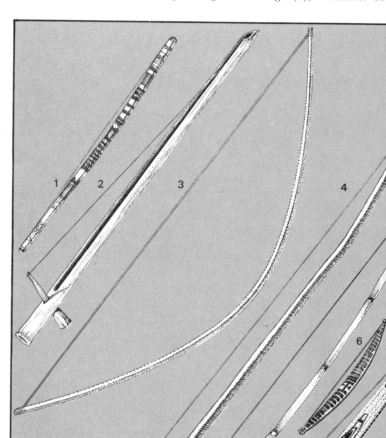

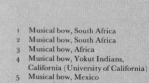

1 Musical bow, South Africa
2 Musical bow, South Africa
3 Musical bow, Africa
4 Musical bow, Yokut Indians, California (University of California)
5 Musical bow, Mexico
6 Musical bow, Brazil
7 Musical bow, Alaska (Museum of the American Indian, New York)
8 Musical bow, Solomon Islands
9 Musical bow, Hawaii

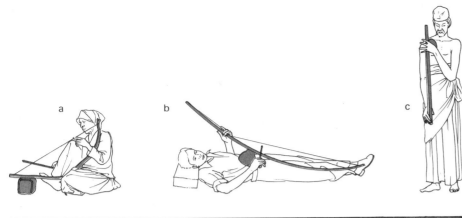

Left Examples of the great variety of positions and techniques adopted when playing the musical bow. The musician from Southern Africa (a) is resting her bow on a tin can to supply a resonator. The musicians from Guam (b) and India (c) have bows with resonators, which are held against the body for extra effect.

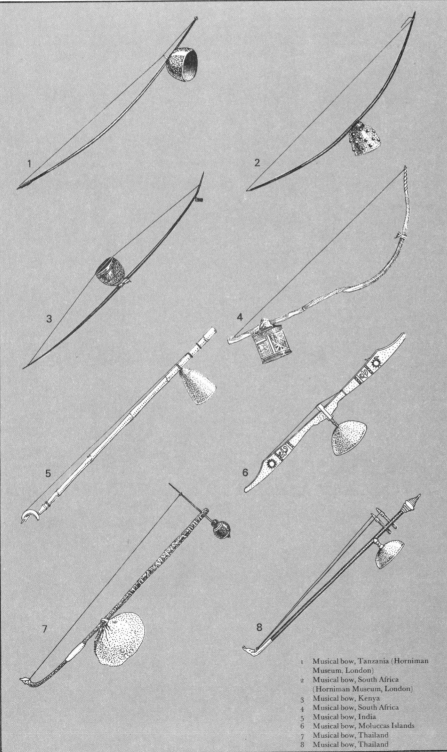

Left Musical bows with attached resonators. Half gourds are the most common form of attached resonator, but other materials include tin cans (4) and half coconut shells (6). Generally the Asian examples (5 to 8) are more sophisticated than those from Africa (1 to 4). The delicately carved end of the bow from India (5) is designed to rest on the player's knee. The examples from Thailand (7 and 8) are thought to be of Laotian origin.

Below Compound musical bows from the Congo (1—in the Horniman Museum, London) and from South Africa (2). Compound bows comprise a number of bows attached to a single resonator, usually made from wood but sometimes from a gourd or some other material. Each bow produces a note of a different pitch.

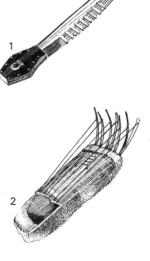

1 Musical bow, Tanzania (Horniman Museum, London)
2 Musical bow, South Africa (Horniman Museum, London)
3 Musical bow, Kenya
4 Musical bow, South Africa
5 Musical bow, India
6 Musical bow, Moluccas Islands
7 Musical bow, Thailand
8 Musical bow, Thailand

©DIAGRAM

Ancient lyres

The lyre is a stringed instrument with a four-sided frame consisting of a soundbox, two arms, and a crossbar. The strings are fastened to the front of the soundbox and run over a bridge to the crossbar. The lyre is first recorded in Sumerian art around 2800 BC but is probably even older. It was a popular instrument in ancient Egypt but is now most closely associated with the ancient Greeks.

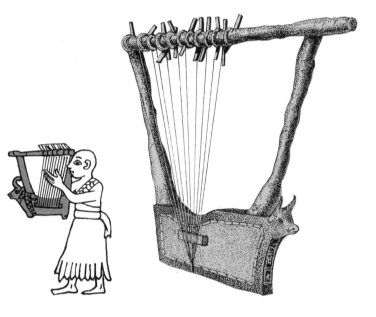

Above Sumerian silver lyre with bull's head carving (reconstructed, in the British Museum). Representations in art show up to 11 strings, which were tuned by levers on the crossbar. Sumerian lyres were held with the crossbar uppermost, and were plucked with the bare fingers.

Below Egyptian lyres. The reconstructed lyre (Berlin Museum) has straight arms similar to Sumerian examples. The drawing from a mural shows a lyre with asymmetrical curved arms, played in the Egyptian way with the crossbar away from the body. Lyres appeared in Egyptian art about 2000 BC.

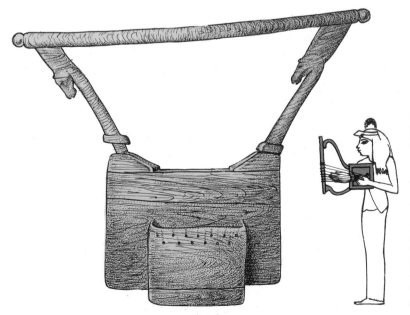

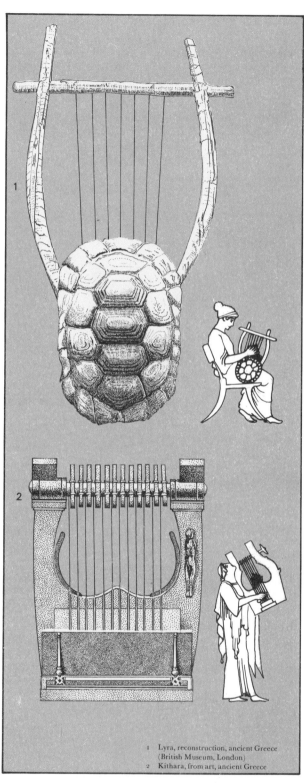

1 Lyra, reconstruction, ancient Greece
   (British Museum, London)
2 Kithara, from art, ancient Greece

Above Greek lyres. The lyra (1) has a bowl-shaped soundbox faced with tortoiseshell. In Greek mythology the first lyra was made from an empty tortoiseshell by Hermes, messenger of the gods. The lyra was essentially an amateur instrument. Professional musicians preferred the kithara (2), a more sophisticated instrument with a larger, box-shaped soundbox made of wood. The god Apollo is often depicted playing a kithara, a symbol of harmony. The kithara, but not the lyra, was later adopted by the Romans.

European lyres

Lyres were known in medieval times in Britain, Germany, France, and Scandinavia. The earliest examples may have been descended from classical instruments, but medieval European lyres have a characteristic appearance with the body, arms, and usually the crossbar, made from a single piece of wood. Plucked lyres have completely died out in Europe, but bowed lyres, a later medieval development, survive in Scandinavia.

Left Anglo-Saxon rote (reconstruction, British Museum), from the 7th century AD ship burial at Sutton Hoo, Suffolk. Similar plucked lyres with six strings are depicted in contemporary illustrations.
Below King David playing a lyre, drawn from an 8th century English manuscript.

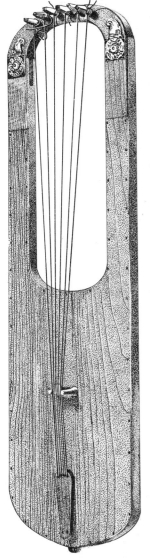

Right Bowed lyres. The crwth (1) is a Welsh bowed lyre that was popular in the Middle Ages and remained in use until the early 19th century. It had four stopped strings over a central fingerboard, and two off-board drone strings. The kanteleharpe (2) is a rare Finnish folk lyre, made from a single piece of wood with an opening cut from the top left hand corner. There are three parallel strings, of which only that at the left is stopped. The tallharpa (3) is a folk lyre of Swedish origin that remained popular in Estonia until the early 20th century. It usually had three or four strings.

Below Tallharpa player.

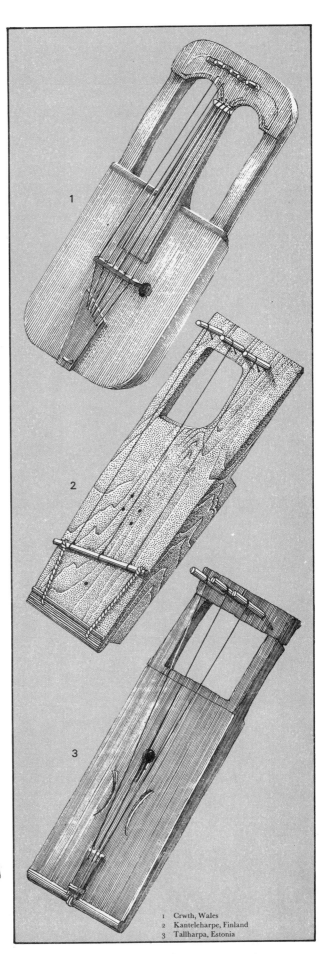

1 Crwth, Wales
2 Kanteleharpe, Finland
3 Tallharpa, Estonia

© DIAGRAM

African lyres

Despite their widespread popularity in ancient times, plucked lyres survive only in the musical cultures of parts of Africa and Siberia. Most interesting are the lyres of Ethiopia, since they demonstrate the two basic lyre types known from earliest times. African lyres are commonly used to accompany singing in religious festivals and in magical rites, particularly those associated with healing.

a   b

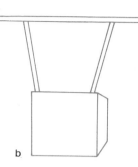

Above Diagrams showing the two basic types of lyre resonator—bowl-shaped (a) and box-shaped (b). Both types are commonly found in modern Ethiopia, but only the bowl-shaped resonator is known in lyres from other parts of Africa. **Right** Ethiopian playing a box-shaped bagana.

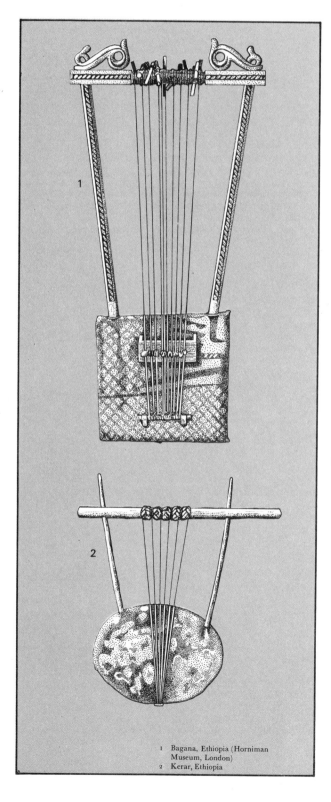

Left Ethiopian lyres— bagana (1) and kerar (2). The bagana is the lyre of the Ethiopian aristocracy and priesthood, while the kerar is a popular folk lyre. Just as in ancient Greece, the box-shaped instrument is more highly esteemed than the bowl-shaped popular instrument.

Below A highly decorated bowl-shaped kerar from Ethiopia (Horniman Museum, London). The six strings diverge from a ring at the base of the resonator. Like the bagana the kerar is played with a leather or claw plectrum, although sometimes the fingers are also used.

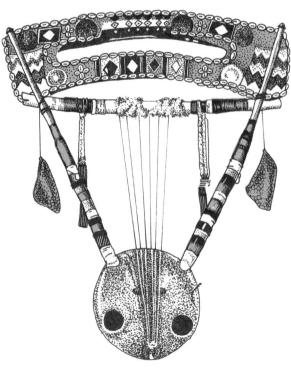

1   Bagana, Ethiopia (Horniman Museum, London)
2   Kerar, Ethiopia

Right A Kenyan musician
playing the obukano, a large
bowl-shaped lyre that has
been described as "the
double bass of East Africa."
This instrument has eight
strings, tuned by adjusting
the rings on the crossbar.
It is played with the fingers.
Smaller lyres are also widely
found in Kenya.

Below Lyres from the Sudan
(left) and Uganda (right).
The Sudanese lyre is called
a kissar—reminiscent of
kithara, the word for one of
the lyres of ancient Greece.
Not all Sudanese lyres are
as primitive as this one. The
Ugandan lyre is decorated
with beads and feathers
(Horniman Museum).

Folk harps

The harp is a plucked stringed instrument in which the strings run at an oblique angle from the soundbox to the instrument's neck. There are three basic forms: the bow or arched harp, the angle harp, and the frame harp. Bow harps are today widely found in Africa and Eastern Asia. Angle harps are common in Africa, but are now extremely rare elsewhere. Frame harps are rarely found outside Europe.

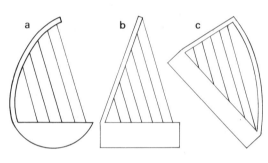

Left Diagrams illustrating the basic difference between the harp (a) and the lyre (b). The strings of the harp run at an oblique angle from the soundbox to the neck attached to it. The strings of the lyre run across the soundbox to a crossbar supported by two arms.

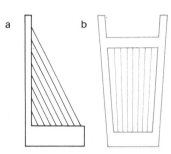

Left Diagrams showing the three basic forms of harp. The bow-shaped harp (a) is the earliest form, thought to have developed from the musical bow. The angle harp (b) was the predecessor of the frame harp (c). The pillar of the frame harp permits a higher string tension than on other harps.

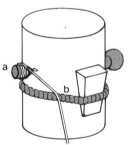

Left Diagram based on a Ugandan bow harp showing two different ways of modifying the sound produced by a string. The string is attached to a peg for tuning (a), and runs over a skin ring (b) that gives a buzzing quality to the sound. Such fittings are quite common on folk harps.

Right Angle harps. The harp from Borneo (1) has a deep box-shaped resonator and is decorated with a carved bird's head. The angle harp fell out of use in the Caucasus in the 19th century, but some examples survive (2). Angle harps are today commonly played in parts of Africa. The Congolese harp (3) is a primitive example with unusual split cane strings. The harp from Gabon (4) has a decorative head that is a common feature of harps from this part of Africa.

Left Harp player from Gabon showing the usual way of holding a folk harp, with the resonator against the body.

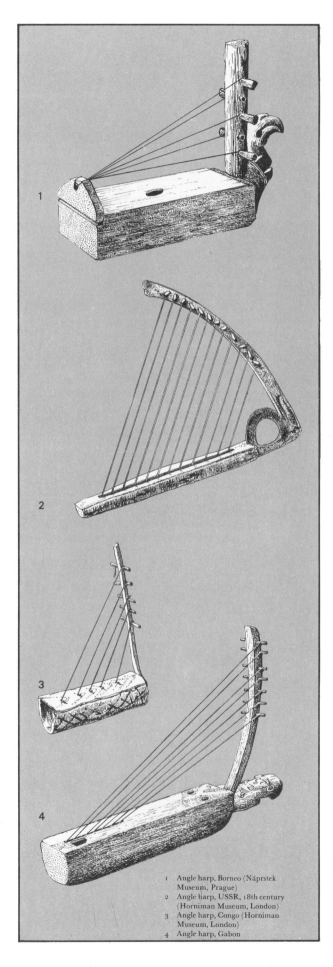

1 Angle harp, Borneo (Náprstek Museum, Prague)
2 Angle harp, USSR, 18th century (Horniman Museum, London)
3 Angle harp, Congo (Horniman Museum, London)
4 Angle harp, Gabon

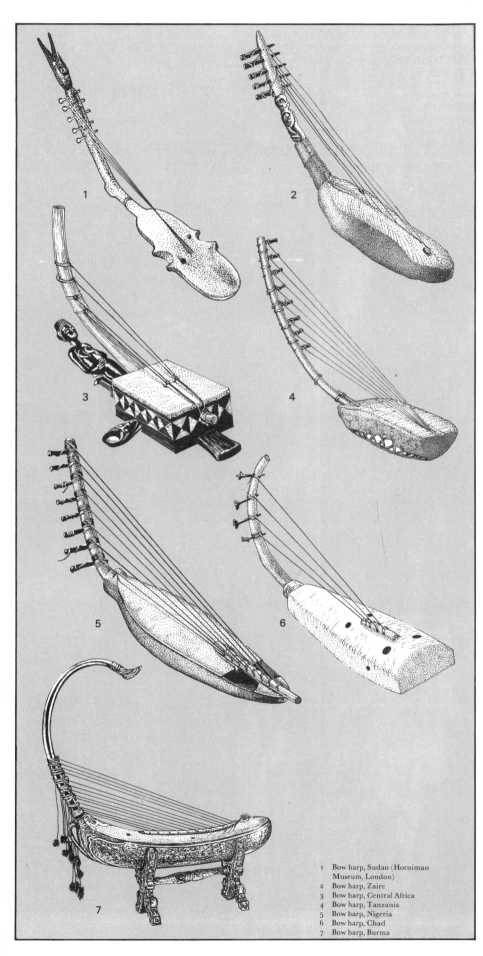

Left Bow harps from Africa and Asia. The Sudanese harp (1) and the harp from Zaire (2) have resonators reminiscent of primitive fiddles. The harp decorated with carved wood figures (3) is musically primitive, lacking either tuning pegs or rings. Less elaborately decorated but easier to tune are the harps from Tanzania (4), Nigeria (5), and Chad (6). The harp from Chad has a large resonator with several sound holes. The beautiful Burmese harp (7) is on a display stand. It is tuned with silk cord attached to the strings and tied around the harp's neck.

Below Three bow harp players from Chad.

Below Liberian loma harp. This unusual instrument has a gourd resonator into which is inserted a stick to serve as the harp's neck. The strings run to the neck from another stick lashed to the base of the neck. A third stick completes the frame and gives the instrument greater strength and stability.

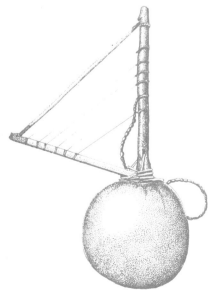

1   Bow harp, Sudan (Horniman Museum, London)
2   Bow harp, Zaire
3   Bow harp, Central Africa
4   Bow harp, Tanzania
5   Bow harp, Nigeria
6   Bow harp, Chad
7   Bow harp, Burma

Historical harps

Bow harps were known in Egypt and Sumeria as early as 3000 BC. Angle harps were a later development, probably originating in Persia and known in Egypt by about 2000 BC. Frame harps developed in Europe in the Middle Ages. The earliest frame harps were small and sturdy with few refinements, but progressive modification eventually resulted in the versatile orchestral instrument of the present day.

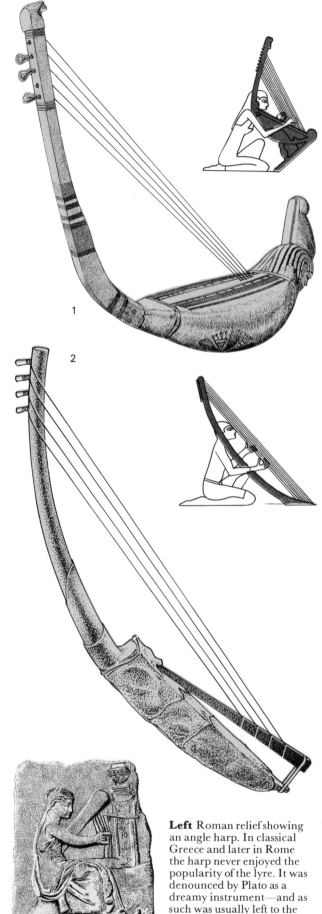

Left An illustration of an Egyptian harp player based on a wall painting in the tomb of Rameses III (c. 1235 BC). This large erect harp was one of a variety of forms found in ancient Egypt. It was played with the resonator resting on the floor. The hieroglyphs record the harper's song.

Right Smaller harps from ancient Egypt. The painted harp (1) dates from about 1250 BC and has a wood resonator. The shoulder harp (2) is less curved and has a string-bearing arm projecting from a parchment covered resonator. (Both these harps, restored, are in the British Museum.)

Left Egyptian angle harp dating from about 1500 BC (in The Louvre, Paris). It is probably the oldest harp so far discovered.
Below Babylonian relief showing musicians with angle harps similar to the Egyptian angle harp. They are holding them with the resonator against the body.

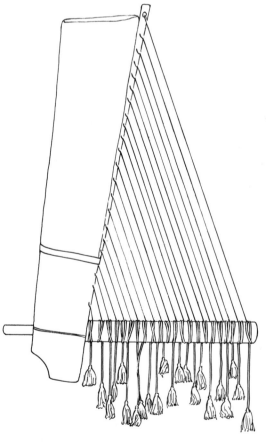

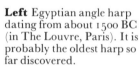

Left Roman relief showing an angle harp. In classical Greece and later in Rome the harp never enjoyed the popularity of the lyre. It was denounced by Plato as a dreamy instrument—and as such was usually left to the women to play.

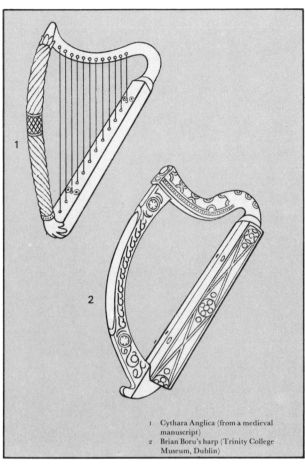

1 Cythara Anglica (from a medieval manuscript)
2 Brian Boru's harp (Trinity College Museum, Dublin)

Left Medieval frame harps. This depiction of the "Cythara Anglica" (1) is based on a manuscript illustration dating from the 12th or 13th century. The "Brian Boru" harp (2) dates from the 11th century and is believed to have belonged to this famous Irish ruler. It is made from carved oak.

Right Modern reconstruction of a medieval harp (Arnold Dolmetsch Ltd).

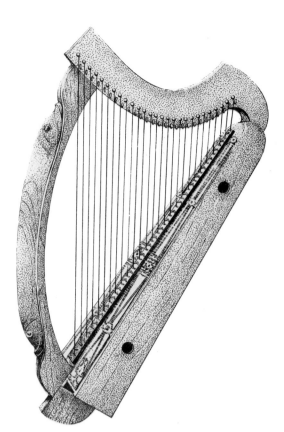

Below Minstrel playing the Irish harp. This important instrument has changed little for a thousand years.

Left One of the oldest surviving Celtic harps—known as Queen Mary's harp (Museum of Antiquities of Scotland, Edinburgh). It is commonly thought to have belonged to Mary Queen of Scots. Probably dating from before the 15th century, it shows strong similarities to Brian Boru's harp.

Right 18th century Italian diatonic harp (Gemeentemuseum, The Hague). Popular as a solo instrument and occasionally used in the orchestra in the 17th and 18th centuries, the diatonic harp had a greater range than the Celtic harp. It was however limited to the notes of a single key.

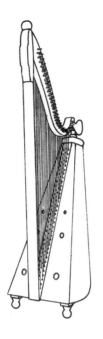

Left A Welsh triple harp. Invented in the 17th century, the triple harp is a chromatic instrument capable of producing all the notes in every key.
Below Diagram of a triple harp string arrangement—with the diatonically tuned strings in the outer rows, and additional semitones in the center row.

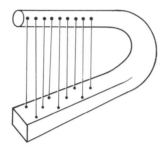

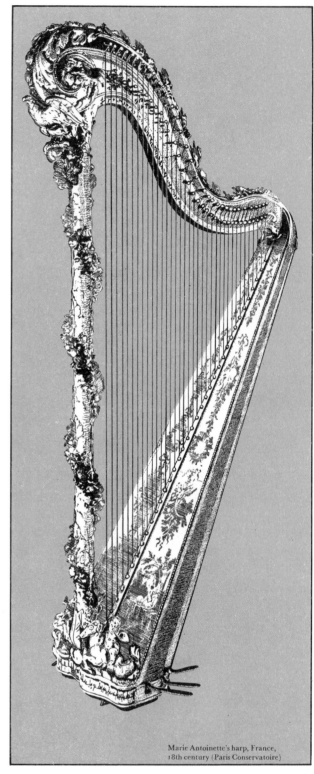

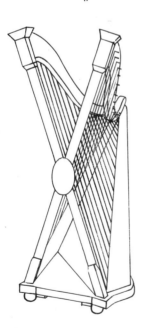

Left Operation of the hook mechanism on the neck of a hooked harp. Turning a hook (center) shortens the vibrating length of the string and raises the note by a semitone. Invented in the late 17th century, the hook harp was another solution to the problem of producing a chromatic harp.

Left An unusual double harp built in the United States in the 19th century (Metropolitan Museum, New York). Some makers have preferred to experiment with chromatic harps that are not dependent on mechanically changing the tuning of the strings. This harp has 45 diatonically tuned strings attached to one neck, and 33 strings providing additional notes attached to the other.

Right Marie Antoinette's harp. Ornamented in the style of Louis XVI, it is thought to have belonged to his Queen. It is a single-action pedal harp.

Marie Antoinette's harp, France, 18th century (Paris Conservatoire)

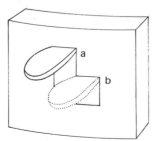

Left Single-action pedal. The chromatic pedal harp is more versatile than the manually operated hooked harp since string tensions are more easily changed during performance. With the pedal in position (a) the strings play their natural note. Position (b) makes a single semitone adjustment.

Right Harp pedal box with single-action pedals. The earliest pedal harps, built about 1720, had only five pedals but the usual number was soon increased to seven —one pedal for each note of the octave. Changing the pedal position alters the pitch of all the strings of the same letter name.

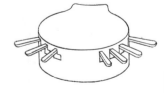

Orchestral harps

The modern harp is a regular member of the symphony orchestra. Its range is the largest of all orchestral instruments, and it is equally effective playing both solo melodies and the rippling chordal accompaniments with which it is most often associated. Interest in the harp as an orchestral instrument was developed in the 19th century by composers such as Wagner and Tchaikovsky, and still continues today.

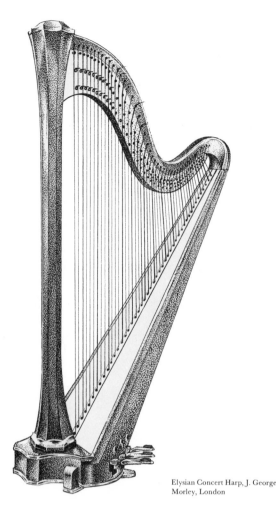

Elysian Concert Harp, J. George Morley, London

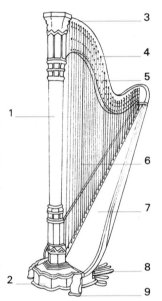

Right A modern concert harp—with double-action pedals. The double-action mechanism, invented in the 19th century, allows the player to raise the pitch of the strings by either a semitone or a tone. This has made it easier for the player to realize the instrument's full potential.

Left Identification of parts of the orchestral harp.

1 Pillar
2 Base
3 Neck
4 Tuning pegs
5 Disks
6 Strings
7 Soundboard
8 Pedals
9 Feet

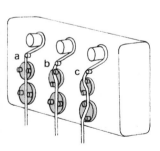

Left Diagram showing the playing position of the hands. The player may pluck strings singly or in chords. Some of the strings are colored to act as guides. Very attractive is the "glissando" effect obtained by running the hands across the strings, plucking each of them in quick succession.

Left Diagram showing the operation of the disk mechanism that changes the pitch of the strings on the modern orchestral harp. In position (a) the disks have no effect on the string which therefore produces its natural note. In position (b) the studs of the top disk shorten the vibrating length of the string and raise its note by a semitone. In position (c) both disks are in contact with the string and raise its note by a full tone.

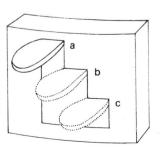

Left Double-action pedal. With the pedal in position (a) the strings produce their natural note. Position (b) raises them a semitone, and (c) a full tone.

Harp

Pitch range

W. A. Mozart   Concerto for flute, harp, and orchestra K. 299
G. Bizet   Carmen
M. Ravel   Introduction et allegro
R. Glière   Concerto for harp op. 74
P. Hindemith   Sonata for harp
F. Martin   Petite symphonie concertante

Tchaikovsky Swan Lake, Scène

Moderato

Orchestral position

© DIAGRAM

Folk lutes

All lutes comprise a resonating belly and a neck, and have strings that run from near the base of the belly along the full length of the neck. Plucked folk lutes are popular in many parts of the world and are made in many different shapes and sizes. Important differences include the relative length of body and neck, the shape of the back, the number of strings, and whether there are frets.

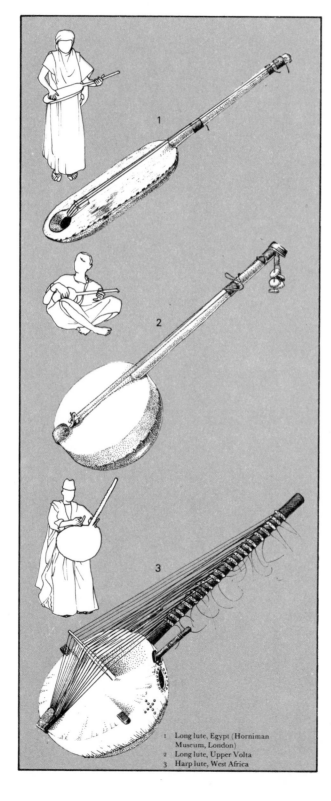

1 Long lute, Egypt (Horniman Museum, London)
2 Long lute, Upper Volta
3 Harp lute, West Africa

Right Neck lengths. Lutes may be subdivided according to their relative neck and body lengths. A "short-necked" lute (a) has a neck that is shorter than its body. In a "long-necked" lute (b) the neck is longer than the body. Sometimes the neck of a lute is simply an elongation of the body.

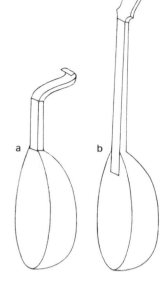

Right Back shapes. Another way of subdividing plucked lutes is according to the shape of their backs. Many folk lutes have rounded backs (a), and in this respect resemble the lute of renaissance Europe. Others have flat backs (b), and so resemble the European classical guitar.

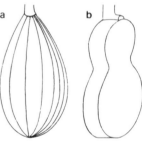

Right Stopping a string. If an instrument has no frets (a), an activated string will vibrate from the instrument's bridge to the point where the player's finger presses the string against the neck. If an instrument is fretted (b), a string will vibrate from the bridge to the fret below the point where finger pressure is applied. The presence of frets therefore simplifies finger stopping by eliminating the need to apply finger pressure at a very precise point. Many folk lutes have gut or metal frets, either fixed into the fingerboard or tied around it.

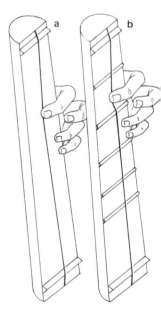

Left African folk lutes. The strings of the Egyptian lute (1) are held in place by leather thongs. The lute from Upper Volta (2) has a gourd resonator and metal jingles. The West African instrument (3) is classified as a harp lute.
Right Strings on the bridge of a harp lute.

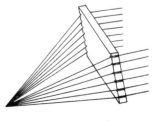

Right Lutes from modern Greece. The short-necked outi (1) is a bass lute with four pairs of strings. Many are unfretted. The more popular long-necked bouzouki (2) is a fretted instrument with strings arranged in double courses.
Far right Greek musician playing a bouzouki.

Right The Romanian cobza (3) has a very short neck, strings diverging into two groups at the bridge, and many small sound holes forming a decorative pattern on the belly. The Yugoslavian uti (4) is a short-necked lute used as a melody instrument.
Far right Uti player from Yugoslavia.

Right The Yugoslavian tambura (5) is a fretted long-necked lute often played in groups. Long-necked lutes were brought to the Balkans by the Turks in the 14th and 15th centuries. The saz (6) and waisted tar (7) are modern Turkish long-necked lutes. Both have movable tied gut frets.

©DIAGRAM

Below Lutes from the Middle East. The ud—from Iraq (1) and Syria (2)—is a short-necked, unfretted, double-strung lute played with a plectrum. Middle Eastern long-necked lutes include the tambur (3) and the tar (4). Both of these are from Iran, with movable frets and four strings.

1 Ud, Iraq
2 Ud, Syria (Horniman Museum, London)
3 Tambur, Iran (Moravian Museum, Brno, Czechoslovakia)
4 Tar, Iran (Moravian Museum, Brno, Czechoslovakia)

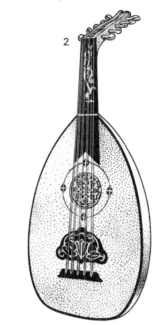
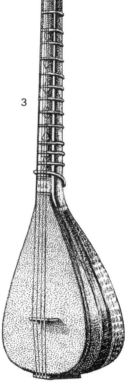
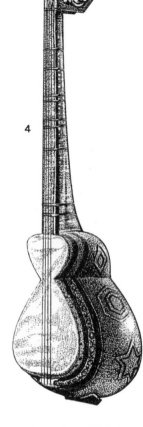

Right The Chinese p'i p'a (1) has frets on the belly and neck, four silk strings, slim lateral tuning pegs, and a shallow rounded back. It has been known for about 2000 years. The Japanese biwa (2) developed from the p'i p'a. Biwas with four strings are most common.

Below Chinese p'i p'a player.

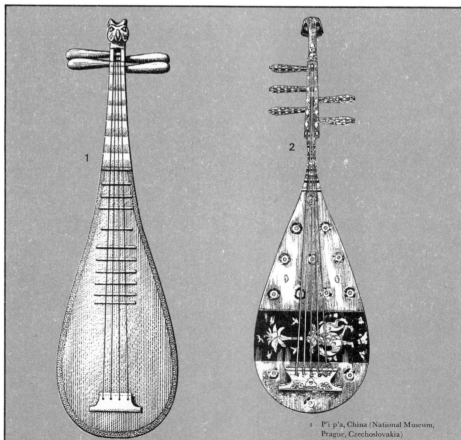

1 P'i p'a, China (National Museum, Prague, Czechoslovakia)
2 Biwa, Japan

Right The sitar (1) and surbahar (2) are North Indian instruments related to the vina, an Indian zither. Played strings run over arched metal frets to the peg-box. Sympathetic strings run under the frets in the troughed neck to lateral pegs.

Below Sitar player.

Right The tambura (3) is the classical drone lute of India. There are four strings and no frets. A movable ivory bridge is used for adjusting the pitch. The mayuri, or peacock sitar (4), is a beautiful South Indian instrument that may be either plucked or bowed.

Below Tambura player.

1 Sitar, India
2 Surbahar, India
3 Tambura, India
4 Mayuri, India (Metropolitan Museum, New York)

© DIAGRAM

Right Flat-backed lutes from Europe. The Russian balalaika (1) has a characteristic triangular belly. The fish-shaped machete (2) is a Portuguese folk guitar. The Ukrainian bandoura (3) is a large lute with stopped strings attached to pegs on the neck, and drone strings running to pegs on the belly. The bandurria (4) is a small Spanish folk instrument.

Below Ukrainian musician playing the bandoura.

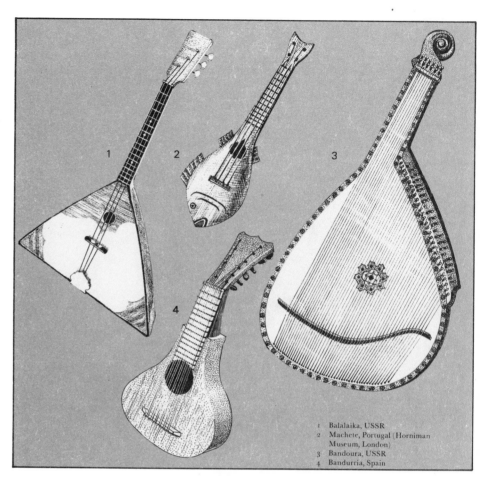

1 Balalaika, USSR
2 Machete, Portugal (Horniman Museum, London)
3 Bandoura, USSR
4 Bandurria, Spain

Right Ramkies—primitive folk guitars from Southern Africa. These home-made instruments were originally made with skin-covered (1) or gourd resonators, but old tin cans were found to be an excellent substitute (2 and 3).

Below Ramkie player from South Africa.

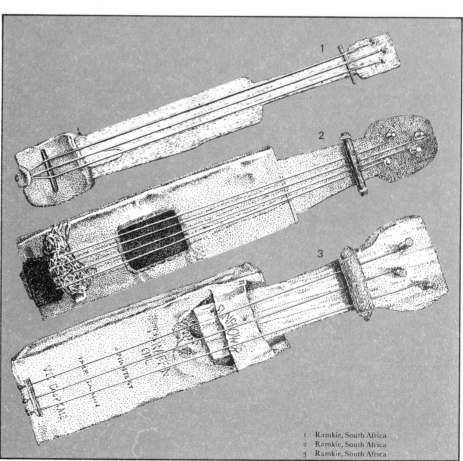

1 Ramkie, South Africa
2 Ramkie, South Africa
3 Ramkie, South Africa

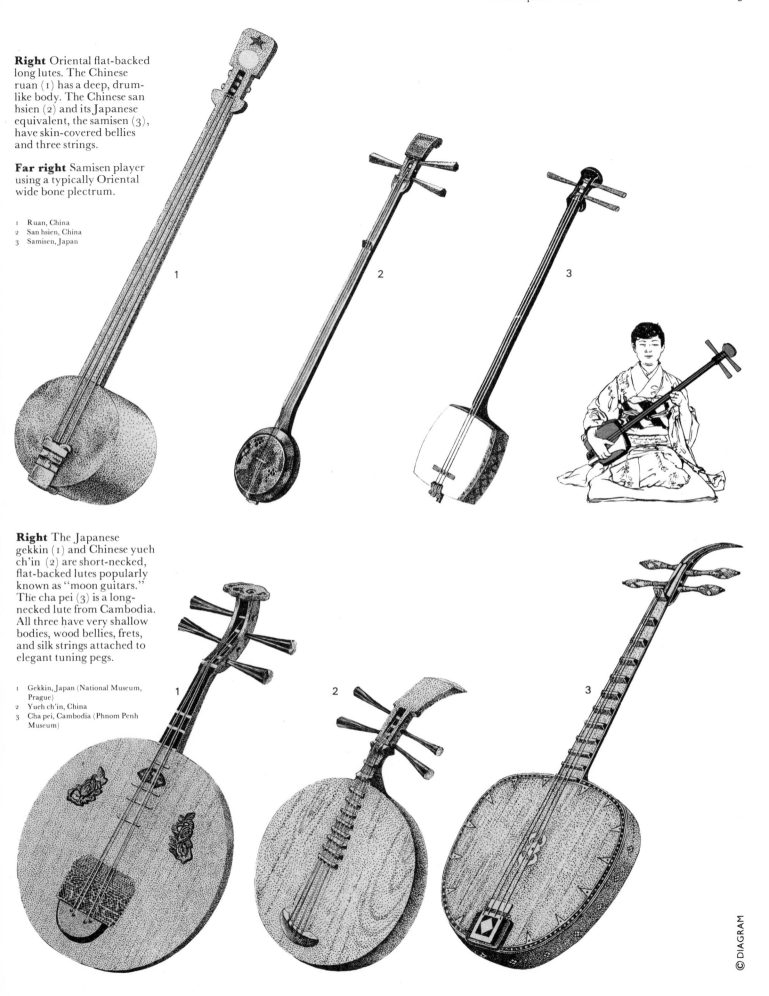

Right Oriental flat-backed long lutes. The Chinese ruan (1) has a deep, drum-like body. The Chinese san hsien (2) and its Japanese equivalent, the samisen (3), have skin-covered bellies and three strings.

Far right Samisen player using a typically Oriental wide bone plectrum.

1 Ruan, China
2 San hsien, China
3 Samisen, Japan

Right The Japanese gekkin (1) and Chinese yueh ch'in (2) are short-necked, flat-backed lutes popularly known as "moon guitars." The cha pei (3) is a long-necked lute from Cambodia. All three have very shallow bodies, wood bellies, frets, and silk strings attached to elegant tuning pegs.

1 Gekkin, Japan (National Museum, Prague)
2 Yueh ch'in, China
3 Cha pei, Cambodia (Phnom Penh Museum)

© DIAGRAM

Renaissance lutes

The lute was one of the most popular instruments of renaissance Europe. Although similar to instruments known as early as 2000 BC in Mesopotamia and 1500 BC in Egypt, the lute appeared in Europe only in the 10th century AD. By the 15th century lutes were in regular use as consort and accompanying instruments, and remained tremendously popular in Western Europe for the next 200 years.

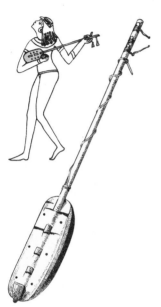

Left Ancient Egyptian long-necked instrument. This lute-like instrument had a cylindrical neck which passed through slits in the hide covering the round-backed sound box. There were three gut strings of which the tuning was regulated by rope wound tightly around linen knots.

Right Lute dating from the late 16th century. This instrument has a single top string—chanterelle—and five double courses. Both strings of each course are tuned to the same pitch, giving a strong tone when plucked together. The neck ends in a bent-back pegbox and has eight frets.

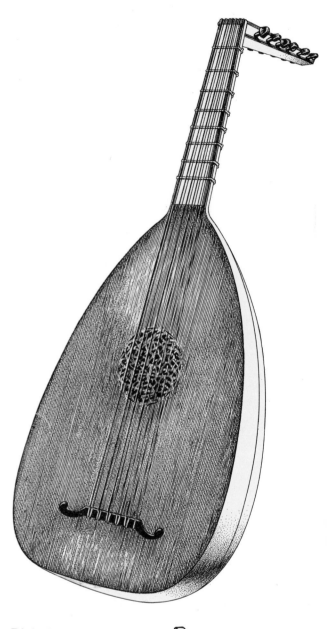

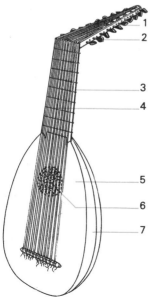

Above 16th century lute tablature—a system of notation. Each horizontal line represents a string, with the top line corresponding to the lowest string. The numbers indicate at which fret the string is to be stopped, and the symbols above the lines indicate the rhythm.

Left Identification of the parts of a renaissance lute. Most, but not all, members of the renaissance lute family were fretted.

1 Pegbox
2 Pegs
3 Neck
4 Frets
5 Belly
6 Sound hole
7 Ribs

Right Pegboxes. Straight (a) or slightly angled (b) pegboxes were found on most instruments of the renaissance lute family. The lute proper, however, was distinguished by its bent-back pegbox (c).
Below Musicians drawn from an 11th century French bas-relief.

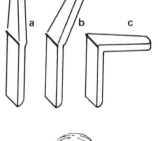

Left Italian lutes. The lute with the wide neck (1) has 20 strings, and dates from the 16th century. The early 17th century lute (2) has 13 strings. Throughout their history lutes have been made with different numbers of strings and frets.
Right A 17th century lute player, or lutenist.

Right 16th century soprano lute (Castello Sforzesco, Milan). Different-sized versions of the standard lute began to appear in the 16th century. This example of a small lute has 12 strings and is beautifully inlaid on its back and neck with ebony, ivory, and mother-of-pearl.

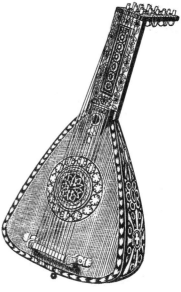

Below Modern reconstruction, by Dolmetsch, of a renaissance lute. It has 19 strings—one chanterelle and nine double courses.

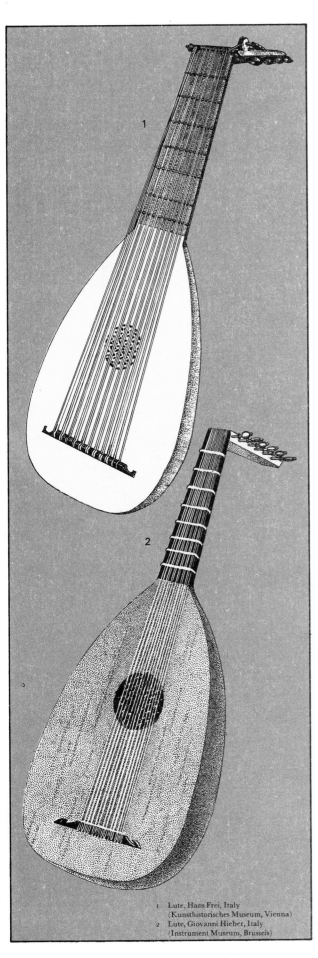

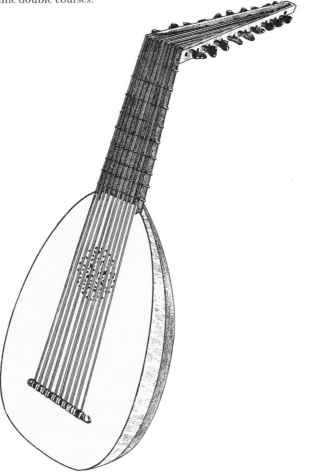

1 Lute, Hans Frei, Italy
   (Kunsthistorisches Museum, Vienna)
2 Lute, Giovanni Hieber, Italy
   (Instrument Museum, Brussels)

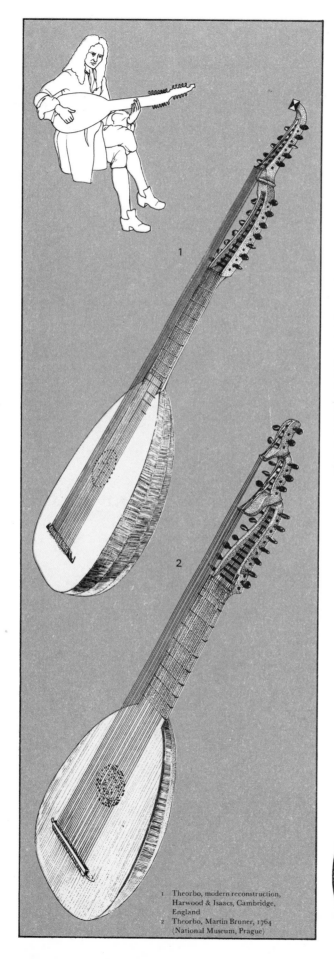

Right Diagrams showing two different theorbo pegbox arrangements. Theorbos were a type of archlute—or bass lute—developed in the 1500s. Archlutes are characterized by their unstopped bass strings attached to additional peg-boxes.

Left Modern reconstruction of a 16th century theorbo (1), and an 18th century theorbo (2). Both these examples have 14 stopped strings and 10 unstopped strings, but theorbos were made with different numbers of strings. By introducing an extra pegbox archlute-makers avoided the use of a single very long pegbox which would have been less able to take the strain of the instrument's longer bass strings. The theorbo enjoyed considerable popularity throughout Europe for about 200 years.

Below Theorbo-lute. This was a hybrid instrument with the bent-back pegbox of the lute and the long bass strings of the theorbo.

1   Theorbo, modern reconstruction, Harwood & Isaacs, Cambridge, England
2   Theorbo, Martin Bruner, 1764 (National Museum, Prague)

Theorbo-lute, Tieffenbrucker, 1610 (Wagner Museum, Lucerne, Switzerland)

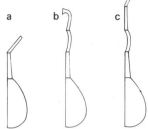

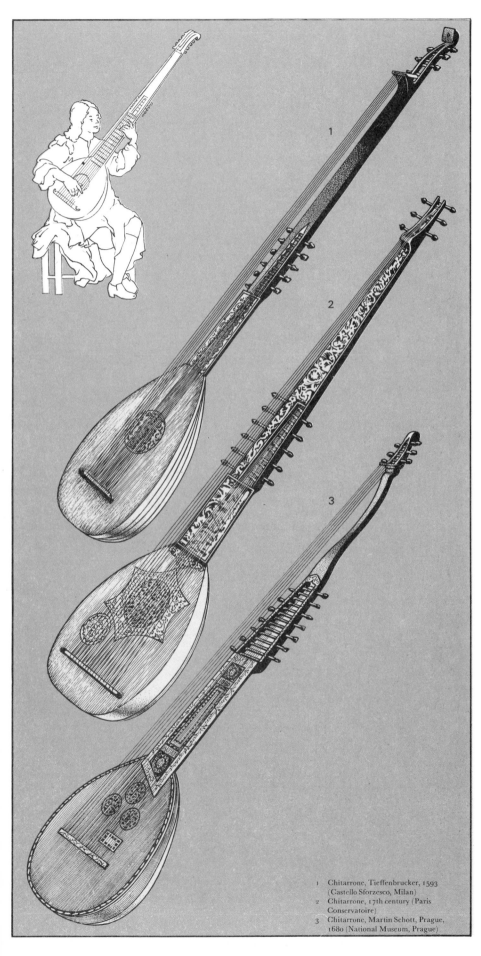

Above Diagram showing the relative proportions and pegbox positions of the renaissance lute (a), theorbo (b), and chitarrone (c).
Left Chitarrones with one, two, and three sound holes. The chitarrone, a type of archlute, is characterized by its very long neck and well-spaced pegboxes.

Below Colascione—a long-necked lute popular in Italy in the 16th and 17th centuries. It had a small, round-backed body, three strings, and a very long neck with up to 24 movable frets. The colascione is thought to have developed from the Eastern long-necked lute.

Colascione, early 17th century (Gemeentemuseum, The Hague, Netherlands)

1 Chitarrone, Tieffenbrucker, 1593 (Castello Sforzesco, Milan)
2 Chitarrone, 17th century (Paris Conservatoire)
3 Chitarrone, Martin Schott, Prague, 1680 (National Museum, Prague)

© DIAGRAM

Below Mandola made by Viventi of Verona in 1696 (Hungarian National Museum, Budapest). The mandola was a small lute with a long, sickle-shaped pegbox. Examples are common in the art of the Middle Ages. The number and tuning of the strings varied.

Right Mandolins from Naples. The mandolin originated in the 18th century and is still played today. The Neapolitan mandolin (1), the classical instrument of the 18th century, had a deeply vaulted back, fretted neck, and four pairs of strings. The mandolone (2), a bass version of the Neapolitan mandolin, had six to eight pairs of metal strings.

1 Neapolitan mandolin, Antonio Vinacci, Naples, 1774 (Carel van Leeuwen Boomkamp collection, Amsterdam)
2 Mandolone, Southern Italy, late 18th century (Carel van Leeuwen Boomkamp collection, Amsterdam)

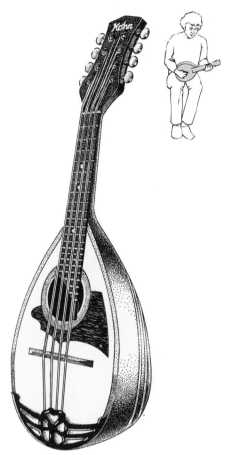

Left Mandolins from Genoa
and Milan. The Genoese
mandolin (1) had six pairs
of strings, and a wider neck
than the Neapolitan
instrument. The Milanese
mandolin (2), known in the
1700s as the pandurina,
had six pairs of strings
and was closely related
to the mandola.

Above Modern mandolin
and mandolin player. The
mandolin has always been
most popular in Italy, often
providing the melody to the
accompaniment of the
guitar. Larger sizes, known
by the names of mandora,
mandocello, and
mandobass, are sometimes
found in mandolin bands.

1 Genoese mandolin, Northern Italy,
   c. 1700 (Carel van Leeuwen
   Boomkamp collection, Amsterdam)
2 Milanese mandolin, Francesco
   Plesber, Milan, 1773 (National
   Museum, Prague)

Citterns

The cittern was a stringed instrument with a flat back and sickle-shaped pegbox developed about 1500. The neck was fretted and the wire strings, varying in number, were plucked with the fingers. Easy to play and cheap to buy, the cittern was more popular with amateurs than with serious musicians who preferred the lute. By the early 19th century the cittern had been ousted from popularity by the guitar.

Right and below 17th and 18th century citterns. The cittern with a decorative figure (1) was made for Archduke Ferdinand of the Tyrol. The cittern from the early 17th century (2) has unusual crown-shaped tuning pegs. The elegant Italian cittern (3) has an ornamental head decoration. The cittern with the complex curved outline (4) has 11 wire strings arranged in three triple courses and one double. The two Dutch citterns (5 and 6) date from the late 18th century. The bass cittern (7) has unstopped bass strings attached to a second pegbox like that on contemporary archlutes.

1　Archduke Ferdinand's cittern, Girolamo de Virchi, Italy, 1574 (Kunsthistorisches Museum, Vienna)
2　Cittern, early 17th century (Paris Conservatoire)
3　Cittern, Italy, 17th century (Ashmolean Museum, Oxford)
4　Cittern, Italy, 17th century (Carel van Leeuwen Boomkamp collection, Amsterdam)
5　Cittern, Johannes Theodorus Cuypers, The Hague, 1782 (Carel van Leeuwen Boomkamp collection, Amsterdam)
6　Cittern, Johannes Theodorus Cuypers, The Hague, 1767 (Carel van Leeuwen Boomkamp collection, Amsterdam)
7　Bass cittern, Renault and Chatelain, Paris, 1789 (Carel van Leeuwen Boomkamp collection, Amsterdam)

Right Unusual citterns.
The theorbized cittern (1)
has two pegboxes like the
theorbo. The keys of the
keyed cittern (2) operate
small hammers that strike
the strings through
perforations in the sound
hole. The lyre-shaped
cittern (3) and bell-shaped
cittern (4) date from around
1700.

1 Theorbized cittern, possibly
   Scandinavia, 17th century
   (Kunsthistorisches Museum,
   Vienna)
2 Keyed cittern, Longman and
   Broderip, England, late 18th century
   (Brussels Conservatoire)
3 Lyre cittern, c.1700 (Kunsthistorisches
   Museum, Vienna)
4 Bell cittern, Joachim Tielke,
   Hamburg, c.1700 (Victoria and
   Albert Museum, London)

Right Larger citterns. The
pandora (1) is a bass
instrument with a deeply
scalloped outline. The very
rare penorcon (2) has no
sound hole. The bass cittern
(3) is a particularly unusual
shape. The orpharion (4) is
characterized by its slanting
frets and string holder.

1 Pandora, 17th century
2 Penorcon, 17th century (Brussels
   Conservatoire)
3 Bass cittern, Germany, 16th century
4 Orpharion, F. Palmer, 1617 (Claudius
   collection, Copenhagen)

©DIAGRAM

Historical guitars

The guitar is a plucked string instrument with a flat back and characteristic waisted outline. Probably introduced to Spain by the Arabs, it was established throughout Europe by the late 14th century. During the 17th century, the guitar rose to prominence as an instrument much easier to play than the then fashionable lute. Its appeal has never waned and it remains a favorite portable accompanying instrument.

Left Gittern, or medieval guitar (British Museum, London). The gittern's body and neck were carved from a single piece of wood. A hole was pierced behind the fingerboard for the player's thumb. The strings, attached to a button at the lower end of the body, passed over a bridge.

Left Vihuela—an important plucked instrument of the Renaissance. The body of the vihuela was guitar-shaped but its strings were tuned like those of a lute. It was confined almost exclusively to Spain, where it was generally associated with the aristocracy.

Right Late 17th century guitar. Developed from the gittern, the earliest guitars had four double courses of strings tuned like the inner four courses of the lute or vihuela. Also popular throughout Europe in the 17th and 18th centuries was a guitar with five double courses of strings. During the 18th century a version with six single strings was introduced, and rapidly acquired popularity because of the simpler playing technique required.

Left Chitarra battente—an Italian form of guitar from the 17th and 18th centuries. It had a deep body and vaulted back, and both the sides and back were made up of long narrow ribs. The strings, usually arranged in five double or triple courses, were metal and played with a plectrum.

Guitar, M. Fux, Vienna, 1692 (National Museum, Prague)

Left Unusual 19th century guitars. The lyre-guitar (1) takes its name from the Greek lyre of classical art. The lyre-shaped guitar (2) has six double courses of strings attached to pegs set around three sides of the pegbox. The guitar with crosswise sympathetic strings (3) was an attempt to improve the instrument's tone. The guitar modified by Ritter (4) has a very short, wide neck and 24 strings. The cut-away soundbox of the guitar (5) made the frets more accessible. The guitar with the extended soundbox (6) was an attempt to produce extra resonance.

Below Lyre-guitar player.

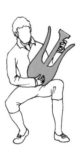

Right Walking stick guitar —one of a number of novelty instruments made in this form during the 19th century. This guitar has four strings and only a very small soundbox (National Museum, Prague).

1 Lyre-guitar, Gennaro, Naples, 1806 (Carel van Leeuwen Boomkamp collection, Amsterdam)
2 Lyre-shaped guitar, England
3 Guitar, José Porcel, Spain, 1867
4 Guitar, modified by Ritter (Horniman Museum, London)
5 Guitar with cut-away soundbox
6 Guitar with extended soundbox

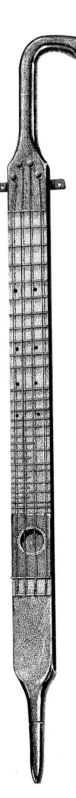

© DIAGRAM

Classical and acoustic guitars

Today the guitar enjoys tremendous popularity in many parts of the world. The non-electric guitar is a light portable instrument that lends itself well to many forms of music. It is ideal for solos and for accompanying singing or other instruments. The classical or Spanish guitar has changed little since the 16th century, but popular folk guitars are now produced in a variety of different styles.

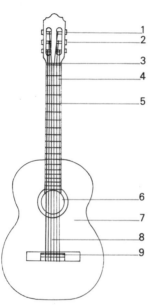

Left Identification of parts of the modern classical guitar.

Right Classical or Spanish guitar. The six strings, traditionally gut, are now often nylon. The player demonstrates the classical playing position, with the guitar held centrally in front of his body. Plucking rather than strumming the strings is the essence of classical playing technique.

1 Machine head
2 Peg
3 Nut
4 Fingerboard
5 Frets
6 Sound hole
7 Body
8 Strings
9 Bridge

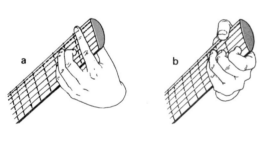

Left Fingering the sixth string. On the classical guitar (a) the player uses "barre" fingering, stopping the string with his index finger. The steel-strung guitar (b) has a narrower fingerboard with an oval cross-section, and the sixth string can be stopped from behind with the thumb.

Guitar

Tuning   Pitch range

M. de Falla   Homenage, pour le tombeau de Claude Debussy
H. Villa-Lobos   Suite popular brasileira
J. Rodrigo   Concierto de Aranjuez
J. Rodrigo   Fantasia para un Gentilhombre
H. W. Henze   Kammermusik, three Tentos

Romance for guitar (anon.)

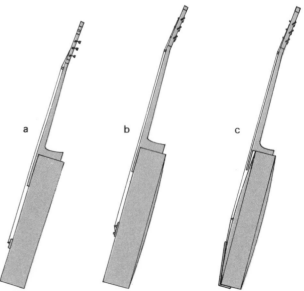

Right Different body shapes of modern guitars. The classical guitar (a) is flat both back and front. The jumbo, or dreadnought, guitar (b) has a bulging back and deeper body than other guitars. The f-hole arch-top guitar (c) bulges both back and front and has arched shoulders.

Right Steel-strung acoustic guitars. The jumbo guitar (1) is a large folk model. This example has the less common very curved outline. The 12-string guitar (2) has a body shape more typical of modern folk guitars. The 12 strings are tuned in six pairs. The dobro (3) has a circular metal resonator on the belly and an internal tone chamber. Popular among early blues singers, the dobro is often played with a "bottleneck" —a tube fitted over a finger on the stopping hand. The f-hole guitar (4) was developed as an alternative to the banjo. It appears as a rhythm instrument in some jazz bands.

Above Player demonstrating a popular playing position for the folk guitar—with the instrument held to the side of the body.

Right Guitar heads. On the traditional guitar (1) the strings are tied to tuning pegs. On most modern guitars (2 and 3) the strings are threaded through machine heads, which fit into the head of the guitar. The string tension is changed by cogs when the tuning pegs are adjusted.

Right Bridges. On the classical guitar (a) the strings are threaded through holes in the bridge and tied. On the modern guitar (b) the strings end in rings that are inserted in holes in the bridge and secured with pins. On type (c) the strings thread through the tailpiece and the bridge is movable.

Right Diagram giving the location of position markers on the guitar neck.
Below Two types of capo tasto—a device fastened to the neck of the guitar to change the vibrating length of the strings. It allows a player to use the same fingering to produce chords in different keys.

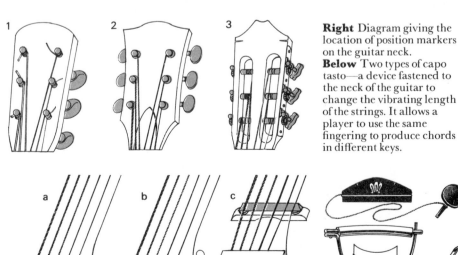

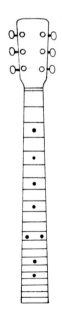

© DIAGRAM

Ukuleles and banjos

The ukulele and banjo are plucked string instruments popular in the jazz bands, music halls, and minstrel shows of the United States and Britain. The ukulele is a small guitar developed in Hawaii in the 19th century from the Portuguese machete. The banjo has its origins in the long-necked lutes brought to America by slaves. Both ukulele and banjo have given rise to a variety of hybrids.

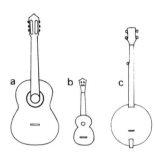

Left Diagram showing the different shapes and sizes of the guitar (a), ukulele (b), and banjo (c). The ukulele resembles the guitar in outline but is very much smaller. The banjo is closer in size to the guitar but has a relatively long neck, a large round belly, and no soundhole.

Right The ukulele (1) has an all wood belly and four gut strings. The banjolele (2) is a small banjo strung like a ukulele. Another hybrid instrument is the flat-backed "mandolin" (3). This has the outline and stringing of the classical mandolin and the flat back of the guitar family.

Left The mandolinetto—a hybrid instrument from the early 20th century. It is essentially a ukulele strung like a mandolin.

Left Guitar-banjo—an unusual modern hybrid from China. The circular section set into the guitar-like body is made of snakeskin and resonates in a similar way to the parchment on the banjo. The guitar-banjo has only three strings.

1 Ukulele
2 Banjolele
3 Flat-backed "mandolin"

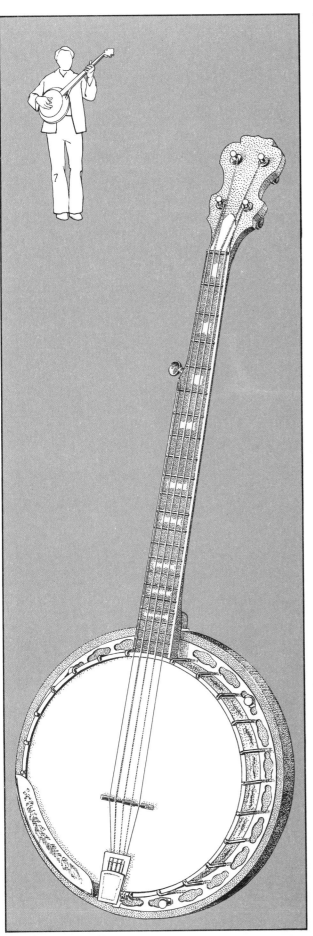

Left Modern "finger style" banjo. The tambourine-like body consists of a circular frame with a parchment belly. The underside is usually left open, but some instruments have detachable resonators. The shorter "thumb string" is used to play the melody, and the other four strings to give a simple accompaniment.

Right Identification of parts of a finger-style banjo.

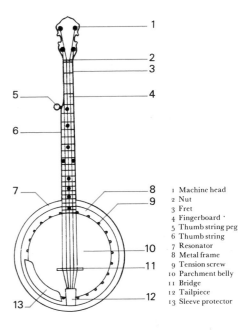

1	Machine head
2	Nut
3	Fret
4	Fingerboard
5	Thumb string peg
6	Thumb string
7	Resonator
8	Metal frame
9	Tension screw
10	Parchment belly
11	Bridge
12	Tailpiece
13	Sleeve protector

Right Different playing styles for the banjo—strumming (a) and plucking, or "finger picking" (b). Some players use a single plectrum of metal, plastic, or even felt. Others wear plectra on the thumb and the first and second fingers.

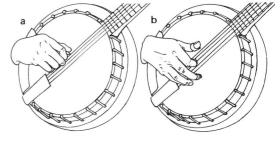

Below Three popular sizes of banjo—tenor (a), long-necked (b), and bass (c). These banjos are plectrum style banjos—with four strings. The tenor banjo, popular as a solo instrument and in jazz bands, is tuned like a violin. The bass is little used except in banjo bands.

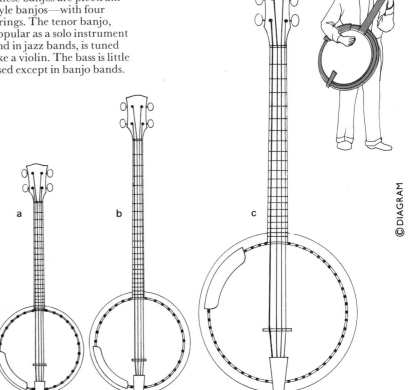

©DIAGRAM

Viols

The viol preceded the violin and was contemporary with it during the 16th century. Although superficially similar to the violin the viol has major distinguishing features, notably its fretted neck characteristic of the renaissance lute. The viol's tone is soft and delicate, and is more suitable for domestic and chamber music than for the concert hall. The viol was superseded by the violin by 1700.

Left Viol player from a 12th century illuminated manuscript.

Below Viol bow and hand position. The viol bow is broader than the modern violin bow. The bow is held with the hand palm outward.

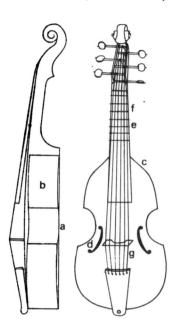

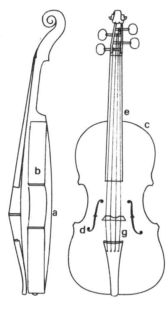

Above Diagram showing differences between the viol and violin. The back (a) of the viol is flat whereas the back of the violin bulges. The ribs (b) of the viol are deeper, the shoulders (c) slope, the soundholes (d) are usually C- rather than F-shaped, the neck (e) is broader, and the fingerboard is fretted (f) with pieces of gut tied round at intervals. The viol has six thin strings (g), whereas the violin has four thicker ones.

Below Diagram showing the different bridge shapes of the viol and the violin. The viol bridge (front) is flatter and less arched than that of the violin. This flatter shape allows the hair of the bow to touch more strings at a stroke, and so makes it easier to play full chords on the viol.

Right The treble and alto viols. The treble viol (1) was the smallest of the regularly used viols. It usually played the upper part in consort music. The alto (2), only slightly larger than the treble, was less common. Both treble and alto viols were held upright on the player's knee.

1 Treble viol, Henry Jay, England, 16th century
2 Alto viol, J. Strong, England, 16th century

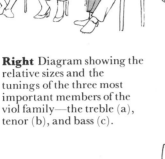

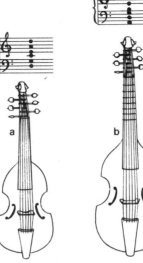

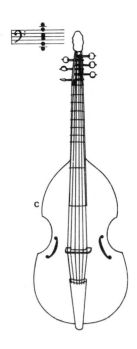

Above Group of 20th century viol players, a sign of the modern revival of interest in this instrument. A consort of viols usually includes two trebles, two tenors, a bass, and a double bass (called a violone). The quiet tone of the viol combines well with recorders and the voice.

Right Diagram showing the relative sizes and the tunings of the three most important members of the viol family—the treble (a), tenor (b), and bass (c).

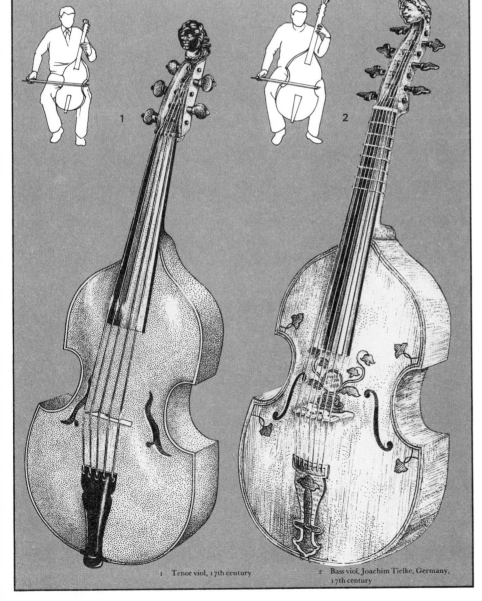

1 Tenor viol, 17th century

2 Bass viol, Joachim Tielke, Germany, 17th century

Left Tenor viol (1) and bass viol (2). These larger viols were in regular use before the smaller versions. The bass viol, the most popular size, was used both as a consort and a solo instrument. It is often referred to as the viola da gamba, although strictly this name applies to all viols.

Below Lyra viol, or viola bastarda. Between the tenor and bass viols in size, this instrument was tuned like the lira da braccio. It sometimes played the second treble part in a consort. Its music was written in tablature rather than notation to facilitate the playing of chords.

©DIAGRAM

Right Viola d'amore (1), violetta (2), and baryton (3). The viola d'amore was one of the most popular instruments in the 18th century. It has sympathetic strings and no frets, and is held like a violin. The name "amore" (love) comes possibly from its romantic tone but more likely from its characteristic cupid decorative device. The violetta is an alto viola d'amore with two sets of sympathetic strings. The baryton (3) is a bass viol with six bowed strings and up to 40 sympathetic strings. Some of the sympathetic strings can be plucked from behind by the left thumb.

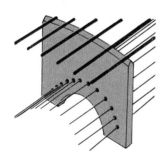

Above Bridge for an instrument with sympathetic strings. The bowed strings, usually made of gut, are supported on the bridge in the usual way. The sympathetic strings, usually made of wire, pass through a series of holes in the bridge. When the bowed strings are sounded, the strings passing through the bridge vibrate in sympathy. Sympathetic strings are a characteristic feature of several instruments in the viol family.

1 Viola d'amore, T. A. Hulinzký, Czechoslovakia, 1769 (National Museum, Prague)
2 Violetta, J. U. Eberle, Czechoslovakia, 1727 (National Museum, Prague)
3 Baryton, Jacques Sainprae, Germany, c. 1720

1 Tromba marina, 17th century
2 Bumbass, Germany, 17th century

Left Tromba marina (1) and bumbass (2). The tromba marina was a large bowed instrument with one string, from which different notes of the harmonic series were produced by lightly touching the string with the left hand. The bumbass was either bowed with a notched stick or plucked.

Below A quinton—a type of five-stringed viol played in the late 18th century.

Folk fiddles

Fiddles are classified as bowed lutes. Folk fiddles of many shapes and sizes are particularly popular in Africa, Asia, and Europe. There are two basic forms—spike fiddles, with long necks, and short-necked fiddles. Spike fiddles are common in the Middle East, Asia, and North Africa but are rarely found elsewhere. Short-necked folk fiddles are commonest in Europe.

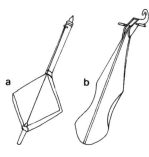

Left Basic fiddle forms—the spike fiddle (a) and the short-necked fiddle (b). The neck of the spike fiddle pierces the body and projects as a spike at the base. The neck and body of the short-necked fiddle are usually made from the same material, often from a single piece of wood.

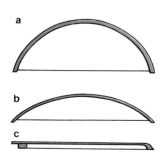

Left Playing positions. The spike fiddle (a) is held vertically, with the spike resting on the player's knee or on the floor. The short-necked fiddle (b) is usually held more or less horizontally, and rested against the player's chest, shoulder, or neck.

Left Three basic types of bow used with folk fiddles—very curved (a), less curved (b), and a straight bow (c) similar to the modern violin bow.

Right Folk fiddles from Africa. The one-stringed fiddles from Mali (1), Ethiopia (2), and Southwest Africa (3) are more versatile than their primitive appearance would suggest. The South African folk fiddles illustrate man's ingenuity in making use of modern materials—a belly made of heavy card (4) and a tin can body (5). The North African rebab (6) is an attractively shaped short-necked fiddle with two strings.

Left Musician from Mali playing a one-stringed fiddle.

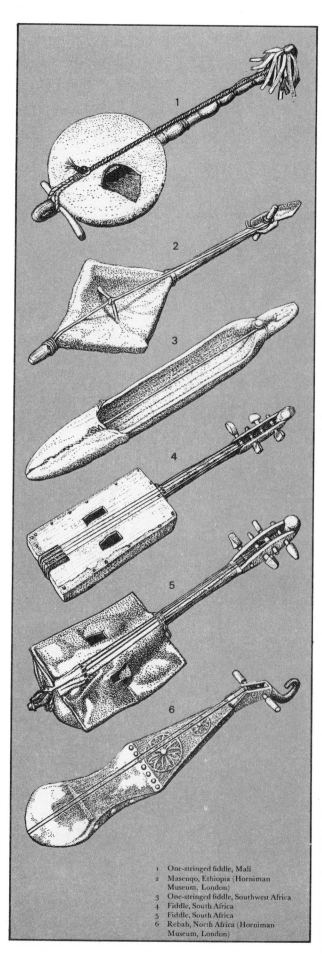

1 One-stringed fiddle, Mali
2 Masenqo, Ethiopia (Horniman Museum, London)
3 One-stringed fiddle, Southwest Africa
4 Fiddle, South Africa
5 Fiddle, South Africa
6 Rebab, North Africa (Horniman Museum, London)

Right American fiddles. The Apache fiddle (1 and 2) is an unusual instrument never very widespread even among these Indians. The highly decorated example has a body made from hollowed out cactus. The Cuban (3) and South American (4) fiddles have hollowed cane bodies.
Below Apache fiddle player.

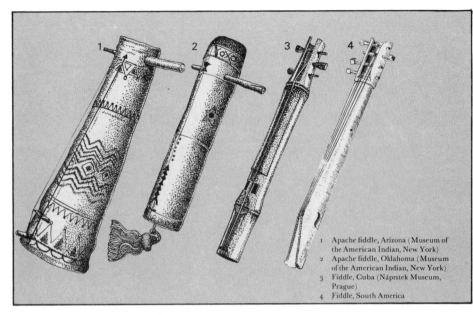

1 Apache fiddle, Arizona (Museum of the American Indian, New York)
2 Apache fiddle, Oklahoma (Museum of the American Indian, New York)
3 Fiddle, Cuba (Náprstek Museum, Prague)
4 Fiddle, South America

Right Spike fiddles from the Middle East. Thought to have originated in Persia, the spike fiddle is today found in a variety of forms throughout the Middle East. The Persian examples (1 and 2) and the Turkish spike fiddle (3) are more sophisticated three-stringed instruments. The more primitive one-stringed examples shown here are from Iraq (4) and Syria (5).

Below Turkish musician playing a spike fiddle.

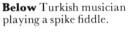

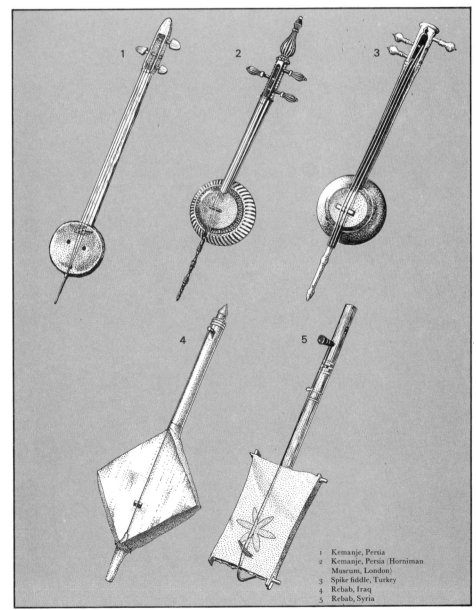

1 Kemanje, Persia
2 Kemanje, Persia (Horniman Museum, London)
3 Spike fiddle, Turkey
4 Rebab, Iraq
5 Rebab, Syria

©DIAGRAM

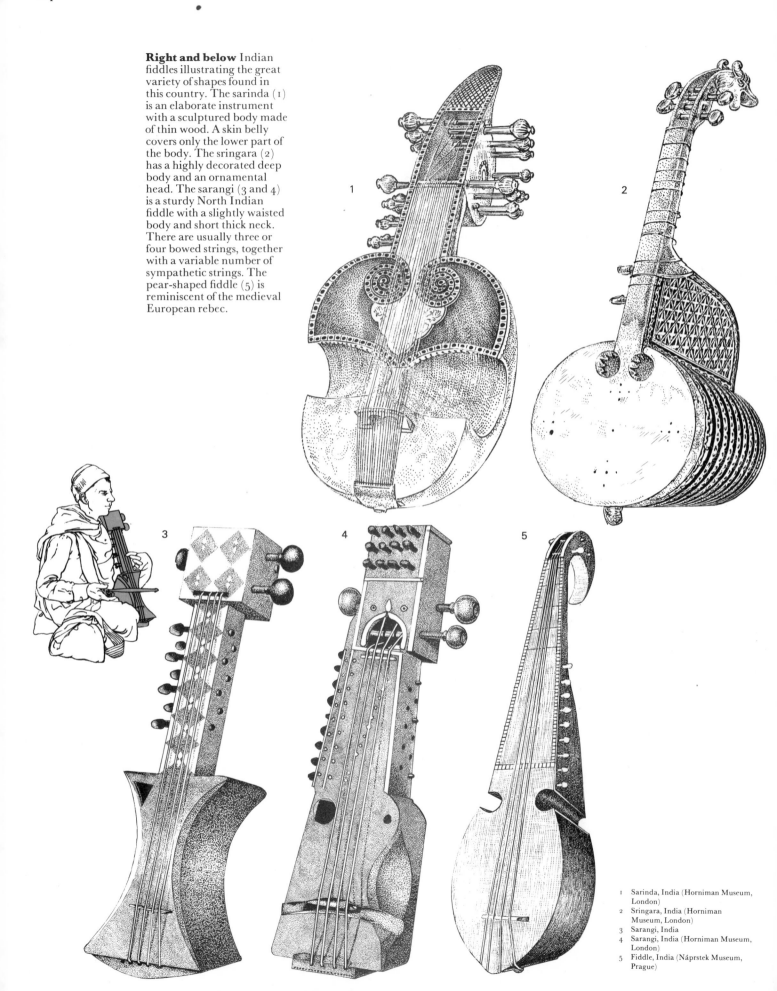

Right and below Indian
fiddles illustrating the great
variety of shapes found in
this country. The sarinda (1)
is an elaborate instrument
with a sculptured body made
of thin wood. A skin belly
covers only the lower part of
the body. The sringara (2)
has a highly decorated deep
body and an ornamental
head. The sarangi (3 and 4)
is a sturdy North Indian
fiddle with a slightly waisted
body and short thick neck.
There are usually three or
four bowed strings, together
with a variable number of
sympathetic strings. The
pear-shaped fiddle (5) is
reminiscent of the medieval
European rebec.

1   Sarinda, India (Horniman Museum,
    London)
2   Sringara, India (Horniman
    Museum, London)
3   Sarangi, India
4   Sarangi, India (Horniman Museum,
    London)
5   Fiddle, India (Náprstek Museum,
    Prague)

Right Asian fiddles. The primitive fiddles (1 and 2) were made by the Gond peoples of Central India. The square-bodied morin-chur (3) from Mongolia is decorated with an ornamental horse's head. The Japanese ko-kiu (4) is a bowed instrument similar in shape to the plucked samisen. The saw-thai from Thailand (5) and the Javanese fiddle (6) are typical spike fiddles with shallow oval bodies. The Cambodian tro-u (7) and the Chinese erh-hu (8) and hu-ch'in (9) each have a bow threaded between the strings.

Below Mongolian street musician with a morin-chur.

1 Primitive fiddle, India (British Museum, London)
2 Primitive fiddle, India (British Museum, London)
3 Morin-chur, Mongolia (National Museum, Prague)
4 Ko-kiu, Japan
5 Saw-thai, Thailand
6 Spike fiddle, Java
7 Tro-u, Cambodia (Phnom Penh Museum)
8 Erh-hu, China (Horniman Museum, London)
9 Hu ch'in, China

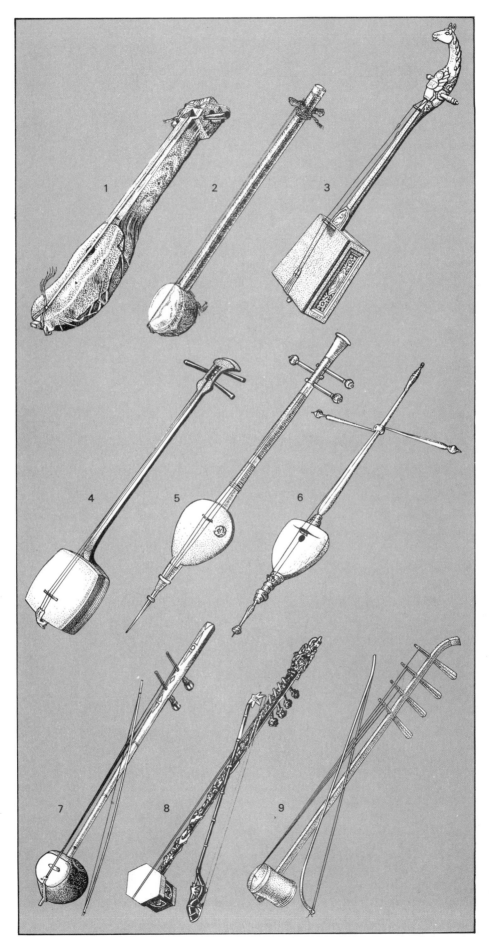

© DIAGRAM

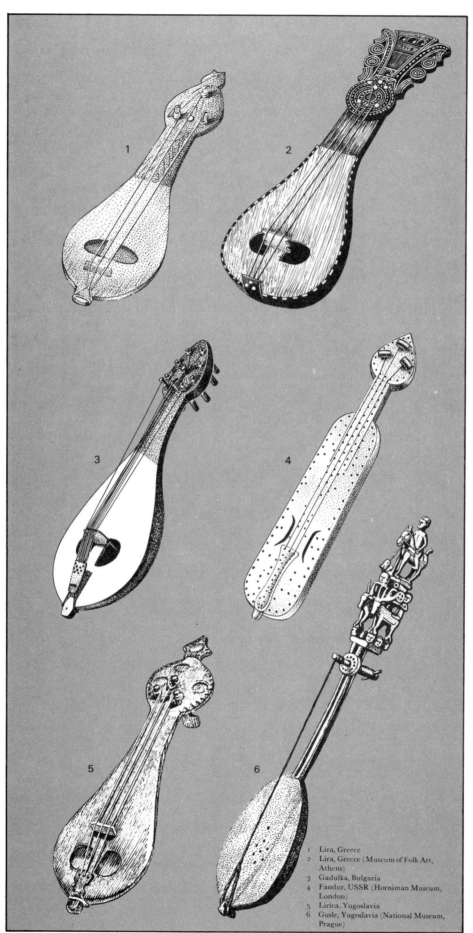

Left Eastern European folk fiddles. The Greek liras (1 and 2) and the Yugoslavian lirica (5) have small pear-shaped bodies, wide necks, and three strings. The Bulgarian gadulka (3) is similar in shape to the lira. The instrument illustrated has both bowed and sympathetic strings, and a bridge with one foot that extends to the back of the instrument to act as a soundpost. The Caucasian fandur (4) has an unusual bottle-shaped body. The Yugoslavian gusle (6) has an ornately carved head, a skin-covered belly, and a single string made of twisted horsehair.

1 Lira, Greece
2 Lira, Greece (Museum of Folk Art, Athens)
3 Gadulka, Bulgaria
4 Fandur, USSR (Horniman Museum, London)
5 Lirica, Yugoslavia
6 Gusle, Yugoslavia (National Museum, Prague)

Above Bulgarian gadulka player. These small fiddles are usually held vertically and rested on the knee.

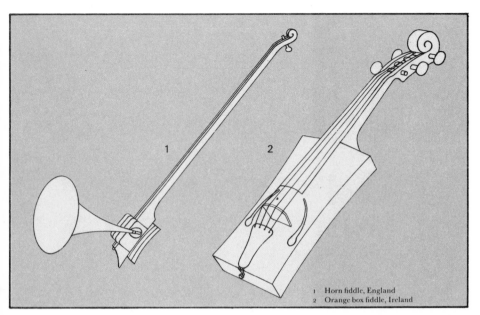

1 Horn fiddle, England
2 Orange box fiddle, Ireland

Left Unusual folk fiddles. The horn fiddle (1), a novelty instrument from the North of England, enjoyed some popularity in the early 20th century. It has a single string and a horn to amplify the sound. The square fiddle from Ireland (2) is a home-made instrument made from an orange box.

1 Fiddle, Poland (Museum of Folk Culture and Art, Warsaw)
2 Guitar-violin
3 Hardangerfele, Norway

Left More sophisticated folk|fiddles adapted from the violin proper. The folk fiddle from Poland (1) has a slim boat-shaped body. The guitar-violin (2) is an interesting hybrid. The Norwegian hardangerfele (3) has a decorated body and neck, and four bowed and four sympathetic strings.

Above Hardangerfele player. The instrument is held in the same way as the violin.

© DIAGRAM

Early fiddles

The bowed instruments of the Middle Ages and the Renaissance were the predecessors of the modern violin. The two main types of medieval bowed instruments, the fiddle and the rebec, were used by troubadours to accompany singing and dancing. The lira da braccio evolved from the fiddle in the late 1400s. It had many features in common with the modern violin, including its waisted profile and regular sound holes.

a   b

Left A selection of medieval fiddles drawn from art of the 12th to 14th centuries. Fiddles appear to have been made in many different shapes and sizes and usually had from three to five strings of which one was a drone. Their many names include vielle, fidel, and fithele.

Above Players of the fiddle (a) and rebec (b). Contemporary sources show a wide variety of playing positions. Most commonly, the instruments were held against the left shoulder or the chest, but occasionally they were held under the chin or upright on the lap.

Right The bow of the early fiddle (a) consisted simply of a pliant stick held taut by horsehair. It was broader and usually shorter than the modern bow (b). The medieval fiddle player sometimes used his thumb to press the hair away from the bow to keep it taut.

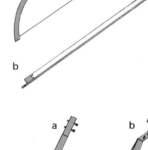

a

b

Right Diagram showing the major differences between instruments of the fiddle type (a) and the rebec type (b). The medieval fiddle had a flat back and a peg disk with front or rear tuning pegs. The rebec had a rounded back and lateral tuning pegs.

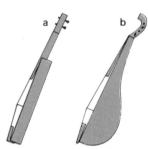

a   b

Below Modern reconstruction of a rebec (Dolmetsch). The rebec, evolved from the Arab rebab, was known in Europe from the 13th century. It had a small pear-shaped body with a rounded back made from a single piece of wood. The neck was short and many examples have a decorative sound hole.

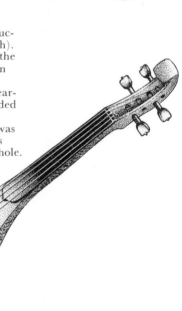

Right Players of the lira da braccio (a) and the lira da gamba (b). The lira da braccio was usually held against the left shoulder. The larger lira da gamba was usually held between the player's knees.

Right Lira da braccio and lira da gamba. The lira da braccio (1), a development of the medieval fiddle, was an important predecessor of the violin. It was characterized by its gently waisted profile and wide fingerboard. It had five fingerboard strings and two off-board drones. The sound holes were C-shaped and later F-shaped. The lira da gamba (2), or lirone, was a bass version of the lira da braccio. It had from nine to 15 fingerboard strings and two off-board drones. In addition to the usual sound holes there was often a central decorative rose.

Below Drawing showing the string arrangement of the lira da braccio. The two drone strings, lying off the fingerboard, were usually tuned one octave apart. Because the fingerboard was wide, the left thumb was probably used to stop the lowest of the fingerboard strings.

1 Lira da braccio, J. Andrea, Verona, 1511 (Kunsthistorisches Museum, Vienna)
2 Lira da gamba, Italy, 17th century (Instrument Museum, Brussels)

© DIAGRAM

Violins

The violin is probably the best known of all Western orchestral instruments. It is the smallest member of the family of bowed stringed instruments that includes the viola, violoncello, and double bass. The violin emerged around 1550 from the medieval fiddle, the rebec, and the lira da braccio, though details of the transition are confused. The early violin proper, however, had four strings, lateral pegs, a waisted body, and f-shaped sound holes—a form that has changed little in 400 years. Violin making began in 16th century Italy and later flourished under makers such as Stradivari and Guarneri. During the 18th century, violinist-composers such as Vivaldi and Tartini expanded the scope of the playing technique, and the perfecting of the bow in the 19th century further increased the possibilities of this most versatile instrument.

Right Violin bows. The bow pioneered by Corelli around 1700 was short and inelastic (a). Tartini's bow of 50 years later was longer and more flexible (b). The Tourte bow, developed in the 19th century and still used today, has an inward-curving stick designed for good balance (c).

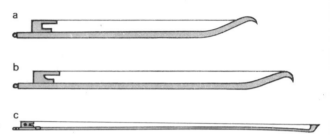

Right Diagram showing the parts of a modern violin and bow.

1 Scroll
2 Peg box
3 Pegs
4 Fingerboard
5 Strings
6 Soundboard
7 Bridge
8 Sound hole
9 E-string tuner
10 Tailpiece
11 Chin rest
12 Button
13 Point
14 Stick
15 Hair
16 Nut
17 Screw

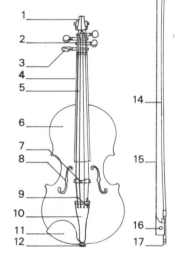

Right Interior of a violin. The soundpost (a), set under the right foot of the bridge, transmits vibrations to the back of the violin. The bass bar (b), glued to the back of the belly; stiffens the body and distributes the vibrations. Without these devices, resonance is reduced and the tone muffled.

Left The Greffuhle violin. Made in 1709, it is a fine example of the craftsmanship of Antonio Stradivari. The ribs and scroll are decorated with delicate inlay work.

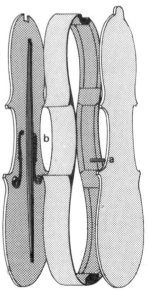

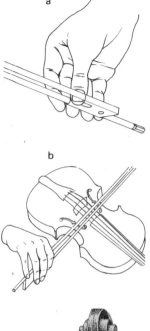

a

b

Left Holding the bow (a) and bowing position (b). The thumb, slightly bent, is inserted between the stick and the hair, close to the nut and opposite the first and second fingers. Different effects can be achieved by varying the method of bowing. The commonest method consists of smooth downstrokes and up-strokes, in which the bow is drawn across the string from nut to point and back again. Other bowing methods include staccato or detached strokes, "hammered" strokes where each stroke is released forcefully, and "jeté" strokes where the bow is allowed to bounce across the strings.

Right Pizzicato action. Sometimes the player is required to pluck the strings between the thumb and forefinger of the right hand, so producing a guitar-like effect. Paganini, the 19th century violinist and composer, introduced the virtuoso technique of plucking the strings with the left hand.

Right Violin mute—used for softening the tone. The mute is a comb-like device with three prongs. Clamped over the bridge, it limits the vibrations of the strings and produces a quiet nasal tone.

Left Modern violin. The demand in the 18th and 19th centuries for a fuller, more brilliant tone led to improvements which have been retained to the present day. These include strings that are thinner and at greater tension, and a higher, more curved bridge that facilitates clean bowing.

Right A comparison of the size of the violin (a) with the larger members of its family—the viola (b), the violoncello (c), and the double bass (d).

a   b   c   d

Violin

Tuning

Pitch range

J. S. Bach	Six solo partitas
A. Vivaldi	Violin concertos
W. A. Mozart	Eine kleine Nachtmusik K.525
J. Brahms	Sonata in G major op. 78
M. Bruch	Concerto in G minor
P. Tchaikovsky	Concerto in D major
A. Berg	Violin concerto

Mendelssohn   Violin concerto, 3rd movement

Orchestral position

The viola is the alto member of the bowed string family and much of its history is shared with the violin. Structurally identical to the violin, though slightly larger, the viola was long overshadowed by the greater technical convenience of the smaller instrument. From the late 1700s composers began to exploit the viola's characteristically mellow tone color, and gave it at last some of the importance it deserves.

Left 18th century viola player. Until the late 1700s the viola enjoyed little importance in the orchestra or chamber group. The later string quartets of Haydn and Mozart are the first pieces in which the viola had an interesting, and often difficult, part to play.

Left Comparative sizes of the viola and violin. The approximate body length of the viola is 17in—about 3in longer than the violin. In relation to the violin, the viola is proportionately small for its pitch—in theory it should be half as long again as the violin.

Right Unusual violas. The viola in the shape of an early fiddle (1) has sloping shoulders reminiscent of the viol. It dates from the 18th century and is probably French. The guitar-shaped viola (2), based on a type devised by Chanot, was made in Paris around 1825.

Left Modern viola. The size of the viola varies from 16–18in; a larger body gives a fuller tone but is more unwieldy in playing. This century has seen the first virtuoso viola players—such as Lionel Tertis and William Primrose—who have done much to increase the instrument's importance.

Viola

Tuning

Pitch range

W. A. Mozart	Sinfonia concertante for violin, viola, and orchestra K. 364
J. Haydn	String quartets
H. Berlioz	Harold in Italy
M. Glinka	Sonata in D minor for viola and piano
R. Strauss	Don Quixote
J. Françaix	Rhapsodie
Hindemith	Concerto for viola and orchestra, 1st movement

Schnelle Halbe

ff

sempre staccato

Orchestral position

Violoncellos

The violoncello, popularly called the cello, is the bass member of the violin family. It is played with a bow shorter and thicker than that of the violin, and is fitted with a retractable spike for resting on the floor. Developed in the 1500s, the cello existed for almost 150 years alongside the tenor viola da gamba whose popularity was slow to fade. From the 1700s the cello became a favorite solo instrument.

Left 18th century continuo player. The baroque cellist was important in both the orchestra and the chamber group. He provided, in conjunction with an organ or harpsichord, a bass line to act as a firm foundation for the instrumental harmonies. This technique was called continuo playing.

Right Comparison of piccolo and full size cellos. The piccolo was a small 18th century version of the standard cello. Intended for solo use, it was tuned like the standard cello although occasionally an extra treble string was added. It appears in some of the cantatas of J. S. Bach.

Left Modern cello. Despite its comparatively large size the cello is one of the most versatile and expressive of all instruments. Good resonance is assured by its large body which is proportionately deeper than that of the violin. It is equally effective in both solo and accompanying passages.

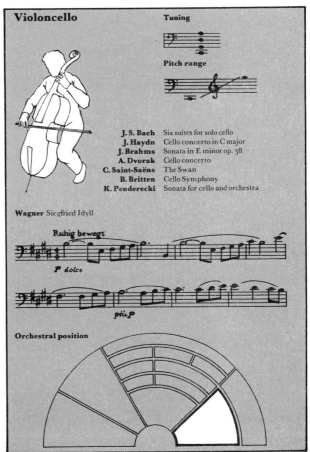

Violoncello

Tuning

Pitch range

J. S. Bach	Six suites for solo cello
J. Haydn	Cello concerto in C major
J. Brahms	Sonata in E minor op. 38
A. Dvorak	Cello concerto
C. Saint-Saëns	The Swan
B. Britten	Cello Symphony
K. Penderecki	Sonata for cello and orchestra

Wagner Siegfried Idyll

Ruhig bewegt

P dolce

più P

Orchestral position

©DIAGRAM

Double basses

The double bass, the deepest member of the violin family, was developed in the 1500s from the violone, the double bass viol. Experiments with body size and number of strings were made in an attempt to simplify the playing technique. Two important types of bow are now in use—the French bow, held "overhand" like the violin bow, and the Simandl bow, named after its inventor, which is held like the viol bow with the palm up.

Left 18th century double bass player. The size of the instrument meant that the player had to stand up in order to reach it comfortably. Most modern players sit on the edge of a stool to play.

Right Two common double bass designs. The instrument with sloping shoulders (a), based on the shape of the earlier viola da gamba, is a typical German design of the 18th century. The violin-shaped design (b) was favored by Italian makers. Instruments of both designs are still played today.

Left Modern double bass. The average double bass played in orchestras and bands is just over 6ft high. Most instruments have four strings, though the range may be extended down by a "C-string attachment"—a device allowing the bass string to be lengthened and stopped mechanically.

a

b

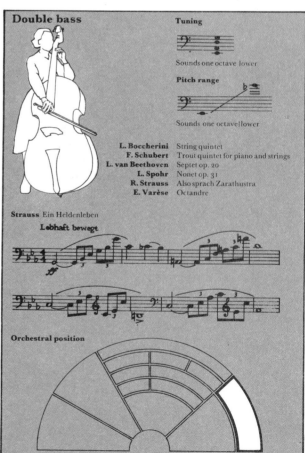

Double bass

Tuning

Sounds one octave lower

Pitch range

Sounds one octave lower

L. Boccherini	String quintet
F. Schubert	Trout quintet for piano and strings
L. van Beethoven	Septet op. 20
L. Spohr	Nonet op. 31
R. Strauss	Also sprach Zarathustra
E. Varèse	Octandre

Strauss Ein Heldenleben

Lebhaft bewegt

Orchestral position

Kits

The kit is a type of very small violin, developed in the 16th century from the rebec. Played throughout Western Europe, it was called sordine in Italy and pochette in France. It remained popular for 200 years especially with dancing masters who could carry the tiny instrument around in a pocket and use it to provide music for lessons. Another less common portable instrument was the walking stick violin.

Left 18th century kit player. The kit was small enough to be kept in the pocket of a man's coat.

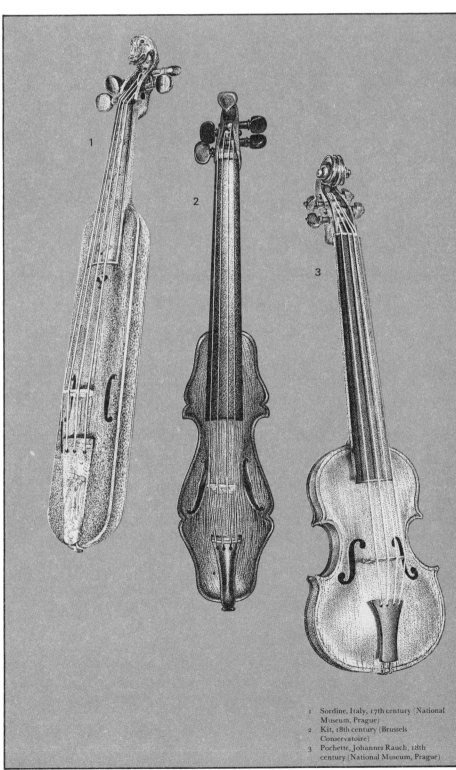

1 Sordine, Italy, 17th century (National Museum, Prague)
2 Kit, 18th century (Brussels Conservatoire)
3 Pochette, Johannes Rauch, 18th century (National Museum, Prague)

Left Examples of the great variety of forms taken by the kit. The 17th century Italian sordine (1) has a common boat-shaped body. The 18th century kit (2) has an elegant curved profile. The 18th century pochette (3) resembles a very small violin with an elongated fingerboard.

Right 19th century walking stick violin (National Museum, Prague). Portable like the kit, the walking stick violin was no more than a novelty instrument. The shaped handle served as a chin rest in playing.

Above Walking stick violin player.

© DIAGRAM

Simple zithers

Zithers are a group of instruments with strings
that run the entire length of the body and parallel
to it. Usually the whole body acts as a resonator
but sometimes a supplementary resonator is
added. There are a great variety of forms, of
which the simplest are ground, trough, tube, raft,
and simple stick zithers. Simple zithers are
commonest in Africa and are most often used as
accompanying instruments.

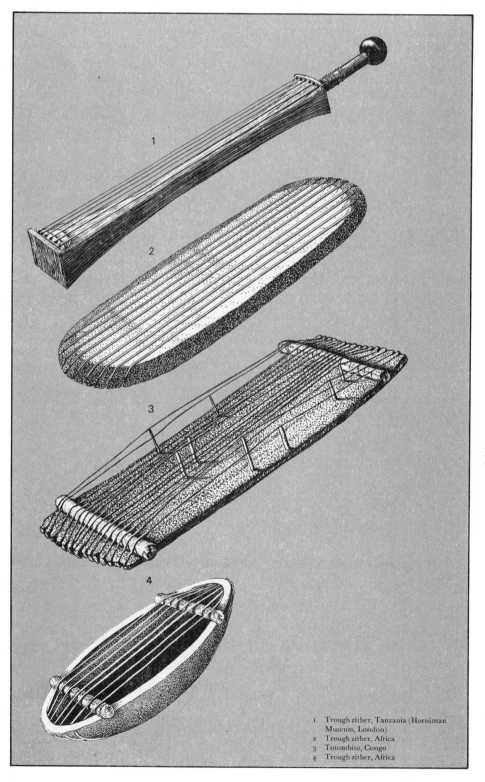

Above Ground zither. This
simple instrument consists of
a string stretched between
posts set in the ground. It is
positioned over a bark-
covered pit that acts as a
resonator, and the strings
are beaten rather than
plucked. Ground zithers are
found in Africa and Southeast Asia.

Left Trough zithers from
Africa. These instruments
usually consist of a hollowed-
out piece of wood with a
single length of string laced
back and forward over the
trough. The Congolese
totombito (3) has individual
bridges to raise the strings
farther from the board.
Below Trough zither player
from Africa.

1 Trough zither, Tanzania (Horniman
  Museum, London)
2 Trough zither, Africa
3 Totombito, Congo
4 Trough zither, Africa

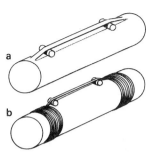

Above Types of tube zither. Idiochord zithers (a) have "strings" cut from the tube and raised over small bridges. Heterochord zithers (b) have separate strings attached to the tube.

Right Idiochord tube zithers from Oceania and Yugoslavia. The one-stringed example from New Britain (1) and the zither from New Guinea (2) are both plucked. The zithers from Yugoslavia (3 and 4) are usually played with a short cane bow similar to the instrument itself.

Right Valihas—tube zithers from Malagasy. Although some examples are idio-chords, heterochord valihas are most common. They are made in a great variety of sizes, and are often decorated. Many have a slit-shaped sound hole cut from the cane tube.
Below A valiha player.

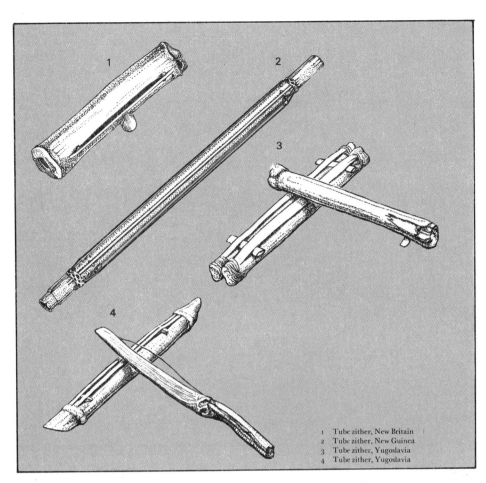

1 Tube zither, New Britain
2 Tube zither, New Guinea
3 Tube zither, Yugoslavia
4 Tube zither, Yugoslavia

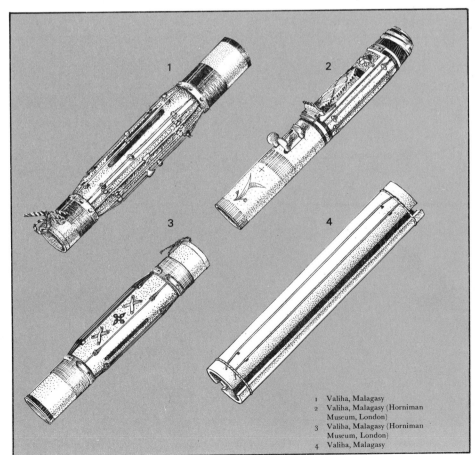

1 Valiha, Malagasy
2 Valiha, Malagasy (Horniman Museum, London)
3 Valiha, Malagasy (Horniman Museum, London)
4 Valiha, Malagasy

©DIAGRAM

218

Right Raft zithers. These popular instruments consist of several idiochord tube zithers bound together in a raft. The East African example (1) has rattling nutshells enclosed in its tubes for extra effect. The Nigerian instrument (2) has a gourd resonator attached to its underside.

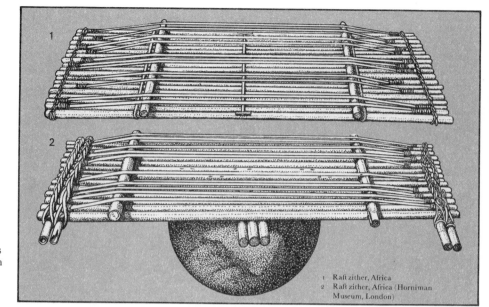

1　Raft zither, Africa
2　Raft zither, Africa (Horniman Museum, London)

Right Simple stick zithers and a harp zither. The Ugandan enzenze (1) and the Congolese instrument (2) are simple stick zithers. Each of them has frets and a single gourd resonator. The mvet (3) is a harp zither from Cameroon. Its strings, made from raffia, run over a tall, vertical bridge.

Below Musician from Cameroon playing a harp zither.

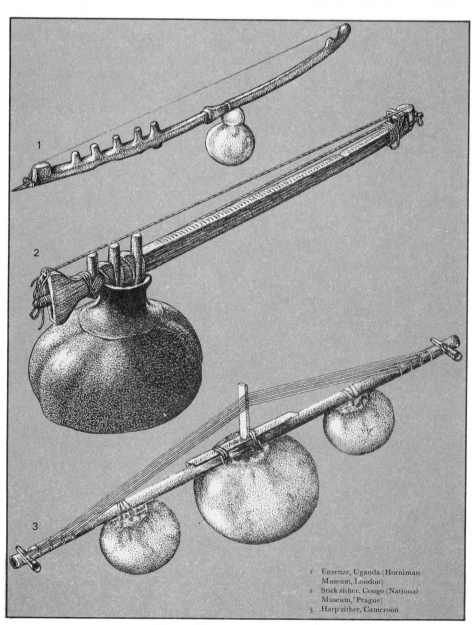

1　Enzenze, Uganda (Horniman Museum, London)
2　Stick zither, Congo (National Museum, Prague)
3　Harp zither, Cameroon

Vinas

The vina, one of the most important of India's
stringed instruments, is a sophisticated type of
stick zither. One form of the instrument, found
throughout India, consists of a stick fingerboard
and two gourd resonators. In the other important
form, popular in Southern India, the stick fingerboard is replaced by a wide neck and one of the
gourds by a wood body. Many examples are
beautifully decorated.

Above Different playing
positions for the vina. Sometimes the instrument is rested
on the floor in front of the
player (a). Other players
prefer to support the instrument with the body (b).

1 Bicitrabin, North India
2 Bin, North India

Left North Indian vinas.
The bicitrabin (1) consists
of a hollow tube and two
gourd resonators. The tube
forms the fingerboard and
is unfretted. The strings are
stopped with a crystal
plectrum. The bin (2) is
similar to the bicitrabin
but has as many as 24 high
frets.

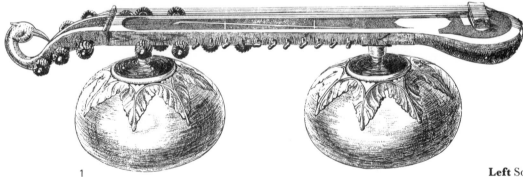

1

Left South Indian vinas.
Both these examples have
wider necks than the bin or
bicitrabin. The vina with
two gourd resonators (1) is
unfretted and has only a
rudimentary body. The
fretted vina (2) represents
the more developed form
with a wood body in place of
a second gourd resonator.

2

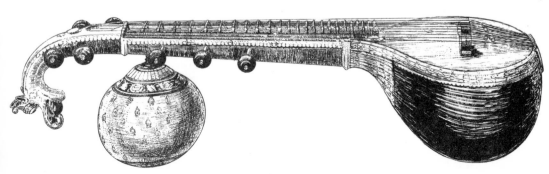

Long zithers

An important group of Far Eastern stringed instruments can conveniently be classified as long zithers. Most of them have long board resonators with a slightly arched surface, but others have long tube resonators. The Chinese ch'in has no bridges, but most long zithers have bridges that are movable. Long zithers are played by plucking, either with the fingertips and thumb or with plectra.

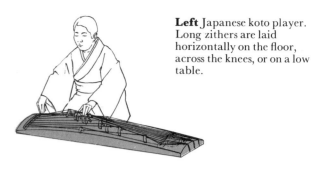

Left Japanese koto player. Long zithers are laid horizontally on the floor, across the knees, or on a low table.

Left Plectra for playing the Japanese koto. The player uses three long ivory plectra —on the thumb and the index and middle fingers of the right hand. The Burmese migyaun and the Thai chakay are usually played with a single plectrum made of ivory, metal, or tortoise-shell.

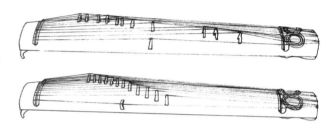

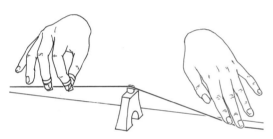

Left Playing technique for long zithers with movable bridges. The player uses his left hand to alter the pitch slightly by pressing on the string behind the bridge while plucking it with his right hand. (On the unfretted ch'in the left hand is used to stop the strings and to produce harmonics.)

Above Movable bridges in different positions on a long zither. The player uses movable wood bridges to change the vibrating length and so alter the pitch of strings. This is important since much Eastern music is based on a variety of scales made up of notes of slightly different pitches.

Below Chinese ch'in (1) and Japanese kotos (2 and 3). The ch'in is the classical long zither of China and was played 2000 years ago. Stopping positions for the seven strings are indicated by ivory disks inlaid in the soundboard. The Japanese koto has 13 silk strings that pass over movable bridges.

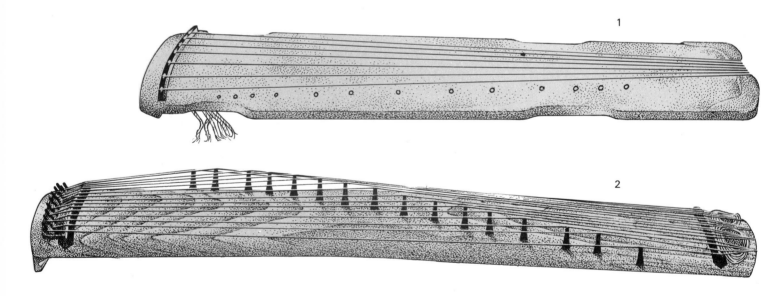

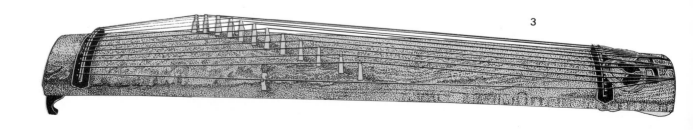

1

2

3

Above Korean kayakeum—
a long zither with silk
strings attached to the
underside of the soundboard.
It has movable bridges.
Right Korean djunadjan—
a smaller instrument with 10
pairs of strings attached to
tuning pegs. There are fixed
bridges at the ends and
movable bridges between.

Right Smaller fretted long
zithers from Asia. The
Bornean zither (1) has a flat
body and a lute-like profile.
The Javanese kachapi (2)
has movable bridges, and
tuning pegs inserted through
the side of the body. The
six-string Korean komungo
(3) corresponds to the
Chinese ch'in. The Burmese
mi gyaun (4) and the Thai
chakay (5) are long tube
zithers in crocodile form.

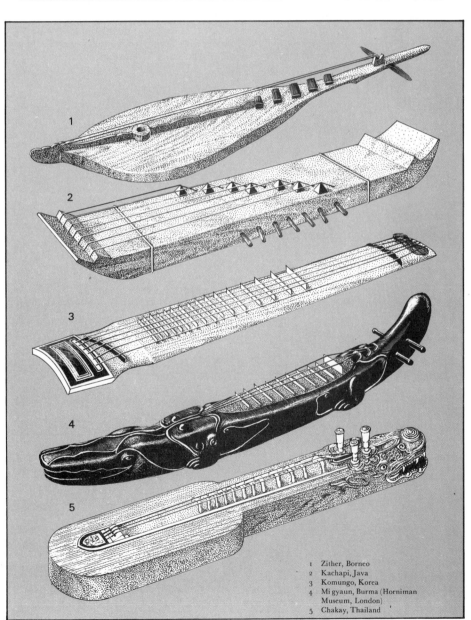

1   Zither, Borneo
2   Kachapi, Java
3   Komungo, Korea
4   Mi gyaun, Burma (Horniman
    Museum, London)
5   Chakay, Thailand

© DIAGRAM

Board zithers

Most European zithers are board zithers with a basic rectangular or trapezoid shape. Strings are stretched across a flat or slightly curved board that forms the top of a box resonator. The most important form in medieval times was the psaltery, a development of the Middle Eastern qanun which reached Europe in the 11th century. Today board zithers are popular folk instruments in many countries.

Left Psaltery player. The instrument is usually laid flat on the knees, or on a table, and is plucked with the fingers or a plectrum.

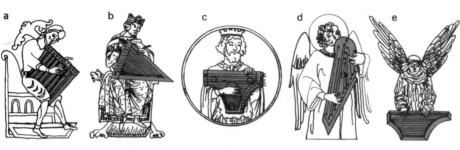

Left History of the psaltery in art. Early psalteries were often square (a) or triangular (b). In the 14th and 15th centuries instruments in the shape of a pig's head— strumento di porco (c)—or a wing (d) were popular. By about 1500 the psaltery had a more modern shape (e).

Left Late 17th century psaltery with decorated case (Castello Sforzesco, Milan). The strings of this trapezoid instrument are attached to tuning pegs at one side and pass over four movable bridges. During the 17th century the psaltery became a favorite with amateur musicians.

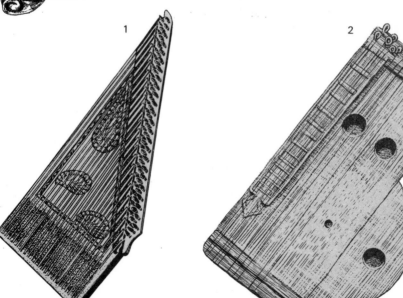

Left The Turkish qanun (1) has changed little since the Middle Ages. The ancestor of most European zithers, this important form of plucked board zither has been known since the 10th century. The Yugoslavian zither (2) is one of a variety of forms of board zither found in this country.

Right Board zithers from Slovakia, Hungary, and France. The Slovakian zither (1) terminates in a violin-like scroll. The strings of the Hungarian zither (2) are attached to pegs along its stepped side. The French épinette des Vosges (3) is played with a plectrum.

Right Different styles of board zither from Scandinavia. The Norwegian langleik (4) and the Swedish hummels (7 and 8) have frets under some of the strings. The Icelandic fidla (5) and langspil (6) are played with a bow. The Finnish kantele (9) has tuning pegs along its wider end.

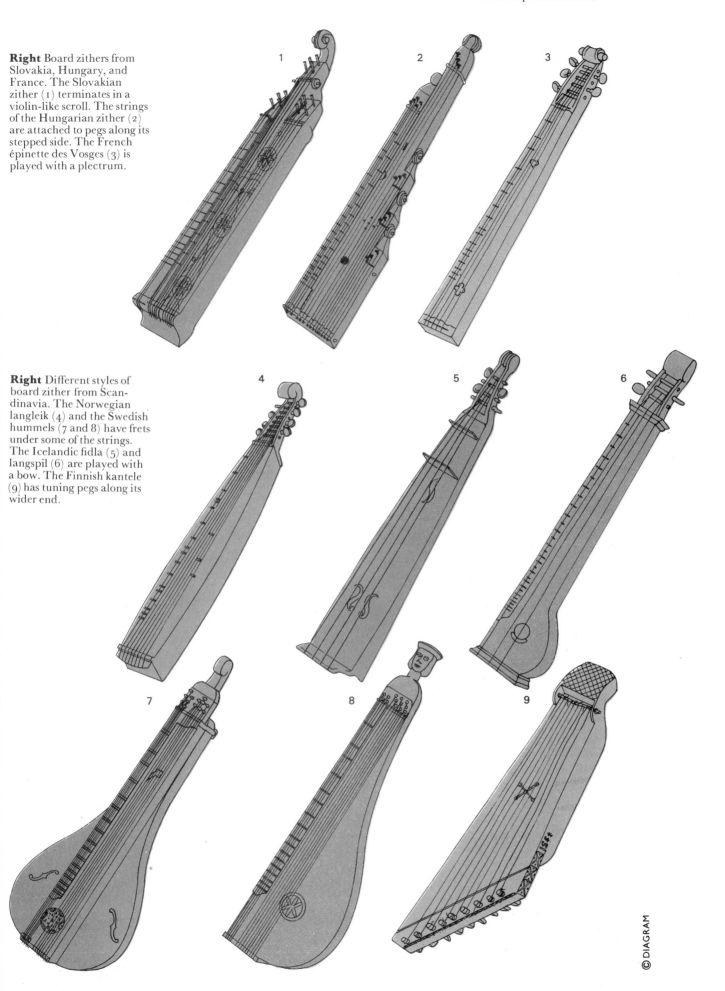

© DIAGRAM

Right Upright board
zithers. The arpanetta or
spitzharfe (1) and the diplo-
kithara (2) were strung on
both sides of the resonator.
They were plucked with
both hands (far right). The
arpanetta was popular in
Germany in the 1600s and
1700s. The diplo-kithara was
developed around 1800 by
Edward Light.

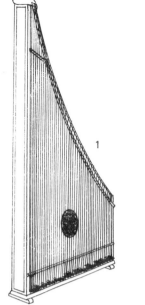
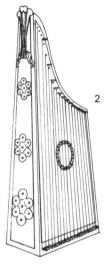

1   Arpanetta, 17th century (Horniman
    Museum)
2   Diplo-kithara, Edward Light, c. 1800
    (National Museum, Berlin)

Right Unusual board
zithers. The aeolian harp (3)
is a zither with a rectangular
box resonator and strings
sounded by the wind. The
strings are all the same length
but of different thicknesses,
and produce chords when
the instrument is placed in a
draught. Stringed instru-
ments sounded by the wind
have been known since
biblical times. The tam-
bourin de Béarn (4), a French
folk instrument, is a stringed
"drum" with gut strings
beaten with a stick. The
bowed zither (5) is a 19th
century German instrument.

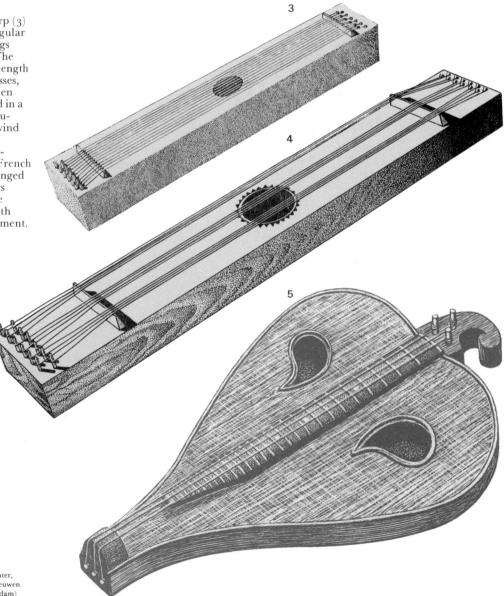

3   Aeolian harp, 18th century
4   Tambourin de Béarn (modern
    reconstruction, Dolmetsch)
5   Bowed zither, Johann Haslwanter,
    Munich, c. 1870 (Carel van Leeuwen
    Boomkamp collection, Amsterdam)

Right Appalachian dulcimer. A plucked zither rather than a true dulcimer, this instrument is played by plucking the strings with one hand. The player uses his other hand or a quill or stick to stop the strings as he plays.

Below Folk musician with an Appalachian dulcimer.

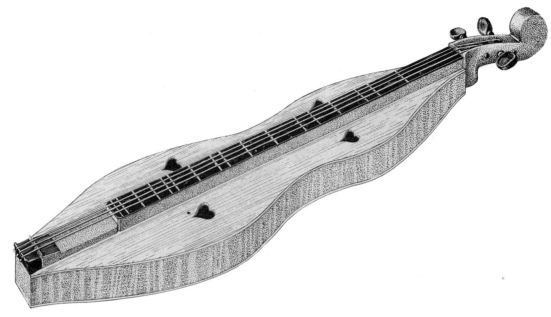

Right Modern concert zither. Its metal melody strings, over a fretted fingerboard, are stopped with the fingers of the left hand and plucked with a plectrum worn on the right thumb. The gut accompanying strings are plucked with the fingers of the right hand.
Below Zither player.

Right Modern chord zither (1) and autoharp (2). Both instruments simplify the playing of accompaniments. The chord zither has strings arranged so that the notes of chords occur in groups. The autoharp has dampers which damp all the strings except those needed to form a particular chord.

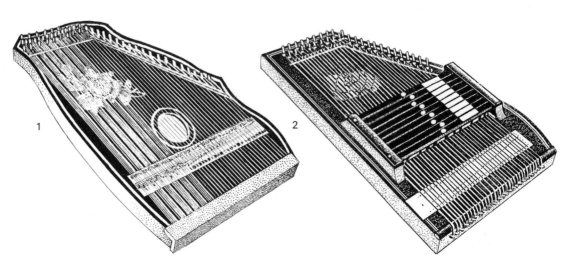

© DIAGRAM

Dulcimers

A dulcimer is a board zither struck with hammers or beaters. Like the plucked board zither it came to Europe from the Middle East in the 11th century. It enjoyed considerable popularity with fashionable European audiences from the 17th to the 19th centuries but now survives only as a folk instrument. The struck board zither was unknown in the Far East until about 1800, when it was introduced by Europeans.

Left Playing the dulcimer. The player uses small beaters or hammers to strike the strings.

Below Smaller dulcimers. The Persian santir (1), Russian chang (2), and Indian santoor (3) have individual movable bridges. The Korean yangum (4) and Swiss hackbrett (5) have long bridges shaped to allow strings over or under them. The Yugoslavian dulcimer (6) has both sorts of bridges.

Right Examples of different types of dulcimer beater. Common styles include straight beaters (a), curved beaters (b), and padded sticks (c). Wood is the most usual material. (The hammer action of the piano is a sophisticated development of the struck dulcimer principle.)

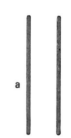

a   b   c

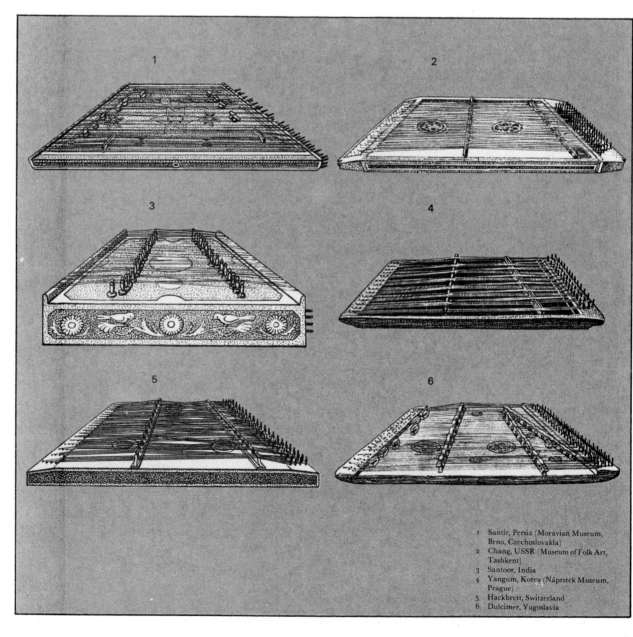

1 Santir, Persia (Moravian Museum, Brno, Czechoslovakia)
2 Chang, USSR (Museum of Folk Art, Tashkent)
3 Santoor, India
4 Yangum, Korea (Náprstek Museum, Prague)
5 Hackbrett, Switzerland
6 Dulcimer, Yugoslavia

Right Iraqi santir and Chinese yang chin. The santir (1) has a deep box resonator with three sound holes. Its metal strings, arranged in triple courses, are attached to tuning pegs in the side of the box. The yang chin (2)—or "foreign zither"—was introduced into China from the West in about 1800. Movable bridges are used to divide its strings into different vibrating lengths.

Right Hungarian cimbalom. Based on a smaller gypsy instrument, the cimbalom was modernized by Schunda in the late 19th century. The strings, in multiple courses, are divided by bridges into different vibrating lengths. Kodaly used the cimbalom in "Háry János."

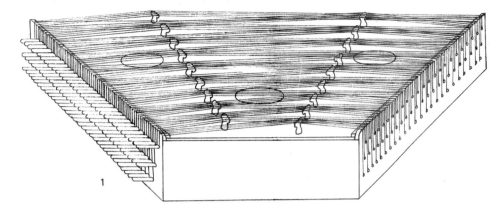

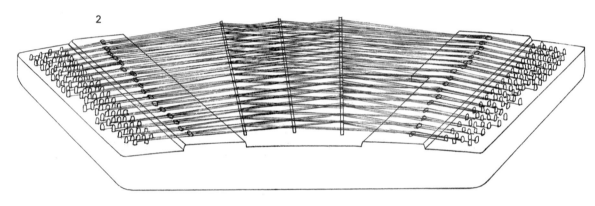

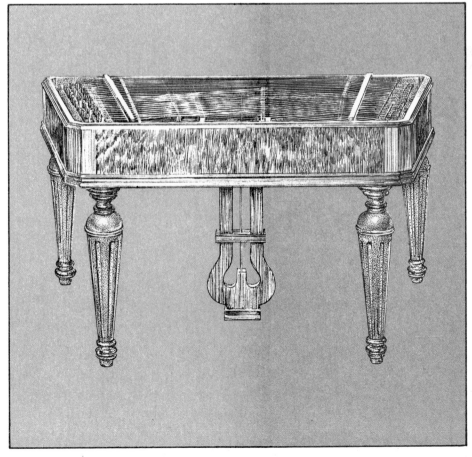

©DIAGRAM

Clavichords

The clavichord was one of the most popular keyboard instruments of the baroque period. Its unique action, developed from that of the simple monochord, made it the most sensitive and responsive keyboard instrument of the time. Its exceptionally quiet tone, however, meant that it was suitable only as a domestic solo instrument. The clavichord remained popular until the 18th century, when it was replaced by the piano.

Right Clavichord action. When the key (a) is depressed, the brass blade or tangent (b) strikes a pair of strings (c), making them vibrate. The tangent remains in contact with the strings until the key is released, so vibrato, or "bebung," can be achieved by varying finger pressure on the key.

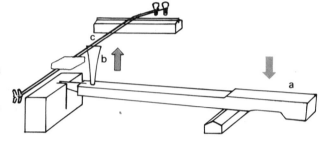

Above Monochord from a 16th century woodcut. The monochord, used for teaching music during the Middle Ages, was first developed by Pythagoras to measure intervals of a scale It consisted of a single string, two fixed bridges resting on a soundboard, and other movable bridges.

Right Diagrams showing the different tangent actions of a fretted and an unfretted clavichord. On the fretted clavichord (a), each pair of strings serves several different tangents. On the later unfretted clavichord (b), each tangent has its own pair of strings. On all clavichords the pitch produced when a key is depressed is determined not by the total length of the strings but by the point at which the tangent strikes them. When the tangent strikes a pair of strings it divides them into two vibrating lengths, one of which is deadened by a damper.

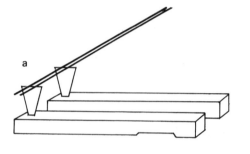

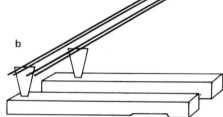

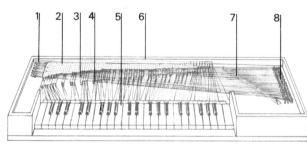

Left Diagram showing the parts of a clavichord.

1 Hitch pins
2 Dampers
3 Strings
4 Tangents
5 Keyboard
6 Case
7 Bridge
8 Tuning pins

Right Fretted clavichord by the Italian instrument maker, Domenico da Pesaro. This example, dating from 1543, is thought to be the oldest dated clavichord. The case is hexagonal and the keyboard protrudes from the side of the instrument.

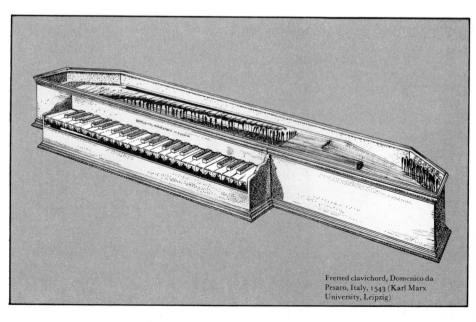

Fretted clavichord, Domenico da Pesaro, Italy, 1543 (Karl Marx University, Leipzig)

Right 17th century Flemish fretted clavichord (Brussels Conservatoire). This instrument has a more typical rectangular case, with a decorative inlaid lid. Small compact instruments of this type were popular in the home, where they were set on a table for playing.
Far right Clavichord player.

Right Unfretted German clavichord. This instrument made in 1767 by Johann Hass, is typical of the large clavichords popular in Germany in the second half of the 18th century. The inside of the lid is decorated with a pastoral scene. The keys are ivory, tortoiseshell, and mother-of-pearl.

Right German pedal clavichord made by Gluck in about 1750. Beneath the standard instrument is a second clavichord operated by pedals. The strings of the pedal clavichord lie underneath its soundboard. Instruments of this type were used by organists for practice purposes.

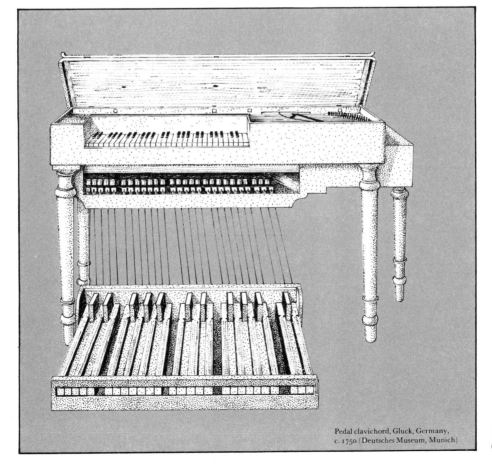

Pedal clavichord, Gluck, Germany, c. 1750 (Deutsches Museum, Munich)

Harpsichords

The harpsichord is the largest and most important plucked-string keyboard instrument. The first successful examples were made in Italy in the 1500s, following almost 200 years of experiments. Later, important manufacturing centers were established in France, Germany, Flanders, and Britain. The bright clear sound of the harpsichord made it a popular solo instrument and a favorite with composers in the 17th and 18th centuries. In addition, the harpsichord player was an important member of the baroque chamber group and orchestra. He directed, or "conducted," the performance from the keyboard, and acted as a continuo player supplying reinforcing harmonies to the instrumental texture. In recent years there has been a revival of interest in the harpsichord, and it can now be heard in performances both of baroque music and of specially written modern works.

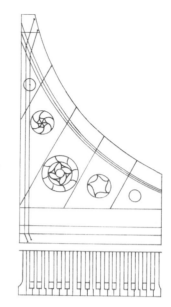

Left The layout of a wing-shaped keyboard instrument, after a drawing in a treatise on musical instruments by Arnaut de Zwolle, c. 1440. Accompanying drawings in Zwolle's treatise give details of mechanism, along with precise instructions for manufacture.

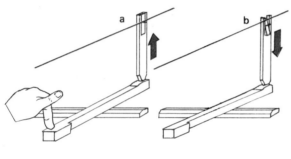

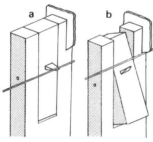

Above Plucking action of the harpsichord. When the key is depressed (a), the quill or leather plectrum in the jack plucks the string as it passes. When the key is released (b), a pivot on the jack makes the plectrum bypass the string.
Left Plectrum plucking (a) and bypassing (b).

Below Identification of parts of a harpsichord.

1 Sound hole
2 Bridge
3 Soundboard
4 Jacks
5 Strings
6 Keyboard

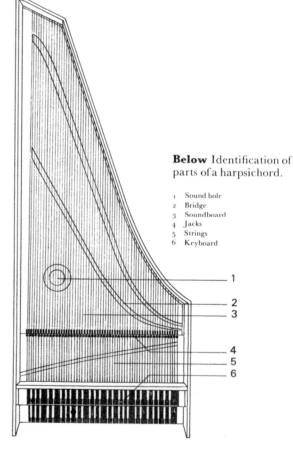

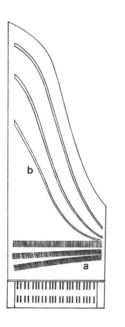

Left Diagram showing the three rows of jacks (a) and curved bridges (b) of a typical 18th century harpsichord. Each row of jacks plucks a different set of strings. Slides, controlled by stops, allow the player to select an "on" or "off" position for each set of jacks.

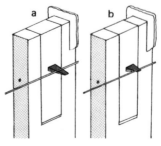

Left Diagram comparing plectra plucking positions. On an ordinary jack (a) the center of the plectrum plucks the string. On a jack brought into operation by the lute stop (b) the tip of the plectrum plucks the string and so produces a thin brittle sound very like that of a lute.

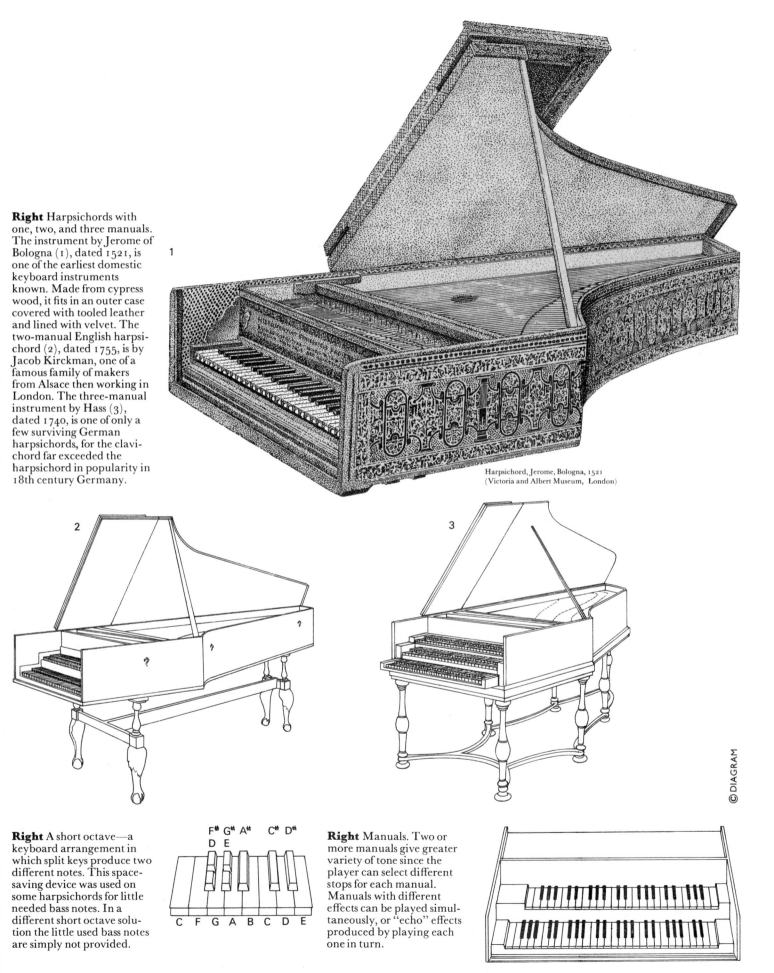

Right Harpsichords with one, two, and three manuals. The instrument by Jerome of Bologna (1), dated 1521, is one of the earliest domestic keyboard instruments known. Made from cypress wood, it fits in an outer case covered with tooled leather and lined with velvet. The two-manual English harpsichord (2), dated 1755, is by Jacob Kirckman, one of a famous family of makers from Alsace then working in London. The three-manual instrument by Hass (3), dated 1740, is one of only a few surviving German harpsichords, for the clavichord far exceeded the harpsichord in popularity in 18th century Germany.

Harpsichord, Jerome, Bologna, 1521
(Victoria and Albert Museum, London)

© DIAGRAM

Right A short octave—a keyboard arrangement in which split keys produce two different notes. This space-saving device was used on some harpsichords for little needed bass notes. In a different short octave solution the little used bass notes are simply not provided.

Right Manuals. Two or more manuals give greater variety of tone since the player can select different stops for each manual. Manuals with different effects can be played simultaneously, or "echo" effects produced by playing each one in turn.

232

Harpsichord

D. Scarlatti	Sonatas
H. Purcell	Suites
J. S. Bach	English Suites
G. F. Handel	Suites
F. Couperin	Ordres
F. Martin	Concerto for harpsichord and small orchestra
F. Poulenc	Concert champêtre

J. S. Bach English Suite in F

Right and below Different styles of harpsichord from France, England, and Portugal. The French example (1) is elaborately painted on the lid, sides, and soundboard. The English harpsichord (2) has a flap in the lid. Operated by the right pedal, this flap is slowly opened and closed to produce crescendo and diminuendo effects. The harpsichord from Portugal (3) is much influenced by Portuguese furniture design.

1 Harpsichord, Stehlin, Paris, 1760 (Smithsonian Institution, Washington DC)
2 Harpsichord, Kirckman, London, 1777 (Fenton House, London)
3 Harpsichord, Antunes, Lisbon, 1789 (Lisbon Conservatoire)

1

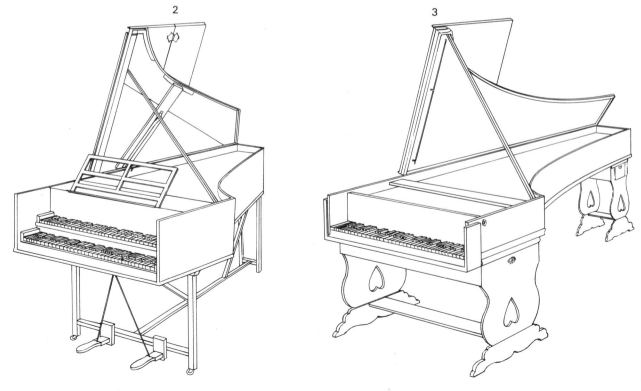

2

3

Right Clavicytherium, or
upright harpsichord (Royal
College of Music, London).
This instrument, dating from
the late 15th century, is
possibly the earliest surviving
stringed keyboard instru-
ment. It has a sophisticated
action in which the jacks do
not return by gravity but
have to be pulled back
mechanically. It has a
painted lid and a relief
landscape on the soundboard.
Far right 18th century
upright harpsichord by de
Lin (Gemeentemuseum,
The Hague). It is decorated
with inlaid and gilded wood.
Such instruments enjoyed
some vogue in the 18th
century.

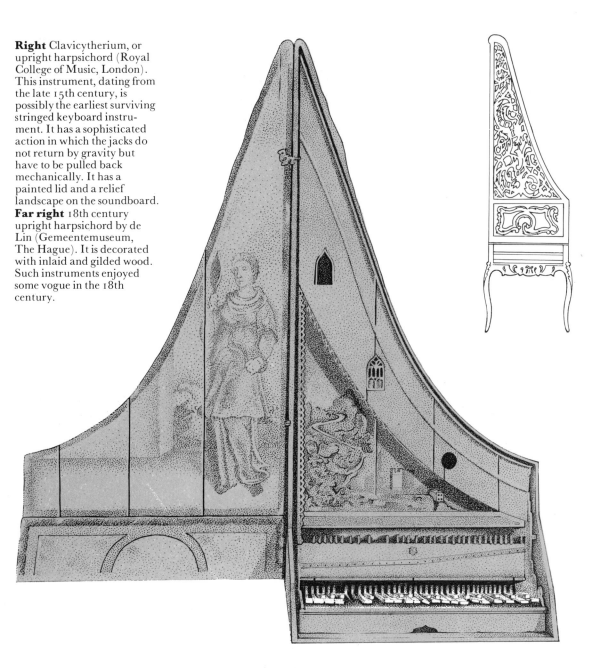

Below Diagram of a
combined piano and harpsichord. This unusual instrument has a piano keyboard
and hammers at one side (a)
and a harpsichord keyboard
and jacks at the other (b).
Each keyboard has its own
strings, though all are
attached to hitch pins along
a common rail.

Below right Claviorgan,
or organ harpsichord, by
Bertolotti of Venice, 1585
(Brussels Conservatoire).
It has a single keyboard,
two sets of strings, and two
rows of jacks—along with
three ranks of pipes, two
wood and one metal,
controlled by levers operated
by the right hand.

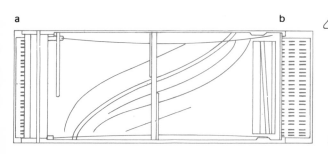

a   b

© DIAGRAM

Virginals and spinets

Virginals and spinets are small keyboard instruments with plucking actions similar to that of the larger harpsichord. The virginal was a popular domestic instrument in 16th and 17th century England, and major composers such as Byrd and Gibbons wrote prolifically for it. The spinet, first popular in Italy in the 16th century, became in the 18th century a favorite instrument throughout Europe.

Right Diagrams comparing the virginal (a) and spinet (b). The virginal usually has a rectangular box-shaped case with strings running almost parallel to the keyboard. The popular form of spinet shown here has a "bentside" case and strings running diagonally away from the keyboard.

a

b

Right Virginal keyboard positions. The small keyboard, a characteristic of the instrument, allows a variety of positions for a single keyboard or the placing of two keyboards side by side.(The larger spinet keyboard usually occupies the whole of one side of the instrument.)

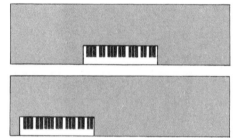

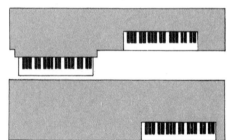

Right Virginal by Andreas Ruckers—one of a famous Flemish family of plucked string instrument makers. Dated 1610 this fine instrument has a single keyboard set to the right of a typical rectangular box-shaped case. Inlaid wood was used for its intricate decoration.

Below Illustration of a virginal player, showing the comparatively small size of this once very popular instrument.

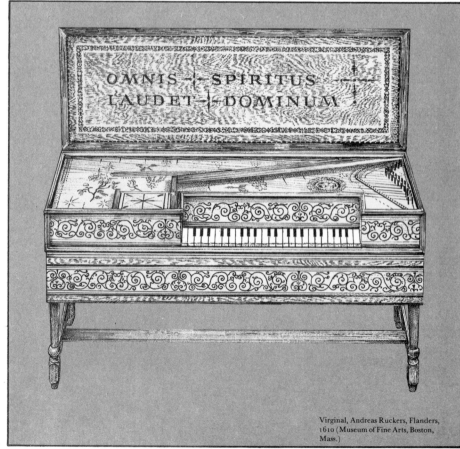

Virginal, Andreas Ruckers, Flanders, 1610 (Museum of Fine Arts, Boston, Mass.)

Right Flemish double virginal made in 1660 by Lodewejck Grauwels (Metropolitan Museum, New York). It is in effect two instruments in a single case. The smaller virginal— known as an ottavino—fits like a drawer under the soundboard of the larger one.

Right 16th century spinet (Castello Sforzesco, Milan). This instrument has an irregular polygonal case supported on a three-legged stand. The keys are inlaid with rare woods, and the date, 1562, and the maker's name, Benedetto Floriani, are carried on a small metal plate above the keyboard.

Right 18th century English spinet by Thomas Hitchcock of London. This instrument has the "bentside" case typical of most spinets. Its walnut case is inlaid with boxwood but lacks the ornate decoration of many contemporary instruments. It has a larger compass than most earlier spinets.

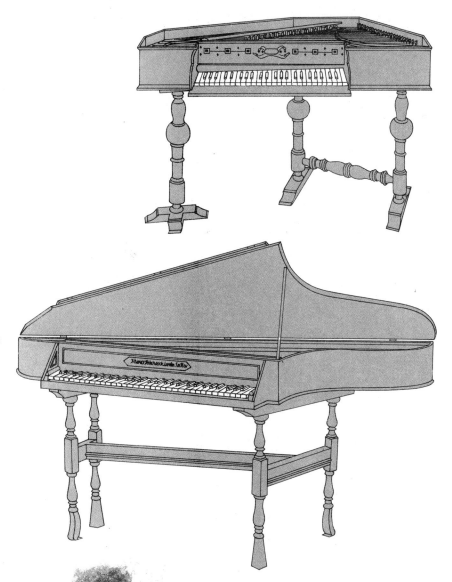

© DIAGRAM

Historical pianos

The piano, or pianoforte, is the most popular of the keyboard instruments. The first piano was made around 1700 by an Italian, Bartolommeo Cristofori, who was experimenting to produce a keyboard instrument that was more responsive to the player's touch than the harpsichord. The new instrument might have passed unnoticed but for the interest of a writer, Scipione Maffei. An article he wrote after a visit to Cristofori's

workshop was later translated into German and probably inspired Gottfried Silbermann to start making pianos. In 1760 Johannes Zumpe, one of Silbermann's pupils, took the art of piano making to England, and there developed his compact "square" piano. Developments in manufacture continued in Europe and America during the next hundred years and led to the modern instrument of today.

Piano, Bartolommeo Cristofori, Florence, 1720 (Metropolitan Museum, New York)

Above Early piano by Bartolommeo Cristofori, inventor of the instrument he called a "gravicembalo col piano e forte" ("harpsichord with soft and loud"). This example has the wing-shaped case of the harpsichord, others had the shape of the clavichord or spinet.

Right Diagrams showing the plucking action of the harpsichord jack (a) and the striking action of the piano hammer (b). The leather-topped hammers of the piano gave a gentler more controlled sound than that produced by the plucking action of the harpsichord jacks.

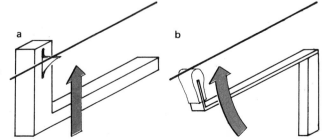

Above Grand piano by Gottfried Silbermann. Made in about 1745, it belonged to King Frederick the Great of Prussia. Silbermann was responsible for a number of minor improvements, but essentially the action used in his pianos was the same as that developed earlier by Cristofori.

Above right "Square" piano by Johannes Zumpe, 1767. His instruments had a compact rectangular case and an action that was a simplified form of that used by Cristofori and Silbermann. The first public solo piano performance was by J. C. Bach on a Zumpe piano in England in 1768.

Below left Grand piano by Johann Andreas Stein, made in the 1770s. His pianos had what came to be known as the "German" or "Viennese" action. They were light to the touch and were fitted with an escapement mechanism. Mozart greatly admired their bright even tone.

Below Grand piano by John Broadwood, 1792. Among the developments introduced by Broadwood were heavier strings and a stronger frame. His "English" action pianos were more resistant to the touch and had a more powerful tone. English action pianos are the ancestors of the modern instrument.

1 Piano, Gottfried Silbermann, Freiberg, c. 1745 (Potsdam-Sanssouci, West Germany)
2 Piano, Johannes Zumpe, London, 1767 (Metropolitan Museum, New York)
3 Piano, Johann Andreas Stein, Augsburg, 1770s (Germanisches Nationalmuseum, Nuremberg, West Germany)
4 Piano, John Broadwood, London, 1792 (Metropolitan Museum, New York)

© DIAGRAM

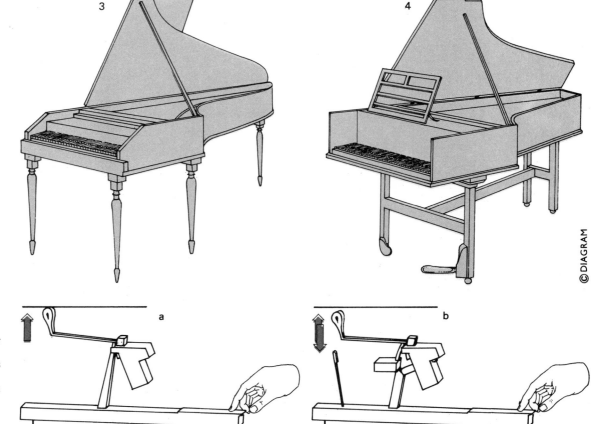

Right Hammer actions. If there is no escapement mechanism (a), the hammer strikes the string when the key is depressed and remains in contact with it until the player releases the key. With an escapement mechanism (b), the hammer returns directly even if the player keeps the key depressed.

238

Right An orphica. Made from 1795 to about 1830, orphicas were small portable pianos. This example has a range of four octaves and would have been played on a small table. Smaller orphicas were made to be played on the player's lap or suspended on a band around his neck.

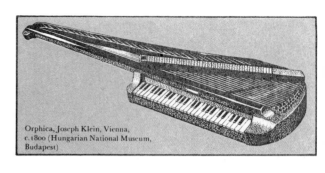

Orphica, Joseph Klein, Vienna, c.1800 (Hungarian National Museum, Budapest)

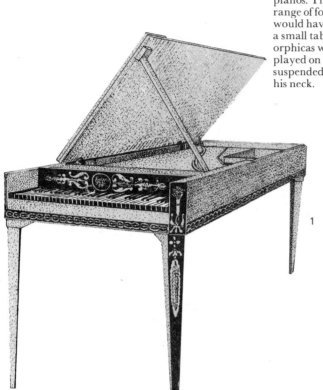

1

2

Above Elegant Czech table piano (1) and a French table piano that belonged to the Duke of Wellington (2). The practice of incorporating pianos in cases with a different function enjoyed some popularity in the 19th century. Other examples combined pianos with desks or sewing tables.

Below The Empire piano (3) is an Austrian instrument made about 1820. Its ornamentation reflects a contemporary interest in classical Greece and Rome. The massive American piano (4) dates from about 1850 and is another example of the influence of fashion on piano case design.

1 Table piano, Leopold Sauer, Prague, early 19th century (City Museum, Prague)
2 Table piano, Jean-Henri Pape, Paris, mid-19th century (Castello Sforzesco, Milan)
3 Empire piano, Conrad Graf, Vienna, c.1820 (Hungarian National Museum, Budapest)
4 Piano, Nunns & Clarke, New York, c.1850 (Metropolitan Museum, New York)

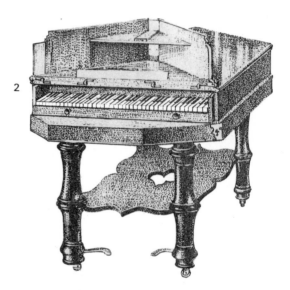

3

4

1

2

3

1 Giraffe piano, Czechoslovakia, early 19th century (National Museum, Prague)
2 Pyramid piano, Conrad Graf, Vienna, 1829 (Gemeentemuseum, The Hague, Netherlands)
3 Harp piano, probably by Kuhn & Ridgeway, Baltimore, 1857 (Smithsonian Institution, Washington DC)

4 Janko piano, C. Goetz, Germany, c. 1890 (Gemeentemuseum, The Hague, Netherlands)
5 Portable grand piano, John Isaac Hawkins, Philadelphia, 1801 (Smithsonian Institution, Washington DC)

Above Giraffe piano (1), pyramid piano (2), and harp piano (3)—three designs developed to save floor space. All were essentially vertical grand pianos, with the strings running from just below keyboard level. Their case heights were thus determined by the length of the longest strings.

Below Janko piano (4) and portable "grand" piano (5). Invented by Paul von Janko in 1882 the Janko keyboard had six rows of keys. Each note could be played by three different keys. Hawkins's portable "grand" was a compact instrument with strings running to the foot of the case.

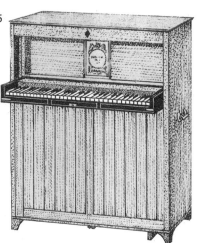

4

5

© DIAGRAM

Modern pianos

The piano is one of the most popular and versatile of all instruments. It has a large pitch range, exceeded only by that of the organ, and is capable of great expressiveness. It remains important in the home where it is used both as a solo and accompanying instrument. The piano appears regularly on the concert platform in solo recitals and in performances of chamber music and concertos.

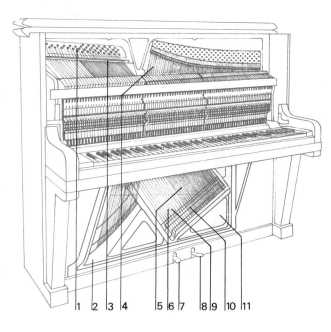

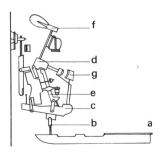

Left The arrangement of strings in a typical upright piano. The one-piece iron frame, invented by Alpheus Babcock in 1825, allows "cross stringing"—an economical arrangement where the bass strings pass at a different level over the strings of the middle and upper registers.

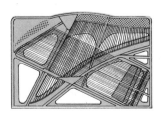

Left Upright action. When the key (a) is depressed, the pivot (b) lifts the lever (c) which then lifts the jack (d). This strikes the butt (e), throwing the hammer (f) against the string. The check (g) catches the hammer halfway on its return to make possible the more rapid repetition of notes.

Above Diagram showing parts of an upright piano. The strings are fixed at one end to tuning pins and are stretched over a cast-iron frame capable of taking a strain of up to 17 tons. Behind the frame is a soundboard which reproduces the strings' vibrations and so increases the volume.

1	Tuning pins
2	Iron frame
3	Bridge
4	Trichords
5	Bichords
6	Single strings
7	Soft pedal
8	Sustaining pedal
9	Bass strings
10	Bridge
11	Soundboard

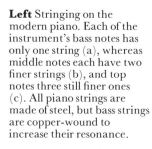

Left Stringing on the modern piano. Each of the instrument's bass notes has only one string (a), whereas middle notes each have two finer strings (b), and top notes three still finer ones (c). All piano strings are made of steel, but bass strings are copper-wound to increase their resonance.

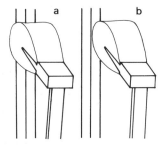

Left The action of the left, or "soft," pedal. When the pedal is not being used, the hammers strike the strings near their center (a). When the pedal is depressed, the hammers shift slightly to the right (b). This reduces contact with the strings and so produces a softer tone.

Above A modern upright piano. Vertically strung pianos were built from the 18th century, but the earliest examples—such as the "pyramid" piano—were essentially grand pianos set on end. The true upright piano was invented by John Isaac Hawkins in Philadelphia around 1800.

Left Diagrams showing damper action. When a key is depressed, the dampers leave the strings (a1, b1). Usually they return to stop the strings vibrating as soon as the finger leaves the key (a2). Depressing the sustaining pedal delays damper action on all strings until the foot is raised (b2).

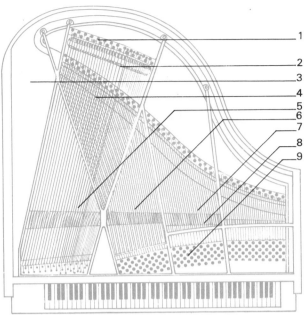

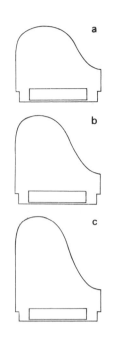

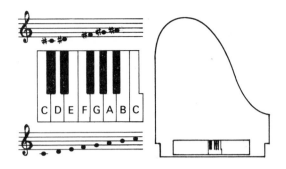

Above Notes comprising an octave on the piano. The keyboard is an excellent device for simplifying the playing of a complex stringed instrument. Keyboard instruments have existed for 700 years, and by the early 1400s the keys were arranged in the same order as on the modern piano.

Above Parts of a modern grand piano. The one-piece iron frame allows the strings to be stretched at high tension, improving the tone quality and responsiveness of the instrument. Small grands are cross-strung to accommodate the long bass strings in a shorter case.

1 Hitch pins
2 Bass bridge
3 Soundboard
4 Long bridge
5 Single strings
6 Bichords
7 Trichords
8 Dampers
9 Wrest pins

Above Diagram showing the three most important sizes of grand piano. The compact miniature or "baby" grand (a) is usually between 5ft 6in and 5ft 10in long. The drawing room or boudoir instrument (b) measures between 6ft and 7ft, and the concert grand (c) is 7ft to 9ft long.

Below Modern concert grand. The grand's main advantages are that its open lid helps project the sound, and the floor under the soundboard reflects rather than absorbs sound. The center pedal, an optional extra, sustains only notes whose keys are depressed when the pedal is applied.

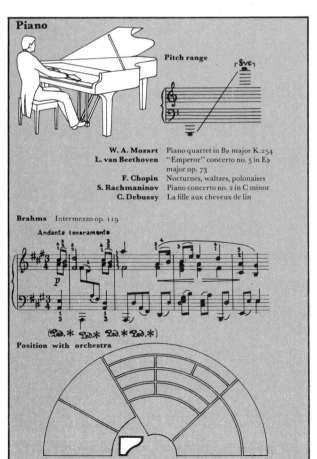

Piano

Pitch range

W. A. Mozart — Piano quartet in B♭ major K.254
L. van Beethoven — "Emperor" concerto no. 5 in E♭ major op. 73
F. Chopin — Nocturnes, waltzes, polonaises
S. Rachmaninov — Piano concerto no. 2 in C minor
C. Debussy — La fille aux cheveux de lin

Brahms Intermezzo op. 119

Andante teneramente

Position with orchestra

Music boxes

The first music boxes were made by Swiss watchmakers in the late 18th century, and by the early 19th century the cylinder-operated music box had become a popular domestic instrument. Later in the 19th century it was ousted from popularity by the disk-operated music box which could play a greater number of tunes on cheap, interchangeable disks. Today, music boxes remain popular as novelties.

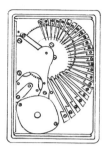

Left Intricate music box mechanism of a tiny musical snuff box dating from the late 18th century. Pins set on the two revolving disks pluck the steel tongues of different lengths to produce a simple tune.

Below The two chief types of music box mechanism— the cylinder (a) and the disk (b). Each has pins on its surface which pluck the required melody tongues when the cylinder or disk is rotated. Disks, cheap and interchangeable, had superseded cylinders by the late 19th century.

a

b

Right Different types of music box from the 19th century. The cylinder music box (1) played several tunes from one cylinder. The bells were sounded as the cylinder rotated. The disk music box (2) by Smulders has a walnut case. Disk music boxes were superseded by the gramophone.

Left Mechanical trumpeter, made in 1810 by Friedrich Kaufmann of Dresden.

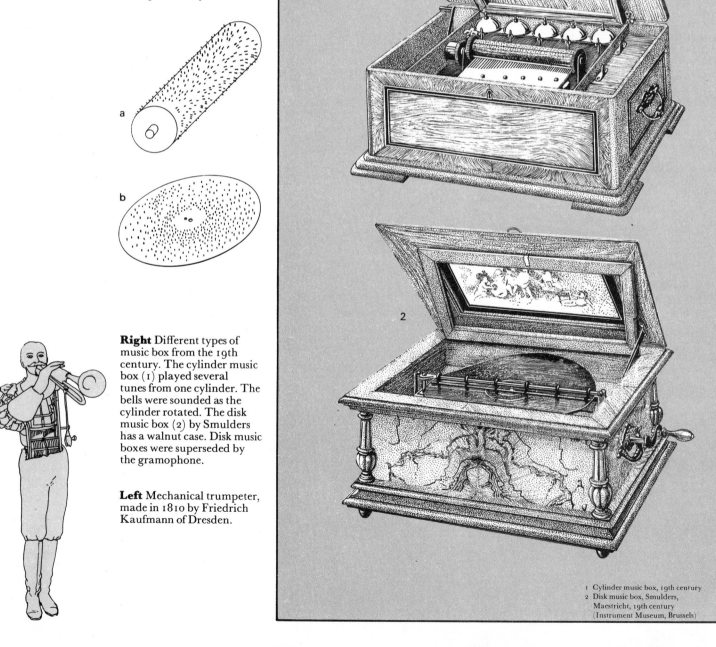

1 Cylinder music box, 19th century
2 Disk music box, Smulders, Maestricht, 19th century
(Instrument Museum, Brussels)

Left Music sheets from 19th century music boxes. Fixed inside the lid, the sheet listed the pieces played by the music box. Often very attractive, they are now collector's items.

Left Small round music box (actual size). Miniature instruments such as this, playing only one simple tune, were popular domestic novelties in the late 19th century. The lids of many examples are decorated with pastoral scenes. Larger boxes, playing more elaborate tunes, were made in a similar style.

1 Symphonium, 19th century
2 Polyphon, 19th century
3 Polyphon, 19th century

Left Automatic disk music boxes—often found as coin-in-the-slot machines in bars and cafes in the late 19th century. The symphonium (1) had several disks changed automatically. The polyphon, produced in a variety of case styles (2 and 3), had a star-wheel to pluck the tongues.

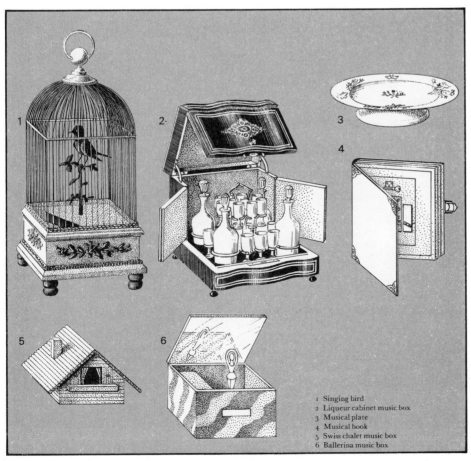

1 Singing bird
2 Liqueur cabinet music box
3 Musical plate
4 Musical book
5 Swiss chalet music box
6 Ballerina music box

Left Novelty music boxes. The 19th century singing bird (1) moved its head and beak to birdsong produced by a mechanism in the base of the cage. The liqueur cabinet (2), plate (3), and book (4) are 19th century novelties. The Swiss chalet (5) and ballerina music box (6) are still popular today.

Right Swiss cuckoo clock—a novelty clockwork "instrument."

© DIAGRAM

Carillons and chimes

Carillons and chimes represent one of the earliest and most successful ways of making music mechanically. The carillon, a set of tuned bells usually hung in a tower, was developed in Northern Europe as early as the 13th century. The bells are struck by means of wires, levers, clockwork, or electricity. On a smaller scale, simple chiming mechanisms have often been included in clocks.

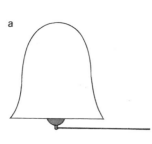

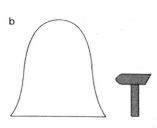

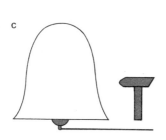

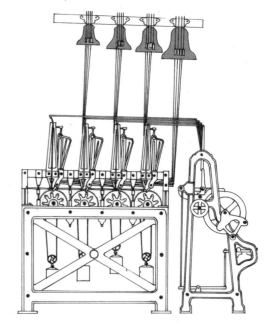

Right Diagram of Collins's chiming mechanism, which in the late 19th century was built into the carillon of Saint Germain in Paris. A complex system of barrels and weights meant that only the lightest finger pressure on the keys was needed to make the hammers strike the bells.

Left Three diagrams showing different carillon striking mechanisms. Most carillon bells are made to sound by either an internal clapper attached to a rope (a) or by an external hammer (b). Occasionally a carillon bell is fitted with alternative types of striking mechanism (c).

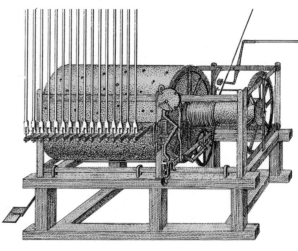

Right Drum and levers of a 19th century clock carillon, taken from a contemporary engraving. The carillon mechanism sounding the bells worked automatically at certain times of the day. This carillon played the tune "Old Hundredth," for which the music and peg pattern are also shown.

Right Diagram showing the mechanism of an automatic carillon. When the drum (a) rotates, the pegs (b) catch the levers (c) and so cause the hammers (d) to strike the bells. The arrangement of the pegs on the drum determines the sequence in which the bells sound—and so produces a tune.

Left Two manual methods of operating a carillon striking mechanism. In the simple system (a) the operator pulls directly on ropes attached to the bell clappers. In the more sophisticated system (b) the ropes are attached to levers arranged like the notes on an organ keyboard.

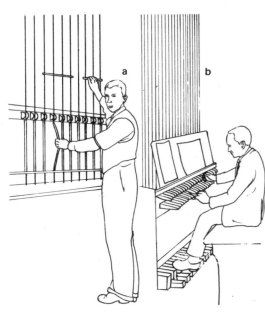

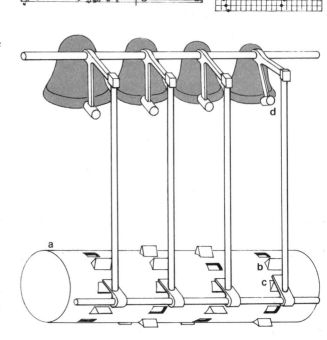

Right An unusual carillon consisting of nine hemispherical bells on an oak frame. Graduated in size, the bells are struck from below by hammers operated directly by ropes or from a keyboard. Bells arranged in this way occupy less space than the more common suspended bells.

Above Jack o'the clock, or quarter boy, in the form of a knight in armor (from Southwold, England). Small figures of this type are frequently found on European clock towers. Operated in conjunction with the clockwork mechanism, they strike bells on the hour and its quarters.

Right Chiming mechanism from a 16th century clock. The drum is turned at appropriate times by the clockwork, and pins on the drum cause the hammers to strike the bells. This produces an attractive tune in which as many as three bells are made to sound simultaneously.

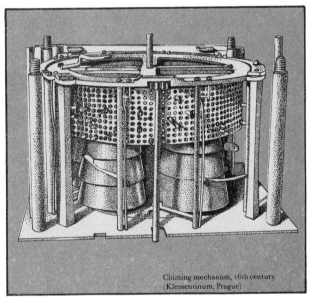

Chiming mechanism, 16th century (Klementinum, Prague)

Left Water clock by Rowland Emett. Erected in a shopping center in Nottingham, England, this 23ft high extravaganza is a most imaginative modern musical timepiece. Times are marked by a musical accompaniment as animals, birds, and butterflies circle the clock faces.

Right Angel chimes—a popular domestic novelty. Heat rising from the candles reaches the windmill-like vanes and causes the upper part of the chime to revolve. Small beaters suspended from each angel strike the bells as they turn.

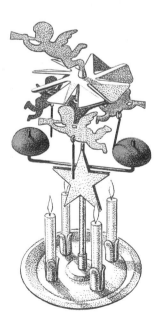

© DIAGRAM

Mechanical music makers

Mechanical music makers fall into two main groups. Instruments of the first group, including the hurdy gurdy and geigenwerk, have strings that are sounded mechanically but are stopped or selected by the player's fingers. The second group, including the automatic violin and the orchestrion, are fully automatic—the player merely selects a cylinder or roll to determine the tune to be played.

Right Hurdy gurdy and nyckelharpa. Known in Europe since medieval times, the hurdy gurdy (1) is a mechanized violin. Its strings, set into vibration by the rotation of a wheel, are stopped by means of a keyboard. Most examples have one or more drone strings which sound continuously. The nyckelharpa (2), a Swedish folk instrument, is bowed manually although the strings are stopped mechanically with keys.

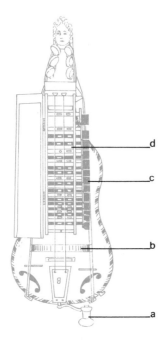

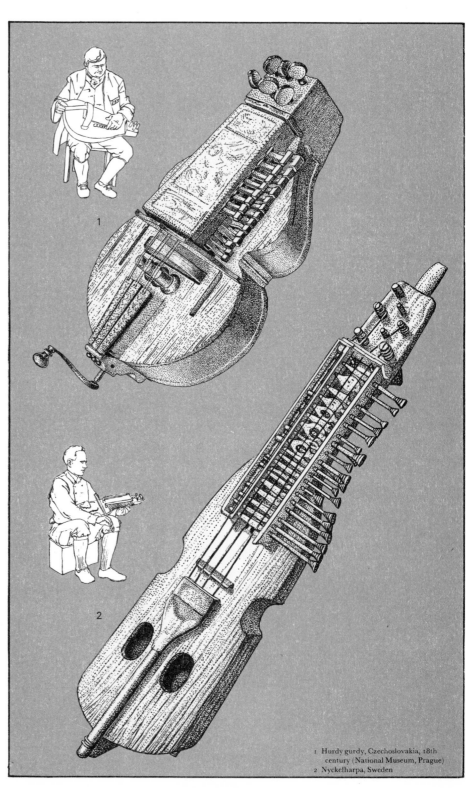

Above Illustration showing the working parts of a hurdy gurdy. Turning the handle (a) causes the wheel (b) to rotate, so setting the strings into vibration. The depression of the keys (c) with the fingers causes tangents (d) to rise and stop the strings, thus determining the pitch.

1 Hurdy gurdy, Czechoslovakia, 18th century (National Museum, Prague)
2 Nyckelharpa, Sweden

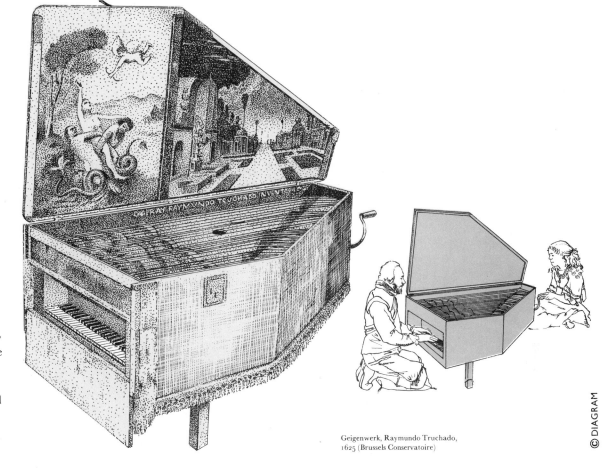

Right Geigenwerk—a mechanical "harpsichord." Invented in Germany in the late 1500s, the geigenwerk had metal strings which vibrated when parchment covered wheels were turned by a handle. Depressing a key caused a string to sound by pressing it against a rotating wheel.

Geigenwerk, Raymundo Truchado, 1625 (Brussels Conservatoire)

© DIAGRAM

Right Automatic instruments "programmed" by holes in a paper music roll. The Mills' Violano-virtuoso (1) had strings made to vibrate by small bows and stopped with metal "fingers." The coin-in-the-slot Link piano (2) had mechanisms for operating a piano, mandolin, triangle, and drums.

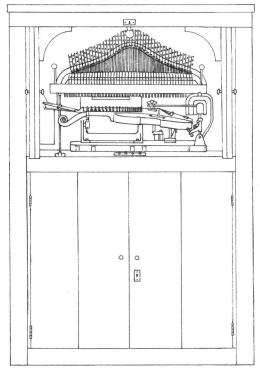

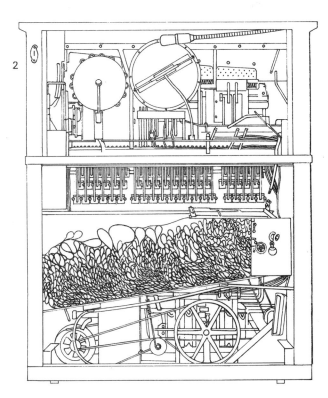

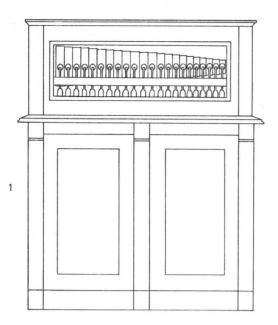

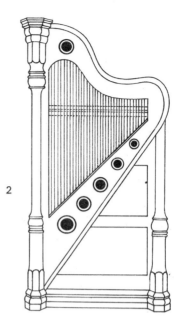

1

2

Left Self-playing xylophone
(1) and automatic harp (2).
The self-playing xylophone,
first made in the USA
around 1900 by DeKleist,
was operated by a pinned
cylinder. The strings of the
automatic harp by
Wurlitzer were plucked by
tiny "fingers" operated by
a perforated music roll.

Left Orchestrion by
Kaufmann. Designed to
imitate instruments of the
orchestra, the orchestrion
consisted of organ pipes
controlled by pinned
cylinders or perforated rolls.
Many sizes and styles were
made throughout the 19th
century by makers in
Germany and the USA.

Automatic pianos

Many types of automatic piano were made in the 19th and early 20th centuries as a result of an interest in mechanical music makers and a popular enthusiasm for piano music. The earliest mechanical piano music was produced by the "piano player"—a device applied to an ordinary piano. Later, fully automatic pianos—player pianos and reproducing pianos—became popular in homes and bars.

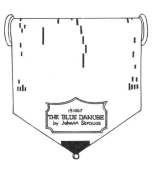

Left Automatic piano roll, with perforations corresponding to the pitch and length of the notes to be produced. Passing over a cylinder pierced with small holes, perforations in the roll allow air to pass through pipes connected to the piano action and so cause the hammers to strike the strings.

Above Illustration taken from an advertisement for a "piano player"—a small cabinet pushed up to the keyboard of an ordinary piano. Felt-covered hammers projecting from the piano player cabinet depressed the piano keys below them in response to a punched music roll.

Right Early 20th century Wurlitzer player piano. Instruments of this type, the most popular of all automatic pianos, had the piano player mechanism built into the piano case. Interchangeable music rolls, each giving several tunes, passed over an electrically rotated cylinder.

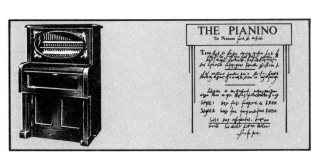

Above Advertisement for a roll-operated Wurlitzer Pianino, popular in the early 1900s as coin-in-the-slot entertainment in bars and cafes. Most instruments of this type were electrically powered, though some manufacturers made models powered by water, gasoline, or clockwork.

Right Reproducing piano—a sophisticated type of player piano capable of reproducing performances by great pianists. Extra holes in the music roll varied the volume of individual notes within a piece, so producing nuances of performance impossible on simpler models.

Mechanical organs

Mechanical organs of all types consist of a set of organ pipes and bellows controlled by mechanical means—usually a barrel. Fitted with pins for short notes and bridges for long notes, barrels may be rotated by hand, clockwork, steam, or electricity. Made for many purposes, mechanical organs range from hand-cranked models for home and church use to the large and elaborate organs made for fairgrounds.

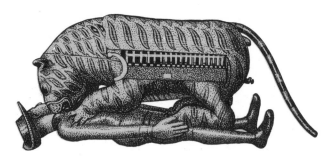

Above Tippoo's tiger—an unusual mechanical organ in the form of a tiger attacking an officer of the British East India Company (Victoria and Albert Museum, London). Captured by the British from Tippoo Sultan in 1799, its pipes produce roars and wails when the handle is turned.

Right 19th century barrel organ. Portable instruments of this type were often used at parties and outdoor gatherings. Spare barrels were stored in the cabinet. Larger versions have sometimes been used in poorer churches as a substitute for a conventional church organ.

Above Organ-grinder—an old street musician with a small barrel organ rested on a stick and held by a strap around his neck.

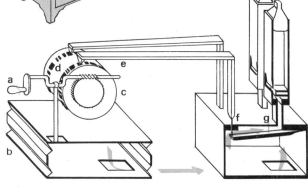

Right How a barrel organ works. Turning the handle (a) pumps the bellows (b) and rotates the barrel (c). Pins and bridges (d) on the barrel's surface lift a pivoted lever (e) which depresses a rod (f). This causes a valve (g) to open, admitting air to the pipes that are to be sounded.

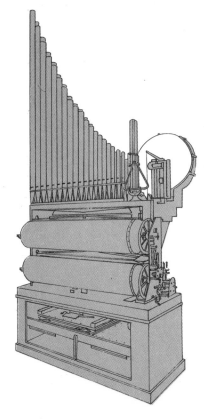

Left Componium (Instrument Museum, Brussels). Made by Winkel of Amsterdam in 1821, this unusual instrument is an orchestrion with a cylinder-operated automatic composing machine capable of improvising variations on a given theme.

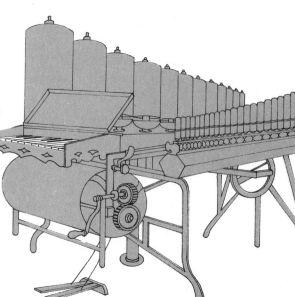

Right Calliope—a steam organ invented by A. S. Denny in the 1850s. It consisted of a set of chromatic whistles sounded by steam from a boiler.

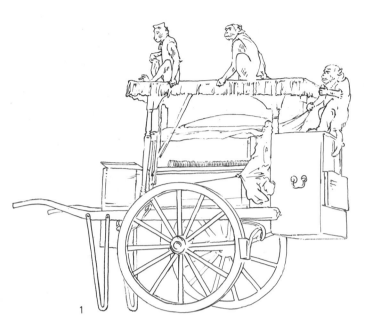

Above Street organs. The hand-cranked barrel organ transported on a hand cart (1) was a common sight in city streets in the late 19th century. Small steam-powered organs, like the English example (2), were mounted on a low trolley.
Right An ornate horse-drawn street organ.

Below A large Marenghi fairground organ, built in 1910 and used for some years in the amusement park in Southend, England. This instrument, an excellent example of its kind, is housed in an elaborate case. Decorative figures at the front strike bells in time with the music.

Electric guitars

An instrument of vast popularity, the electric guitar has been an innovating force behind modern rock groups. Although developed from the acoustic guitar, the modern electric guitar bears only a superficial resemblance to its predecessor. In the electric guitar vibrations of the strings are converted electronically into sound, and a variety of equipment has been developed for effects and amplification.

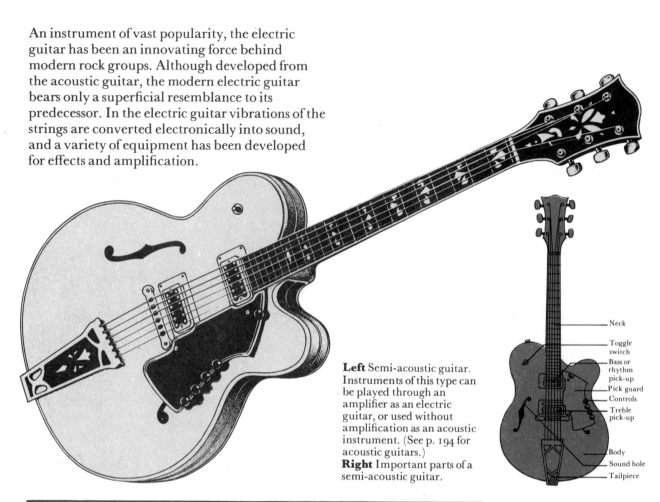

Left Semi-acoustic guitar. Instruments of this type can be played through an amplifier as an electric guitar, or used without amplification as an acoustic instrument. (See p. 194 for acoustic guitars.)
Right Important parts of a semi-acoustic guitar.

Neck
Toggle switch
Bass or rhythm pick-up
Pick guard
Controls
Treble pick-up
Body
Sound hole
Tailpiece

1 Solid-body guitar
2 Double-neck guitar

Left Solid body (1) and double-neck guitar (2). The solid-body instrument shown here is a shape first made by Gibson for Les Paul. The double-neck guitar shown can be used as a six-string or fuller sounding 12-string instrument. Other double-necks are combined six-string and four-string bass models. In electric guitars the body acts only as a string-bearer, and in theory these instruments could be any shape. Tone quality is determined by electronic controls and amplification.
Below Holding a guitar.

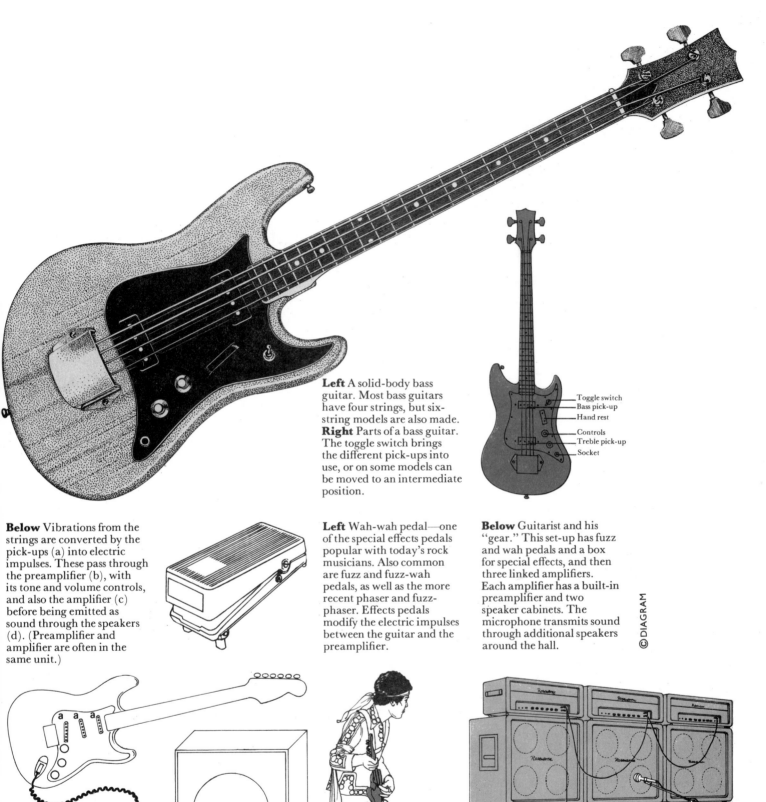

Left A solid-body bass guitar. Most bass guitars have four strings, but six-string models are also made.
Right Parts of a bass guitar. The toggle switch brings the different pick-ups into use, or on some models can be moved to an intermediate position.

Toggle switch
Bass pick-up
Hand rest
Controls
Treble pick-up
Socket

Below Vibrations from the strings are converted by the pick-ups (a) into electric impulses. These pass through the preamplifier (b), with its tone and volume controls, and also the amplifier (c) before being emitted as sound through the speakers (d). (Preamplifier and amplifier are often in the same unit.)

Left Wah-wah pedal—one of the special effects pedals popular with today's rock musicians. Also common are fuzz and fuzz-wah pedals, as well as the more recent phaser and fuzz-phaser. Effects pedals modify the electric impulses between the guitar and the preamplifier.

Below Guitarist and his "gear." This set-up has fuzz and wah pedals and a box for special effects, and then three linked amplifiers. Each amplifier has a built-in preamplifier and two speaker cabinets. The microphone transmits sound through additional speakers around the hall.

© DIAGRAM

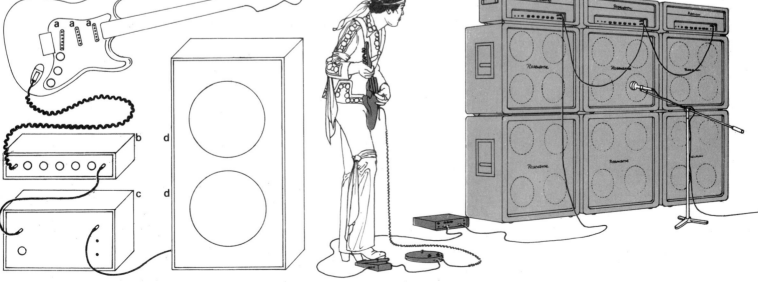

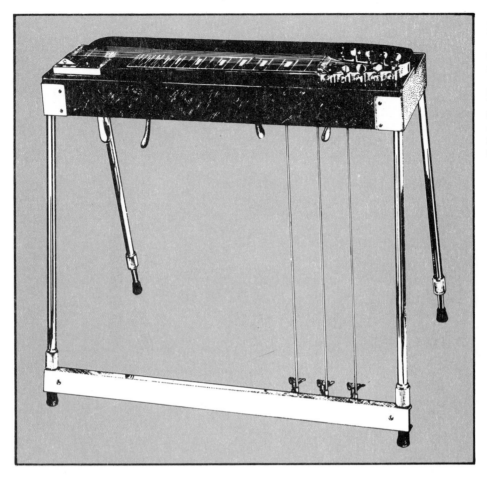

Left Single-neck pedal steel guitar. Used in country and western and some rock music, the pedal steel guitar has floor pedals and knee levers for changing string tunings during play. There are usually one to four knee levers and up to eight floor pedals. Double-neck pedal steel guitars are also popular.

Below Pedal steel guitar player. The instrument's characteristic sound is produced by sliding a metal bar—or "steel"—up and down the strings.

1 Hawaiian guitar
2 Electric mandolin

Left Hawaiian guitar (1) and electric mandolin (2) The Hawaiian guitar, like the pedal steel guitar, has no frets although indicators are painted on the fingerboard. The electric mandolin is a semi-acoustic instrument played with or without amplification. Its strings are tuned in pairs.

Below Hawaiian guitar player. Rested on a stand or across the knees, the Hawaiian guitar is played with a "steel" or sometimes with a tube known as a "bottleneck."

Instruments in which sound is produced by conventional means such as strings or reeds and then amplified or modified electrically are classified as electro-mechanical instruments. The simplest examples have small microphones mounted on the instrument itself which serve to amplify the sound produced. The vibraphone, played in orchestral music and modern jazz, has electrically operated sound-modifying fans.

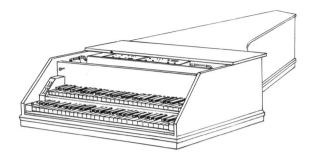

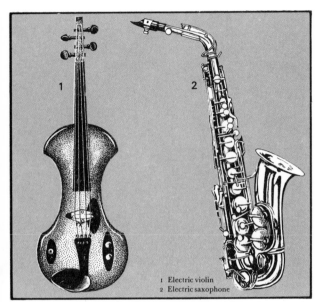

1 Electric violin
2 Electric saxophone

Left Contemporary electro-mechanical instruments. The electric violin (1) has controls for tone and volume, and an internal pick-up. It is played with a bow in the usual way. The electric saxophone (2) has a pick-up on the reed, and a volume control and socket near the mouthpiece.

Below Vibraphone. Used in the orchestral works of major modern composers, the vibraphone resembles the orchestral xylophone in external appearance. Its characteristic vibrato effect is produced by the rotation of electrically operated fans at the upper ends of the resonator tubes.

Above Electric harpsichord. This interesting instrument, now in the Instrument Museum in Brussels, was made by Neupert of Nuremberg. It has the usual harpsichord action. Amplification is by means of microphones in a box over the strings and speakers near the instrument's lid.

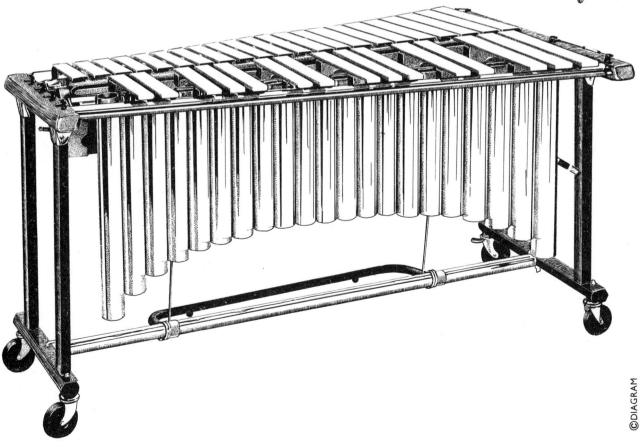

©DIAGRAM

Electric organs

Unlike a traditional organ which produces sound by forcing air through pipes, the electric organ creates sound from signals produced by the oscillations of electronic circuits. These signals are amplified, and then transmitted through speakers. The absence of pipes makes electric organs very compact, and many recent models without pedalboards are easily portable.

Right Parts of an electric organ. The two manuals—great (1) and swell (2)—can be used for contrasting effects, and the pedalboard (3) provides a bass line. The stops and drawbars (4) alter the tone quality by emphasizing selected harmonics. The pre-set buttons (5) bring into operation an entire set of pre-selected stops. The foot pedal (6) is used for volume control.

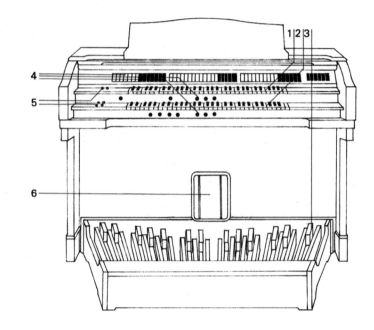

Right How an electric organ works. The oscillations of the tone generator (1) produce an electronic signal which is then modified by the stops and foot pedal. The signal, boosted by the preamplifier (2), passes through the amplifier (3) before being emitted through the speaker (4).

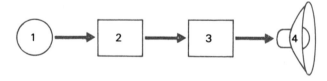

Right Automatic chord selection buttons from a Gulbransen organ. Arranged on a pull-out tray below the lower manual, these buttons operate the pedals. Used in conjunction with a "walking bass" control, patterns of selected chords may be sounded in time with the melody.

Right Pedalboard—with pedals arranged like the notes of the keyboard. Individual notes can be sounded, but more often a special device is used to produce a four or eight note rhythm pattern by touching only one pedal. Common patterns include boogie and Latin American.

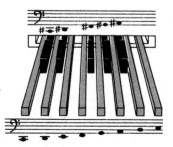

Right Tubon and player. The tubon is an unusual portable electric instrument operating on the same principles as the electric organ.

Right Gulbransen President electric organ, with swell and great manuals, a two-octave pedalboard, and a wide variety of stops. Although most commonly used for popular music, large electric organs are also frequently found in churches as a substitute for a pipe organ.

Right Electric-organ player.
Below Small two-manual electric organ. The great versatility of these portable instruments makes them very popular with rock musicians. Special stops and tabs controlling the manuals produce different effects, such as "wah-wahs," glissandos, and arpeggios.

Right Electric-piano player.
Below Modern electric piano. Similar to the electric organ, this instrument is also popular with rock bands. Its keys respond to touch pressure—a gentle touch gives a quiet note, a firm touch a loud note. Drawbars produce harpsichord and honky-tonk effects.

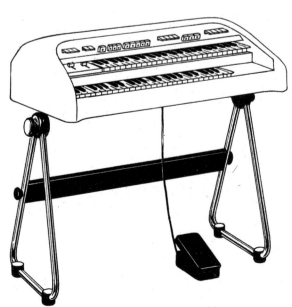

Radio-electric instruments

Radio-electric instruments are characterized by having an electronic sound source. The theremin and ondes martenot, first made in the 1920s, are found only rarely today, but the synthesizer which dates from the 1940s is becoming increasingly popular. Unlike traditional musical composition, "synthetic" music can technically generate, modify, and shape electrical sounds into a piece of music.

Above Ondes martenot—an unusual electronic instrument invented in the 1920s by Maurice Martenot. Controlled by a keyboard, it also has a ribbon device for special "sweeping" effects. Vibrations of the transducer strings give the instrument's characteristic lingering sound.

Right How an ondes martenot works. A keyboard (1) and ribbon (2) control the oscillators (3 and 4). Signals from the oscillators are first mixed in the detector (5), and then pass through an amplifier (6) and tone controls (7) before being emitted as sound through a speaker (8).

Left Theremin—developed in the 1920s and named after its inventor. Signals produced by oscillators are modified by the position of the player's hands. Volume is controlled by the proximity of the left hand to the metal loop, and pitch by moving the right hand toward or away from the rod.

Right Tape recorder of the type found in electronic music studios for composing and performing electronic music. This apparatus consists of a standard two-track stereophonic tape recorder with a sound-wave generator and oscillograph mounted above it.

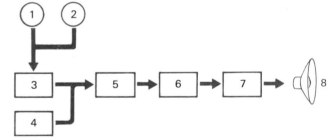

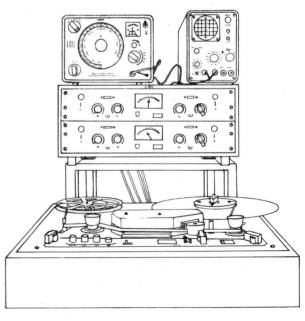

Right Moog Sonic Six—a small portable synthesizer. In most synthesizers the front panel includes controls for the oscillators (which produce electric impulses), mixers (which combine two or more sounds), filters (which emphasize or suppress groups of harmonics), amplifiers (which vary loudness), and a control device, usually a keyboard.

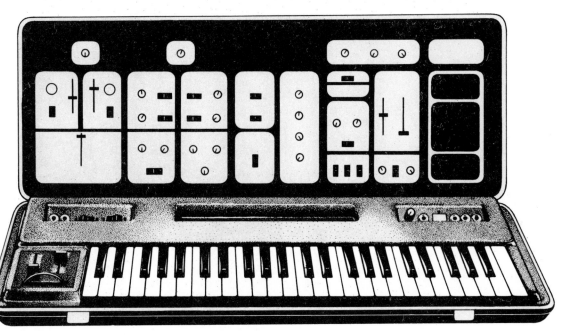

Left Diagram showing how a typical synthesizer works. The oscillators (1, 2, and 3), together with a noise source (4) and external input (5), produce signals which pass through contour generators (6 and 7), a filter (8), and amplifiers (9 and 10) before being emitted through one or more speakers (11).

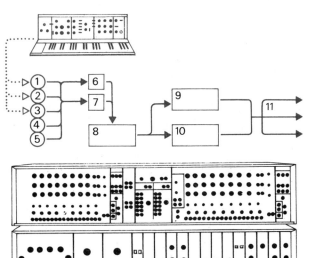

Left Synthesizer with incorporated sequencer for programmed control. Larger models can control every aspect of sound production —pitch, duration, rhythm, and volume. The "attack," "decay," and tone color controls allow the operator to simulate the sounds of traditional instruments.

Right Rock musician using a synthesizer in conjunction with an electric organ. Many groups employ someone to travel with them whose job is to connect, repair, and maintain the electronic equipment. In performances, the blending of the group is achieved by a musician at the mixer board.

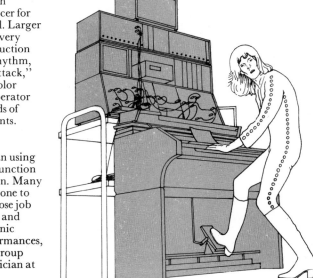

©DIAGRAM

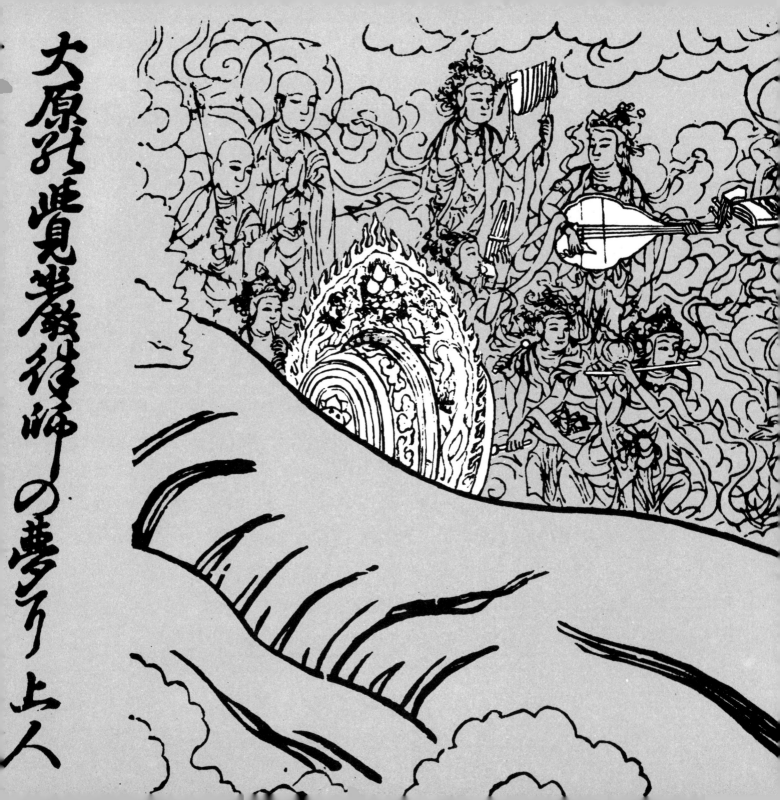

大原孝覧夢厳律師の夢ヨリ上人

Africa

Music permeates almost every aspect of African tribal life. Important simply as entertainment it is also an integral part of many ceremonies and rituals, particularly those connected with birth, initiation, marriage, and death. The art of performance is taken very seriously by many African peoples, and musicians, notably drummers, are usually trained from a very young age. Instruments of every kind are found in sub-Saharan Africa. Idiophones, especially rattles and xylophones, are very important, and along with flutes, trumpets, and horns, are popular ensemble instruments. Drums of every type are played throughout the continent and in some tribes have considerable ritual significance. Chordophones, including bows, harps, lyres, lutes, fiddles, and zithers, are found in most areas and are commonly used as solo or accompanying instruments.

Right Horn player in bronze from the Benin culture of West Africa.

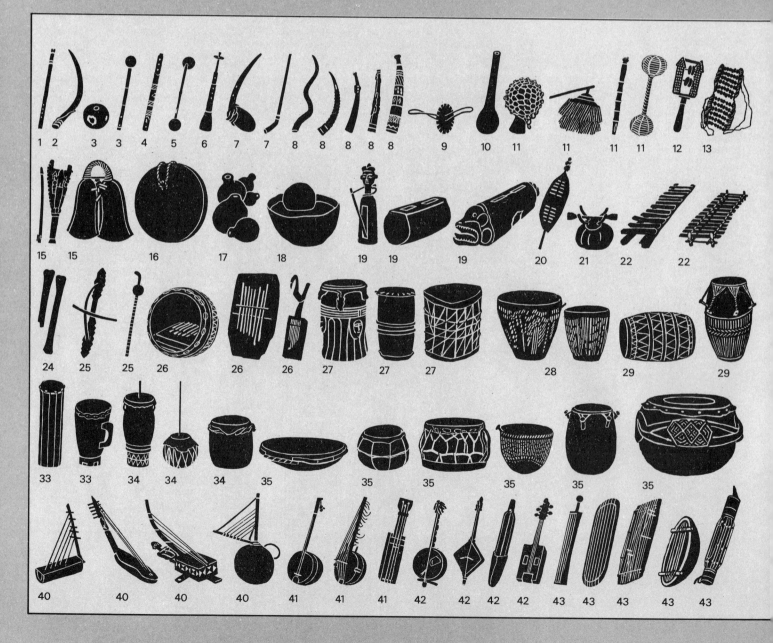

Left Ethiopian sistrum player and drummer from a mural in Aksum cathedral.

Right Player of a long drum—a brass figure from Dahomey, West Africa.

Africa

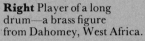

13   13   13   14   14   14   14   14   14

22   22   23   23   24   24

30   31   31   31   32   32   32   32   33   33

36   37   37   37   37   37   38   38   39   39   39

43   43   43   43   43

Aerophones

1 End-blown flute (16)
2 Whistle (20)
3 Vessel flutes (21)
4 Side-blown flute (22)
5 Folk clarinet (37)
6 Folk shawm (45)
7 Simple trumpets (58, 59)
8 Simple horns (66, 67)
9 Buzzer (77)

Idiophones

10 Stamping stick (92)
11 Rattles (94–96)
12 Sistrum (97)
13 Jingles (98, 99)
14 Clapper bells (100, 101)
15 Struck bells (105)
16 Gong (106)
17 Percussion vessels (112)
18 Water drum (113)
19 Slit drums (114)
20 Percussion shield (117)
21 Percussion bar (117)
22 Xylophones (118, 119)
23 Clappers (126)
24 Friction instruments (128)
25 Scrapers (130, 131)
26 Sansas (133)

Membranophones

27 Cylindrical drums (143)
28 Conical drums (145)
29 Barrel drums (146)
30 Waisted drum (148)
31 Goblet drums (150)
32 Footed drums (151)
33 Long drums (152)
34 Friction drums (155)
35 Kettledrums (156)
36 Mirliton (161)

Chordophones

37 Musical bows (166, 167)
38 Multiple bows (167)
39 Lyres (170, 171)
40 Folk harps (172, 173)
41 Folk lutes (178, 182)
42 Folk fiddles (202)
43 Simple zithers (216–218)

(Numbers in brackets are page numbers of main entries.)

©DIAGRAM

The Americas

A survey of musical instruments in the Americas reveals a fascinating diversity of styles and influences. In North America the Indians have generally restricted their music making to ceremonies and ritual, believing that many of their instruments have magical significance. Drums and rattles are the instruments of greatest prestige, while the flute is the only common melody instrument. The Indians of Central and South America play a variety of wind instruments as well as rattles and drums, but there appear to have been no indigenous stringed instruments. Beginning with the introduction of the guitar and harp by the Spaniards, many foreign instruments have been absorbed, modified, and developed in the Americas. Important among these are African folk instruments brought by slaves and the instruments of later immigrants from Europe and elsewhere.

Below Details from Indian paintings—an Arapaho Indian with a bone whistle, and an Indian from the Southwest playing a drum with a painted skin.

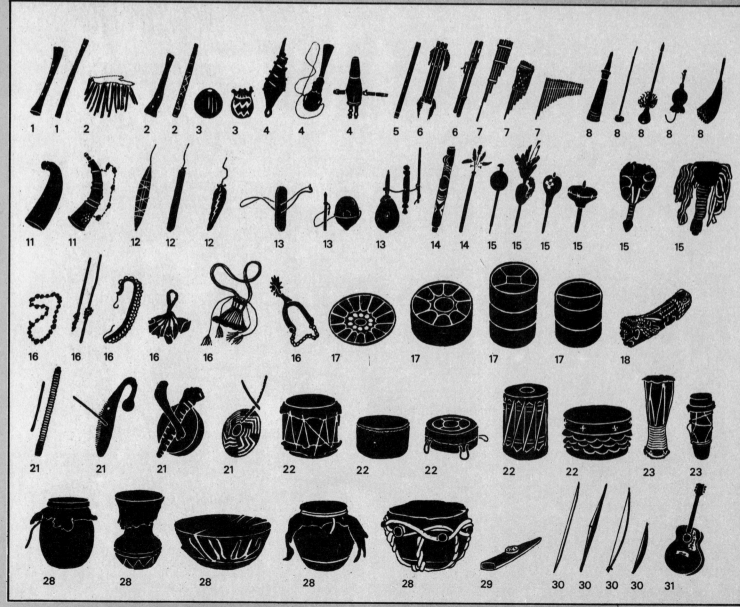

Below Pueblo Indians making music—using two gourd rattles during the Green Corn ceremony, and a cylindrical drum for accompanying the Hot Cornhusk dance.

Below Detail from a Mexican mural, showing musicians with a small drum, footed drum, and rattles.
Right Panpiper from the Inca civilization of Peru.

The Americas

Aerophones

1 End-blown flutes (16, 17)
2 Whistle flutes (18, 19)
3 Vessel flutes (20)
4 Whistles (20)
5 Side-blown flute (22)
6 Multiple flutes (24, 25)
7 Panpipes (27)
8 Folk clarinets (36, 37)
9 Multiple clarinet (39)
10 Simple trumpets (58, 59)
11 Simple horns (67)
12 Bull-roarers (76)
13 Buzzers (77)

Idiophones

14 Stamping sticks (92)
15 Rattles (94–97)
16 Jingles (98, 99)
17 Steel drums (111)
18 Slit drums (115)
19 Marimba (119)
20 Friction instrument (128)
21 Scrapers (130, 131)

Membranophones

22 Cylindrical drums (142)
23 Conical drums (145)
24 Barrel drum (146)
25 Footed drums (151)
26 Long drums (152)
27 Frame drums (154)
28 Kettledrums (157)
29 Kazoo (161)

Chordophones

30 Musical bows (166)
31 Guitars (195)
32 Ukulele (196)
33 Banjo (197)
34 Folk fiddles (203)
35 Appalachian dulcimer (225)

(Numbers in brackets are page numbers of main entries.)

9 10 10 10 10 10 10 10 10 10 10 10

15 15 15 15 15 15′ 15 15 15 15

18 18 18 19 20

24 25 25 26 26 27 27 27

31 31 32 33 34 34 34 34 35

© DIAGRAM

Europe

The folk music culture of Europe is both rich and varied. Different countries, large and small, have their own traditional instruments and their characteristic musical styles. Most instruments are used for entertainment, and particularly for the accompaniment of singing and dancing. Drone instruments, such as the hurdy gurdy and bagpipes, and "harmonic" instruments, like the guitar and zither, provide a fuller sounding accompaniment and for this reason have been especially popular. Instruments of the shawm family, including the piffaro and bombarde, have survived in several areas, while flutes of many types are common in Eastern Europe. Also popular in Eastern Europe are fiddles and lutes, many of which originated in the Middle East. Zithers are a favorite solo and accompanying instrument in Alpine and Scandinavian countries.

Above Illustration from an accordion advertisement, and a figure with a hurdy gurdy.

Right 19th century French popular print of dancing music makers at a carnival.

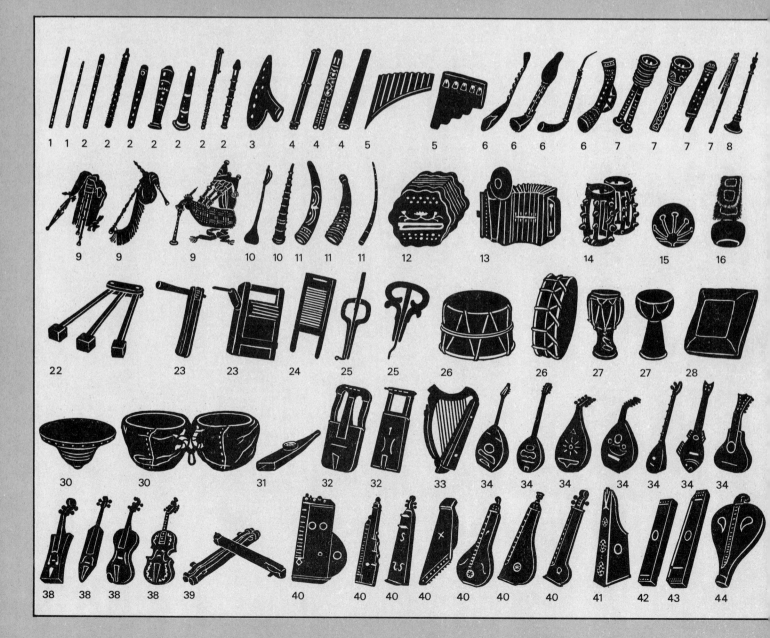

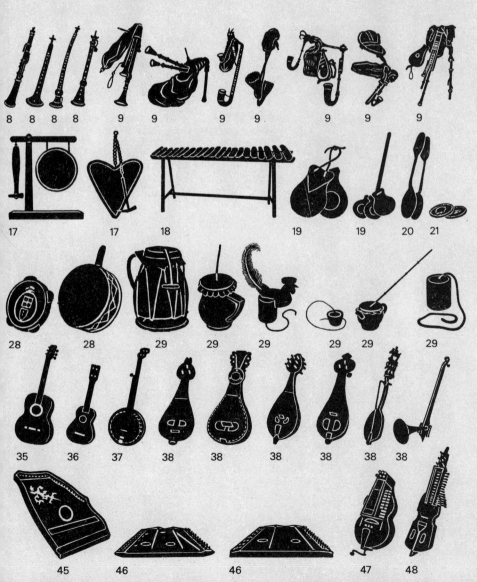

Europe

Aerophones

1 End-blown flutes (17)
2 Whistle flutes (18, 19)
3 Ocarina (21)
4 Multiple flutes (25)
5 Panpipes (27)
6 Folk clarinets (37)
7 Multiple clarinets (38, 39)
8 Folk shawms (44)
9 Bagpipes (55–57)
10 Simple trumpets (58)
11 Simple horns (66, 67)
12 Concertina (80)
13 Accordion (81)

Idiophones

14 Jingles (99)
15 Pellet bell (100)
16 Clapper bell (100)
17 Gongs (106)
18 Lithophone (121)
19 Castanets (125)
20 Spoons (127)
21 Coins (127)
22 Clapper (127)
23 Cog rattles (131)
24 Washboard (131)
25 Jew's harps (132)

Membranophones

26 Cylindrical drums (143)
27 Goblet drums (150)
28 Frame drums (154)
29 Friction drums (155)
30 Kettledrums (157)
31 Kazoo (161)

Chordophones

32 Lyres (169)
33 Harp (175)
34 Folk lutes (179, 182)
35 Guitar (194)
36 Ukulele (196)
37 Banjo (197)
38 Folk fiddles (206, 207)
39 Simple zither (217)
40 Board zithers (222, 223)
41 Upright zither (224)
42 Aeolian harp (224)
43 Tambourin de Béarn (224)
44 Bowed zither (224)
45 Chord zither (225)
46 Dulcimers (226)

Mechanical

47 Hurdy gurdy (248)
48 Nyckelharpa (248)

(Numbers in brackets are page
numbers of main entries.)

©DIAGRAM

Middle East, North Africa, USSR

The music of the countries of the Middle East and North Africa, while showing regional variations, is dominated by the cultural traditions of Islam. Classical music characteristically uses the lute, psaltery, spike fiddle, flute, and drums as its principal instruments, while reed pipes are common in folk music. Russian instruments show a diversity of forms reflecting a wide range of influence.

Right Russian musician playing a dumbrak—a folk lute of Middle Eastern origin.

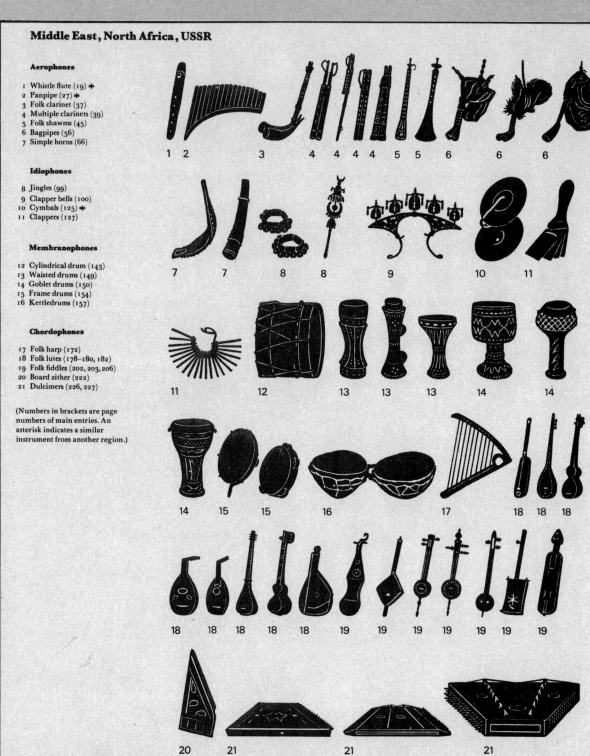

Middle East, North Africa, USSR

Aerophones

1 Whistle flute (19) ✲
2 Panpipe (27) ✲
3 Folk clarinet (37)
4 Multiple clarinets (39)
5 Folk shawms (45)
6 Bagpipes (56)
7 Simple horns (66)

Idiophones

8 Jingles (99)
9 Clapper bells (100)
10 Cymbals (125) ✲
11 Clappers (127)

Membranophones

12 Cylindrical drum (143)
13 Waisted drums (149)
14 Goblet drums (150)
15 Frame drums (154)
16 Kettledrums (157)

Chordophones

17 Folk harp (172)
18 Folk lutes (178–180, 182)
19 Folk fiddles (202, 203, 206)
20 Board zither (222)
21 Dulcimers (226, 227)

(Numbers in brackets are page numbers of main entries. An asterisk indicates a similar instrument from another region.)

India

Indian classical music is closely related to the musical culture of the Middle East. In its most characteristic form, a group of two or three players improvise on set rhythmic and melodic patterns known as talas and ragas. The sitar and vina are popular solo instruments, while the tambura and tabla are used for accompaniment. Fiddles, reed pipes, and drums are commonly found as folk instruments.

Right Part of an 11th century relief showing dancers and musicians of the god Indra.

India

Aerophones

1 Whistle flute (18)
2 Side-blown flute (22)
3 Folk clarinets (37)
4 Multiple clarinet (38)
5 Folk shawms (45)
6 Bagpipe (56)
7 Simple horns (67)

Idiophones

8 Rattle (97)
9 Jingles (99)
10 Clapper bell (101)
11 Gongs (106)
12 Cymbals (125)✛
13 Scraper (130)
14 Jew's harp (132)

Membranophones

15 Tabla (144)
16 Double drum (144)
17 Barrel drums (146)
18 Waisted drums (148)
19 Goblet drum (150)
20 Long drums (152)
21 Frame drums (154)
22 Kettledrums (157)

Chordophones

23 Musical bow (167)
24 Sitar (181)
25 Folk lutes (181)
26 Folk fiddles (204, 205)
27 Vinas (219)
28 Dulcimer (226)

(Numbers in brackets are page numbers of main entries. An asterisk indicates a similar instrument from another region.)

1 2 3   3   4 5   5   6   7   7   7   8 9   9

9   10   11   11   12   13 14   15   15

16   17   17   17   17   17   18   18   18   19

20   20   21   21   22   22   22   22

22   23 24   25   25   25   26   26   26   26

26   26   26   27   27   27   27   28

© DIAGRAM

Far East

The major influence on the music of a vast area of Southeast Asia has been the classical music of China. Chinese classical music, based on sophisticated theories dating back 3000 years, has greatly influenced the musical development of neighboring countries, and instruments that originated in China are now found in similar forms elsewhere. Among the most distinctive instruments of mainland Southeast Asia and Japan are spike fiddles, gongs, mouth organs with bamboo pipes, and lutes and long zithers plucked with large plectra. A significant contribution to the musical life of this part of the world has been made by specific groups of instruments played in association with court entertainments, religious ceremonies, and theatrical performances. Also important is solo music for lutes like the p'ip'a and biwa and zithers such as the ch'in and koto.

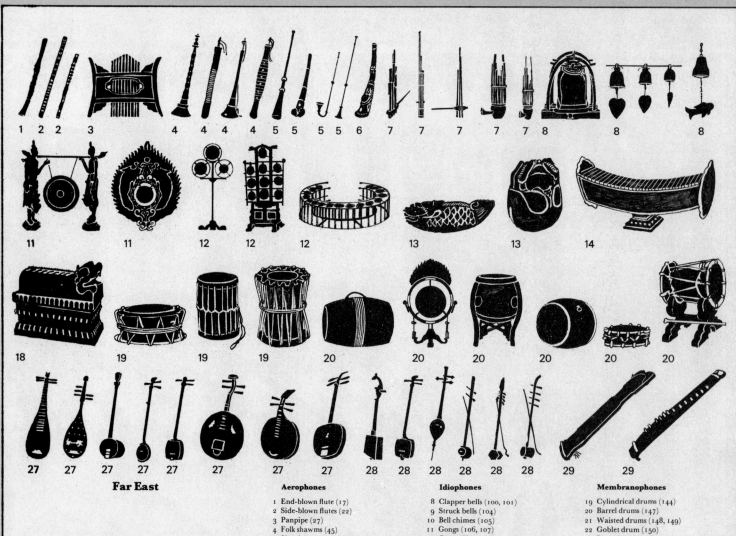

Far East

Aerophones
1 End-blown flute (17)
2 Side-blown flutes (22)
3 Panpipe (27)
4 Folk shawms (45)
5 Simple trumpets (58, 59)
6 Simple horn (67)
7 Mouth organs (78)

Idiophones
8 Clapper bells (100, 101)
9 Struck bells (104)
10 Bell chimes (105)
11 Gongs (106, 107)
12 Gong chimes (109)
13 Slit drums (115)
14 Xylophone (120)
15 Lithophone (121)
16 Cymbals (125)
17 Clappers (127)
18 Scraper (131)

Membranophones
19 Cylindrical drums (144)
20 Barrel drums (147)
21 Waisted drums (148, 149)
22 Goblet drum (150)
23 Long drum (152)
24 Frame drum (154)

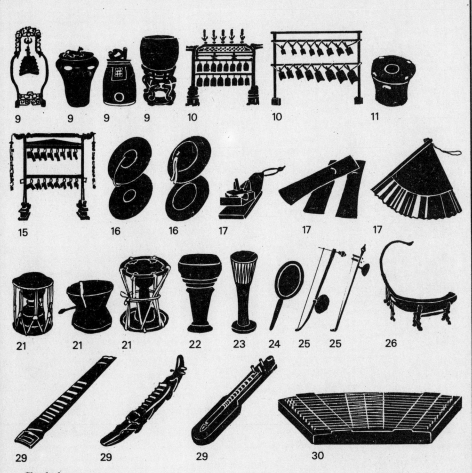

Chordophones

25 Musical bows (167)
26 Folk harp (173)
27 Folk lutes (180, 183)
28 Folk fiddles (205)
29 Long zithers (220, 221)
30 Dulcimer (227)

(Numbers in brackets are page
numbers of main entry.)

Above Peking street
peddlers—from a thesis
published in the 1930s.

Above 19th century
Japanese caricature of a
dancing samisen player.

©DIAGRAM

Indonesia

Music in Indonesia centers on the gamelan ensemble—an instrumental group of variable size and function used in association with state ritual, religious ceremonies, and drama. Tuned percussion instruments—notably gongs, gong chimes, and metallophones—are most important, while drums, flutes, and fiddles are also found. Although notation exists, performances are usually improvised or played from memory.

Left Detail taken from a carved wall frieze Barabudur, Java.

Indonesia

Aerophones

1 Folk shawm (45)

Idiophones

2 Anklung (97)
3 Jingle (99)
4 Clapper bell (101)
5 Gong (107)
6 Gong chimes (108, 109)
7 Xylophone (120)
8 Saron (122)
9 Gansas (122)
10 Genders (123)
11 Cymbals (125)
12 Clappers (126, 127)

Membranophones

13 Cylindrical drum (144)
14 Conical drums (145)
15 Barrel drums (147)
16 Frame drums (154)

Chordophones

17 Folk fiddle (205)

(Numbers in brackets are page numbers of main entry.)

Oceania

Tribal customs and practices dominate the music of Oceania. Particularly important among the many instruments used for ritual and signaling are primitive idiophones such as stamping sticks and scrapers. Slit drums and the distinctive long-bodied drums of New Guinea are thought to have magical powers and are often decorated with carvings. Flutes, jew's harps, and trumpets are also characteristic of the region.

Right Musicians from an Australian aboriginal cave painting.

Oceania

Aerophones

1 End-blown flute (16)
2 Vessel flute (20)
3 Nose flute (23)
4 Simple trumpets (58, 59)
5 Simple horn (67)
6 Bull-roarers (76)
7 Mouth organ (78)

Idiophones

8 Stamping sticks (92)
9 Stamping board (93)
10 Rattle (94)
11 Clapper bell (101)
12 Percussion vessels (112, 113)
13 Slit drums (116)
14 Trough drum (116)
15 Clappers (126, 127)
16 Friction instruments (128)
17 Scrapers (130)
18 Jew's harp (132)

Membranophones

19 Cylindrical drum (144)
20 Waisted drums (148)
21 Footed drums (151)
22 Long drums (153)
23 Kettledrum (157)

Chordophones

24 Musical bows (166)
25 Folk harp (172)
26 Simple zithers (217)

(Numbers in brackets are page numbers of main entry.)

1 2 3 4 4 4 4 4 5 6 6 6 7

8 8 9 10 11 12 12 13

13 13 14 15 15 15

16 16 17 17 18 18 18 19

20 20 21 21 22 22 22 22 22

23 24 25 26 26

© DIAGRAM

Ancient instruments

The history of musical instruments began many thousands of years ago when early man first used natural objects as sound makers. Later, civilized societies developed more sophisticated instruments.

Left Musicians with lyres, tambourine, and cymbals, drawn from an Assyrian relief of the 7th century BC.

Musical instruments are known to have existed in Europe over 25,000 years ago. The earliest examples were simple rhythm instruments used to emphasize man's own rhythm "instruments" of clapping hands and stamping feet. Many wind instruments, too, have a very long history. Bone, stone, wood, clay, and later metal were all used for making ancient instruments, which were generally employed in signaling and ritual.

The development of higher civilizations in the Middle East and Europe led to the evolution of more sophisticated instruments used for entertainment purposes. Contemporary literary and visual sources, together with surviving examples, prove the existence of a wide variety of instruments, and it is known that the ancient Greeks and Romans in particular regarded their makers and performers with the highest esteem.

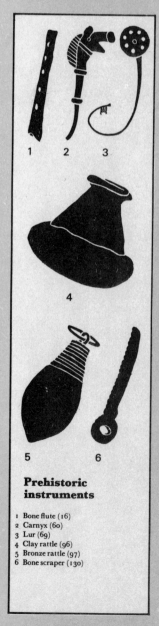

Prehistoric instruments

1 Bone flute (16)
2 Carnyx (60)
3 Lur (69)
4 Clay rattle (96)
5 Bronze rattle (97)
6 Bone scraper (130)

Middle East and Europe

Assyria and Sumeria

1 Trumpet (60)
2 Bell (101)
3 Cymbals (124)
4 Lyre (168)

(Numbers in brackets are page numbers of main entries. An asterisk indicates a similar instrument from another region.)

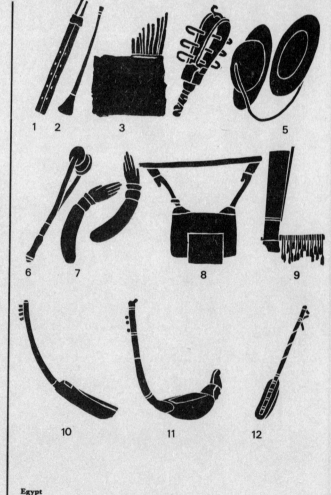

Egypt

1 Double clarinet (39)
2 Trumpet (60)
3 Hydraulis (82)*
4 Sistrum (97)
5 Cymbals (124)
6 Crotals (124)
7 Clappers (126)
8 Lyre (168)
9 Angle harp (174)
10 Shoulder harp (174)
11 Bow harp (174)
12 Lute (184)

Above Greek lyre player depicted on pottery.

Right Roman trumpet players from a relief on Trajan's column.

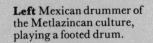

Left Mexican drummer of the Metlazincan culture, playing a footed drum.

The Indian civilizations of Central and South America developed a rich musical culture of their own in the centuries before the arrival of the first Europeans. Flutes, including whistles and panpipes, were most important and a great variety of examples survive in museums. Rattles, scrapers, and drums were also significant, but interestingly there is no evidence of any stringed instruments at all.

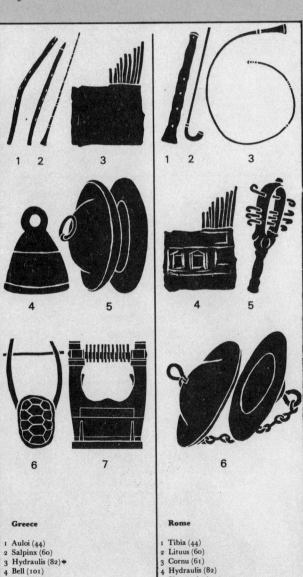

Greece

1 Auloi (44)
2 Salpinx (60)
3 Hydraulis (82)*
4 Bell (101)
5 Cymbals (124)
6 Lyra (168)
7 Kithara (168)

Rome

1 Tibia (44)
2 Lituus (60)
3 Cornu (61)
4 Hydraulis (82)
5 Sistrum (97)
6 Cymbals (124)

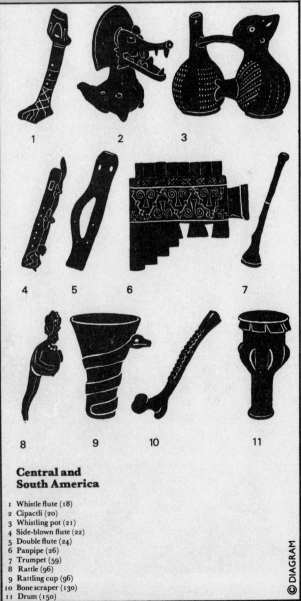

Central and South America

1 Whistle flute (18)
2 Cipactli (20)
3 Whistling pot (21)
4 Side-blown flute (22)
5 Double flute (24)
6 Panpipe (26)
7 Trumpet (59)
8 Rattle (96)
9 Rattling cup (96)
10 Bone scraper (130)
11 Drum (150)

© DIAGRAM

Medieval instruments

Evidence from manuscripts, paintings, and church windows has been pieced together to provide an impression of the musical life of medieval Europe. Few instruments survive from this period, and sources suggest that the musical culture was less rich than that of the ancient civilizations of Greece and Rome. Certainly there was no clear distinction between folk and art music. Instruments were used mainly for the accompaniment of the voice, and drone instruments such as the hurdy gurdy and bagpipes were favorites with medieval minstrels and troubadours. Very important in this period were Middle Eastern influences on the instruments of Western Europe. The Arab conquest of Spain and the return of Crusaders from the Middle East resulted in the introduction of previously unknown instruments and in modifications to those already in use.

Left Medieval monarch playing a harp to the accompaniment of two horn players.

Above Lyre player from a romanesque pillar at Cluny, France.

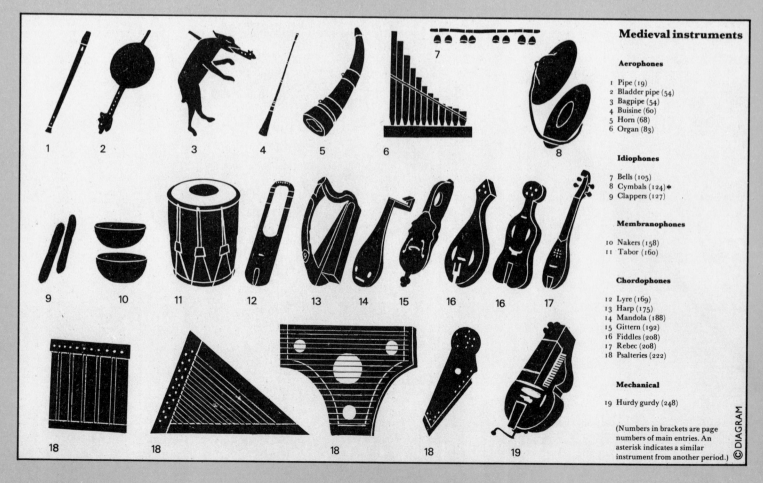

Medieval instruments

Aerophones

1 Pipe (19)
2 Bladder pipe (54)
3 Bagpipe (54)
4 Buisine (60)
5 Horn (68)
6 Organ (83)

Idiophones

7 Bells (105)
8 Cymbals (124)*
9 Clappers (127)

Membranophones

10 Nakers (158)
11 Tabor (160)

Chordophones

12 Lyre (169)
13 Harp (175)
14 Mandola (188)
15 Gittern (192)
16 Fiddles (208)
17 Rebec (208)
18 Psalteries (222)

Mechanical

19 Hurdy gurdy (248)

(Numbers in brackets are page numbers of main entries. An asterisk indicates a similar instrument from another period.)

© DIAGRAM

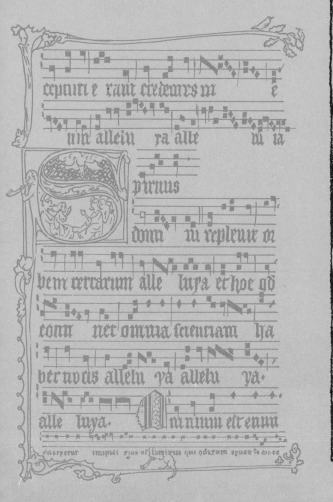

Above Angels playing horns in a 14th century manuscript illustration.
Below A typical medieval music manuscript in which the melody is indicated by symbols—called neumes—positioned on sets of four lines. This system was the forerunner of modern staff notation.

Right German woodcut showing Apollo surrounded by an assembly of gods. Apollo is playing a fiddle while the deities play a variety of instruments including bagpipes, horns, a lute, and a harp.

Renaissance instruments

In contrast with the Middle Ages the Renaissance was a period of intense musical activity in Europe. The most significant of the many musical developments in the years 1450 to 1650 was the rise in the importance of instrumental music. Beginning with the replacement of one or more of the melodic lines in a vocal piece, composers went on to write truly independent parts for instruments. A wealth of music was specially written for consorts—small groups of instruments such as recorders and viols—and also for keyboards such as the harpsichord and organ. The rise of opera around 1600 in Italy was an important influence on the development of instrumental music. Opera orchestras were assembled to accompany the singers, and composers first began to exploit the specific tone colors of individual instruments.

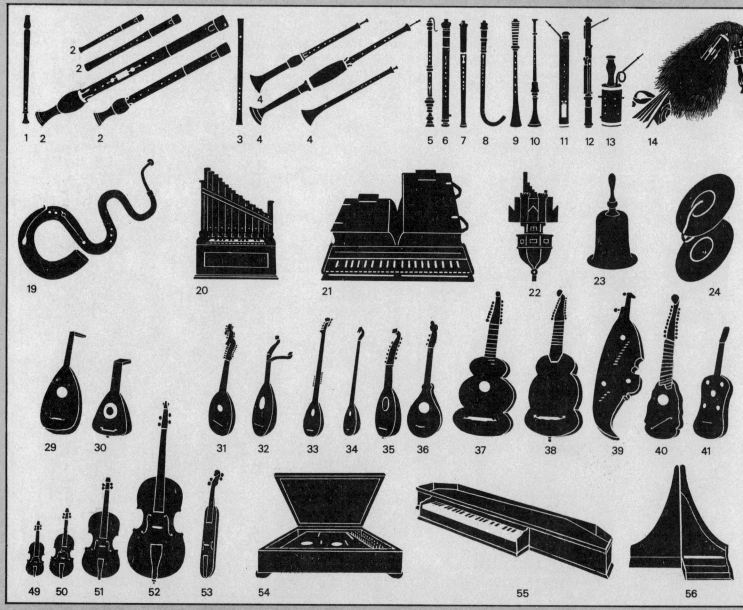

Left Woodcut from "Theorica Musicae," 1492, by Franchinus Gafurius. A reflection of contemporary interest in the theory of music, this illustration shows experiments concerning the mathematical relationship of musical intervals.

Right Group of renaissance musicians taken from an early 17th century title page. The ensemble includes a keyboard, violin, viol, trombone, lute, recorders, and voices.

Renaissance instruments

Aerophones

1 Pipe (19)
2 Renaissance recorders (28)
3 Flute (32)
4 Shawms (46)
5 Bassanello (46)
6 Courtaut (47)
7 Cornemuse (47)
8 Crumhorn (47)
9 Rauschpfeife (47)
10 Deutsche schalmei (47)
11 Curtal (47)
12 Sordone (47)
13 Racket (47)
14 Musette (55)
15 Trumpet (61)
16 Trombone (64)
17 Horn (68)
18 Cornetts (72)
19 Serpent (72)
20 Portative organ (83)
21 Regal (83)
22 Swallow's nest organ (85)

Idiophones

23 Handbell (102)
24 Cymbals (124)*
25 Clappers (127)*

Membranophones

26 Long drum (159)*
27 Kettledrum (159)*
28 Side drum (159)*

(Numbers in brackets are page numbers of main entries. An asterisk indicates a similar instrument from another period.)

Chordophones

29 Lute (184)
30 Soprano lute (185)
31 Theorbo (186)
32 Theorbo–lute (186)
33 Chitarrone (187)
34 Colascione (187)
35 Mandola (188)
36 Cittern (190)
37 Pandora (191)
38 Penorcon (191)
39 Bass cittern (191)
40 Orpharion (191)
41 Vihuela (192)
42 Guitar (192)
43 Viols (199)
44 Viola d'amore (200)
45 Baryton (200)
46 Tromba marina (201)
47 Lira da braccio (209)
48 Lira da gamba (209)
49 Violin (210)
50 Viola (212)
51 Violoncello (213)
52 Double bass (214)
53 Sordine (215)
54 Psaltery (222)
55 Clavichord (228)
56 Clavicytherium (233)
57 Harpsichord (231)
58 Virginal (234)
59 Spinet (235)

Baroque and classical instruments

The baroque period, after 1650, saw the regular use of an ensemble which became the nucleus of the modern orchestra. It included the modern string group, flutes or recorders, oboes, bassoons, trumpets, and horns. Also characteristic was the continuo of keyboard and cello or bassoon provided to give a firm bass line and strengthen the harmonies. With the transition to the classical period, around 1750, the continuo was abandoned and the orchestra enlarged with the addition of clarinets and occasionally trombones. The baroque contrapuntal style, characterized by the interweaving of melodies played by different instruments, was in the classical period replaced by a style in which the emphasis was on melody and bass. Another important classical development was the enthusiastic adoption by most composers of the newly developed pianoforte.

Left Horn player in 18th century Viennese porcelain.

Left Engraving showing violin and virginal players from the title page of a 1663 book of lessons for the virginal by John Playford.

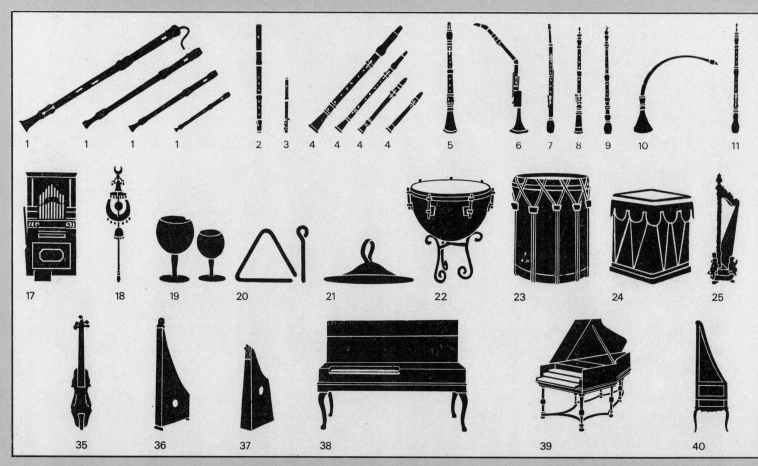

Above Cherub musicians playing panpipes and trumpets, taken from a title page of 1770.

Right A humorous title page from an early 19th century edition of Mozart's divertimento "A Musical Joke," K.522, scored for two violins, viola, double bass, and two horns.

Right Illustrations from "Gabinetto Armonico" an 18th century book on musical instruments by Filippo Bonanni.

Baroque and classical instruments

Aerophones

1 Baroque recorders (29)
2 Flute (32)
3 Piccolo (33)
4 Chalumeaux (40)
5 Clarinet (40)
6 Basset horn (42)
7 Clarinet d'amore (42)
8 Oboe (48)
9 Oboe d'amore (49)
10 Cor anglais (49)
11 Oboe da caccia (49)
12 Bassoon (52)
13 Contrabassoon (52)
14 Natural trumpet (61)
15 Slide trombone (65)
16 Natural horn (68)
17 Chamber organ (84)

Idiophones

18 Jingling johnny (99)
19 Musical glasses (129)
20 Triangle (136)
21 Cymbal (136)

Membranophones

22 Kettledrum (158)
23 Long drum (159)
24 Side drum (159)

Chordophones

25 Diatonic harp (175)
26 Lute (184)
27 Mandolin (188)
28 Cittern (190)
29 Guitar (192)
30 Chitarra battente (192)
31 Violin (211)
32 Viola (212)
33 Violoncello (213)
34 Double bass (214)
35 Kit (215)
36 Arpanetta (224)
37 Diplo-kithara (224)
38 Clavichord (229)
39 Harpsichord (231)
40 Upright harpsichord (233)
41 Spinet (235)
42 Piano (236)
43 Square piano (237)

(Numbers in brackets are page numbers of main entries.)

©DIAGRAM

Romantic instruments

The outstanding features of the romantic period, after 1830, were the rise of the virtuoso and the increasing influence of art and literature on music. The extraordinary technical gifts of such virtuoso performers as Paganini and Liszt encouraged composers to write more demanding parts both for soloists and the orchestral group as a whole. Interest in art and literature led composers to write descriptive pieces in the form of symphonic poems and concert overtures which were freer both in content and construction than the traditional symphony or concerto. Experiments in the field of instrument making gave rise to significant improvements to such instruments as the flute, trumpet, and piano. Several new instruments were also developed in the period, but only a few, like the tuba and saxophone, have survived to the 20th century.

Above Members of the Distin family playing saxhorns made for them by Adolphe Sax in 1844.

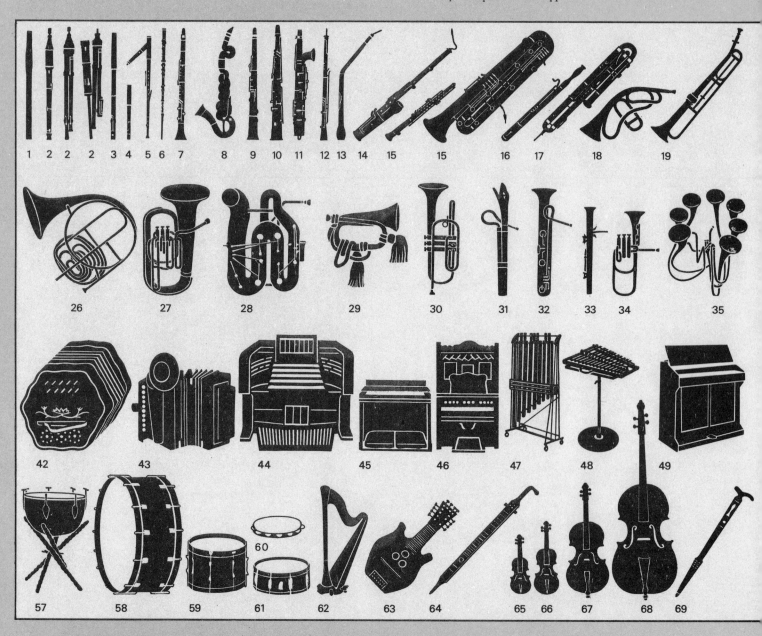

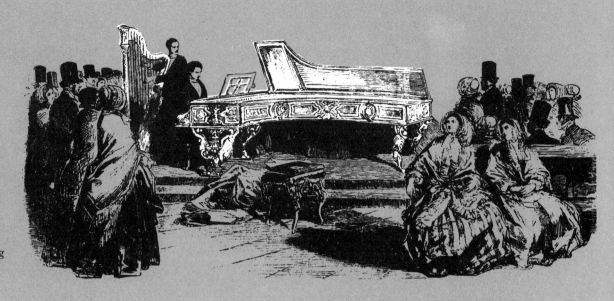

Right Detail from a 19th century illustration showing a demonstration of Erard pianos and harps.

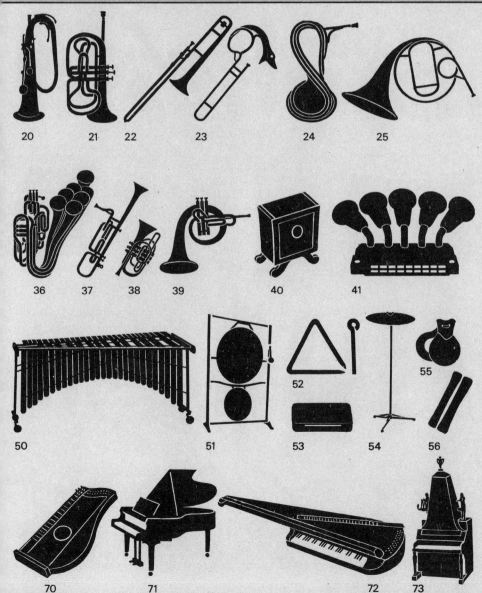

Romantic instruments

Aerophones

1 Fife (23)
2 Flageolets (31)
3 Flute (32)
4 Piccolo (33)
5 Bass flute (33)
6 Walking stick flute (35)
7 Clarinet (41)
8 Bass clarinet (42)
9 Tarogato (42)
10 Heckelclarina (42)
11 Octavin (43)
12 Oboe (48)
13 Cor anglais (49)
14 Baritone oboe (49)
15 Sarrusophones (51)
16 Bassoon (52)
17 Contrabassoon (53)
18 Hand trumpet (62)*
19 Slide trumpet (62)*
20 Keyed trumpet (62)*
21 Valved trumpet (62)
22 Slide trombone (65)
23 Buccin trombone (64)
24 Hand horn (69)
25 Crook horn (69)
26 Omnitonic horn (69)
27 Tuba (71)
28 Serpent (72)
29 Bugle (73)
30 Cornet (73)
31 Basshorn (74)
32 Ophicleide (74)
33 Tuba-Dupré (74)
34 Saxhorn (74)
35 Alto horn (74)
36 Tenor trombone (74)
37 Clavicor (74)
38 Alto marching horn (75)
39 Könighorn (75)
40 Symphonium (79)
41 Mouth organ (79)
42 Concertina (80)
43 Accordion (81)
44 Organ (85)
45 Harmonium (87)
46 Parlor organ (87)

Idiophones

47 Tubular bells (134)
48 Glockenspiel (134)
49 Celeste (134)
50 Xylophone (135)
51 Gongs (136)
52 Triangle (136)
53 Wood block (136)
54 Cymbal (136)*
55 Castanets (136)
56 Claves (136)

Membranophones

57 Kettledrum (158)
58 Bass drum (159)*
59 Tenor drum (159)*
60 Tambourine (159)*
61 Side drum (159)*

Chordophones

62 Pedal harp (177)
63 Guitar (193)
64 Walking stick guitar (193)
65 Violin (211)
66 Viola (212)
67 Violoncello (213)
68 Double bass (214)
69 Walking stick violin (215)
70 Zither (225)
71 Grand piano (241)
72 Orphica (238)
73 Pyramid piano (239)

(Numbers in brackets are page numbers of main entries. An asterisk indicates a similar instrument from another period.)

© DIAGRAM

Modern instruments

Instrumental music of the 20th century may be divided into two broad groups. The first includes pieces for traditional resources in conventional forms such as the symphony, concerto, and sonata. The other comprises avant garde or "modern" music in which tapes and electronically produced sounds are used to supplement traditional instruments. Two new types of instrument have made an impact on modern music and helped to bridge the gap between "popular" and "serious" musical styles. The first group—electro-mechanical—includes instruments such as the electric guitar in which the sound is produced mechanically but amplified or modified by electrical means. The second group comprises radio-electric instruments such as the electric organ and synthesizer in which the sound itself is produced electronically.

Below Illustration from an early 20th century advertisement for an automatic piano.

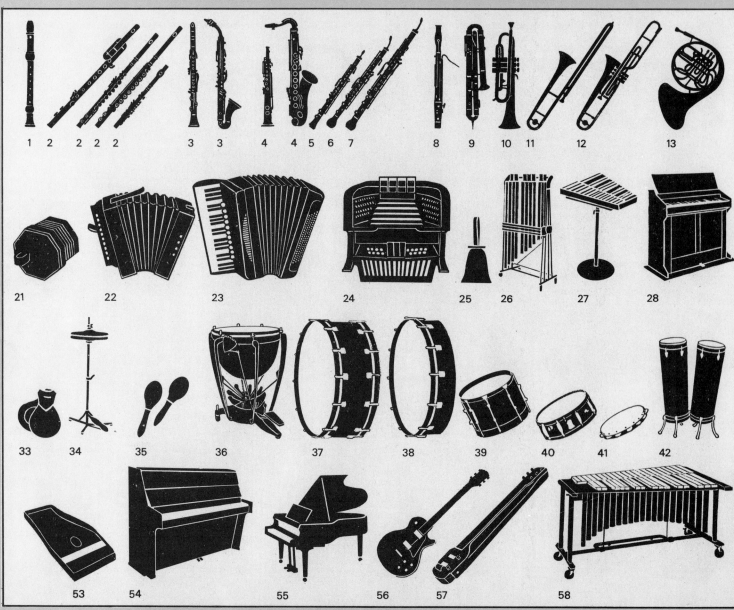

Left King Oliver's Creole Jazz Band in 1923 — one of the greatest of all traditional jazz groups.
Right The Beatles — the sound of the '60s from Liverpool, England.

Right Avant garde score. Inspired by the symbols on the score, any number of musicians play unspecified instruments in any sequence for any length of time.

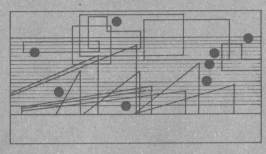

Modern instruments

Aerophones

1 Recorder (29)
2 Flutes (34)
3 Clarinets (41)
4 Saxophones (43)
5 Oboe (50)
6 Oboe d'amore (50)
7 Cor anglais (50)
8 Bassoon (53)
9 Contrabassoon (53)
10 Trumpet (63)
11 Trombone (65)
12 Valve trombone (65)
13 Horn (70)
14 Tuba (71)
15 Bugle (73)*
16 Cornet (73)
17 Sousaphone (75)
18 Euphonium (75)
19 Mouth organs (79)
20 Melodica (79)
21 Concertina (80)
22 Melodeon (80)
23 Accordion (81)
24 Organ (85)

Idiophones

25 Handbell (102)
26 Tubular bells (134)
27 Glockenspiel (134)
28 Celeste (134)
29 Xylophone (135)
30 Gongs (136)
31 Triangle (136)
32 Claves (136)
33 Castanets (136)
34 Cymbals (136)
35 Maracas (137)

Membranophones

36 Timpani (158)
37 Bass drum (159)
38 Gong drum (159)
39 Tenor drum (159)
40 Side drum (159)
41 Tambourine (159)
42 Cocktail drums (160)
43 Timbales (160)

Chordophones

44 Harp (177)
45 Mandolin (189)
46 Guitar (194)
47 Ukulele (196)
48 Banjo (197)
49 Violin (211)
50 Viola (212)
51 Violoncello (213)
52 Double bass (214)
53 Zither (225)
54 Upright piano (240)
55 Grand piano (241)

Electrical

56 Electric guitar (254)
57 Hawaiian guitar (256)
58 Vibraphone (257)
59 Electric organ (259)
60 Ondes martenot (260)
61 Synthesizer (261)

(Numbers in brackets are page numbers of main entries. An asterisk indicates a similar instrument from another period.)

©DIAGRAM

Orchestral and chamber groups

The orchestra is the best known of all Western instrumental groups. Most major cities of the world have at least one full-sized orchestra giving regular performances of a wide variety of music. The exact instrumental resources employed at any performance vary according to the style of music being played. Most baroque pieces require only a small "chamber" orchestra, while works dating from the 19th and 20th centuries usually require a much larger orchestra. The majority of the orchestral repertory is made up of symphonies, overtures, and concertos. As well as in the concert hall, orchestras may be heard in theaters and churches taking part in performances of opera, ballet, and oratorios. Also popular with concert goers are small ensembles of different kinds used for the performance of chamber works.

Left Chronology of the introduction of instruments into the orchestra. Dates are approximate — instruments were used sporadically in the orchestra before being adopted as regular members.

Below "The triumphs of Maximilian" — a woodcut of 1512 showing a group of Renaissance musicians.

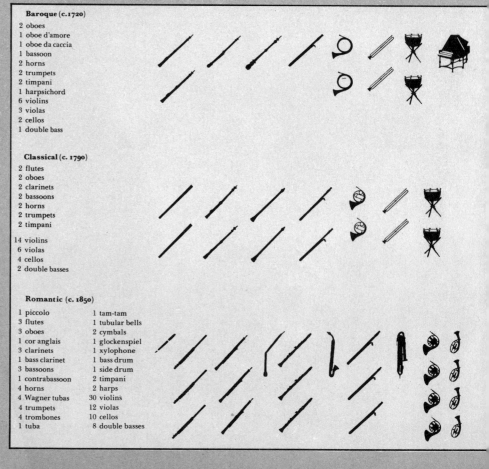

Right Instruments of the orchestra at different periods, and an illustration of a large 19th century orchestra. The basis of the small baroque orchestra was the string group and continuo. Oboes and bassoons appeared regularly while the oboe d'amore and oboe da caccia were popular additions. Trumpets, timpani, and horns were used only sparingly. The typical classical orchestra had no continuo, but a large string group and two each of flutes, oboes, clarinets, bassoons, horns, trumpets, and timpani. The romantic orchestra included enlarged string, wind, and brass groups, and new instruments like the tuba, harp, and celeste. Wagner and Berlioz are the composers most often associated with such vast resources. The orchestra retained these massive proportions until the early 1900s when numbers were reduced for both artistic and economic reasons.

Timeline (left margin)

1650

Violin, viola, cello, harpsichord

Oboe, bassoon

1700

Double bass

Recorder, flute, trumpet, timpani, horn

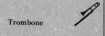

Trombone

Bass drum, side drum, cymbals, triangle

1800

Piccolo, cor anglais, bass clarinet, contrabassoon

Harp

Glockenspiel, tuba, xylophone, tam-tam, celeste

1900

Vibraphone

1930

Baroque (c.1720)

2 oboes
1 oboe d'amore
1 oboe da caccia
1 bassoon
2 horns
2 trumpets
2 timpani
1 harpsichord
6 violins
3 violas
2 cellos
1 double bass

Classical (c. 1790)

2 flutes
2 oboes
2 clarinets
2 bassoons
2 horns
2 trumpets
2 timpani

14 violins
6 violas
4 cellos
2 double basses

Romantic (c. 1850)

1 piccolo	1 tam-tam
3 flutes	1 tubular bells
3 oboes	2 cymbals
1 cor anglais	1 glockenspiel
3 clarinets	1 xylophone
1 bass clarinet	1 bass drum
3 bassoons	1 side drum
1 contrabassoon	2 timpani
4 horns	2 harps
4 Wagner tubas	30 violins
4 trumpets	12 violas
4 trombones	10 cellos
1 tuba	8 double basses

Right Typical chamber groups for music of the 18th and 19th centuries. Chamber groups have from two to ten performers, each playing a different part. Baroque sonatas for solo instruments such as the oboe or flute have a cello and harpsichord accompaniment (a). (Similar in style are trio sonatas featuring two treble instruments — oboes, flutes, recorders, or violins — with cello and keyboard continuo). String trios for violin, viola, and cello (b) and string quartets for two violins, viola, and cello (c) were particularly popular in the classical period. If one of the string instruments of the trio is replaced by a piano (d), the work is called a piano trio. Solo sonatas of the classical period usually feature one melody instrument with piano accompaniment (e). The wind quintet, a common grouping of wind and brass, consists of a flute, oboe, clarinet, bassoon, and horn (f).

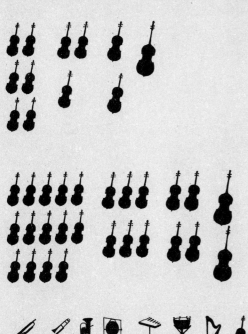

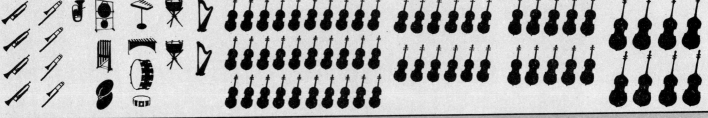

Orchestral instruments

Piccolo (34)
Flute (34)
Oboe (50)
Oboe d'amore (50)
Oboe da caccia (49)
Cor anglais (50)
Clarinet (41)
Bass clarinet (41)
Bassoon (53)
Contrabassoon (53)
Horn (70)
Wagner tuba (70)
Trumpet (63)
Trombone (65)
Tuba (71)
Tam-tam (136)
Tubular bells (134)
Cymbals (136)
Glockenspiel (134)
Xylophone (135)
Bass drum (159)
Side drum (159)
Timpani (158)
Harpsichord (231)
Harp (177)
Violin (211)
Viola (212)
Cello (213)
Double bass (214)

(Main entry page numbers in brackets.)

©DIAGRAM

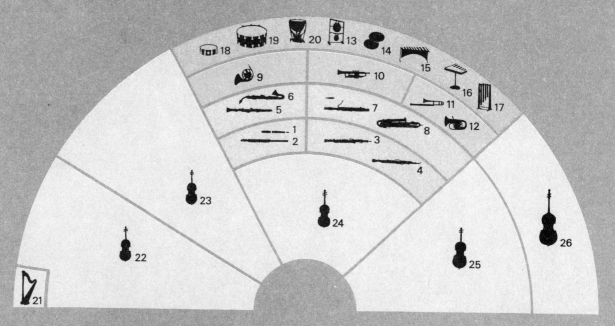

Above Usual orchestral seating plan. Instruments of the four "families" — woodwind, brass, percussion, and strings — are positioned in groups. This arrangement helps blend the tone colors of individual instruments, and helps the musicians play together in their groups.

Below The comparative pitch ranges of common orchestral instruments, shown in relation to the piano keyboard. In the case of instruments — like the clarinet and trumpet — for which written notation differs from actual sound, the diagram gives the actual sound produced.

Woodwind	**Brass**	**Percussion**	**Strings**
1 Piccolo	9 Horns	13 Tam-tam	21 Harp
2 Flutes	10 Trumpets	14 Cymbals	22 1st violins
3 Oboes	11 Trombones	15 Xylophone	23 2nd violins
4 Cor anglais	12 Tuba	16 Glockenspiel	24 Violas
5 Clarinets		17 Tubular bells	25 Cellos
6 Bass clarinet		18 Side drum	26 Double basses
7 Bassoons		19 Bass drum	
8 Contrabassoon		20 Timpani	

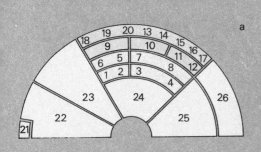

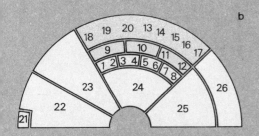

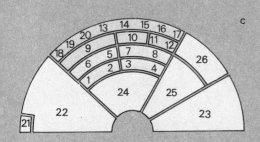

a

b

c

Left Alternative seating plans for an orchestra. The commonest plan (a) has flutes, oboes, clarinets, and bassoons in a block at the center of the orchestra. Some conductors, however, prefer these players in a single line (b), while others favor the separation of first and second violins (c).

Right The opening of an orchestral score — Wagner's "Grosser Festmarsch". Most composers follow the same instrument order for scores — woodwind, brass, percussion, and strings. Within the different families, higher pitched instruments appear above lower pitched ones.

Below Language dictionary for common orchestral instruments. Baroque and classical composers of different nationalities generally used only Italian for annotating their scores. In the 19th and 20th centuries some composers have preferred to use their own language.

Italian	English	German	French
Flauto piccolo	Piccolo	Kleine Flöte	Petite flûte
Flauto	Flute	Flöte	Flûte
Oboe	Oboe	Oboe	Hautbois
Corno inglese	Cor anglais	Englisches Horn	Cor anglais
Clarinetto	Clarinet	Klarinette	Clarinette
Clarinetto basso	Bass clarinet	Bassklarinette	Clarinette basse
Fagotto	Bassoon	Fagott	Basson
Contrafagotto	Contrabassoon	Kontrafagott	Contrebasson
Corno	Horn	Horn	Cor
Tromba	Trumpet	Trompete	Trompette
Trombone	Trombone	Posaune	Trombone
Tuba	Tuba	Tuben	Bombardon
Tam-tam	Tam-tam	Tam-tam	Tam-tam
Piatti	Cymbals	Becken	Cymbales
Silofono	Xylophone	Xylophon	Xylophon
Campanette	Glockenspiel	Glockenspiel	Jeu de timbres
Campane tubulari	Tubular bells	Röhrenglocken	Cloches tubulaires
Tamburo militare	Side drum	Kleine Trommel	Tambour militaire
Gran cassa	Bass drum	Grosse Trommel	Grosse caisse
Timpani	Timpani	Pauken	Timbales
Arpa	Harp	Harfe	Harpe
Violino	Violin	Geige	Violon
Viola	Viola	Bratsche	Viole
Violoncello	Violoncello	Violoncello	Violoncelle
Contrabasso	Double bass	Kontrabass	Contrebasse
Pianoforte	Pianoforte	Klavier	Pianoforte
Clavicembalo	Harpsichord	Klavizimbel	Clavecin
Chitarra	Guitar	Gitarre	Guitare
Organo	Organ	Orgel	Orgue

©DIAGRAM

1 kleine Flöte.

3 grosse Flöten.

3 Hoboen.

3 Clarinetten (in C.)

3 Fagotte und 1 Contrafagott.

4 Hörner. (F (F)

3 Trompeten.

1 Basstrompete in C.

3 Posaunen.

1 Contrabasstuba.

3 Pauken (G.C.D.)

(Triangel, Becken, kleine u. grosse Trommel. Tamtam.)

Violinen.

Bratschen.

Violoncelle

Contrabässe.

Military and marching bands

The military and marching bands of the present day have their origins in the instruments — horns, trumpets, drums, and cymbals — used by ancient armies for signaling and for raising morale. Modern bands include a wide variety of instruments — woodwind, brass, percussion, and drums — and have a more strictly musical function, being well suited to playing popular tunes and hymns as well as military marches.

Right Military musicians of the past — Irish bagpiper (a), mounted drum and trumpet players (b), and foot drummer (c). Such musicians formerly accompanied armies right on to the battlefield. The military instrumentalist of today is generally seen on ceremonial occasions.

Right Diagram showing a typical marching order for a small military band. The 30 musicians are arranged in rows, with the brass at the front, cymbals and drum in the center, and woodwind at the rear. The trombones are on the front row to allow free movement of their slides.

Below Instruments of a marching band arranged by type, and a line of military bandsmen in typical marching order. Woodwind, brass, percussion, and drums are well suited to marching use — strings are not found because of the difficulty of playing such instruments on the move.

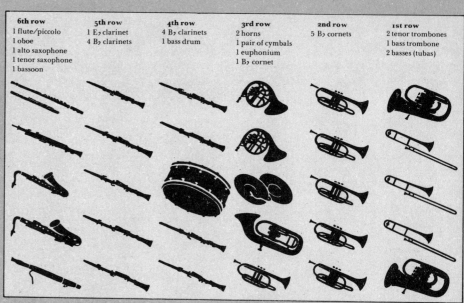

6th row	5th row	4th row	3rd row	2nd row	1st row
1 flute/piccolo	1 E♭ clarinet	4 B♭ clarinets	2 horns	5 B♭ cornets	2 tenor trombones
1 oboe	4 B♭ clarinets	1 bass drum	1 pair of cymbals		1 bass trombone
1 alto saxophone			1 euphonium		2 basses (tubas)
1 tenor saxophone			1 B♭ cornet		
1 bassoon					

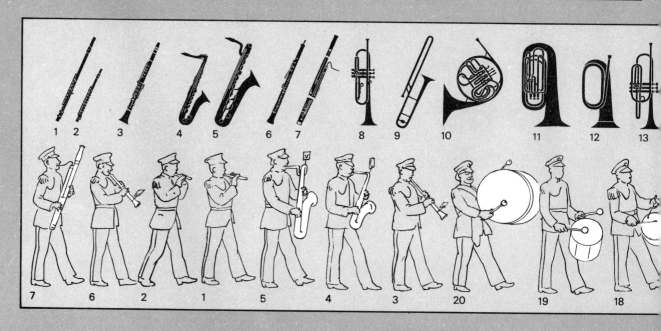

1 2 3 4 5 6 7 8 9 10 11 12 13

7 6 2 1 5 4 3 20 19 18

Right Instrumentalists from marching bands based on the combination of drums with one other instrument. The band of bagpipes and drums (a) is a feature of Scottish army regiments. The less well known fife and drum combination (b) has been popular in Ireland since around 1500.

Right Four members of a Salvation Army band (a) are representative of the growth of non-military marching bands in the late 19th century. Many town and works bands date from this time. Baton-twirling majorettes (b) are often seen at the head of popular marching bands in the USA.

Right Advertisement for the band of John Philip Sousa. Formed in 1892, this famous American band made a successful world tour in 1910. Its repertory of stirring marches — many of them composed by Sousa himself — helped bring about a considerable rise in band music standards.

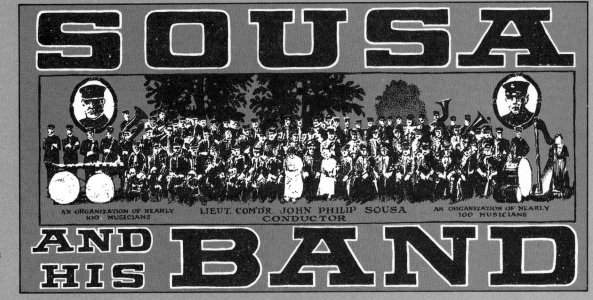

SOUSA AND HIS BAND

AN ORGANIZATION OF NEARLY 100 MUSICIANS   LIEUT. COMD'R. JOHN PHILIP SOUSA CONDUCTOR   AN ORGANIZATION OF NEARLY 100 MUSICIANS

Marching band instruments

1	Flute (34)	11	Marching tuba (71)
2	Piccolo (34)	12	Bugle (73)
3	Clarinet (41)	13	Cornet (73)
4	Alto saxophone (43)	14	Mellophone (73)
5	Tenor saxophone (43)	15	Euphonium (75)
6	Oboe (50)	16	Glockenspiel (123)
7	Bassoon (53)	17	Cymbals (136)
8	Trumpet (63)	18	Side drum (160)
9	Trombone (65)	19	Tenor drum (160)
10	Horn (70)	20	Bass drum (160)

(Main entry page numbers in brackets.)

©DIAGRAM

Popular bands

Bands playing music for popular entertainment have shown enormous variations in size, composition, and musical style. Essentially shaped by popular taste, they can provide a fascinating insight into the nature of the society that produced them. The last hundred years have been particularly rich in the development of popular bands — producing sounds as varied as jazz, the big band sound, and rock.

Right A detail from a 16th century German engraving shows music for outdoor dancing provided by a renaissance group of wind and string instruments.
Left A silhouette depicts a small orchestra playing Strauss waltzes in a typical 19th century Viennese concert garden.

Palm court orchestra

1 Violin (211)
2 Viola (212)
3 Cello (213)
4 Double bass (214)
5 Piano (240)

(Main entry page numbers in brackets.)

Left A small "palm court" orchestra. Traditionally associated with the elegant "thé dansant" popular in the first decades of the 20th century, these small string orchestras are still sometimes found providing gentle background music in hotels and restaurants in America and Europe.

Dance band

1 Clarinet (41)
2 Saxophone (43)
3 Trumpet (62)
4 Trombone (64)
5 Xylophone (135)
6 Cymbals (136)
7 Bass drum (159)
8 Side drum (159)
9 Tenor drum (159)
10 Violin (211)
11 Double bass (214)
12 Piano (240)

Left A popular dance band. Since dancing became a widespread popular pastime in the 1920s numerous instrumental combinations have been used for its accompaniment. A typical small band might consist of clarinet, piano, double bass, and drums. Larger groups have as many as 20 players.

Right Instruments and musicians of a traditional jazz band typical of New Orleans bands in the early days of jazz. Not included here but also common in jazz bands are the cornet and saxophone. Many jazz musicians won international fame with the development of the recording industry.

Below A big band. Bands of this type, of which the Glenn Miller Orchestra is the most famous, enjoyed their greatest popularity in the 1940s and early '50s. Featuring a large number of brass and wind instruments, they played music in a wide variety of styles ranging from dixieland to "bop."

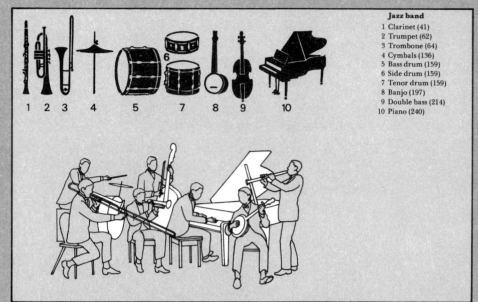

Jazz band
1 Clarinet (41)
2 Trumpet (62)
3 Trombone (64)
4 Cymbals (136)
5 Bass drum (159)
6 Side drum (159)
7 Tenor drum (159)
8 Banjo (197)
9 Double bass (214)
10 Piano (240)

Big band
1 Clarinet (41)
2 Saxophone (43)
3 Trumpet (62)
4 Trombone (64)
5 Accordion (81)
6 Cymbals (136)
7 Bass drum (159)
8 Side drum (159)
9 Tenor drum (159)
10 Guitar (194)
11 Violin (211)
12 Cello (213)
13 Double bass (214)
14 Piano (240)

Right A modern rock group. In addition to the original rock instruments — electric guitars and drums — many modern groups have added other recently invented instruments — electric pianos, organs, and synthesizers — to give greater variety and depth to their music.

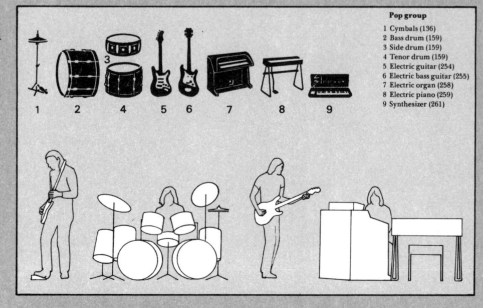

Pop group
1 Cymbals (136)
2 Bass drum (159)
3 Side drum (159)
4 Tenor drum (159)
5 Electric guitar (254)
6 Electric bass guitar (255)
7 Electric organ (258)
8 Electric piano (259)
9 Synthesizer (261)

© DIAGRAM

Groups around the world

All over the world people enjoy making music in groups. Sometimes these groups are informal gatherings of amateur musicians playing any instruments of their choice. Other groups — like the Indian sitar, tambura, and tabla — are formal ensembles with their own classical traditions. Two larger groups of very great importance in their own countries are the gagaku ensemble of Japan and the gamelan of Indonesia.

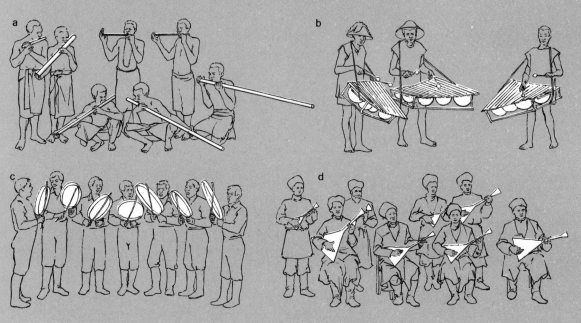

Left Examples of groups made up of musicians all playing the same type of instrument. Usually the instruments are of different sizes to provide variety of tone. The group of side-blown flute players (a) is from New Guinea — where these instruments are important in magic and ritual. Xylophone ensembles (b) are found accompanying dancing in Central and Southern Africa. Eskimos sometimes use frame drums of different sizes (c) to accompany their primarily vocal music. Russian balalaika orchestras (d) have been very popular on their tours of the West.

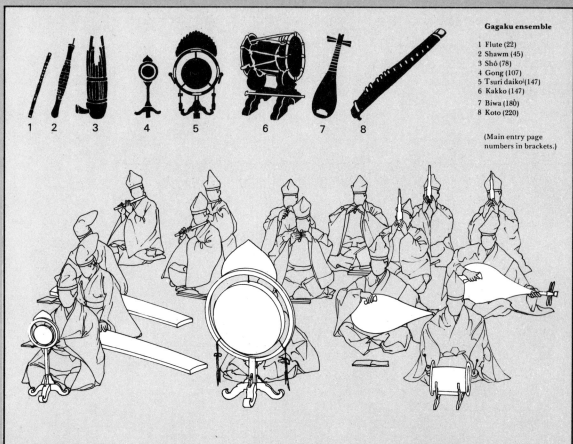

Gagaku ensemble

1 Flute (22)
2 Shawm (45)
3 Shô (78)
4 Gong (107)
5 Tsuri daiko (147)
6 Kakko (147)
7 Biwa (180)
8 Koto (220)

(Main entry page numbers in brackets.)

Left Japanese gagaku ensemble. Gagaku is the classical music of Japan. The melody is played by the shawms and side-blown flutes and reinforced and harmonized in a simple fashion by the shô. Biwas and kotos are used to play an abstracted version of the melody and sometimes provide a simple accompaniment. The percussion instruments — gong and drums — emphasize the strong beats and add stability to the rhythm.

Right Popular one-man "ensembles". The banjo and mouth organ (a) are often played together by US folk musicians. The pipe and tabor combination (b) survives in Europe from the Middle Ages. In Bolivia musicians combine drum and panpipes (c). One-man bands (d) include a great variety of instruments.

Right Popular two-man ensembles — drummer and shawm player from Albania (a), fiddle and accordion players from Scotland (b), bagpipe and shawm players from Italy (c), and lute and fiddle players from Greece (d). Similar combinations are found in many different countries.

Right Indian classical ensemble comprising sitar, tabla, and tambura. The sitar plays complex improvisations based on set rhythmic and melodic patterns known as talas and ragas. The tambura, which plays a continuous drone, and the tabla provide the accompaniment.

Indian classical ensemble

1 Tabla (144)
2 Tambura (181)
3 Sitar (181)

Right Instruments and musicians from a Javanese gamelan orchestra. Also found elsewhere in Indonesia — notably in Bali — gamelan orchestras vary considerably in size and composition. Each gamelan is essentially made up of tuned percussion instruments — although the leader plays a spike fiddle. The gamelan is used in conjunction with religious and state ceremonies and to accompany acting and puppetry. All performances are from memory.

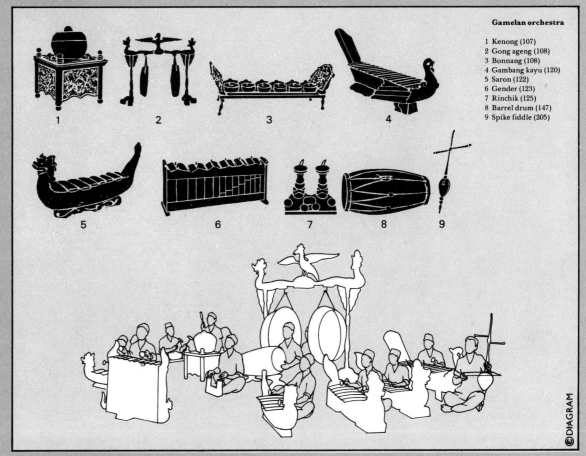

Gamelan orchestra

1 Kenong (107)
2 Gong ageng (108)
3 Bonnang (108)
4 Gambang kayu (120)
5 Saron (122)
6 Gender (123)
7 Rinchik (125)
8 Barrel drum (147)
9 Spike fiddle (205)

©DIAGRAM

Fig. 4

Fig. 7

Fig. 2.

Fig. 1.

Fig. 5.

Makers, virtuosi, writers

Amati family

Amati is one of the most famous names in the history of violin making. Three generations of this ancient and noble Italian family made their home town of Cremona the violin center of Europe in the 16th and 17th centuries. Andrea Amati (c.1511-c.1579) was one of the first people to make violins, and may even have been the instrument's inventor. The first instruments he made were almost certainly three-stringed fiddles, but by the 1560s it is recorded that the French court ordered from him a complete string band of 38 instruments — violins, violas, and cellos. Andrea's sons Antonio (1550-1638) and Girolamo (1551-1635) worked together and produced many fine instruments that still survive. Girolamo used the Latin form of his name, Hieronymus, when labeling instruments. Nicolo Amati (1596-1684), son of Girolamo, was the greatest maker of the family, and his instruments are renowned for their sweetness of tone. He had many pupils, of whom the greatest was Antonio Stradivari.

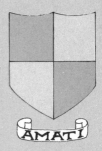

Antonius, & Hieronym. Fr. Amati
Cremonen. Andreæ fil. F. 1637,

Louis Armstrong

Louis Armstrong — widely known by his nickname "Satchmo," short for "Satchel Mouth" — was one of the world's greatest and best known trumpet players. He was born in New Orleans on July 4, 1900 and died 71 years later in New York City. As a child he had a number of brushes with the law, and it was in a reform school that he first learned to play the trumpet. In 1922 he went to Chicago to play the cornet in King Oliver's Creole Jazz Band. After only three years he formed his own group, and his success mushroomed from then on. Satchmo was both an innovator and technician par excellence, setting an extraordinary record when he sounded a high C on the trumpet a staggering 280 times in succession. He is probably mainly remembered, however, for his authentic swing style, which gained him admirers, young and old alike, in countries throughout the world. Some critics have called him the "Einstein of Jazz" — most people simply remember him as an affable, ebullient man who through his trumpet had the ability to create tremendous vitality and style.

Hector Berlioz

Hector Berlioz (1803-69), a Frenchman, was a major composer of the romantic period. His main contributions were the development of the genre known as the "dramatic symphony" and his imaginative handling of the distinctive tone colors of the many instruments that made up a typical orchestra of the romantic period. Berlioz' symphonies — of which the best known is probably his "Symphonie Fantastique" written in 1830 — were dramatic stories in which people and actions could be identified through the expression of various instruments. Berlioz also introduced new attitudes toward rhythm, melody, and structure, and his innovative ideas have continued to affect composers to the present day. Berlioz' handling of vast and imaginative resources in his compositions is legendary — for example in the overture to "Les Francs-Juges" he requested a total of 467 instruments and a chorus of 360 voices. Another expression of Berlioz' interest in the distinctive tone colors of different instruments is to be found in his major literary treatise on instrumentation and orchestration.

Theobald Boehm

Theobald Boehm (1793-1881), a flute maker from Munich, made several fundamental improvements to this instrument. Despite earlier experiments by other makers, the flute at the start of Boehm's career was difficult to finger and comparatively weak in tone. Boehm's first flutes had a conical bore but in 1847 he changed to a cylindrical bore — the shape now generally used. Boehm also increased the size of the finger holes and so further improved the flute's tone quality and carrying power. Even more important he devised a rational system of rings and keys for the instrument. As a result of Boehm's work, keys for covering and uncovering the holes lie easily under the fingertips while the holes themselves are in their best acoustic position where they would otherwise be difficult to reach. In 1842 the French clarinetist, Hyacinth Klosé, adapted Boehm's system to the clarinet, and "Boehm" clarinets are the most popular type in use today. Boehm also introduced all-metal flutes, which have largely replaced wood flutes because of their greater power and durability.

John Broadwood

John Broadwood (1732-1812) was one of the greatest early piano makers. Born in Scotland, he trained as a cabinet-maker before going to London to seek his fortune. He found it in the workshops of Burkat Shudi, a Swiss harpsichord maker. Eight years later, in 1769, Broadwood married Shudi's daughter. The following year his father-in-law took him into partnership and the business was operated under the name of Shudi and Broadwood until 1795. This same business, under the name of John Broadwood and Sons, survives to the present day — making it the oldest keyboard instrument makers still in existence. Broadwood began making pianos in 1773, starting with square models based on those by Zumpe. In 1777 he helped build the first English grand piano, and in the 1780s patented two inventions that have been generally adopted — the application of the pedals of the harpsichord to the grand piano and the introduction of a separate bridge for the bass strings.

Bartolommeo Cristofori

Bartolommeo Cristofori (1655-1731) was the inventor of the fortepiano, now known as the pianoforte or simply piano. He was born in Padua, Italy, where he made a reputation as a harpsichord maker. About 1687 Prince Ferdinand, son of Grand Duke Cosimo III of Florence, invited Cristofori to move to Florence in his service. There Cristofori appears to have helped the prince in organizing music, as well as in making instruments. By 1709 Cristofori had already made four of the instruments

he described as "gravicembalo col piano e forte" — that is "harpsichord with soft and loud". The new instruments had strings struck by hammers instead of being plucked as in the harpsichord. This gave the player greater control over volume, allowing him indeed to play soft or loud as required. Prince Ferdinand died in 1713, but Cristofori remained in the family's service, taking charge in 1716 of the collection of 84 musical instruments left by the prince. In this collection were seven harpsichords by Cristofori.

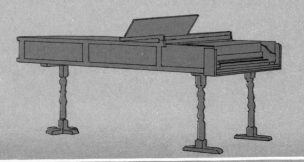

Johann Christoph Denner

Johann Christoph Denner (1655-1707) is best remembered today for his development of the clarinet. The son of a horn tuner, Johann Christoph learned his father's trade in Nuremberg and soon established a reputation for himself as a maker of fine recorders, flutes, oboes, and bassoons. Improvements that he made to the simple single-reed folk instrument, the chalumeau, are thought to have helped him in his development of the first clarinets around 1700. These early clarinets, with the body shape of a treble recorder, had finger keys, and a "speaker key" to extend the range upward. According to Johann Walther, writing in 1732, the early clarinet sounded "rather like a trumpet from a distance." The important work begun by Johann Christoph was continued by his two sons who joined him in his flourishing business. As well as making instruments, they acted as salesmen, traveling through Europe and helping to popularize the new instrument after their father's death.

D

Arnold Dolmetsch

Arnold Dolmetsch (1858-1940), a French-born British musician, did much to revive the use of obsolete instruments. Arnold was born in Le Mans, and learned to build pianos and organs in the workshops of his father and grandfather. He also kept up the family tradition of clavichord playing. After studying music in Brussels and London, Dolmetsch made harpsichords for Chickering in Boston, Massachusetts, and then for Gaveau in Paris. He settled in England in 1914, published a book on interpreting 17th and 18th century music, and devoted the rest of his life to reestablishing instruments of the 15th to 18th centuries. At Haslemere, Surrey, Dolmetsch made modern versions of many of these instruments and taught people to play them — especially the recorder, which now enjoys worldwide popularity largely thanks to his efforts. In 1925 Dolmetsch started the annual Haslemere Festival of old instruments and their music. In 1928 the Dolmetsch Foundation was formed to support and extend Arnold's work. Since his death, his son Carl and other members of the family have carried on his crusade.

Sébastien Erard

Sébastien Erard (1752-1831) made the first French pianos, and invented the "double escapement" mechanism which is the basis of all modern piano actions. Erard was born in Strasbourg and learned harpsichord making in Paris. A mechanical harpsichord constructed by him attracted the attention of the Duchesse de Villeroi, who gave him a workshop at her château. There, in 1777, he made his first pianoforte. After a time in London during the French Revolution, Erard returned to Paris in 1796, when he made his first grand piano on the English pattern. In 1821 he produced his double-escapement action, the culmination of years of experiment. This action was more complicated than earlier actions, but also more robust, and it allowed the hammers to fall back so quickly that performers could now play rapidly repeated notes. The firm founded by Sébastien was carried on by his nephew Pierre (1796-1855), who further developed the action of the concert harp, on which Sébastien had taken out several patents between 1792 and 1810. The result of their labors was an instrument that was stronger in tone and easier to play in different keys.

Benjamin Franklin

Benjamin Franklin (1706-1790), American printer, publisher, inventor, and statesman, found time in his extraordinarily busy life to develop a new instrument from the musical glasses. After hearing a performance on the musical glasses, which were tuned by varying the amount of water in each one and played by rubbing the rims with moistened fingers, Franklin went on to invent a ready-tuned instrument that was also easier to play. It consisted of 24 glass bowls gradated in size to give different pitches. The bowls were mounted horizontally on a long spindle so that their lower rims dipped into a trough of water. A pedal mechanism, like that of a treadle sewing machine, was used to turn the bowls on the spindle — so keeping the rims moist for playing. The player produced the required pitches by touching the rims of the rotating bowls with his fingers. Franklin built his instrument in 1761, and gave it the name "armonica." The glass harmonica — as we now call Franklin's brainchild — became widely popular, and Mozart, Haydn, and Beethoven all wrote music for it.

Guarneri family

Guarneri is the name of a family of Italian violin makers based in Cremona. Andrea Guarneri (c.1626-1698), the first violin maker of the family, was a pupil of Nicolo Amati and a colleague of Antonio Stradivari. Andrea's elder son Pietro (1655-1720), a very fine craftsman, settled in Mantua and is generally called "Peter of Mantua" to distinguish him from his nephew of the same name. Giuseppe (1666-c.1740), younger son of Andrea, made many remarkable instruments, some of them almost as good as Stradivari's. His labels call him "Joseph filius Andreae." Giuseppe's elder son Pietro (1695-1762) is generally known as "Peter of Venice" to distinguish him from his uncle. Many of his instruments resemble those of the elder Pietro. Giuseppe's younger son, also Giuseppe (1698-1762), was by far the greatest maker of the family, and many players rank his violins with Stradivari's. He is often known as "Joseph del Gesù" from his use of labels bearing a cross and the letters "I.H.S." standing for "Jesus Hominum Salvator." More than 70 of his total output of about 200 instruments survive.

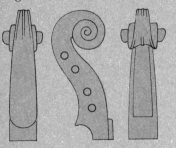

Andreas Guarnerius fecit Cremonæ sub titulo Sanctæ Teresiæ 16

Heckel family

Heckel is the name of a German family of wind instrument makers. Johann Adam Heckel (c.1812-1877) started the family firm at Biebrich on Rhine in 1831. He did much to redesign the bassoon — work carried on after his death by his son Wilhelm (1856-1909). By 1880 Wilhelm had produced an instrument with a smooth, even tone which made it so popular that this type of bassoon is still the most widely used. Wilhelm also remodeled the contrabassoon and made it a more playable, less clumsy instrument. Besides improving old instruments, Wilhelm helped to invent new ones. Best known among these is the heckelphone, a kind of oboe between the bassoon and cor anglais in pitch, which was designed by Wilhelm in collaboration with his son Wilhelm Hermann (1879-1952). The heckelphone consists of a wood tube with a conical bore, ending in a globular bell closed by a perforated stopper. A bent metal crook carries a double reed similar to that of the bassoon. The heckelphone made its debut in Richard Strauss's opera "Salome" in 1905, but has never become widely popular.

Hotteterre family

Hotteterre is the name of a large French family of wind instrument and hurdy gurdy makers. More than 20 of them are known to have made or played a variety of instruments including recorders, flutes, oboes and bassoons. Outstanding among them was Jean Hotteterre IV (1648-1732). Jean was a maker of bagpipes, but is best known for the improvements he made to woodwind instruments, in particular to the flute and oboe. His most important contribution to the development of the flute was the introduction of a conical bore for the body and cylindrical bore for the head. This gave a pure, sweet tone, less shrill than that of the flute's near relative the fife. Hotteterre made his flutes and oboes in three sections instead of one section as before. This meant that they could be tuned by shortening or lengthening at the joints, which were reinforced with ornamental ivory bands. In addition to improving the flute, Jean played an important part in developing the oboe — a mellow, quiet toned instrument that was better suited to indoor music than its forerunner the shawm.

Kirckman family

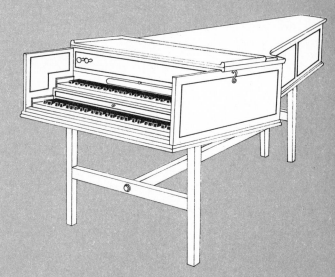

Kirckman is the name of a leading family of harpsichord and piano makers founded by Jacob Kirckman (1710-1792). Jacob was born at Bischweiler, near Strasbourg, and emigrated to England in the early 1730s. There he worked for Hermann Tabel, a Flemish harpsichord maker trained by the famous Ruckers family. Tabel died in 1738, and within a month Kirckman had married his widow and taken over the business. He made the most of his opportunities, for as well as constructing excellent harpsichords he became a moneylender and pawnbroker, and reputedly left a fortune of £200,000. His instruments incorporated the Venetian swell — a series of shutters over the soundboard activated by a pedal and giving a similar effect to that of an organ swell. Jacob's nephew Abraham (1737-1794) joined the business in 1772, and in the 1770s the family began to make pianos. These instruments, bearing labels that dropped the "c" of Kirckman, shared certain features with Kirckman harpsichords and even sounded rather like them.

Franz Liszt

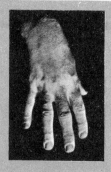

Franz Liszt (1811-1886), a Hungarian, was a pianist of astonishing virtuosity and a composer of great originality. The first popularizer of the solo piano recital, he revealed a technical prowess that led composers to write increasingly taxing pieces for the piano. Liszt's own compositions included piano concertos, rhapsodies, church works, and transcriptions. His innovations included a pioneering one-movement sonata and a use of chromatic harmony foreshadowing 20th century atonalism. Liszt also introduced the symphonic poem and inspired the development of the leitmotiv, or recurrent theme, by his son-in-law Richard Wagner. Having begun his career as a child prodigy, Liszt studied and performed in Vienna before touring Western Europe. He came to win immense adulation and had a succession of mistresses. In 1865, however, he took minor orders and much of his most experimental music was written during this last phase of his life.

Neuschel family

Neuschel is the name of a family of German brass instrument makers responsible for the development of the trombone from the medieval trumpet. The trombone, or sackbut as it was originally called, was first described and depicted in the last quarter of the 15th century. Documents of the same period mention Hans Neuschel, a master brass worker of Nuremberg, as the first important maker and player of the instrument. Doppelmayr wrote that Hans's outstanding craftsmanship earned him such a reputation that he received orders from the royal courts of several European countries. Among his distinguished customers was Pope Leo X for whom he made some silver trombones. After Hans's death in 1533, younger members of the family, Hans and Jörg, took over the business. Jörg, the youngest, was the last member of the Neuschel family to carry on the craft of instrument making. His customers included several European Kings, and the Electors of Saxony and the Rhineland. The only surviving Neuschel trombone, an elegant and beautifully made instrument dating from 1557, was made by Jörg.

Niccolò Paganini

Niccolò Paganini (1782-1840) enjoys a place in musical history as the greatest violin virtuoso of the 19th century. Born in Genoa, Italy, he began studying under his father, made his first public appearance in 1793, and by 1797 was touring Lombardy. In 1805 he became director of music in Piombino. Written at this time were his caprices for unaccompanied violin. These fully exploited new tuning and fingering techniques and made extensive use of pizzicato and harmonics — novelties that were to transform virtuoso violin playing and to influence piano music, partly through transcriptions of his works by Schumann. Paganini also wrote violin concertos, variations, and string quartets. Much of his music lacks depth and is flashily brilliant, reflecting the demonic quality of Paganini's own playing. Coupled with his gambling, love affairs, and romantic physical appearance, Paganini's "possessed" performances created a popular image of a man under the devil's influence. Many of his performances were in Italy, but a visit to Vienna in 1828 established Paganini as the idol of Europe, the first of many such "pop" stars.

Michael Praetorius

Michael Praetorius (1571-1621) is our chief single source of knowledge for the musical instruments of his day. Born at Kreuzberg, Thuringia, he studied at Frankfurt on Oder and eventually became organist and choirmaster to the Duke of Brunswick. Praetorius composed prolifically, favoring lavish, Italian-influenced settings for voices and instruments. All told he produced more than 40 volumes of works, notably "Musae Sionae," which alone has 1,244 choral pieces. He also published "Terpsichore," a large collection of colorful dance tunes. But the work for which he is chiefly remembered is the "Syntagma Musicum," a major treatise on music comprising three completed parts. Part 1 is an account of ancient and ecclesiastical music and ancient secular instruments. Part 2 describes contemporary musical instruments: their form, compass, tone, and quality. Part 3 outlines principles of contemporary secular composition. The "Syntagma" has proved invaluable in helping modern makers recreate some of the instruments of the early 1600s.

Mstislav Rostropovich

Mstislav Leopoldovich Rostropovich is arguably the natural successor to the world's first outstanding solo cellist, Spain's Pablo Casals (1876-1973). Born in 1927 in Baku, USSR, Rostropovich studied in Moscow under Shostakovich, became professor at Moscow Conservatory in 1960, and gained many major international awards. In 1965 he became the first cellist to sell out New York City's Carnegie Hall, and by the 1970s had a huge following in the West — admired as teacher and conductor as well as cellist. Critics agree that Rostropovich's greatness as a performer lies in his subordination of supreme technical mastery to unsurpassed eloquence of interpretation. An interesting aspect of his playing is that Rostropovich holds the cello at 45° — less upright than most players — leaving him freer for fingering and bowing. He once said his wish was "to make the cello as beloved an instrument as the violin and piano," but added "this cannot be until there are more and great new works for cello." Compositions written for him by Britten, Prokofiev, and Shostakovich have helped Rostropovich realize his dream.

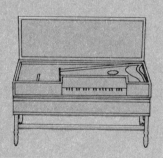

Ruckers family

Ruckers is the name of a family of Flemish harpsichord makers active in Antwerp about 1580-1670. They are thought to have made the earliest harpsichords with two manuals and a regular 4ft stop. The first outstanding member of the family was Hans Ruckers (c.1550-c.1625), whose instruments had a beauty of tone that won them a lasting reputation throughout Europe. At least some of Hans' innovations sprang from his expertise as an organ tuner. For example, he introduced an octave stop and a harp stop to give the harpsichord a greater variety of tone color. Hans passed on his skills to his sons Jan (1578-1643) and Andries (1579-c.1640); and Andries' own son, Andries II, carried on the Ruckers tradition. The main types of instrument produced by the Ruckers family were harpsichords with one manual and two manuals, and virginals with the keyboard to the right or to the left. Many of these instruments were beautifully decorated, with panels of imitation marble, detailed scroll-work, and painted pastoral scenes.

Adolphe Sax

"Adolphe" (Antoine Joseph) Sax (1814-1894), a Belgian instrument maker, invented several families of wind instruments of which the saxophone and saxhorn are the best known. Sax was born at Dinant, and studied the flute and clarinet at Brussels. Setting out to improve on the tone of the bass clarinet, he developed a new instrument — the saxophone — which he patented in Paris in 1846. Made in several sizes, the saxophone is a metal instrument with a conical bore, clarinet-type mouthpiece, and single reed. It is easy to play and soon became popular with military bands and then with the jazz bands of the early 1900s. To replace the existing motley collection of valved brass band instruments Sax also invented another family of instruments — saxhorns — which had broad, bugle-like conical bores. The deeper saxhorns are still in regular brass band use. Adolphe's other inventions included the saxtuba, and the short-lived saxotromba family with its trumpet-like sound. Sax failed to exploit his inventions commercially, and died poor.

Andrés Segovia

Andrés Segovia, born in 1893, revolutionized the role of the classical guitar by setting a new high playing standard and vastly enlarging the guitar repertoire. Born at Linares, Spain, Segovia was largely self taught, but also studied in Granada, where he gave his first performance in 1909. Later he began touring widely in Europe and the Americas, making his New York City debut in 1928. Audiences were entranced by the century's first classical guitarist to reveal a truly virtuoso technique, to which he added a new intensity of expression. Breaking with Spanish classical tradition, Segovia proved his instrument's capabilities by playing his own compositions and masterly transcriptions of demanding works for other instruments, especially lute and harpsichord works by Bach, Couperin, and Rameau. Segovia's success inspired Castelnuovo-Tedesco, Falla, Roussel, Villa-Lobos, and others to write works for him. As a result of his pioneering work the classical guitar has shaken off its old image as an accompanist's instrument, and earned its solo role in the modern concert hall.

Ravi Shankar

Ravi Shankar is the world's best-known exponent and popularizer of that expressive classical Indian instrument the sitar. Ravi was born in 1920 in Benares (Varanasi), a famous seat of Hindu culture. He began his career as a musician and dancer with the troupe led by his brother Uday Shankar. Touring abroad he made contacts with Western music that have helped him bridge the gap between the two cultures. After years of intensive study in India Ravi emerged as an outstandingly creative performer of classical Indian music. He also became music director of All India Radio, founded India's National Orchestra of Chamber Music, composed ballet scores, orchestrated Indian music, and was responsible for the music of leading Indian motion pictures. But he made his greatest impact on the West in the 1960s when he appeared as the Beatles' guest star. Soon, sitar was joining guitar in the world of "pop" and Ravi's concerts began attracting a huge following of youthful devotees seeking through his playing an insight into the mysticism of the East.

Gottfried Silbermann

Gottfried Silbermann (1683-1753) built some of the finest 18th century German organs and helped to save the early piano from obscurity. After studying organ building with his brother Andreas (1678-1734), Gottfried won a contract to design an organ for the cathedral at Freiberg near Dresden. The Freiberg organ, the first of 47 organs built by him in his native Saxony, blended the best of German, French, and Italian practices, and won him many admirers. Indeed, in the early 1900s rediscovery of the

soft, radiant tones of such instruments led to the slogan "Back to Silbermann" and a stampede away from the massive sounds of many 19th century organs. Silbermann also built harpsichords and clavichords, and in 1733, impressed by an account of Cristofori's invention, completed the first piano ever made in Germany. His interest in pianos continued, and in 1747 Johann Sebastian Bach reported favorably after trying out three Silbermann grands.

Antonio Stradivari

Antonio Stradivari (1644-1737) was one of the greatest and most prolific of all violin makers. He spent his life in Cremona, Italy — where he worked for Nicolo Amati until about 1680. In all Stradivari made some 1200 violins, violas, and cellos, of which some fine examples survive. Two of his 11 children, Francesco (1671-1743) and Omobono (1679-1742), followed him, but their work is less distinguished. The importance of Stradivari lay not only in his superb craftsmanship and unerring choice of fine wood, but in his modifications to the basic design of the violin — lowering the arch of the belly, strengthening the corner blocks, accentuating the curvature of the middle ribs, modifying the sound holes, and enlarging the scroll. Stradivari's early violins followed the Amati pattern, but he later adopted a pattern with a slightly longer body. His greatest instruments, made after 1707, combine great power with beauty of tone and ease of playing.

Caspar Tieffenbrucker

Caspar Tieffenbrucker (c.1514-c.1570), sometimes known as Gaspard Duiffopbrugcar, was the most important member of a large Bavarian family of instrument makers. Probably born in Füssen, which is still a center of violin making, he subsequently moved to Lyon in France and there set up a prosperous business as a maker of lutes and viols. His instruments were famous for their exquisite inlaid work, and several of his viols still survive today. Tieffenbrucker's good fortune came to an end, however, when in 1566 he was turned out of his house to make way for extensions to the city's fortifications. He was unable to obtain compensation, and his widow and children were left poor after his death. The business, however, was carried on for some years by his son Jehan and other members of the family. In the 1820s, 250 years after Tieffenbrucker's death, the French maker Jean-Baptiste Vuillaume produced a number of violins carved and inlaid in the style of Tieffenbrucker — and until recently collectors and players alike have been confused by this imitation.

Antonio de Torres Jurado

Antonio de Torres Jurado (1817-1892) was the Spanish instrument maker responsible for the design of the modern guitar. A pupil of José Pernas in Granada, Torres embarked around 1850 on a career of guitar making. He continued until his death, with an interruption of 11 years when his poor financial state forced him to do other work. His early guitars were built according to the design and proportions used since about 1700, but by the late 1850s he had made important adjustments both to the construction and dimensions of the instrument. He concentrated his efforts on producing a better tone by improving the top soundboard, and also standardized the string length to approximately 26in — the length still used today. He perfected the use of fan barring — a set of reinforcing bars radiating from the sound hole on the underside of the soundboard — which distributed the vibrations and enriched the tone. Torres's innovations, and the outstanding technical achievements of the guitarist Tarrega, resulted in the establishment of a national school of guitar making and playing in Spain.

François Tourte

François Tourte (1747 - 1835) was a French craftsman responsible for the design of the modern violin bow. One of an important family of Parisian bow makers, François concentrated his efforts on improving and eventually standardizing the material, proportions, and weight of the bow. He found that Pernambuco wood from Brazil, which is both strong and light, was the ideal material for the bow's stick. Instead of cutting the stick ready curved, Tourte bent the wood by heating it, and made it curve in toward the hair. He standardized the bow's length to approximately 29½in, adjusting the height of the point and nut to achieve perfect balance. Most of these major improvements were made around 1780, and Tourte was both encouraged and advised in his work by the distinguished violinist Viotti, who arrived in Paris from Italy in 1782. Often called the "Stradivari of the bow," Tourte worked to within a few years of his death at the age of 87. The perfected Tourte bow, combining stiffness with resilience, gave a full, rich tone, and its design has remained virtually unaltered to the present day.

Charles Wheatstone

Sir Charles Wheatstone (1802 - 1875), a British physicist chiefly remembered for his work on the electric telegraph, is important in music history for his invention of the symphonium and concertina, two important free-reed instruments. The son of a Gloucester music seller, he was apprenticed at the age of 14 to his uncle, an instrument maker. Though he had little formal scientific training, Charles soon developed an interest in acoustics and the scientific principles of wind instruments, and spent much of his time experimenting in different branches of physics. In 1829 he patented his symphonium — a type of mouth organ in which the reeds were contained in a small metal box that had finger buttons at each side and a blow hole at the front. Wheatstone experimented with silver, gold, and steel for the instrument's reeds in his attempts to obtain a pure and steady tone. The application of bellows to the symphonium led to the development in 1844 of the concertina — the instrument with which Wheatstone is most often associated.

Rudolph Wurlitzer

Wurlitzer is almost certainly the best-known name in the history of mechanical music makers. In its heyday, from the 1890s to the 1930s, the company founded by Rudolph Wurlitzer distributed and manufactured a wide range of mechanical instruments including coin-operated pianos and huge theater organs. Rudolph was born in Germany in 1831, where his father was an instrument maker. At the age of 22 Rudolph went to America where he had a succession of different jobs before he became established. Then, realizing the business possibilities for selling comparatively cheap, German-made instruments in America, he sent his savings to his father in return for musical instruments. These Rudolph sold at a high profit — the Wurlitzers were in business. After concentrating initially on conventional instruments, Rudolph turned his attentions in the 1880s and 1890s to music boxes and other mechanical music makers. Among his greatest marketing successes was the coin-operated piano, invented in 1899 by another German, Eugene DeKleist. After Rudolph's retirement, his sons Howard and Farny took over the running of the firm.

Bibliography

Aalst, J. A. van Chinese Music (Paragon)
Albrecht, G. Musikinstrumente und wie man sie spielt (Atlantis Verlag)
Apel, W. (ed) Harvard Dictionary of Music (Harvard University Press)
Baines, A. Bagpipes (Oxford University Press)
Baines, A. Musical Instruments through the Ages (Walker)
Baines, A. Woodwind Instruments and their History (Faber)
Bate, P. The Flute (Benn)
Bate, P. The Oboe (Benn)
Bate, P. The Trumpet and Trombone (Benn)
Bebey, F. African Music (Harrap)
Bellow, A. Illustrated History of the Guitar (Colombo)
Blades, J. Percussion Instruments and their History (Faber)
Bonanni, G. Antique Musical Instruments and their Players (Dover)
Boomkamp, C. van L. Descriptive Catalog of Collection (Fritz Knuf)
Bowers, Q. D. Put another Nickel in (Bonanza)
Boyden, D. D. History of Violin Playing (Oxford University Press)
Bragard, R. and de Hen, F. Les Instruments de Musique (A. de Visscher)
Buchner, A. Folk Music Instruments of the World (Octopus)
Buchner, A. Musical Instruments: an Illustrated History (Crown)
Buchner, A. Musical Instruments through the Ages (Spring Books)
Camp, J. Bell Ringing (David and Charles)
Caron, N. and Safvate, D. Iran: les Traditions Musicales
    (Buchet/Chastel)
Carr, R. and Tyler, T. The Beatles: an Illustrated Record (New English
    Library)
Carrington, J. F. Talking Drums of Africa (Negro Universities Press)
Carse, A. Musical Wind Instruments (Da Capo)
Chedd, G. Sound (Aldus)
Clark, J. E. T. Musical Boxes (Cornish Bros)
Clemenicic, R. Old Musical Instruments (Octopus)
Coleman, S. N. Bells (Day)
Coleman, S. N. The Book of Bells (Day)
Collinson, F. The Bagpipe (Routledge and Kegan Paul)
Cooper, M. The Concise Encyclopedia of Music and Musicians
    (Hawthorn)
Cowling, E. The Cello (Batsford)
Crowhurst, N. H. Electronic Musical Instruments (Foulsham-Tab)
Crowley, T. E. Discovering Mechanical Music (Shire Publications)
Danielou, A. Inde du Nord (Buchet/Chastel)
Darlow, D. Musical Instruments (A. and C. Black)
Donington, R. The Instruments of Music (Methuen)
Ellington, E. K. Music is my Mistress (W. H. Allen)
Fagg, W. The Raffles Gamelan (British Museum)
Farmer, H. G. The Organ of the Ancients (William Reeves)
Fox, C. Jazz in perspective (BBC)
Fox, L. Instruments of Popular Music (Lutterworth)

Museums

Kunsthistorisches Museum, Vienna, Austria
Brussels Conservatoire, Belgium
Instrument Museum, Brussels, Belgium
Phnom Penh Museum, Cambodia
Gold Museum, Bank of the Republic, Bogotá, Colombia
Archeological Museum, San José, Costa Rica
Moravian Museum, Brno, Czechoslovakia
City Museum, Prague, Czechoslovakia
Náprstek Museum, Prague, Czechoslovakia
National Museum, Prague, Czechoslovakia
National Museum, Copenhagen, Denmark
Cairo Museum, Egypt
National Museum, Helsinki, Finland
Conservatoire de Musique, Paris, France
The Louvre, Paris, France
Musée de l'Homme, Paris, France
Instrument Museum, Leipzig, East Germany
Karl Marx University, Leipzig, East Germany
Museum für Völkerkunde, Leipzig, East Germany
Potsdam-Sanssouci, East Germany
Museum für Völkerkunde, Berlin, West Germany
Bavarian National Museum, Munich, West Germany
Deutsches Museum, Munich, West Germany
Germanisches Nationalmuseum, Nuremberg, West Germany

Fox, L. Instruments of Professional Music (Lutterworth)
Fraenkel, G. (ed) Decorative Title Pages (Dover)
Galpin, F. Old English Instruments of Music (Methuen)
Galpin Society Journal
Geiringer, K. Musical Instruments (George, Allen, and Unwin)
Goff, J. le Le Moyen Age (Bordas)
Gregory, R. The Horn (Faber)
Gregory, R. The Trombone (Faber)
Grove's Dictionary of Music and Musicians (Macmillan)
Haacke, W. Organs of the World (George, Allen, and Unwin)
Harrison, F. and Rimmer, J. European Musical Instruments
    (Studio Vista)
Hindley, G. Musical Instruments (Hamlyn)
Hipkins, A. J. Musical Instruments (A. and C. Black)
Hofmann, C. American Indians Sing (Day)
Hollis, H. R. The Piano (David and Charles)
Hooreman, P. Musiciens à travers les temps (Fernand Nathan)
Horniman Museum Musical Instruments (Inner London Education
    Authority)
Horniman Museum Wind Instruments of European Art Music (Inner
    London Education Authority)
Hosier, J. Instruments of the Orchestra (Oxford University Press)
Hunt, E. The Recorder and its Music (Barrie and Jenkins)
Izikowitz, K. G. Musical Instruments of the South American Indians
    (Galpin Society)
Jaffrenou, G. Folk Harps (Model and Allied Publications)
Jenkins, J. Ethnic Musical Instruments (Evelyn)
Junius, M. M. The Sitar (Heinrichshofen's Verlag, Wilhelmshaven)
Karolyi, O. Introducing Music (Penguin)
Keepnews, O. and Grauer, B. Pictorial History of Jazz (Crown)
Kendall, A. The World of Musical Instruments (Hamlyn)
Khe, T. V. Vietnam (Buchet/Chastel)
Kinsky, G. (ed) A History of Music in Pictures (Dent)
Kirby, P. The Musical Instruments of the Native Races of South Africa
    (Witwatersrand University Press)
Kobola, A. Tradicijska narodna glazbala Jugoslavije (Školska Knjiga)
Kroll, O. The Clarinet (Batsford)
Kunst, J. Music in Java (Martinus Nijhoff)
Kunst, J. Music in New Guinea (Martinus Nijhoff)
Langwill, L. The Bassoon and Contrabassoon (Benn)
Langwill, L. and Boston, N. Church and Chamber Barrel Organs
    (Langwill)
Larousse Encyclopedia of Music (Hamlyn)
McCarthy, A. Big Band Jazz (Barrie and Jenkins)
MacMahon, D. Brass, Woodwind, and Strings (Nelson)
McPhee, C. Music in Bali (Yale University Press)

Malm, W. Japanese Music and Musical Instruments (Tuttle)
Malm, W. Musical Cultures of the Pacific and Southeast Asia (Prentice
    Hall)
Manga, J. Hungarian Folk Song and Instruments (Corvina Press)
Marcuse, S. A Survey of Musical Instruments (Harper and Row)
Marcuse, S. Musical Instruments: A Comprehensive Dictionary
    (Norton)
Mason, B. Drums, Tomtoms and Rattles (Dover)
Musikgeschichte in Bildern, vols I-IV (Deutscher Verlag für Musik,
    Leipzig)
Nelson, S. M. The Violin and Viola (Benn)
Nketia, J. The Music of Africa (Gollancz)
Ord-Hume, A. Clockwork Music (George, Allen and Unwin)
Oxford Histories (Oxford University Press)
Paganelli, S. Musical Instruments from the Renaissance to the 19th
    century (Hamlyn)
Panum, H. Stringed instruments of the Middle Ages (William Reeves)
Pape, W. Instrumentenhandbuch (Musikverlag Hans Gerig)
Paumgartner, B. Das Instrumentale Ensemble (Atlantis Verlag)
Peinkofer, K. and Tannigel, F. Handbuch des Schlagzeugs (B. Schott's
    Söhne)
Piston, W. Orchestration (Norton)
Powne, M. Ethiopian Music (Oxford University Press)
Quantz, J. J. On Playing the Flute (Faber)
Reinhard, K. Turquie (Buchet/Chastel)
Rendall, G. The Clarinet (Benn)
Rensch, R. The Harp (Philosophical Library, New York)
Rimmer, J. Ancient Musical Instruments of Western Asia (British
    Museum)
Rockstro, W. The Flute (Rudall Carte)
Russell, R. The Harpsichord and Clavichord (Faber)
Rust, B. The Dance Bands (Ian Allan)
Sachs, C. The History of Musical Instruments (Dent)
Schmidt, L. Volksmusik (Residenz Verlag)
Scuro, V. Presenting the Marching Band (Dodd, Mead)
Seeger, P. Steel Drums (Oak)
Simon, G. T. Simon says (Arlington House)
Stevens, S. and Warshofsky, F. Sound and Hearing (Time-Life)
Stites, R. S. The Arts and Man (McGraw-Hill)
Sumner, W. L. The Organ (Macdonald)
Tallis, D. Musical Boxes (Muller)
Thomson, J. Your Book of the Recorder (Faber)
Tracey, H. Chopi Musicians (Oxford University Press)
Vertkov, K. Blagodatov, G. Yazovitskaya E. Atlas of Musical Instruments
    of the Peoples Inhabiting the USSR (State Publishers, Moscow)
Webb, G. The Cylinder Musical Box Handbook (Faber)

Index

End papers Selection of illustrations from Michael Praetorius's "Theatrum Instrumentorum, seu sciagraphia," published in Germany in 1620 as an appendix to "Syntagma Musicum."

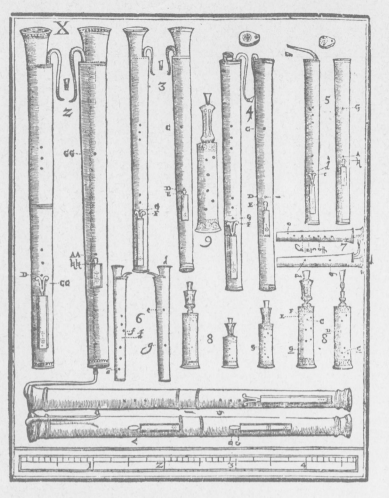

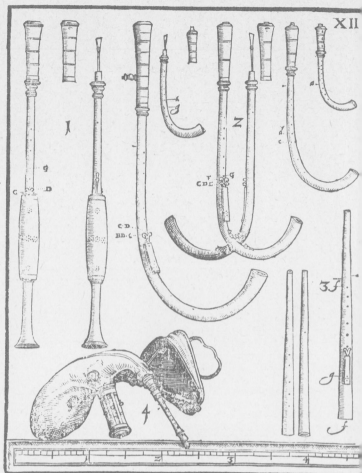

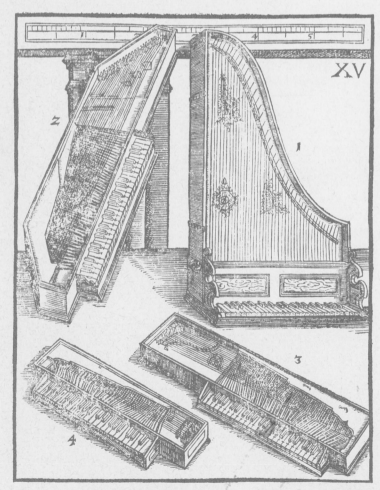

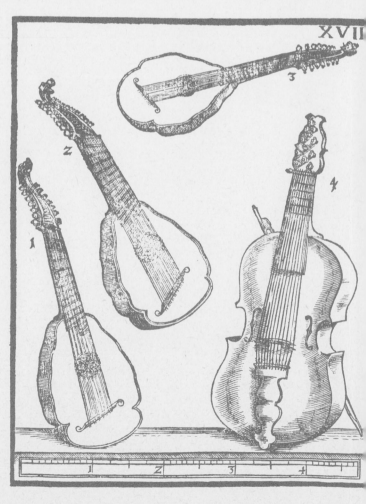